# Monitoring the EU Accession Process:

## *Judicial Independence*

**COUNTRY REPORTS**

BULGARIA
CZECH REPUBLIC
ESTONIA
HUNGARY
LATVIA
LITHUANIA
POLAND
ROMANIA
SLOVAKIA
SLOVENIA

*2001*

*Published by*

OPEN SOCIETY INSTITUTE

Oktober 6 u. 12
H–1051 Budapest
Hungary

400 West 59th Street
New York, NY 10019
USA

© OSI/EU Accession Monitoring Program, 2001
All rights reserved.

*Second Edition*

EU ACCESSION MONITORING PROGRAM

Oktober 6 u. 12
H–1051 Budapest
Hungary

*Website*
<www.eumap.org>

The EU Accession Monitoring Program
gratefully acknowledges the support of the Ford Foundation

ISBN: 1-891385-20-8

Library of Congress Cataloging-in-Publication Data.
A CIP catalog record for this book is available upon request.

Copies of the book can be ordered from the CEU Press.
<ceupress@ceupress.com>

*Printed in Budapest, Hungary, December 2001.*
*Design & Layout by Createch Ltd.*

# Table of Contents

Acknowledgements ....................................................... 7

Preface ........................................................................ 9

Foreword ................................................................... 11

Judicial Independence in the EU Accession Process .... 13

Judicial Independence in Bulgaria ............................... 69

Judicial Independence in the Czech Republic .......... 109

Judicial Independence in Estonia ............................. 147

Judicial Independence in Hungary ........................... 185

Judicial Independence in Latvia ............................... 225

Judicial Independence in Lithuania .......................... 267

Judicial Independence in Poland .............................. 307

Judicial Independence in Romania ........................... 349

Judicial Independence in Slovakia ............................ 395

Judicial Independence in Slovenia ............................ 431

# Acknowledgements

The EU Accession Monitoring Program of the Open Society Institute would like to acknowledge the contribution of the following individuals in researching and drafting our monitoring reports. Final responsibility for the content of the reports rests with the Program.

| | | |
|---|---|---|
| **Bulgaria** | Alexander Arabadjiev | *Former Member of the Constitutional Court of Bulgaria* |
| **Czech Republic** | Lucie Atkins | *Central European University* |
| **Estonia** | Jaan Ginter | *University of Tartu* |
| **Hungary** | Zoltan Fleck | *ELTE Eotvos Lorant University of Sciences* |
| **Latvia** | Anita Usacka | *Constitutional Court of Latvia* |
| **Lithuania** | Linas Sesickas | *Bernotas & Dominas GLIMSTEDT* |
| **Poland** | Hanna Suchocka | *Member of Parliament* |
| **Romania** | Horatiu Dumitru | *Musat & Asociatii* |
| | Monica Macovei | *Romanian Helsinki Committee* |
| **Slovakia** | Jan Hrubala | *Center for Enviromental and Public Advocacy* |
| **Slovenia** | Ales Zalar | *Slovenian Judges Association* |

*We would like to thank the following individuals for their review and critique of earlier drafts of these reports:*
Aija Branta, Bill Burke-White, Venelin Ganev, Zdenek Hraba, Daiga Iljanova, Matjaz Jager, Peter Kresak, Ants Kull, Ieva Morica, Wiktor Osiatynski, Peep Pruks, Cornelio Sommaruga, Balazs Toth, Renate Weber, Marek Zubik

The Constitutional and Legal Policy Institute also made a significant contribution to the reports.

Advisory Board Members: Judicial Independence

| | |
|---|---|
| Giuseppe Di Federico | *University of Bologna* |
| Lech Garlicki | *Constitutional Tribunal of Poland* |
| Ernst Markel | *Supreme Court of Austria; European Association of Judges* |
| Andras Sajo | *Central European University* |
| Stefan Trechsel | *University of Zurich* |

OSI also held roundtable meetings in many candidate States to invite expert critique and commentary on the draft reports from representatives of the governments, the Commission Delegations, and civil society. Lists of participants from these meetings are available from the EU Accession Monitoring program <euaccession@osi.hu>.

The EU Accession Monitoring Program

| | |
|---|---|
| Rachel Guglielmo | *Program Director* |
| Karoly Bard | *Legal Consultant* |
| Henrikas Mickevicius | *Legal Consultant* |
| Timothy Waters | *Legal Consultant* |
| James A. Goldston | *Deputy Director, Open Society Institute* |
| Andrea Gurubi Watterson | *Program Assistant* |

# Preface

The EU Accession Monitoring Program of the Open Society Institute was initiated in 2000 to encourage independent monitoring of the process by which the European Union is considering applications for membership from the ten candidate States of Central and Eastern Europe. The Program aims to contribute to this historic process by producing monitoring reports to complement the evaluations already being conducted by the European Commission, as reflected in its annual "Regular Reports" on candidate States' progress towards meeting accession criteria. The enlargement of the European Union is a positive development, and independent monitoring is one means of magnifying its beneficial effects, both within the candidate States and in the EU itself.

In keeping with the larger aims of the Open Society Institute, the Program is monitoring compliance with the political criteria for membership as defined by the European Council in Copenhagen in 1993:

> *Membership requires that the candidate country has achieved stability of institutions guaranteeing democracy, the rule of law, human rights and respect for and protection of minorities.*

In order to determine specific topics for monitoring, the Program looked to the Regular Reports to identify certain aspects of the political criteria frequently highlighted by the Commission itself: minority rights, judicial independence, and corruption. Monitoring was also initiated on a fourth topic of importance to both the Commission and OSI: equal opportunities for women and men.

Monitoring reports were elaborated by independent experts and/or organisations in each of the ten candidate countries on the basis of a methodology developed by OSI with the assistance of an international advisory board. This methodology draws upon existing international and European standards for judicial independence to provide a framework for analysis of corresponding legislation, institutions and practice in the candidate States.

First drafts of each report were reviewed by a national expert and the international advisory board. Subsequently, round-table meetings were organised in nine candidate

States to invite critique of the drafts from government officials, civil society organisations, judicial representatives, and from the Commission itself. Where it was not possible to organise a round-table, the draft was submitted for comment by mail. The final reports underwent significant revision on the basis of the comments and criticisms received during this process. The Program assumes full editorial responsibility for their final content.

# Foreword

Since 7 November 2000 the European Union has its own Charter of human rights. Although this document lacks legal force, it is a banner professing the Union's allegiance to the fundamental values of the modern world, and a statement of its member States' common purpose. It may be seen as an affirmation of this commitment that in considering candidate States for membership an assessment is made of their progress in the area of human rights.

I do not hesitate to affirm that the independence of the judiciary is a cornerstone, not only of respect for human rights, but also of the rule of law. Yet in international instruments for the protection of human rights, the independence and impartiality of the judiciary have an inconspicuous place. They are almost hidden in Article 6 of the European Convention for the Protection of Human Rights and Fundamental Freedoms and Article 14 of the International Covenant on Civil and Political Rights.

The actual importance of judicial independence is, however, of a different category from other – individual – rights. We are faced here with a fundamental principle of the organisation of a State, the basic "stuff that constitutions are made of". It is neither the legislative nor the executive branch that ultimately prevents a descent into totalitarianism. An independent judiciary sustains the rule of law without pursuing the aims of a particular political party, and does not hesitate to decide in favour of the weak.

Modern democracies cannot function without a minimum amount of co-operation from their citizens. They must be given the feeling of "*tua res agitur*" ("this is all about *you*") with regard to the political entities in which they live, whether it be the commune or town, the province or the State. This requires a fundamental trust in the correct functioning of the institutions – with "correct" meaning according to the law.

There are very good reasons to apply an increased degree of scrutiny with regard to countries that have lived under communism for two generations. The role of the judiciary in those times is well known: "judgement by telephone" is the widely known expression for their "method of interpretation". When, following the fall of the Iron Curtain, the first seminars on fair trials were organised for lawyers from Central and Eastern Europe, some participants had no idea what an independent judiciary involved. I was asked, "How is the judge supposed to know which way to decide?"

In attempting to answer such fundamental questions, members of the Union have discovered that simply transferring technical knowledge or providing financial assistance for judicial infrastructure, while necessary, is not sufficient. Even more, they need, and properly ought, to clarify their common values and standards – to identify and articulate what judicial independence means for democratic States in 21$^{st}$ century Europe.

Considerable progress has been achieved over the last ten years. Yet, the process certainly is not completed, and beyond the candidate States, there are further challenges. Practising lawyers from the accession region have told me that there is still quite a way to go, in part because of the difficult economic circumstances that make reform on even basic matters such as ensuring decent salaries for judges so hard to sustain.

The present study, prepared by the Open Society Institute, is an excellent beginning, and a provocative challenge. The study has been undertaken with extraordinary care; very detailed questionnaires were prepared, competent national reporters were engaged and their work was also supervised by an international advisory board. It presents no doubt by far the most elaborate and accurate picture of the independence of the judiciary in the countries covered. Perhaps it will serve as an example for further studies of similar questions, not only in candidate States, but also in the present EU member States. By raising important questions, and setting forth fact-based findings, these reports may assist the strengthening of the independence of the judiciary and the rule of law in the whole Union. What more could one ask?

*Stefan Trechsel*
*Professor of Criminal Law and Procedure at the University of Zurich,*
*former President of the European Commission of Human Rights*

OPEN SOCIETY INSTITUTE 2001

# Judicial Independence in the EU Accession Process

# Table of Contents

I. Introduction ........................................................ 16
   A. The Importance of Judicial Independence .... 16
   B. Achieving Independence
      and Accountability ...................................... 18
   C. Issue Areas for the Candidate States ........... 20
      1. Weak Commitment to a Culture
         Based on the Rule of Law ..................... 21
      2. Insufficient Institutional
         Independence ....................................... 23
      3. Undue Executive Interference .............. 24
   D. Using Accession to Identify Developing
      European Standards .................................... 26
      1. Existing EU Standards ......................... 27
      2. International Standards ....................... 28
      3. Developing Standards for the Union ..... 31

II. Constitutional and Legal Foundations
    of Judicial Independence ................................. 33
   A. Guarantees of the Separation of Powers,
      or Independence ......................................... 33
   B. Representation of the Judiciary .................. 34
   C. Extraordinary and Military Courts ............. 35
   D. The Role of Constitutional Courts ............. 36
   E. Rules on Incompatibility ........................... 37

III. Administration of the Court System
     and Judicial Independence .............................. 40
   A. Loci of Administrative Responsibility ........ 40
      1. Principal Administration
         by the Ministry of Justice .................... 41
      2. Administration by a Judicial Council ... 42

| | | |
|---|---|---|
| IV. | Financial Autonomy and Level of Funding ...... 46 | |
| | A. Budgeting Process ........ 46 | |
| | B. Work Conditions ........ 48 | |
| | C. Compensation ........ 49 | |
| V. | Judicial Office ........ 51 | |
| | A. Selection Process ........ 51 | |
| | B. Tenure, Retirement, Transfer, and Removal ........ 54 | |
| |     1. Tenure ........ 54 | |
| |     2. Retirement ........ 55 | |
| |     3. Transfer ........ 55 | |
| |     4. Removal ........ 56 | |
| | C. Evaluation and Promotion ........ 57 | |
| | D. Discipline ........ 58 | |
| VI. | Intra-Judicial Relations ........ 61 | |
| | A. Relations with Superior Courts ........ 61 | |
| | B. Case Management ........ 62 | |
| VII. | Enforcement and Corruption ........ 64 | |
| | A. Enforcement ........ 64 | |
| | B. Corruption ........ 65 | |
| VIII. | Recommendations ........ 66 | |

# Judicial Independence in the EU Accession Process

## I. Introduction

This Overview and the accompanying Country Reports assess the state of judicial independence in ten countries applying for membership in the European Union, in light of the Union's own evolving standards.

When one considers that prior to 1989 each candidate State had a judiciary politically subordinated to the Government and the ruling Communist party, the progress achieved in reforming the court systems of these States has been impressive. Of course, just over ten years after the political transformation, the organisational reform of the courts and the elaboration of guarantees of judicial independence are still in progress.

The European Commission has identified progressive improvement in the role and functioning of the courts as one of the political criteria by which prospective members are to be considered. The Commission has repeatedly expressed concern about the slow pace of court reform in the candidate States. The major problems it has identified have been the considerable backlog of pending cases, the length of proceedings, and deficiencies in the execution of judgements.

In short, the Reports primarily urge candidate States to increase the efficient processing of claims before their courts. The Commission has paid less attention to what distinguishes the judiciary from other branches of the State: the need for courts and judges to be independent and impartial. None of the candidate States considered in these Reports has a fully effective *and* fully independent court system.

### A. The Importance of Judicial Independence

The Copenhagen criteria do not explicitly mention judicial independence, and yet it is difficult to imagine how a State could achieve "stability of institutions guaranteeing ...the rule of law" without an independent judiciary, or how it could effectively combat corruption without impartial judges. It is clear that the EU values both judicial independence[1] and judges' impartiality.[2]

Moreover, if efficiency is understood not simply as the speed with which cases are decided but the quality of those decisions and their contribution to the goals of a just society, then the degree to which the independence and impartiality of the judiciary and individual judges are guaranteed becomes a crucial measure of performance.

The judiciary occupies a unique position in a democratic society. It is called upon to decide disputes that cannot or should not be left to the political branches[3] or private individuals. It upholds the law for all – and in so doing, it also safeguards the rights of individuals and minority groups of all types against the excesses of majoritarianism. This sometimes requires judges to confront the interests of the political branches or powerful individuals, but because judges are not democratically elected, they must derive their authority and legitimacy from different sources than do the political branches; one of judges' most important sources of legitimacy and authority is their independence.

Meaningful independence (and public perception of that independence) is essential to the judiciary's legitimacy as a guarantor of rights and freedoms. If the judiciary is not independent of the executive and legislature, it cannot properly restrain those branches. If courts are not seen as independent (and impartial), citizens will not turn to them to resolve their problems, but may seek recourse through political or extralegal means.

---

[1] For example, on 24 April 2001, EU Commissioner for Enlargement Guenter Verheugen told journalists in Brussels that the EU is worried by possible infringements of the judiciary's independence in Romania; two days later, in Bucharest, he reiterated the EU's concerns and promised to continue monitoring the matter. *Adevarul*, 27 April 2001; *Romania Libera*, 28 April 2001.

[2] These Reports assess both judicial independence and judicial impartiality, which requires that judges not have any prejudicial connections to or views of any party to a dispute, whether because of involvement in a previous stage of the case or a personal pecuniary connection to a party or the issue. While analytically distinct concepts, in practical application independence and impartiality are closely related and raise analogous problems. Compare D.J. Harris, M. O'Boyle, and C. Warbrick, *Law of the European Convention on Human Rights* (1995), p. 234. See e.g. *Piersack v. Belgium*, ECHR Judgement of 1 October 1982 (App. No. 8692/79), A 53; *Daktaras v. Lithuania*, ECHR Judgement of 10 October 2000 (App. No. 42095/98 [2000]) (finding a violation of Article 6(1) in a case in which the President of the Criminal Division of the Supreme Court both lodged a cassation petition and convened the Chamber hearing the case; and holding that a tribunal must be impartial from an objective viewpoint – that is, it must offer sufficient guarantees to exclude any legitimate doubt as to its impartiality).

[3] For convenience, these Reports refer to the "political branches", meaning the whole of the legislative and executive branches. This includes the civil service, which is professional rather than political, but whose senior management is politically appointed.

The legislature and the executive themselves have a direct interest in judicial independence; they often need the judiciary to resolve problems which do not have easy political solutions – but the judiciary can do this only if all parties see it as a neutral arbiter, independent of the branches and parties which have turned to it in the first place.

The importance of judicial independence extends beyond the political; economists have noted the importance of an independent and impartial judiciary to a stable and prosperous economy. Individuals and institutions must be able to rely on predictable justice – free of the vagaries of political interference or economic influence by either party – in the adjudication of their claims. In societies struggling to reform their economies, judicial independence contributes to the confidence, security and predictability of economic transactions.

## B. Achieving Independence and Accountability

In the communist period, the judiciary's position was defined by its political subordination, but an independent judiciary must be incorporated into society in a different fashion, not only freeing it, but also integrating it as an equal member.

Independence serves important social needs; it is not, properly speaking, an end in itself or a way to secure the professional position of judges for their own benefit, but rather a means to achieve the goals of a just and prosperous society. For this reason, independence needs to be complemented with means to ensure that judges and the judiciary as a whole comport with society's democratic principles and legitimate interests: even as they are independent, in other words, judges need to be accountable to society.

It is sometimes suggested that accountability and independence are inherently contradictory. In fact there need be no contradiction between them because the initial grant of independence is actually limited, extending only to judges' core decision-making function within their court,[4] and to such further areas as are necessary to ensure that there is no improper influence on that function. Indeed, unless judges are somehow accountable, society will likely view their independence as a danger and seek to curtail it.

As judges are given limited independence for specific, if fundamental, social purposes, and not for its own sake, accountability to society and the instrumental independence

---

[4] Compare e.g., Lord Irvine of Lairg, "Introduction", Judicial Organisation in Europe (Council of Europe, May 2000), p. 7 ("Central to the rule of law is the basic conception that judges must be independent of government, with absolute power *over the decisions taken in their own courts*, which can only be overturned by equally absolute decisions of senior judges in higher courts[.]")(emphasis added).

which society affords judges can be, to a great extent, complementary. This is achieved by precisely defining spheres of competence, creating transparency without control, and encouraging free debate about, without improperly interfering with, judicial decisions.

*Defining Competence*: The judiciary's proper roles include settling disputes among private parties, and also ensuring the justice and legality of the acts of the democratically accountable branches; courts therefore serve a monitoring or policing function. Since a monitor who is not independent of those being monitored cannot be effective, it is necessary to define spheres of competence in which judges may act without fear of influence from the political branches or parties to disputes. Judges' core competence is the power to decide cases requiring application or interpretation of law. Where influence or restrictions on judges do not impair that function,[5] either directly or indirectly, or where they actually contribute to independence,[6] they are acceptable.

*Creating Non-Controlling Transparency*: Judicial independence requires that the points of contact between the judiciary and the outside world are transparent and regularised: transparent, so that observers can see clearly the effects of the interaction, and regularised, so that to as great a degree as possible, decisions can be anticipated with some certainty.[7] A marginally greater level of political involvement in personnel and administrative concerns is acceptable where it is governed by objective, transparent rules promulgated in advance and applied uniformly.

External influence is best directed through "soft" methods aimed at ensuring that the judiciary, the other branches, and society remain apprised of each others' views on judicial

---

[5] Thus, societies may for example provide for the removal of physically or mentally incompetent judges or judges who have committed violent crimes. Compare "United Nations Basic Principles on the Independence of the Judiciary", adopted by the seventh United Nations Congress on the Prevention of Crime and the Treatment of Offenders held in Milan from 26 August to 6 September 1985 and endorsed by General Assembly Resolutions 40/32 of 29 November 1985 and 40/146 of 13 December 1985 (hereafter "UN Basic Principles", Art. 18 (judges shall be subject to removal for incapacity or behaviour rendering them unfit to discharge their duties); Recommendation No. R. (94) 12 of the Committee of Ministers to Member States on the Independence, Efficiency and Role of Judges, 1994 RGE 648 94 (hereafter "CoE Recommendations"), Principles V.3.c. (judges' responsibility to withdraw from cases due to health problems or the "interests of justice") and VI.2 (providing for removal due to incapacity or criminal behaviour).

[6] Legitimate restrictions actually preserve judicial independence and impartiality by insulating the judge from pressures. Thus, society may require that judges be impartial and follow ethical codes designed to ensure that they have no improper contacts with parties to cases. See e.g. UN Basic Principles, Art. 15 (providing that "[t]he judiciary shall be bound by professional secrecy with regard to their deliberations and to confidential information acquired in the course of their duties…").

[7] Legitimacy is also partly derived from transparent appointment procedures and operations. Indeed, it can be argued that these elements of legitimacy should logically precede the full grant of independence.

affairs without directly intervening in judges' activities. Judges' decision-making and administrative functions should be transparent, with regular reporting to the legislature and executive on the use of budgeted funds and the activities of the courts. Accountability within the judiciary – through appeals and uniformity decisions – should also be transparent. Requiring judges to issue reasoned opinions allows the public to follow the courts' processes without intervening.[8]

*Allowing Public Debate*: Criticism of judicial decisions, and of judicial institutions, is an important aspect of accountability that is consistent with judges' core independence. Judges are afforded independent discretion to decide difficult cases; that does not mean that everyone agrees with each decision. Yet in some of the candidate States, judges seem to believe that criticism from any quarter is an infringement on their independence. To be sure, the very purpose of courts is to provide regularised, fair venues for distributing justice, and unchecked public pressure on a judge to decide a particular way in a particular case defeats that purpose; even when channelled through the media, it can place undue pressure upon judges.[9]

Yet media criticism is one effective way to convey different views to the judiciary, even about particular judgements, without violating its freedom to adjudicate. So long as public commentary on cases does not cross into advocacy for disregarding judicial outcomes, or suggestions that judges ought not have the right to rule as they see fit, it should not be seen as undue interference.

Even criticism by the executive or legislature is appropriate, if conveyed in a spirit which unambiguously confirms the judiciary's right to decide freely, and the full preparedness of the other branches to uphold and execute its judgements. In a society in which such sentiments are not automatically assumed, it may be appropriate for public officials to qualify any criticisms they make with explicit reaffirmation of their support for the principle of judicial independence.

## C. Issue Areas for the Candidate States

Judicial reforms begun in the early 1990s have not occurred in isolation; they are part of a larger political and social restructuring in each candidate State that is still continuing.

---

[8] Written opinions are a good example of society's prerogative to make rules outside the core decision-making competence: requiring a written opinion places a burden on judges, but does not restrict their right to decide how they see fit – it only requires them to inform society of the reasons underlying decisions.

[9] See UN Basic Principles, Art. 2; CoE Recommendations, Principle I.2.d.

Judicial independence must be understood in this larger context. While each State presents a unique set of circumstances, a number of common features mark the region as a whole and should be kept in mind when developing standards designed to encompass all of Europe's efforts to achieve a real degree of judicial independence.

Significant progress has been made towards the goal of a truly independent judiciary integrated in and accountable to a democratic society. In each State, constitutional and legislative guarantees of the judiciary's independence are in place and accepted, and the traditional civil law systems of the region have been revitalised, with the courts playing an increasingly active role. Novel institutional arrangements to increase the autonomy of the judiciary in its relations with the other branches of the State have been developed in several States. The status of the judiciary has been considerably enhanced through improvements in salary and expansion of its sphere of competence. At the same time, the average speed with which judges dispose of cases has also improved. Courts are increasingly viewed as legitimate fora for the determination of disputes.

The areas in which the candidate States still fall short – and the causes – are many, and vary from State to State. Notwithstanding the significant progress noted above, three broad problems continue to impair the development of fully independent judiciaries across the accession region: 1) weak commitment to a culture based on the rule of law; 2) insufficient institutional independence of and material support for the judiciary; and 3) undue executive interference with the administration of the judiciary. In all these areas, the elaboration of clear EU standards is essential to the success of reform.

## 1. *Weak Commitment to a Culture Based on the Rule of Law*

One legacy of the pre-1989 period common throughout the region is a weak commitment to a culture based on the rule of law. All the candidate States were ruled by communist dictatorships from just after the end of the Second World War until the end of the 1980s. Although the severity of the regimes differed greatly over time and from State to State, in all of them, the pre-war civil law system and judiciary[10] were subordinated to the executive and through it to the supra-political authority of the Communist Party.[11] In these systems based on the unity of power, the subordination of judges to politicians and of law to politics extended from mundane administration to matters at

---

[10] Even prior to the communist period, the principles of the rule of law and separation of powers were only partly respected throughout most of the region.

[11] Forms commonly found in some civil law systems – such as combination of judicial and prosecutorial functions, full review, uniformity of decision, and civil service status for judges – were retained in the communist period.

the core of judicial decision-making. The continuing effects of this history on public and political ideas about the judiciary, and on judges' view of their role, should not be underestimated.

In the communist period, judges were generally viewed as functionaries, and few individuals imagined a judge might issue a decision fundamentally at odds with the official political line. These perceptions persist; many politicians and citizens still assume that judicial processes should or do hew to current political priorities and that judges implement State policy.[12] These perceptions contribute to popular distrust of judges.

There is also a widespread perception that corruption – another symptom of a weak legal system – is endemic in the judiciary of several candidate States, as in some member States. Rapid and destabilising economic changes, the weakness of new political institutions, and the legacy of a system in which the law was not an impartial protector of rights have encouraged corrupt practices in all walks of life, including adjudication and enforcement. Indeed, anecdotal evidence suggests that corruption among judges and administrative staff is particularly acute in Bulgaria, the Czech Republic, Latvia, Lithuania, Romania, and Slovakia, though it is widely thought to be present in all candidate States;[13] certainly, perceptions of corruption further reduce trust in the courts.

This lack of public and political trust can have serious consequences for judicial independence, as it undermines support for needed reforms and can encourage incursions on judicial prerogatives. In Bulgaria, for instance, a number of initiatives threaten judges' independence. A draft law proposes to abolish judges' right to appeal adverse disciplinary rulings, and the principal Act regulating the judicial system has been amended twice in order to alter the composition of the country's judicial council prior to the expiry of its members' terms. Consideration is even being given to lifting judges' constitutional immunity from prosecution in order to curb perceived widespread corruption. Decisions in the Czech Republic (1996), Lithuania (1998) and Hungary (2000) to extend lustration screening procedures against judges in part responded to continuing distrust of judges who had served under communism. However, so many years after the transitions began, such decisions raise inevitable concerns that screening is politically motivated. In Slovenia in 1999, some Members of Parliament sought unsuccessfully to abolish judicial tenure, arguing that it encourages inefficient adjudication.

---

[12] Political actors have attempted to influence the outcome of individual cases (Latvia, Poland), remove individual judges or court presidents (Slovenia), alter the composition of judicial governance bodies through legislation (Bulgaria) or otherwise restore executive control over the judiciary (Estonia, Hungary, Slovenia). Reference by politicians to "shared responsibilities" is also quite frequent.

[13] In the absence of clear definitions and standards, even within the EU, it is difficult to establish actual levels of corruption.

In many candidate States, relations between the media and the judiciary are quite strained,[14] reflecting an imperfectly developed understanding of the two institutions' roles in a democratic society. For their part, judges frequently interpret any criticism as an improper intrusion on their independence. At the same time, accusations by judges that journalists lack the necessary knowledge in matters of law and are unaware of the value of judicial independence have some basis.[15]

## 2. Insufficient Institutional Independence

Meaningful judicial independence rests not only on large principles and social attitudes, but on careful attention to the effects of administrative structures regulating the judiciary.

Courts are often poorly positioned to defend themselves against incursions on their independence, because they have little influence over the institutions which administer their budget and individual judges' careers. Although independence is not incompatible with executive or legislative oversight, at a minimum courts should have meaningful involvement in their own administration, while procedures for budgeting, discipline and administration should be designed to circumscribe legislative and executive discretion.

The problem of insufficient institutional independence is especially acute in the Czech Republic, Estonia, Latvia, and Romania, as well as Slovakia, where the situation is in flux following recent constitutional amendments.

Many candidate States have developed independent judicial councils to administer the judiciary on matters such as discipline, court management, appointments and promotions. Councils can be a useful solution to the problems of executive interference. Some councils, however, while nominally independent, are composed primarily of individuals appointed by the executive or legislature; it is reasonable to question these councils' ability to represent or administer the judiciary. Where States choose not to create truly independent judicial councils, they must ensure that the alternatives contain explicit and robust institutional guarantees for the neutrality of procedures applied to the judiciary, provide judges with meaningful input, and ensure that independence is maintained in fact.

---

[14] In Slovenia, however, the media has advocated strengthening judicial independence and supported judges' efforts to persuade Parliament to adopt an adequate budget for the judiciary in 1999.

[15] It is reported from several countries that the media do a poor job of informing the public about criminal cases and legal concepts, such as the presumption of innocence. The tension between media and courts is partly due to the lack of appropriate channels of communication; as it is generally forbidden for judges to comment on the cases they try, court spokesmen might be employed to bridge the gap.

Even where candidate States have created independent bodies or vested the judiciary with administrative powers, they have almost always maintained the budget process as a matter of executive and legislative discretion, not limited by clear procedures and without significant input from judges. Judges chronically short of funds are more susceptible to outside influence from parties prepared to offer bribes for preferential treatment. In turn, this makes the judiciary less trustworthy as a neutral arbiter, and reduces public support.

Standards for the proper level of material support for the judiciary are necessarily contextual, and of course it is both normal and proper that ultimate budgetary authority should rest with the legislature. Nonetheless, one can identify in international norms a requirement – and in European practice a determination – that courts shall have sufficient funding to ensure their smooth operation[16] and that judges earn a salary comporting with the dignity an independent judiciary requires.[17] This means that judicial salaries should be competitive with the professional alternatives available to judges, and that judges should not be made vulnerable to influence due to economic need. One of the best ways to ensure this is for legislatures and executives to commit to particular levels of funding, and to incorporate judicial submissions into the budget deliberation process.

Many of the candidate States fall short of these standards, especially in the provision of materials;[18] salaries, however, have improved considerably. While no candidate State has achieved fully satisfactory levels of material support, standards remain particularly low in Bulgaria, Latvia, Lithuania, Romania, and Slovakia, and to some degree in Poland.

Of course, insufficient institutional independence and material support are in part symptoms of the larger problem of executive control; where another branch is responsible for the judiciary, it will always have incentives and opportunities to make the judiciary a lower priority, unless public expectations demand otherwise.

## 3. Undue Executive Interference

A related legacy of the pre-1989 period, and one of the most prominent threats to the consolidation of fully independent judiciaries in the candidate States, is the continuing, pervasive influence of the executive, and especially Ministries of Justice, in the adminis-

---

[16] See UN Basic Principles, Art. 7; UCJ, Art. 14.

[17] See UN Basic Principles, Art. 11; CoE Recommendations, Principle III.1.b.; UCJ, Art. 13.

[18] There is tremendous variation within each country, with some courts being well-supplied and others receiving little assistance. This variation itself opens up opportunities for targeted and improper influence through selective financial support.

tration of the judiciary and in the selection, promotion, and disciplining of judges. Even in States in which there have been legislative changes increasing the formal independence of the judiciary, there has been an observable tendency for the executive to try to retain or reclaim powers through appointments, influence on the composition of judicial oversight bodies, and new legislation.

The problem of ministerial control is especially acute in the same countries in which the judiciary's institutional independence is poorly established: the Czech Republic, Estonia, Latvia, and Romania. Elsewhere, there are still concerns, and only in Hungary and perhaps Slovenia has this problem been minimised. Lithuania is in transition towards a system giving the courts full administrative autonomy; in Slovakia, the executive retains almost total administrative control at present, but recent constitutional amendments seem to require the creation of a judicial council with far-reaching administrative authority.

There is no absolute reason why the executive cannot be involved in, or even principally responsible for judicial administration – in many member States it is. However, absent an established and proven tradition of forbearance by the executive in its relations with the courts, such involvement should be discouraged. The specific historical circumstances of the region show that the interaction of executive and judiciary often harms judicial independence. Because the Ministry of Justice was the agent of control over the judiciary under the Communists and judges operated in a culture of deference, it may be preferable to make an unambiguous break with that tradition, rather than trusting to internal institutional reform.

Part of the solution is to clearly insulate the judiciary from undue executive (or legislative) involvement through unambiguous constitutional guarantees and the creation of institutions – within the judiciary or with substantial judicial representation – to administer the judiciary and judges' careers in a neutral manner. In most States, the broad outlines of such systems are formally in place, although important legislative and institutional improvements can still be made. Locating independent administrative bodies at the constitutional level helps to insulate them from politically motivated alteration. In addition, courts should be given the means to develop their management expertise, so as to remove one of the principal arguments for continued executive involvement. This is an area in which international support could be of critical importance.

Equally important, however, is an atmospheric change: The continuing assumption – both in the other branches and in the judiciary – that executive involvement in judicial administration is both necessary (because the judiciary is ill-prepared to administer itself) and desirable must be confronted and rejected. Politicians must publicly affirm the importance of an independent judiciary, enact legislation supporting it, and refrain from making inroads on the judiciary's prerogatives. Judges must refute political criticisms, not by censuring them, but by demonstrating that they are prepared to administer themselves with professionalism and restraint, and to make themselves accountable to society.

## D. Using Accession to Identify Developing European Standards

Many of the issues identified in these Reports are only *potential* opportunities for undue interference. It is an indication of the still unsettled status of the judiciary in these States that these potential problems – emanating from structures similar or even identical to those in more mature democracies, including some in the EU – continue to generate legitimate concern. In some other countries, time and practice have occasionally confirmed that the risk is only theoretical, and that the general respect for rule of law, the dignity of judicial office, and the proven interest of other branches in supporting independence are sufficient to ensure that interference does not occur.[19]

Determining the acceptability of a given arrangement requires clear articulation and understanding of the standards the EU wishes to apply to itself and its candidates. The candidate States are under an effective obligation to fulfil the Copenhagen criteria, but the EU has yet to elaborate any standards by which candidate States' efforts – or member States' continuing performance – can be measured. More precise standards are necessary to encourage a uniformly high level of respect for judicial independence across Europe.

This is not a problem; it is an historic opportunity. The accession process not only provides impetus to the candidate States to further solidify their transitions to the rule of law, it also encourages the EU as a whole to recognise common standards upon which continuing membership is properly grounded. By identifying political criteria for membership, the EU emphasises that it is more than an economic partnership of convenience, but a true community of values shared across Europe; it is the challenge of accession which makes it possible to express and advance those values.

Within the proper limits of its legal authority, the EU should identify European-wide standards by which it intends to measure judicial independence on a continuing basis. These should include the few required minimums, the few prohibited practices, and the much more numerous options for achieving judicial independence which comport with the Union's principles and goals for itself.

---

[19] Compare UCJ, Art. 11 (2) (requiring that provisions for the administration of the judiciary and disciplinary proceedings must be carried out by independent bodies "[w]here this is not ensured in other ways that are rooted in established and proven tradition[.]").

Such standards need to reaffirm universal and European values while taking proper account of the differing historical and political contexts throughout the continent. To distinguish between formal and real risks to judicial independence, they must address and account for law and practice in the candidate States and the member States. At the same time they must define the core guiding principles essential to the preservation of judicial independence in any context. Both within Europe and beyond, standards exist or can be identified.

## 1. *Existing EU Standards*

The EU has not developed extensive or definitive legal standards or recommendations for judicial independence. The recent Charter of Fundamental Rights of the European Union[20] "recognises"[21] standards that would guarantee the right to a fair hearing before an independent and impartial tribunal established by law, and to an effective remedy.[22] However, while the European Council "would like to see the Charter disseminated as widely as possibly amongst the Union's citizens[,]"[23] the Charter is not binding and as yet has no defined legal status.

Where the EU has been silent, however, the current member States' own varied domestic practice provides important guidance and a basis for developing an objective assessment consistent with the EU's values.

To the degree that member States' own judicial structures have been generally supposed to fall within the (undefined) bounds of acceptable practice, they may provide examples which candidate States could emulate to bring their systems within acceptable bounds. So, for example, arrangements for the judiciary modelled upon a current member State's system – in the way that Romania's system has borrowed heavily from French models – might reasonably suggest that the candidate State's practice was at least as acceptable as that member State's, unless there were compelling contextual reasons to conclude otherwise. To a significant degree, the member States provide 15 models presumptively in accord with the as yet unvoiced standards of the Union.

---

[20] Charter of Fundamental Rights of the European Union, *signed and proclaimed by* the Presidents of the European Parliament, the Council and the Commission at the European Council meeting in Nice, on 7 December 2000 (2000/C 364/01) (hereafter "EU Charter on Fundamental Rights").

[21] EU Charter of Fundamental Rights, Preamble.

[22] EU Charter of Fundamental Rights, Art. 47.

[23] "Citizens' rights – fundamental rights", portal site of the European Union, <http://europa.eu.int/abc/cit1_en.htm> (accessed on 23 August 2001).

At the same time, in some cases, the combination of particular factors which distinguish the candidate States – especially the debilitating legacy of communism and the unsettled political transition – may suggest or require solutions which would be unacceptable in current member States. It is conceivable that a practice identical to one in a member State might be inadequate; for example, the United Kingdom's "unwritten constitution" might not provide sufficient clarity in a country emerging from communist rule. It may be, in other words, that simply copying member States' practice will not be sufficient *or* necessary to create truly independent judiciaries. However, where a practice departs from a common standard, the burden should be on the deviating State clearly to explain itself.

It is not within the scope of these current Reports to conduct a comprehensive survey of member States' practice relating to an independent judiciary. Yet until clear EU standards are elaborated, this will be the most effective means of clarifying, for all States, what the content of Europe's commitment to judicial independence ought to look like, and EU recommendations to the candidate States should be grounded upon such an analysis.

## 2. *International Standards*

In addition, there are a number of internationally recognised standards, in the form of recommended guidelines, emanating from bodies generally enjoying a high level of support from the EU and its member States. These guidelines offer points of reference in assessing State performance in supporting judicial independence.

Taken as a whole, these standards identify the basic principles embodying judicial independence: the individual judge's authority to decide cases free of interference; separation of powers and entrenchment of judicial independence in the constitutional order; administrative independence and inclusion of judges in the budget process; the "fundamental independence" of the judiciary (that is, protection against arbitrary abolition of courts or revision of their decisions); and intra-judicial independence (that is, judges' right to make decisions without undue interference from higher courts). In addition, the standards address the related issue of judicial impartiality and note the responsibility of an independent judiciary to be accountable to society.

### a. *International Covenant on Civil and Political Rights, Article 14*

Article 14 of the International Covenant on Civil and Political Rights[24] – the ICCPR – establishes a universal right to a hearing before a "competent, independent, and impartial

---

[24] International Covenant on Civil and Political Rights, adopted and opened for signature, ratification and accession by General Assembly resolution 2200A (XXI) of December 1966, entered into force 23 March 1976.

tribunal established by law[,]" which implies that States are obliged to create the conditions for judges to adjudicate independently. The general principles in the ICCPR do not elaborate on the content of independence or impartiality in any detail; the General Comment of the Human Rights Committee on Article 14 suggests a more detailed range of requirements, however.[25]

b.   *UN Basic Principles*

Among the most prominent standards are the UN Basic Principles on the Independence of the Judiciary, adopted in 1985. As a resolution of the General Assembly, the Basic Principles represent a non-binding formulation of the community of States' minimum aspirations for the judiciary; it would be difficult to contemplate a legitimate and independent judicial system fundamentally at odds with the Basic Principles.

c.   *Council of Europe Recommendations*

The Council of Europe's Recommendations on the Independence, Efficiency and Role of Judges were adopted in 1994. They establish minimal standards similar in content to the Basic Principles, although the CoE Recommendations provide considerably more elaboration about options for fulfilling its recommendations.

The Council of Europe Recommendations, adopted when the process of political transformation and integration of the candidate States was already well underway or anticipated, are an expression of recommended obligations for the States in the Council of Europe. Although they draw upon the same international sources as do the Basic Principles, they are a European product, and as such reflect more closely the values and aspirations of the EU and the candidate States – all members of the Council of Europe. The Recommendations are, for example, much more explicit in suggesting the appropriateness of self-governing judicial councils as a means of administering the judiciary and in proposing rules for case allocation.

d.   *ECHR Jurisprudence*

Article 6 of the Council of Europe's Convention for the Protection of Human Rights and Fundamental Freedoms[26] – known as the European Convention on Human Rights

---

[25] Office of the High Commisioner for Human Rights, "Equality before the courts and the right to a fair and public hearing by an independent court established by law (Art. 14)": 13/04/84. CCPR General comment 13. (General Comments) (21st session, 1984).

[26] European Convention for the Protection of Human Rights and Fundamental Freedoms (*signed* 4 November 1950; *entered into force* 3 September 1953; amended 21 September 1970, 20 December 1971, and 1 January 1990, 213 UNTS 221, ETS 5), Art. 6 (1) ("[E]veryone is entitled to a fair and public hearing...by an independent and impartial tribunal established by law.").

– elaborates standards for court proceedings, which have implications for judicial independence. Article 6 is binding on States which have ratified the Convention, including all member States and candidate States.

Building upon Article 6, cases arising before the European Court of Human Rights (ECHR) established under the Convention address questions of judicial independence and impartiality. Prominent among them are *Findlay v. United Kingdom* and *Bryan v. United Kingdom*.[27] The *Bryan* judgement sets forth a number of principles essential to the independence of the judiciary:

37. In order to establish whether a body can be considered "independent", regard must be had, *inter alia*, to the manner of appointment of its members and to their term of office, to the existence of guarantees against outside pressures and to the question whether the body presents an appearance of independence.[28]

Other ECHR cases also address an important aspect of judicial independence that often receives less attention: the threat to an individual judge's independence from within the judicial hierarchy itself – what is known as internal or intra-judicial independence. *Sramek v. Austria*, establishes that full independence also requires a sufficient organisational separation from the executive branch.[29] In general, ECHR jurisprudence tends to look to the substantive conditions for an independent judiciary, rather than considering the formal provisions of law determinative.[30]

ECHR jurisprudence is binding on the individual member States who are before the Court in their capacities as States Parties to the Convention in the particular case. More broadly, though, ECHR cases provide clear guidance to other States Parties about acceptable models and practices for their judiciaries. Since Maastricht, it has been clear that "the Union shall respect fundamental rights, as guaranteed by the European Convention for the Protection of Human Rights and Fundamental Freedoms ... and as they result from the constitutional traditions common to the member States, as general principles of Community Law."[31] ECHR decisions interpreting the text of the Convention are generally accorded great weight, even though the European Court

---

[27] *Findlay v. United Kingdom*, ECHR Judgement of 25 February 1997 (No. 110/1995/16/706), Reports 1997-1. *Bryan v. United Kingdom*, ECHR Judgement of 22 November 1995 (No. 44/1994/491/573), A335-A.

[28] *Bryan v. United Kingdom*, para. 37.

[29] See *Sramek v. Austria*, ECHR Judgement of 22 October 1984 (No. 5/1983/61/95), A84, para. 74.

[30] See D.J. Harris, M. O'Boyle, and C. Warbrick, *Law of the European Convention on Human Rights* (1995), pp. 232–33.

[31] Art. F(2), Treaty of Maastricht, renumbered Art. 6(2), Treaty of Amsterdam.

of Justice – the European Union's supreme judicial body – is not legally obliged to follow them.[32]

### e.  Judges' Association Charters

Of some further assistance in formulating standards relating to judicial independence are the guidelines proposed by international judges' associations, in particular the European Charter on the Statute for Judges, adopted by the European Association of Judges,[33] and the Universal Charter of the Judge, adopted by the International Association of Judges.[34] Both Charters identify an expansive range of aspirational rights and obligations designed to promote maximum judicial independence; in so doing, they advocate a model considerably more weighted in favour of judicial autonomy over accountability than can be reconciled with most State practice, among member States or elsewhere.

## 3.  Developing Standards for the Union

One should be cognisant of the limits of these standards when assessing judicial independence in individual States, or when extrapolating to the EU's position. The international standards are non-binding recommendations; absent clear, binding EU requirements, they provide valuable indicia of judicial independence, but no more.

As a consequence, individual States are left with broad discretion in designing institutions to ensure judicial independence. The EU might usefully clarify existing standards, where possible within its mandate, for the whole Union. Taking the EU Charter of Fundamental Rights as a starting point, this should include a clear statement both of the binding rules which the EU is prepared to call on members and candidates to respect, and of the areas in which it has no interest as a Union. It might include instances of the range of acceptable practices, with reference to existing examples.

In giving voice to its standards, the EU should ensure that each allows a qualitative assessment as to whether judicial independence is in fact being respected. Constitutional, legislative, and institutional provisions are meaningless if judges nonetheless feel

---

[32]  See Opinion of Darnon AG in Case 374/87, <u>Orkem</u> (1989), ECR 3351, cited in D. Spielmann, "Comparing ECJ and ECHR Case Law", in P. Alston, ed., *The EU and Human Rights*, 1999, p. 762.

[33]  The Charter (hereafter "ECSJ"), established in 1998, is not a Council of Europe document, but was developed by the European Association of Judges under the Council's auspices through the THEMIS Plan, and published by the Council [DAJ/DOC (98) 23]. Both the European Association of Judges for Democracy and Freedom (MEDEL) and the *Ecole Nationale de la Magistrature* of France (ENM) participated in the development of the ECSJ.

[34]  Hereafter UCJ.

compelled to rule in a particular party's favour. Contrariwise, the absence of any particular provision does not necessarily mean a State is failing to meet its obligations, if the total circumstances show that independence nonetheless obtains. This is particularly so given the multiplicity of approaches within the EU to forming judicial bodies.

In applying its standards, the Commission's assessments should be qualitiative and fair. No State should be told it is failing to develop an independent judiciary without also being told why it is failing, and what it can do to remedy the matter.

## II. Constitutional and Legal Foundations of Judicial Independence

### A. Guarantees of the Separation of Powers or Independence

Most standards on judicial independence recommend that the independent role of the judiciary and individual judges be defined in the constitution of the State, or at an equivalent level.[35] Although not necessary to a system of judicial independence – as EU member States' own practice shows – formally establishing in the constitution that the judiciary is a separate power or is independent of the legislative and executive branches helps protect against politically motivated interference. Lack of constitutional clarity leaves the judiciary continually at risk of incursion by other branches. At a minimum, where the judiciary does not formally constitute a separate and equal branch, the superior branch must embrace limits on its own action such that judges considering cases are able to exercise their own judgement, subject only to the provisions of the law itself.[36]

Basic guarantees of judicial independence are set forth in the Constitutions of all the candidate States, while statutory provisions on the courts sometimes form part of the constitutional order and enjoy special status.[37] Some of the candidate States' Constitutions explicitly declare the separation of powers among executive, legislative, and judicial branches (Bulgaria, Slovenia), while a few (Estonia, Poland) also provide for a "balance" of powers. There is no express separation of powers in the Czech, Hungarian, Latvian, Romanian, or Slovak Constitutions. Consistent with international standards,[38] some Constitutions also formally guarantee the *independence* of the judicial branch as such (Bulgaria, Poland)

---

[35] See e.g. UN Basic Principles, Art. 1; CoE Recommendations, Principle 1 (2)(a); UCJ, Art. 2; ECSJ, Art. 1, 2. *But note* the ECHR generally finds no violation where the judiciary has substantive – though not formal or textual – independence, as is the case in some member States. See *Sramek v. Austria*, para. 38 (1984). In connection with removing a court or tribunal official, that it is sufficient if protections against removal are "recognised in fact and that the other necessary guarantees are present." See *Campbell and Fell v. UK*, ECHR Judgement of 28 June 1984, A80, para. 80.

[36] UN Basic Principles, Arts. 1, 2, 4; CoE Recommendations, Art. 2(a)–(b); UCJ, Arts. 1–4. None of the international standards refer to separation of powers, calling instead for *independent* judges or judiciaries.

[37] In Slovenia and Hungary, for example, adoption and amendment of the law on the organisation of courts require a special quorum of Parliament.

[38] UN Basic Principles, Art. 1. There is no consistent member State practice on a formal declaration of the judiciary's independence.

or of the courts (Estonia,[39] Lithuania,[40] Slovakia[41]); other Constitutions do not.[42] In accordance with European standards,[43] all Constitutions proclaim the independence of individual judges. Accordingly, in the performance of their judicial duties judges are subordinated only to the Constitution and the law.

Notwithstanding their textual diversity, all Constitutions provide distinctive tasks for each branch or for judges, and in practice all candidate States consider their judiciaries effectively separate. In any event, it should be clear that the judiciary can operate independently even where it is not formally identified as a *separate* power, as long as it enjoys explicit and robust guarantees of independence.

In spite of this, explicit reference in the Constitution to separation of powers or to the institutional independence of the judiciary in some form seems preferable as a safeguard against attempts to weaken judicial independence. Indeed, because past circumstances have shaped the political and legal cultures of the candidate States quite differently from those of most member States, an explicit separation of powers seems essential. Comprehensive separation of the branches would prove effective in shielding courts from the potentially negative effects of political processes still undergoing transformation, and give Constitutional Courts a powerful argument to defend judicial independence.

## B. Representation of the Judiciary

If a State fails to identify a clear representative for the judiciary in its relations with the other branches, it runs the risk that significant constitutional and legislative protections of independence will be eroded, as there will be no interlocutor to restrain the other branches from acting in ways which limit the scope of judicial prerogatives.

---

[39] The reference is to "courts" – a term which has not been defined. CONST. REP. ESTONIA, Art. 146.

[40] The Constitution provides that "judges and courts" are independent "[w]hen administering justice." CONST. REP. LITHUANIA, Art. 109.

[41] The references are to courts and judges, not the branch as a whole. CONST. REP. SLOVAKIA, Arts. 141 (1) and 144 (1).

[42] There is no such provision in the Constitutions of Hungary, Latvia, or Slovenia. However, in Latvia the Law on Judicial Power proclaims that "an independent judicial power exists alongside the legislative and the executive power." Law on Judicial Power, Art. 1 (1). Moreover, the Constitutional Court has clearly elaborated a principle of the separation of powers. Decision of the Constitutional Court, Case No. 04-07 (99), State Gazette, 29 March 2000. In Hungary, the Constitution defines the functions of the judiciary in such a way as to imply its separation (CONST. REP. HUNGARY, Chap. X.), and it has been so interpreted by the Constitutional Court. Decision 51/1992 (X.23) of the Constitutional Court (ruling that there can be no political connections between the judiciary and the political branches).

[43] CoE Recommendations, Principle I.

There is no consensus practice within the EU as to how the judiciary is to be represented in its relations with the other branches of the State. In some member States, a clearly defined constitutional representative is identified, while in others representation is more informal. In some, the judiciary is represented by the executive; in others, it represents itself, through special bodies such as a judicial council, or through the higher courts. Independent bodies are the preferred approach of the international judges associations; councils can also be an effective means of including lower court judges in the representation process, and are increasingly employed in member States.

Likewise, among the candidate States several models of judicial representation are employed: representation by the Ministry of Justice (Czech Republic, Estonia, Latvia); by the Ministry and the judicial council (Poland, Romania, Slovakia,[44] Slovenia); by the leading courts alone (Lithuania[45]) or by the judicial council alone (Bulgaria, Hungary). However, many of these bodies are only informal representatives of the judiciary (as in the Czech Republic, Estonia, and Poland), since their functions are not clearly defined in the Constitutions or laws, and representative functions are often in fact dispersed among different institutions or individuals.[46]

Althought each of these models can in theory be effective in representing the judiciary, in practice excessive reliance on the executive branch creates the risk that the judiciary will be given lesser priority in negotiations on a range of issues on which the interests of the judiciary and the executive may conflict, from budgets to resolution of disputes over competencies. A separate and independent branch ought to represent itself, and not rely on the other branches for that representation.

## C. Extraordinary and Military Courts

A basic precondition of judicial independence is that only courts established by law should be permitted to administer justice,[47] and this principle is set forth in all the candidate States' Constitutions. Bulgaria, Estonia, and Slovenia expressly prohibit the establishment of extraordinary courts. Lithuania restricts the establishment of extraordinary courts to special circumstances.

---

[44] Pending implementation of the February 2000 constitutional amendment creating a judicial council, the judiciary is represented by the Minister and the President of the Supreme Court.

[45] The representational function is in transition, following a 1999 constitutional court decision which invalidated parts of the courts law, which has yet to be replaced.

[46] In many States the Supreme Court is represented separately.

[47] See e.g. EU Charter of Fundamental Rights, Art. 47; ICCPR, Art. 14; UN Basic Principles, Art. 5, European Convention on Human Rights, Article 6(1).

In certain states, military courts which are insufficiently independent from the executive exercise broad jurisdiction over cases which properly should be brought before civilian courts.[48] Military courts, traditionally a means of skirting formal judicial protections, have been abolished in the Czech Republic, Lithuania and Slovenia.[49] In Bulgaria, Romania and Slovakia,[50] military courts continue to exercise broad powers, including over cases brought against the police.[51] Poland also has military courts, and in Hungary, military judges sit within the regular court system.

Because military courts generally have a closer connection to the executive through the military hierarchy, they pose two problems. First, military judges in these courts have less independence. Second, the operation of military courts reduces the jurisdiction falling under civilian courts protected by guarantees of independence, or may create an alternative forum whose jurisdiction is vaguely defined.

## D. The Role of Constitutional Courts

Reviewing legislation and measures taken by the executive for compliance with the Constitution is the prerogative of the new constitutional courts in most candidate States;[52] throughout the last decade, constitutional court decisions played a major role in defining the competences and the independence of courts.[53] Consistent with member State practice, constitutional courts in the candidate countries are normally outside the ordinary court system, and are not considered courts in the strict sense. Parliamentary and executive involvement in the selection of constitutional court judges is therefore generally more direct, and the justices always serve limited terms.[54]

---

[48] Military courts are subject to the same requirements of judicial independence as civilian courts. Compare *Findlay v. United Kingdom*, ECHR Judgement of 25 February 1997 (No. 110/1995/16/706), Reports 1997-1. See Office of the High Commisioner for Human Rights, "Equality before the courts and the right to a fair and public hearing by an independent court established by law" (Art. 14): 13/04/84. CCPR General comment 13. (General Comments) (21st session, 1984).

[49] Latvia allows military courts, but has not passed the requisite legislation to allow their operation.

[50] Military courts in Slovakia are considered to form part of the regular court system.

[51] There has been some improvement in Romania, in that the Supreme Court is now the court of last resort for military court cases.

[52] In Estonia the Constitutional Review Chamber of the Supreme Court exercises the functions of a constitutional court.

[53] A Constitutional Court decision was decisive in the reform of Lithuania's system of judicial administration, for example, while Court rulings have clarified questions of the separation of powers or the judiciary's independence in Hungary and Latvia.

[54] In Estonia, justices of the Constitutional Review Chamber are elected to five-year terms from among the Supreme Court justices by the Supreme Court *en banc*.

In part as a consequence of their closer connections to political matters, the relation between the constitutional courts and ordinary courts is problematic in some countries, centring on questions about whether the ordinary courts are subject to constitutional court rulings and whether interpretation of laws is the exclusive prerogative of constitutional courts. In Hungary, representatives of the judiciary have strongly criticised the Ministry of Justice for proposing a Government bill which would allow the Constitutional Court to review decisions of the Supreme Court aimed at ensuring uniform interpretation of legal provisions. The Supreme Court (in Romania) and lower courts (in Poland) have rejected the view that decisions of the Constitutional Court bind the judicial branch.

Where States establish a separate quasi-judicial institution like a constitutional court, closely connected to the executive or the legislature, then that court's influence over the judiciary must be limited in the same way as for the political branches to ensure that it does not unduly interfere with judges' proper scope of decision-making. Vesting judicial review in the ordinary courts (as in Estonia) eliminates the risk that other branches will influence the judiciary through this channel.

Of course, to the degree one considers a constitutional court to have proper adjudicative functions, it should have guarantees of its independence just as any ordinary court.

## E.  Rules on Incompatibility

Personal or professional affiliations outside the judiciary inevitably raise the potential for conflicts of interest that can make it difficult for judges to remain impartial. Where those affiliations are with another branch, it may also be difficult for judges to remain truly independent without jeopardising their careers outside the judiciary. Most standards therefore explicitly recommend limitations on judges' outside activities,[55] although the jurisprudence of the ECHR and the practice of member States do not support an absolute prohibition against judges working in the political branches.[56]

Most candidate States place restrictions on judges' holding offices in the executive, parliament, or the civil service. Not all crossover is prohibited, however; several countries allow judges to work within the Ministry of Justice (Czech Republic, Poland, Slovakia).

---

[55] UCJ, Art. 7 (1). UN Basic Principles, Art. 8, suggests that judges' rights of association and assembly may be limited by the requirement that they "preserve the dignity of their office and the impartiality and independence of the judiciary." These same standards do not exclude judges' associations. UCJ, Art. 12; UN Basic Principles, Art. 9.

[56] See e.g. *Ettl v. Austria*, ECHR Judgement of 23 April 1987 (No. 12/1985/98/146), A 117, para. 38; *Engel and Others v. Netherlands*, ECHR Judgement of 23 November 1976, A 22.

In the Czech Republic and Slovakia, judges routinely work in the Ministry of Justice while retaining their status as judges; Estonia and Latvia are planning to introduce the practice. In Poland, judges may work for the Ministry and continue to adjudicate cases; such a practice seriously undermines judges' independence.

Rules on incompatibility also limit the ability of judges to hold elective office – the practice in most, but not all member States. In general, judges who wish to hold elective office must resign from the bench. However, in some candidate States a judge may merely suspend service (Slovakia, Slovenia) and then return to the judiciary later. This encourages an unduly close relationship with the other branches.

The rules on incompatibility notwithstanding, in several States judges may be appointed to different commissions or committees for elections (Bulgaria, Latvia, Poland, Romania) or human rights (Latvia, where a member of the Supreme Court is a consultant). Obviously, the opportunity to select particular judges to serve on committees affords other branches an opportunity to reward or punish judges for inappropriate reasons. In Bulgaria, commission work can provide significant remuneration, which increases the potential for inappropriate incentives and influence. Preferably, commission work should not be remunerated.

It is common among candidate States – as among member States – that judges are not allowed to be members of political parties or to be engaged in political activities. Although the ban on party membership was introduced as a reaction to the communist past, the prohibition is still perceived as a genuine guarantee of independence. In the member States, too, limitations on judges' political affiliations are common. There are no such prohibitions in the Czech Republic[57] and Slovenia.

All candidate States place restrictions on judges' outside commercial or professional activities; all allow judges to engage in academic, scientific or artistic work. These provisions are consistent with international standards, and generally contribute to ensuring that judges are impartial, and are seen to be.

*Disclosure*: Although there are no international or European standards on the practice, financial disclosure may be an effective way to increase the accountability of judges and combat corruption without impinging upon their independence. In order to enhance transparency of judicial income and with the aim of preventing corruption, some candidate States have introduced acceptable disclosure rules for all judges (Lithuania, Poland, Slovakia). This is particularly important in countries where allegations of judicial

---

[57] Except for constitutional court judges, who may not join parties.

corruption are relatively frequent. However, in some countries, current disclosure rules are not sufficient (Bulgaria, Romania). Thus in Romania, judges at the beginning and the end of their office have to file a *secret* financial declaration; obviously this will do little to curb corruption so long as the results are not made public. There are no disclosure requirements in Slovenia or the Czech Republic.

## III. Administration of the Court System and Judicial Independence

### A. Loci of Administrative Responsibility[58]

Unless bodies responsible for administering the courts are prevented from using their authority to influence judges' decision-making, judicial independence will, over time, be undermined. Vesting administrative authority in another branch unnecessarily increases the incentives and opportunities to exert undue influence. Granting independent bodies self-administrative powers under transparent procedures would reduce the risk of political interference, while still allowing political representation that encourages accountability.

There is no consensus practice among member States as to how the judiciary is to be administered. In some member States, the judiciary is administered by the executive; in others, it fulfils these functions itself, through special bodies or the higher courts. International standards are not in consensus on the recommended form of administration, as some explicitly call for the judiciary to be administered by an independent body representing judges,[59] while others merely call for it to be organised in such a way as not to compromise the independence of judges, but do not identify a clearly preferable method,[60] or allow for a variety of models.[61] All the standards suggest that at a minimum, the judiciary should have some form of meaningful input into its administration.

---

[58] This Section principally focuses on the bodies responsible for general issues of administration. Specific issues of self-governance – such as appointments, case management discipline, and budgeting – are considered in separate Sections, and only mentioned here in passing.

[59] ECSJ, Art. 6.

[60] UCJ, Art. 11(1), but noting further that "[w]here this is not ensured in...ways that are rooted in established and proven tradition, judicial independence...would be carried out by independent bodies that include substantial judicial representation." Id., Art. 11(2).

[61] CoE Recommendations, Art. 2(c).

Among the candidate States several models are in use:[62] administration by the Ministry of Justice (Czech Republic, Estonia, Latvia,[63] Slovakia[64]); administration by the Ministry and at least to some extent the judicial council (Bulgaria, Poland, Romania, Slovenia[65]); and administration by the judicial council (Hungary). In Lithuania, the situation is in considerable flux following a 1999 Constitutional Court ruling that invalidated parts of the courts law, but has yet to be replaced; in the interim, the advisory Council of Judges has taken on certain managerial tasks pending completion of a new law on the judiciary.

All the States have vested at least some administrative responsibilities in court presidents or councils; however, in general, administrative authority has not been fully transferred from the executive, and budgetary responsibility remains very much in the hands of the legislative and executive branches.[66] An independent judiciary is possible under each of these systems, as the experience of member States partly shows, so long as the administrative body is prevented, by transparent procedures, from interfering with the core decision-making independence of the judge.

## 1. *Principal Administration by the Ministry of Justice*

In some candidate States, the Ministry of Justice is the principal administrator of the judiciary (Czech Republic, Estonia, Latvia, Slovakia). This model has allowed the executive indirectly to affect core judicial decision-making through its control of what should be purely administrative decisions, both legally and beyond its formal mandate.

In some other States in which the Ministry of Justice retains an important role alongside other bodies (Poland, Romania, Slovenia), an avenue for improper executive interference in judicial administration remains open. In Poland, for example, a number of tasks, such as administrative supervision of court presidents, review of case backlogs, and

---

[62] This list is quite similar to that above concerning the Representation of the Judiciary; although some States, such as Slovenia, divide these functions, they are generally joined in the same body.

[63] The Conference of Judges, as a self-governing organisation, also has some very limited advisory and election powers. It examines issues of judicial practice and submits requests to the Supreme Court Plenum for explanations on application of law; it elects members of the Judicial Qualification Board and the Judicial Disciplinary Board.

[64] Slovakia has recently amended its Constitution in a manner that requires reform of the administrative supervision of the courts, but the necessary implementing legislation has not been passed.

[65] Slovenia's system divides administrative authority among a judicial council, the Ministry of Justice, and the Supreme Court.

[66] Budgetary powers are discussed at length in Section IV, below.

elaboration of the judiciary's draft budget remain with the Ministry of Justice. In Slovenia, the Minister of Justice, who retains only limited supervisory powers over the administrative activity of court presidents, recently attempted to extend his competence to assessing the efficiency of courts' operations,[67] which would have opened up the possibility for the executive to selectively scrutinise courts. In Romania, judges report that inspectors from the Ministry intimidate them and interfere with their decisional independence by examining case files to verify the correct application of the law.[68]

## 2. Administration by a Judicial Council

One alternative to control by any one branch is to establish completely independent bodies not located within any branch. As in France and Italy, most candidate States have established judicial councils – usually composed of members appointed or elected by the various branches – to administer some of the functions of the judiciary. Some – Bulgaria, Hungary, Poland, Romania, and Slovenia – have vested their councils with substantial powers to varying degrees.

Although not the only means of ensuring administrative independence, councils can limit the role of the executive and legislature in the daily work of courts, thus removing one of the principal avenues for outside influence, while at the same time allowing some representation of views and interests from outside the judiciary. The international judges' associations recommend independent bodies representing judges as the most effective way to ensure judicial independence,[69] and several member States have such councils.

However, not all candidate States' councils work in the same way. The design of a council affects its ability to ensure judicial independence – many councils (such as Bulgaria's) have too few resources or personnel to take over administrative responsibilities formerly handled by large ministerial staffs. Hungary has accorded its council nearly exclusive authority, while four other States divide administrative powers between the council and the Ministry of Justice. In other States, councils exercise only limited administrative, supervisory, disciplinary, or advisory functions.

---

[67] The opposition of the Supreme Court, the Association of Judges and the Judicial Council forced the Government to withdraw the proposal.

[68] Information from five district court judges, April 2001, Bucharest; statement of participants at OSI roundtable meeting, 26 March, 2001, Bucharest. *Explanatory Note: OSI held roundtable meetings in a number of candidate countries to invite critique of country reports in draft form. Experts present included representatives of the government, the Commission Delegations, representatives of the judiciary, and civil society organisations. References to this meeting should not be understood as endorsement of any particular point of view by any one participant.*

[69] UCJ, Art. 11(2); ECSJ, Art. 6.

*a.    Councils with Nearly Exclusive Authority: Hungary*

On one end of the spectrum is Hungary's powerful National Council of Justice, which exercises most of the judicial functions previously performed by the Ministry of Justice. The Council is in charge of tasks related to the administration of courts and the selection, promotion, evaluation and training of judges; court presidents and panels have some responsibilities as well. The Council's budgetary responsibility is much more limited; it submits a draft budget for the courts to the Government.

According to some critics the operations of the Council – which has a large staff – are overly bureaucratic and actually increase the administrative burden on judges. Some argue that it is actually the Office of the Council which wields real power, and not the Council itself. Many of the employees of the Office used to work at the Ministry of Justice, and it has been alleged that their mentality still reflects that of the prior system, when courts were clearly subordinated to the bureaucracy of the Ministry.

*b.    Councils with Broad Responsibility: Bulgaria, Poland*

Continuing down the spectrum from maximum responsibility, two States have created judicial councils with broad powers relating to the independence of the judiciary. Bulgaria's Supreme Judicial Council has very broad formal competencies: it determines the number of judges, submits a draft budget for the judiciary to the Government, makes proposals to the State President concerning appointment of the Presidents of the Supreme Court and of the Supreme Administrative Court, and acts as the disciplinary authority for the judiciary. The Council appoints and dismisses judges, and can lift judges' immunity if requested by the General Prosecutor. However, the Bulgarian Council represents the entire magistracy, including prosecutors and investigators. In addition, the Council only meets occasionally and has very limited staffing and resources, which has left the door open for the executive with its greater resources. The Ministry indeed maintains effective control of many administrative functions, and in certain areas, the dual sources of administrative authority have created confusion.

The National Judicial Council of Poland has less power than its counterpart in Bulgaria. It has competence over some personnel and status issues, such as reviewing applications for judicial posts, making recommendations to the State President for appointments, and deciding on the transfer of judges. As noted above, responsibility for budgets, supervision of court presidents, and training remain with the Ministry of Justice.

*c.    Mixed Systems: Slovenia*

In Slovenia, administration is divided among the Supreme Court, the Ministry of Justice, and the Judicial Council. The Council decides most significant personnel and status issues affecting the judiciary; the Supreme Court submits the courts' budget to the executive, although the Council gives Parliament an advisory opinion on the budget.

### d. Councils with Limited Powers: Lithuania, Romania

Other States have created councils whose administrative powers – and powers to ensure judicial independence – are more limited. In Lithuania, the Council of Judges advises the State President concerning appointment, promotion, transfer and dismissal of judges, and elects the members of the Judges' Examination Commission. Upon receipt of a complaint from a judge, the Council makes an assessment as to whether judicial independence has been violated. The draft Law on Courts would significantly expand the administrative authority of the Council of Judges and a new National Court Administration, substantially reducing the influence of the executive. In the absence of a new Law on Courts, the Council has in practice taken on somewhat broader powers than are defined in its formal remit.

In Romania, the Superior Council of the Magistracy acts as a disciplinary agency and nominates judges for appointment by the State President, but has no other administrative or supervisory powers, which remain with the Ministry of Justice.

### e. Advisory Councils: Slovakia

Slovakia's Council of Judges is a purely advisory body; its ability to support judicial independence rests on publicity and inter-branch relationships. A recent amendment to the Constitution expands the Council's powers to include nomination of judicial candidates, assignment and transfer of judges, proposals for the removal of judges, and establishment of disciplinary tribunals. However, enabling legislation has not yet been passed, and the precise scope of the Council's new powers is not clear.

### f. Composition of Judicial Councils

Just as the powers of the councils are varied, so are the modes of their formation, which may have a significant impact on their independence and effectiveness. Obviously, if the purpose of a council is to minimise the influence of the political branches, it does little good to populate it with appointees directly beholden to the Government or Parliament.

Most councils have a mixed composition – including judges and some combination of prosecutors, lawyers, or State officials – and divide the power to elect members among the judiciary, executive and legislature. This ensures accountability through meaningful involvement of the political branches, and a measure of independence for the judiciary. Some councils have a majority of judges (Hungary, 10 to 5;[70] Lithuania,

---

[70] The Supreme Court elects one delegate and nine judges are elected by the plenary sessions of judges organised on the regional level. The Council has five permanent non-judge members: the Minister of Justice, the General Prosecutor, the President of the National Bar Association and two members of Parliament.

all;[71] Poland, 17 to 8;[72] Romania, 10 to 5;[73] Slovenia, 6 to 5[74]), while in Bulgaria judges have only minority representation.[75] Creating a council with a majority for the executive or legislature can defeat the purpose of separating administrative functions from the political branches.

Some States (Hungary, Lithuania, Slovenia) ensure that the whole judiciary is represented – a procedure which may help reduce the risk of illegitimate internal interference with judicial independence by giving judges of all levels a voice on the administrative or rule-making body – while Romania gives disproportionate weight to the higher judiciary, which does little to diminish the risks of intra-judicial interference.

---

[71] All members are judges; however, the executive may have some influence on the composition of the Council as the State President and the Minister of Justice each appoint two judges to the Council.

[72] Four members elected from the Sejm, two from the Senate, as well as the Minister of Justice.

[73] In Romania, the Council represents the magistracy, including prosecutors. In that context, it is appropriate that judges have only part of the representation – although, of course, a joint administration for judges and prosecutors subject to the executive poses its own problems for judicial independence.

[74] Five lawyers elected by the National Assembly.

[75] The 25-seat Council has 13 representatives of the magistracy, but this includes judges, prosecutors, and investigators, so there are only about six judges (counting the Presidents of the Supreme and Supreme Administrative Courts *ex officio*). Eleven of the 12 non-magistracy seats are elected by Parliament, and the General Prosecutor is a member *ex officio*; thus, members beholden to the legislature or executive hold a clear majority.

## IV. Financial Autonomy and Level of Funding

### A. Budgeting Process

Whatever the constitutional posture of a State towards judicial independence, the judiciary's freedom to operate independently can be seriously undermined if it is unduly beholden to other branches for its material well-being. Parliament can alter the overall funding of the courts; the executive can distribute funds unevenly among courts. Although it is normal – and entirely consistent with European practice[76] – for the judiciary to receive funding solely through parliamentary appropriations and executive disbursements, these processes can be used to punish or reward courts for the behaviour of particular judges. The mere knowledge that this can happen may operate to discourage judges from ruling against the other branches' wishes.

In the candidate States, responsibility for formulating the budget for the judiciary and allocating it to individual courts is, as a general rule, in the competence of the same body that controls the administrative operation of the ordinary court system.[77] Accordingly, where the Ministry of Justice has full or shared administrative control of the courts, it formulates the judiciary's budget, allocates resources to individual courts, and supervises how resources are spent (Czech Republic, Estonia, Latvia, Poland, Romania, Slovakia).

Where judicial councils exercise significant administrative control over courts (Bulgaria, Hungary), they are involved in the budgeting process to a significant degree. In Hungary the National Council of Justice drafts the courts' budget and submits it to the Government. The Government is not bound by the Council's draft, though it is obliged to give Parliament reasons for deviating from the Council's proposal.[78] In Bulgaria the draft budget of the judicial branch is drawn up by the Supreme Judicial Council. The Bulgarian

---

[76] International standards are largely silent on the specific role of the judiciary in the budgeting process. UN Basic Principles, Art. 7, provides only that the State shall ensure adequate resources, but does not recommend a particular process. The UCJ requires that the judiciary have an opportunity to "take part in or to be heard on decisions" relating to the its material support. Art. 14.

[77] In most of the candidate States, higher courts have separate budget chapters (except the Czech Republic); constitutional courts have separate chapters in all candidate States. In Lithuania, the Constitutional Court ruled that the courts' financial independence required the Government to create a separate budget for them rather than allocating their funding through the Ministry of Justice. Ruling of the Constitutional Court of 21 December 1999, Official Gazette, 1999, No. 109-3192.

[78] It has been reported that the Government has not always complied with this requirement.

constitutional court has held that the Government is obliged to incorporate the Council's proposal into the draft budget without alteration and submit it to the National Assembly. However, the Government may also formulate its own proposals and objections, and in practice Parliament has adopted the Government version.

In Slovenia the National Council of Justice and the Supreme Court share responsibilities for budgetary issues: the Supreme Court prepares and submits the budget to the Government; during parliamentary debate, representatives of the Supreme Court and the Council participate in the sessions of the competent parliamentary committee. Lithuania is in transition, with courts submitting their budgets directly to the Ministry of Finance.

There is no evidence that these models guarantee more effective representation of the judiciary's material interests than other approaches. In no case does a council have effective control over the budget proposal for the judiciary as a whole, and of course budgets are ultimately subject to legislative determination. In all these countries judges are left without representation at the crucial stage when the budget is discussed in the Cabinet. In Slovenia in 1998, for example, the refusal of the Minister of Justice to take part in budget negotiations almost resulted in the closure of district and regional courts.

Clear and detailed protections should be in place to ensure that funding is not used to punish judges or to chill their decision-making. Placing authority for the preparation of budget recommendations in the hands of an independent body – such as a judicial council – can limit the executive's ability to curtail judicial independence. Parliament will still appropriate funding, but solutions such as mandatory funding levels or multi-year or block appropriations can reduce the scope for legislative interference.

Where budgets are prepared without significant involvement by judges, leading politicians should publicly demonstrate support for depoliticisation of court funding through appropriate legislation and executive action. The political branches should commit to specified levels of funding, or specified and objective formulae for determining funding which remove the issue from the political sphere. At all levels, high levels of transparency and greater regular input from judges in budget preparations would raise the costs for parties seeking to influence the judiciary through budgetary pressure.

There is no clear standard concerning the proper level of funding for the judiciary as a proportion of the State budget. It may be possible to derive a standard about protecting funding levels against arbitrary reduction.[79] While it is difficult to identify a common

---

[79] Compare UCJ, Art. 13 (1); ECSJ, Art. 8.

approach, no member State has reduced the budget for administering the courts in recent decades.[80] (In this regard, Poland is of note: the judiciary's percentage share of the current budget – 1.37 – is reduced to 1.29 in the next budget.) However, even in candidate States whose funding for the judiciary has remained steady, the effective amount of funding has declined, since the increased number of judges and dramatic expansion of the courts' caseload has not been accompanied by a proportional increase in budget allotments.

## B. Work Conditions

International standards call for courts to have sufficient funding to ensure their smooth operation,[81] and member State practice is consistent with those standards. It is evident that well-trained, knowledgeable and skilful judges who are not overworked are in a better position to resist undue influence than their less competent colleagues. Poor work conditions can threaten judicial independence; in some cases, the standards may be so low as to dramatically reduce the efficiency of the courts, increase the incentives for corruption as a means of circumventing inefficient and overworked courts, and therefore increase public and political support for closer control of the judiciary's operations. In addition, poor work conditions can limit judges' ability to defend their independence by forcing them to devote excessive effort to basic issues of administrative upkeep, and can threaten their impartiality by making them reliant on assistance from outside parties.

Although salaries in the candidate States have generally increased over the past decade, the conditions under which judges perform their duties are still poor. Many judges work in dilapidated offices with minimal equipment or staff support; in some cases, even basic legal texts, such as official gazettes, are not available. In parts of Romania, for example, four to six judges share a single office. In Bulgaria, Latvia, Lithuania, and Slovakia extremely poor conditions are reported, and in Poland, small courts are much better equipped than large courts. Poor conditions are reported from all countries. There are often considerable differences among courts in any single country, and courts in the capitals often suffer the greatest shortage of space.

In almost every country, the caseload of the average judge appears to have increased substantially since 1990. Staffing levels, material resources and improvements in technology have not kept pace with the immense increase in the number of cases to be handled by courts. In Latvia, these heavy caseloads and the resulting backlogs appear

---

[80] Information from Giuseppe Di Federico, Director of the Research Institute on Judicial Systems of the National Research Council, University of Bologna.

[81] See UN Basic Principles, Art. 7; UCJ, Art. 14.

to contribute to routine violations of procedural guarantees (such as timely appeals and review of pre-trial detention), weakening public support for the work of the judiciary.[82]

It seems that the candidate States have largely failed so far to remedy the under-investment during four decades of communism. Partly as a consequence of this the courts remain unacceptably inefficient, subject to corruption, and therefore more exposed to incursions on their independence. Poland and Hungary in particular have made some progress in countering these problems, though there too conditions are poor.

## C. Compensation

A sufficient salary is a necessary safeguard against the risk that impoverished judges will be compelled to sell justice to make ends meet; in addition, salary often correlates with prestige, which can help inoculate judges against attempts at improper influence, especially from parties to disputes. Although judicial salaries need not match those of the political branch exactly, there is a good argument that ensuring equivalent salaries usefully reinforces the perception of equality among the separate branches. International standards variously call for salaries to be "commensurate with the dignity of [the] profession"[83] or simply "adequate[.]"[84] However, protection against salary reductions is generally not provided for in member States.[85]

In all candidate States, judges' salaries have been increased considerably over the last ten years and they are now usually more or less comparable to those of members of Parliament or civil servants in leading positions.[86] In Latvia, for instance, the salary of Supreme

---

[82] Although there are differences across the region, each country suffers to some degree from the problem of backlogs deriving from increased workloads. In Estonia the backlogs are linked to the situation of the Russian population, as it is in the mostly Russian-speaking industrial north-east where a disproportionate number of judicial posts have gone unfilled, leaving the existing judges extremely overburdened. In Hungary and Latvia the capitals suffer from the heaviest overload.

[83] CoE Recommendations, Principle III.1.b.

[84] UN Basic Principles, Art. 11; ECSJ, Art. 8 (where adequate means that it must "ensure that the Judge has true economic independence...").

[85] Only Ireland constitutionally prohibits cutting judges' salaries. Information from Ernst Markel, Presiding Justice of the Supreme Court of Austria.

[86] In Poland judges, who receive lower pay than Members of Parliament, have filed more than 500 claims before the courts and the Constitutional Tribunal invoking provisions of the Constitution requiring that judges' compensation corresponds to the dignity of their office and their responsibilities, claiming that these provisions require the various branches' salaries to be equivalent. In its review of the question, the Tribunal did not find any such violation.

Court justices is equal to the highest amount civil servants in the first category receive, while regional court judges get 85 percent of that amount; salaries are supplemented by additional payments varying according to the judge's level, although judges sometimes do not receive the full amount of the supplemental payments to which they are entitled. Judges in Poland and Slovenia in particular have raised complaints that their salaries are incommensurate with their positions.

# V. Judicial Office

The procedures for regulating the course of a judge's career – from appointment through various promotions to retirement – should, properly, be insulated from political considerations; yet unless proper safeguards are in place, the discretion which inevitably attaches to the decisions affecting the judge's career provides opportunities for other actors to punish or reward judges based on the substance of their rulings.

## A. Selection Process

Over time, a purely political process for selecting new judges can skew the judiciary unduly in favour of the body controlling selections, especially if that body exercises continuing institutional influence on judges' careers. Yet denying the political branches any say in the selection of judges risks isolating the judiciary from the democratic society which it serves – and indeed, the potential intrusion is relatively minor, as, by itself, bias in selection does not restrict the judge's subsequent independence on the bench. Certainly, international standards and member State practice do not prohibit the involvement of the political branches in initital selection of judges.[87]

Among candidate States, there are two aspects of the selection process that are problematic from the point of view of judicial independence: probationary periods for new and untested judges,[88] and political involvement in appointments to higher courts.

*Probationary Periods and New Judges*: Probationary appointment is seen in many countries of Europe as a necessary means of screening out individuals unfit for office and not as a threat to judicial independence. Several member States employ probationary periods during which guarantees of independence are restricted. It is often

---

[87] See *Campbell and Fell v. UK*, ECHR Judgement of 28 June 1984, A80 (holding that appointment by the executive is permissible and even normal). Compare UN Basic Principles, Art. 10 (requiring that appointees be persons of "integrity and ability" and that selection not be for "improper motives" or discriminatory); CoE Recommendations, Principle I.2.c. (recommending that the selecting authority be "independent of the government and the administration[,]" but noting that "constitutional or legal provisions or tradition" may allow judges to be appointed by political authorities and recommending in such cases that the process be transparent and independent in practice); UCJ, Art. 9 (requiring appointment according to objective criteria based on proper professional qualification[,]" but also implicitly allowing for this to be done by political bodies in accordance with "established and proven tradition[.]").

[88] Probationary periods can be considered as a problem of tenure.

noted that new judges lack sufficient experience and maturity responsibly to handle a broad grant of independence. Certainly, because society grants independence to judges in order to secure impartial decisions on important issues, it may reasonably expect that its judges are prepared to use their independence responsibly, and not as a license.

Although there are important variations, in most of the candidate States the path to a judgeship requires a probationary period of several years before a decision concerning a life appointment is made; the Czech Republic, Slovakia, and Slovenia alone grant permanent tenure upon appointment.[89]

Clearly, however, for the duration of the probationary period judges may feel an incentive to consider the effects upon their careers of decisions that displease officials in charge of determining who receives permanent appointment. The gains in ensuring a high quality corps of judges must be weighed against the potential for harm to judicial independence. This is especially the case as there are a number of steps States could take to improve the quality and professional maturity of incoming judges, thus obviating or minimising the need for post-appointment intrusions on judicial independence.

Rather than persist in limiting independence on the grounds that young new judges are unable to handle it, States might work to alter the profile of incoming judges to eliminate the problem of judicial irresponsibility at the outset, in recognition of the fact that judicial independence has taken on a newly recognised importance in a democratic society. In other words, guarantees of independence would not be limited to accommodate the pool of judges, but the other way around. The system would aim to produce judges who can adjudicate responsibly, not limit their ability to do so on the grounds that they cannot.

Ideally, transparent and neutral approval procedures – preferably vested in a body not involved in the further evaluation or promotion of judges during their careers – should be applied to probationers; the political acceptability or preferability of judges' rulings should play no part in the determination. Specifically, training for candidates should be extended, and age limits and experience requirements increased where possible.[90] Expanding the period of in-court training (during which candidates exercise

---

[89] Poland does not have formal probationary periods, but inasmuch as candidates for judgeships must first work as assessors – and exercise adjudicatory powers like a judge – in effect the problems attached to probation can occur there as well.

[90] Where financial resources allow, increasing judicial salaries – besides its inoculatory effects against corruption – can also encourage older, more established attorneys with greater life experience to consider judicial careers, thus reducing the problems associated with young judges.

no core decisional powers by themselves) and reducing the period of probation, as in the German model, or even eliminating probation altogether, can minimise the potential for improper and unnecessary interference. In general, the decision about judges' maturity should be made before they begin working, while mechanisms for removal afterwards should be disfavoured, as they inevitably open the door to abuse, which chills the decisional independence of all judges, including those who are competent.

Where probation is retained, it should be understood that it is only a mechanism to weed out incompetent judges, and cannot have any political content. Therefore, it seems improper to vest any decisional authority in the political branches after they have made the initial appointment.[91] Instead, since evaluating probation is a technical matter, it ought to be done by a commission composed of judges and legal professionals applying clear and neutral criteria. And, of course, since the purpose of probation is to identify incompetent judges, there is little reason to keep probationary restrictions in place for several years.

*Appointments to Higher Courts*: In many candidate States Supreme Court justices and constitutional court judges are appointed by parliamentary vote.[92] These processes are inherently political, and because appointment to these courts is effectively a form of promotion from lower courts, lower court judges may feel incentives to rule in ways which please the political authorities responsible for elevating judges to higher courts – a problem noted in Estonia in connection with its Supreme Court. Supreme Court judges in Romania are appointed by the State President for *renewable* six-year terms, which opens the door to influence like that experienced by probationary judges.

Although the process of selecting judges can never be completely isolated from political considerations – and need not be – political involvement in selection should be cabined within neutral, objective, and transparent standards. Dividing the selection process into nominating and appointing phases, with different bodies or branches responsible for each phase, can limit the risks of undue political influence.[93] Judicial independence is compatible with a wide range of selection processes so long as they are coupled with an unambiguous commitment to the principles that judges, once selected, are no

---

[91] In Estonia, for example, the State President makes initial appointments, but has no involvement in the decision to review a judge at the end of the probationary period – thus keeping the decisional authority in the hands of legal professionals.

[92] In Estonia, Supreme Court judges are elected by Parliament upon the proposal of the President of the Supreme Court, who is also elected by Parliament, upon the nomination of the State President.

[93] See CoE Recommendations, Principle I.2.c(2); but see ECJS, Art. 4 ("No outside influence and, in particular, no political influence, must play any part in the appointment of Judges.").

longer beholden to their political supporters for maintenance in their position, and must not be the subject of attempts to influence decisions in a particular case.[94]

## B. Tenure, Retirement, Transfer, and Removal

### 1. Tenure

If judges believe that their job security depends upon the decision of a political actor, they may feel pressure to rule in a manner showing their loyalty and worthiness. Apart from the probationary period, ordinary judges have tenured irremovability until retirement in all candidate States; this is seen as an essential guarantee of independence, in accordance with the consensus practice among EU member States[95] and international standards.[96]

There are countervailing tendencies, however. In Slovenia members of Parliament have questioned the rationale of permanent tenure and proposed a constitutional amendment to abolish judicial tenure, though it is unlikely to pass.[97] The principle of lustration – though probably a unique case – can threaten judges' security of tenure.[98]

Throughout the region, most of the provisions dealing with judicial tenure seem designed, on their face at least, to respond to legitimate administrative and disciplinary concerns and to the need for accountability. Again, as with other administrative matters, clarity and objectivity of standards are probably more important than the specific requirements.

---

[94] The obvious exception is the institution of (re-)elected judges. However, with the possible exception of the quasi-political constitutional court and probationary regular judges, a clear preference against re-election of judges following the expiry of their term, where they do not have life tenure, would seem in concert with European values. Compare CoE Recommendations, Principle I.3. At a minimum, if a judge is subject to renewal, including through the probationary mechanism, that renewal must not be contingent, in any fashion, on the substantive conclusions the judge reached in any particular case.

[95] Information from Giuseppe Di Federico, Director of the Research Institute on Judicial Systems of the National Research Council, University of Bologna. The consensus practice applies to professional judges, not lay judges (such as justices of the peace in Italy, or administrative tribunal magistrates in England).

[96] UN Basic Principles, Arts. 11, 12.

[97] According to the author of the proposal, judicial backlogs are a result of judges' permanent term, which is not counterbalanced by adequate mechanisms for judicial accountability.

[98] See Section V.B.4.a.

## 2. Retirement

In most candidate States judges may be permitted to continue on the bench after reaching the normal retirement age at the discretion of the judicial administration,[99] a practice which introduces unnecessary risks to judges' independence.[100]

If judges' living standards drop dramatically following retirement, the possibility of extension may present a genuine threat to judicial independence, particularly if there are no precisely defined criteria for continuation. It is possible that selective extension will be used to remove politically undesirable judges, or to encourage pliability. This risk is particularly salient in Bulgaria, where a proposal to dismiss a judge after the retirement age does not have to be supported by reasons and where, at the same time, judges have incentives to continue working as pensions are very small. Similar problems obtain in the Czech Republic, Latvia, Romania[101] and Slovakia. Adequate pensions would reduce concerns about discretionary retirement, although the best approach is to mandate a retirement age without exception; the political branches should not have the discretion to retain or release judges after they become eligible for retirement.

## 3. Transfer

The security offered by tenure may be vitiated if judges can be transferred without cause. All member States restrict the practice of permanently transferring judges without their consent to disciplinary reasons or re-organisations that eliminate courts;[102] however, the rules for temporary transfers are much less restricted.

Generally among candidate States, judges may not be transferred from one court to another during their term in office without their consent; transfers are generally permitted under limited circumstances such as disciplinary sanctions or the reorganisation of courts. Some States allow temporary transfers without a judge's consent

---

[99] No extension beyond mandatory retirement is allowed in Estonia, Hungary, Lithuania and Slovenia.

[100] International standards would seem to favour a strict mandatory retirement. See UN Basic Principles, Art. 12; CoE Recommendations, Principle I.3.

[101] Romania does have a mandatory retirement age for judges; however, the retirement age for the popoulation as a whole is lower , and judges may serve up to the higher maximum retirement age for judges only at the discretion of the judge's court president (with the exception of Supreme Court justices).

[102] Compare CoE Recommendations, Principle I.2.f (providing that "[a] case should not be withdrawn from a judge without valid reasons...").

(Lithuania[103]), sometimes without sufficient procedural guarantees (as in Bulgaria and Hungary[104]).

## 4. Removal

Permanent removal of judges is generally performed by the appointing or electing body, and, consistent with international standards[105] and most EU practice,[106] is generally limited to instances in which judges have been found guilty of a criminal offence,[107] have seriously breached their obligations, or for health reasons are permanently prevented from performing their duties. The provisions generally seem procedurally sound.

### a. Lustration

In most candidate States, the composition of the judiciary has changed considerably since the end of Communism. The number of judges has increased substantially, and in most countries their average age is quite young, due to mandatory or encouraged voluntary retirement of judges politically active during the communist period (Czech Republic, Poland), political screening processes for judges (Czech Republic, Estonia), administration of oaths (Estonia) or declarations (Poland) concerning activities during the communist period, and active recruitment of younger candidates (Romania).

The process of politically motivated screening is by no means complete. For example, in 2000 Hungary extended its existing lustration law, screening certain officials who

---

[103] Under the draft Law on Courts the State president, on the advice of the Council of Judges, would be able to transfer judges for up to six months without their consent, if necessary to ensure the functioning of the court. However, it is not clear how often such a transfer could occur.

[104] The National Council of Justice may transfer a judge once every three years to another court for up to one year in "the interests of the administration of justice." Act LXVII on the Legal Status and Remuneration of Judges, 1997, Art. 17.

[105] UN Basic Principles, Art. 18; CoE Recommendations, Principle VI.2.

[106] In most member States, removal may be effected only on disciplinary or disability grounds, or upon penal conviction for serious offences. There are two main exceptions. In England and Wales judges sitting in the High Court and the Court of Appeals may be removed by the Crown following a vote by both houses of Parliament, but this rather complex procedure has been successfully invoked on only one occasion. A similar procedure in Germany, with impeachment by the *Bundestag* and a final decision by the Constitutional Court, has never been employed. Information from Giuseppe Di Federico, Director of the Research Institute on Judicial Systems of the National Research Council, University of Bologna.

[107] In Bulgaria the judge must be sentenced to imprisonment.

worked in the communist regime, to include ordinary judges.[108] There is concern that submitting judges to ideological screening ten years after the change in regime has no legitimate purpose.[109]

Because it may allow the legislature or executive to remove sitting judges from office based on political or ideological criteria, lustration or screening represents a potentially serious intrusion into the independence of the judiciary. Judges are forced out of office, sometimes without having violated any law, without regard to their competence. Such actions might violate international norms concerning the independence of judges.[110]

However, the relatively limited exercise of lustration seen in candidate States in the past decade does not seem to violate any standard embraced by the EU. Germany still has screening and lustration provisions in place, and most judges who served in the German Democratic Republic have resigned their posts. This has not generated any reaction from the EU or member States.[111] In addition, a number of member States have provisions screening or barring from public office "Nazis", "fascists", or their collaborators.

Considered in the context of the rapid transition from communist systems that denied the independence of the judiciary and actively involved judges in systems of political oppression, a tailored and temporally limited screening seems compatible with the *creation* of an independent judiciary. However, where lustration is expanded over time, or is increasingly unrelated to precisely defined activity during the communist period, as in Hungary, it may interfere with the *maintenance* of an independent judiciary.

## C. Evaluation and Promotion

As with initial selection procedures, where standards for promotion[112] are not regularised and transparent, promotion and the rewards it brings can be held out as an incentive for a judge to issue rulings pleasing to those deciding which judges advance. In addition,

---

[108] The original version from 1994 only covered the President of the Supreme Court.

[109] The Czech Republic and Lithuania extended lustration laws covering judges in 1996 and 1998, respectively.

[110] See UN Basic Principles, Art. 10; CoE Recommendations, Principles I.2.c. and VI.2.

[111] Information from Giuseppe Di Federico, Director of the Research Institute on Judicial Systems of the National Research Council, University of Bologna.

[112] This Section considers both promotion in salary and rank within a court and appointments to higher courts, which, consistent with practice in many member States, is not formally considered a promotion in most candidate States.

because higher judges review lower court decisions, and often have administrative authority, there are added incentives for political actors to influence the advancement of judges to higher positions if clear and neutral procedures are not in place to prevent them.

International standards call for advancement to be based on factors such as experience and ability.[113] Within member States with career systems similar to those in the candidate States, advancement is based on specific norms intended to regulate the process in a fair way,[114] although nowhere is discretion fully eliminated by formal regulation.

Judicial posts in the candidate States are usually filled by career judges who are progressively promoted. Although it is reported that assessments for promotion are in most cases made on objective criteria, such as the judge's integrity, ability and experience, there are considerable differences in the precision and clarity with which criteria for assessing performance are defined. Lack of clear criteria increases the risk of arbitrary, politically biased decisions. Moreover, assessments often consider the rate of reversal by higher courts. While this may be a relevant factor in certain contexts, where higher court judges have influence on promotions (as in Estonia), excessive reliance on this criterion may encourage undue deference by lower judges interested in promotion, which may impinge upon their decisional independence.

In Bulgaria, Latvia, and Slovenia,[115] criteria for assessment and promotion are poorly defined. In Romania, by contrast, criteria for assessing judges' performance are clear and detailed, while few quantitative measures of performance are set except caseload and time served; however an exceptionally high reversal rate may lead to a poor assessment rating.

## D. Discipline

Simplistic models of judicial independence might suppose that *any* attempt to punish a judge infringes judicial independence. This is certainly not the view of the international standards,[116] nor does it comport with member States' practice. When a judge acts in

---

[113] UN Basic Principles, Art. 13; CoE Recommendations, Principle I.2.c. (noting also that it is preferable for evaluative decisions to be made by the judiciary itself); UCJ, Art. 9; ECSJ, Art. 5.

[114] Information from Giuseppe Di Federico, Director of the Research Institute on Judicial Systems of the National Research Council, University of Bologna.

[115] In Slovakia, under a recent amendment to the Constitution, appointments would be made by the State President upon nomination by the Judicial Council. However, the Minister of Justice would still appoint court presidents, and there would be no clear assessment standards.

[116] See UN Basic Principles, Art. 17–20; CoE Recommendations, Principle VI; UCJ, Art. 11.

a manner inconsistent with judicial office, accountability requires disciplinary action or removal; independence requires only that this be done in a way which, over time, does not discourage other judges in the free exercise of their judicial function.

The candidate States' laws on judicial conduct generally oblige judges to refrain from conduct that compromises the dignity of judicial office. For example, Bulgaria's provisions – which sanction unjustified delays,[117] acts that diminish the reputation of the judicial branch, and offences and omissions in the discharge of their official duties[118] – are fairly typical of those in other candidate States, although there is considerable variation in their precision. In Slovakia, there are no detailed rules on what constitutes a disciplinary offence, whereas in Romania the law is quite specific.

This general imprecision in elaborating grounds for disciplinary action stems in part from the absence of official codes of judicial ethics. Certainly, this is not a problem only in the candidate States; in general, member States do not have enforceable codes of judicial ethics which would lay out precisely the grounds for disciplinary action. Usually, norms regulating behaviour on and off the bench are framed by the legislature in general terms and leave room for discretion, the exercise of which has not raised serious concerns.[119]

In all candidate States except Romania and Slovenia,[120] codes of ethics have only unofficial status and do not constitute direct grounds for disciplinary action. In Hungary none have been adopted. The Romanian regulation is unique in that the Law on the Organisation of the Judiciary explicitly states that grave violations of the rules of the Magistrates' Code of Ethics also qualify as disciplinary offences.

In theory, insufficiently formulated rules of conduct invite prosecution of judges for trumped-up disciplinary offences.[121] This is to some extent counterbalanced by procedural safeguards consistent with international standards[122] and legislative practice among EU States. Thus, in all candidate States judges have the right to present their arguments

---

[117] Undue delay is one of the most common causes for disciplinary proceedings in most candidate States.

[118] Bulgaria's Judicial System Act, Art. 168.

[119] Information from Giuseppe Di Federico, Director of the Research Institute on Judicial Systems of the National Research Council, University of Bologna.

[120] Some ethical principles are identified in the Judicial Service Act (Arts. 37–39); moreover a draft Code of Judicial Ethics was adopted by the Slovenian Association of Judges on 8 June 2001.

[121] An example of the potential for this kind of problem may be a case from Estonia, in 2000, in which the Ministry of Justice initiated disciplinary proceedings against a judge, alleging unnecessary delay in a court case. The Ministry was itself a party to the case in question. The judge was ultimately cleared of wrongdoing. Judges' Disciplinary Commission, Estonia, Case No. 3-8-11-1.

[122] UN Basic Principles, Arts. 17, 19; CoE Recommendations, Principle, VI; UCJ, Art. 11(3); ECSJ, Art. 9.

at oral hearings; they may be assisted by counsel and may appeal against decisions of the disciplinary body (except in Latvia; Bulgaria is currently considering a ban on appeals).

Indeed, in practice it is not arbitrary disciplinary punishment which raises concerns across the region, but rather the *reluctance* of disciplinary bodies – composed in most countries of fellow judges – to find judges responsible for offences.[123] Disciplinary accountability should not be seen as a threat to judicial independence. On the contrary, an insufficiently self-critical approach and failure to enforce ethical rules jeopardise independence by weakening public trust and encouraging the other branches to limit their support for judicial independence, as has been seen in Bulgaria and to a lesser degree in Slovenia.

---

[123] In Slovenia, for example, although disciplinary proceedings against judges have been initiated on a number of occasions, no judge has been convicted of a disciplinary transgression; instead, some judges have quietly resigned following investigations. The procedures strongly favour confidentiality – valuable in protecting public confidence in *individual* judges, but damaging to its confidence in the whole judiciary's accountability. In Poland, too, procedures favour confidentiality over accountability.

## VI. Intra-Judicial Relations

Individual judges' freedom to decide cases before them as they see proper can be affected not only by the legislature and executive, but also by actors within the judiciary itself. Although international standards recognise that there are appropriate limits on judicial independence in the form of appellate proceedings,[124] they also reaffirm the decisional independence of individual judges,[125] who may feel constrained in the exercise of their independent judgement by the expectations of higher courts if, as is often the case, members of those courts exercise control over the career path of lower judges.

### A. Relations with Superior Courts

An individual judge's decisional independence may be unduly interfered with by higher judges or courts, as well as by other branches of the State. Numerous instances in which higher courts have administrative authority over lower judges are noted elsewhere in this Report. In addition, higher judges may influence lower court judges through informal consultations which, though not always violating a judge's independence, do limit transparency and accountability in the decision-making process.

As in civil law countries in general, including those within the EU, uniformity of judicial decisions is highly valued and is enforced through various mechanisms in the candidate States. Each State maintains a comprehensive system of appeal. As a general rule, appeal courts review the judgements brought before them in full, checking both whether the facts have been correctly established and whether the inferior court made a correct legal assessment.[126] Most candidate States also provide for a cassation review on procedural grounds. In addition appeal courts in most countries may give specific instructions on how to proceed on re-trial,[127] as well as binding general directives concerning the application of law.[128] Many judges consider binding instructions in particular to be an attempt by the higher courts to limit individual judges' scope of deliberative freedom, in a manner

---

[124] UN Basic Principles, Art. 4; CoE Recommendations, Principle I.2.i.; UCJ, Art. 4.

[125] UCJ, Art. 1, 2, 4; CJE, Art. 1. See *Findlay v. United Kingdom*, paras. 75–77.

[126] In the Czech Republic, as of 1 January 2001 the system of full appeal was replaced by the partial appeal system, which reviews only the legality of lower court decisions.

[127] In Estonia this right is limited. In the Czech Republic and Hungary, the appeal court may also order that criminal cases be re-tried by a different panel.

[128] Except Estonia and Slovakia, although in Slovakia the Supreme Court publicises selected cases of general importance to which courts are expected, but not legally required, to conform.

which ought properly be done only by legislation. However, binding instructions do not necessarily limit judges' independence.

Outside of these entirely legitimate mechanisms for ensuring accurate and consistent results, however, judges often employ informal consultations. In the majority of candidate countries there is no prohibition against lower court judges consulting with those of higher courts.[129] In Romania, higher courts are forbidden to give lower court judges instructions regarding a case outside the appeals process; nevertheless lower court judges regularly consult with higher court judges on particular cases. These practices encourage uniformity of decision, but often at the cost of reducing transparency and accountability, as well as (where such "consultations" take place at the initiative of higher court judges) curtailing lower courts' decisional independence. (This is a particular problem where higher court judges decide on promotions and rates of reversal are considered in the assessment process, as in Estonia.)

## B. Case Management

The nominally administrative task of case management can have important effects for judicial independence and impartiality; during the communist period, case assignment was one area in which political intervention was most prevalent. The power to assign cases can be used to ensure favourable or unfavourable hearings; it can also be used to punish uncooperative judges. International standards recommend that caseload administration be a purely internal matter;[130] all member States leave case assignment to the judiciary, but there is no consensus practice on using neutral procedures.[131]

Generally among candidate States, the authority supervising court administration also has the task of setting overall norms for caseloads. Thus in Slovenia and Hungary the Judicial Councils determine the norms, but in the Czech Republic the Ministry of Justice sets each court's or judge's caseload, with court presidents ensuring compliance – which means the executive influences caseload administration, contrary to international standards.

---

[129] The Czech Republic and Romania do have such prohibitions.

[130] UN Basic Principles, Art. 14; CoE Recommendations, Principle I.2.e. (recommending random distribution).

[131] Information from Giuseppe Di Federico, Director of the Research Institute on Judicial Systems of the National Research Council, University of Bologna.

There has been an encouraging development towards random assignment of cases as a further guarantee of impartiality and independence. In Estonia, Lithuania[132] and Slovenia random assignment is already the rule; in Hungary and Slovakia some court presidents employ random allocation, and the Czech Republic and Latvia have recently introduced random assignment systems. In Bulgaria and Romania court presidents assign cases at their discretion, and the assignment system remains insufficiently transparent, with considerable room for court shopping and bribery.

---

[132] In Lithuania, the court president may select from among three methods for assigning cases, and may change methods once a year.

# VII. Enforcement and Corruption

## A. Enforcement

There are no clear international standards on enforcement of judicial decisions, although the general requirement that judges' decisions not be subject to revision[133] could be understood as implying the need for them to be enforced. In general the standards assume that courts should be supported in their work.[134]

Enforcement is not necessarily a judicial function, and may be a responsibility of the executive. However, where court rulings are not respected, individuals will inevitably come to view the courts as ineffective, and will seek alternative fora for their disputes, decreasing courts' legitimacy. In practice, citizens gain no benefits from guarantees of judicial independence if judges' decisions have no impact. Contrariwise, effective enforcement improves public confidence in and support for independent courts.

All the candidate States face problems with enforcement, especially of civil judgements. In part this is a consequence of courts' expanded competencies and concomitant increases in the caseload that have not been matched by modernisation of the enforcement system.[135] Enforcement mechanisms have generally not been subject to the same degree of sweeping reform as other elements of the judicial process, although some States (Czech Republic, Estonia, Slovakia) have reformed their systems for enforcement (such as by introducing private enforcement) in an effort to improve efficiency.

In some States, such as Romania, Bulgaria, and Slovenia, even decisions requiring action by the Government are sometimes ignored, or enforcement is seriously delayed. (In no case does it appear that candidate States refused to enforce final criminal judgements.) In Bulgaria, for example, the Supreme Administrative Court has had to resort to imposing statutory fines on high officials – including regional governors and even cabinet ministers – following their failure to fulfill obligations arising from court

---

[133] UN Basic Principle, Art. 4; CoE Recommendations, Principle I.2.a.i.

[134] The European Court of Human Rights has held that failure to execute a court judgement may breach Article 6 (1) of the European Convention on Human Rights. See e.g. *Hornsby v. Greece*, ECHR Judgement of 19 March 1997 (App. No. 18357/91), Reports 1997/II (noting also that execution is to be considered "an integral part of the trial", para. 40).

[135] For example, in Lithuania between 1994 and 1999 the number of cases subject to execution increased more than 200 percent, while the number of court bailiffs increased only 30 percent.

decisions. In Slovenia, non-compliance with court decisions is partly a matter of governmental policy in response to budget limitations, as the Ministry of Finance must sign off on any judicial or non-judicial settlement to which the Government agrees. In a similar manner, as of the end of 2000, thirteen rulings of the Constitutional Court were not being enforced because Parliament had failed to enact new legislation.[136]

## B. Corruption

Society's interest in having judges adjudicate cases free of undue influence is not only threatened by other State actors; in many countries, bribery and intimidation by private parties pose an equal or even greater threat. All international standards seek to ensure that judges decide cases impartially, relying only on the facts and the law.[137] All member States have provisions against bribing or intimidating judges, and also against judges administering justice in exchange for money; nonetheless, in some member States, corruption and the threat it poses to judges' impartiality are considered serious problems.

Likewise, there is a widespread perception that corruption is endemic in the judiciary of several candidate States, especially in Bulgaria, the Czech Republic, Latvia, Lithuania, Romania, and Slovakia. Certainly, all candidate States have sanctions against corrupt activity in the courts, but supervisory mechanisms to ensure judges' impartiality – such as disclosure of assets and clear rules on recusement – as well as transparent procedures for tracking cases to prevent delays (a common cause of bribes) are weak in most States.

---

[136] Legal Information Centre of the Constitutional Court, Report No. 143/00-1 from 27 March 2001,

[137] UN Basic Principles, Art. 2; CoE Recommendations, Principle I.2.d (also calling for sanctions against "persons seeking to influence judges in any manner"); UCJ, Art. 3 and 5; ECSJ, Arts. 2–3.

# VIII. Recommendations

This Overview suggests a number of ways in which the accession process could contribute to judicial independence in the candidate countries and the EU itself. Following are several of the most important; all begin from the premise that accession is a positive development whose potential to spark needed reform should be reinforced.

## To the European Union

### Clear Standards

The EU should clarify requirements and standards for judicial independence. It or its member States acting individually should make the UN Basic Principles and CoE Recommendations binding.

### Member States' Practices

A comprehensive survey of member States' practice relating to an independent judiciary should form one of the bases of any effort to elaborate EU standards clarifying, for all States, the content of Europe's commitment to judicial independence; EU recommendations to the candidate States should be grounded upon such standards.

## To EU Candidate States

### Legal Culture and Judicial Capacity

In candidate States, the continuing assumption that political involvement in judicial administration is necessary and desirable must be confronted and rejected. Courts should be given the means to develop their management expertise to counter arguments for executive involvement. International support could be of critical importance in this area.

### Political Support

Politicians must publicly affirm the importance of an independent judiciary by enacting legislation supporting it, and refrain from making inroads on the judiciary's prerogatives.

*Accountability to Criticism*

Judges must refute political criticism, not by censuring all complaints, but by demonstrating that they are prepared to administer themselves with professionalism and restraint, and to make themselves accountable to society.

*Constitutional Guarantees*

Constitutional guarantees should unambiguously identify independence and separation of powers, and independent administrative bodies should be given constitutional status.

*Constitutional Courts*

Where States establish a separate quasi-judicial institution like a constitutional court closely connected to the executive or the legislative, ordinary courts should be protected against political intrusions on their independence, just as against any other political body.

*Judicial Councils*

States should consider creating independent judicial councils to administer the judiciary. Where States choose not to create such councils, they must ensure that the alternatives contain robust institutional guarantees for the neutrality of procedures applied to the judiciary, and that judges have meaningful input in their administration and discipline.

*Remuneration*

Judges' salaries should be competitive with the professional alternatives available to them; judges should have the materials necessary for effective adjudication.

*Funding*

Clear and detailed protections should be in place to ensure that funding is not used to punish judges or to chill independent judicial decision-making. Placing some or all authority for preparing budget recommendations with an independent body – such as a judicial council – can limit the executive's ability to curtail judicial independence.

Where budgets are kept in the competence of the legislature and executive, those branches should commit to specified levels of funding, or specified, objective and non-political formulae for determining funding. Leading politicians should publicly support the depoliticisation of court funding with appropriate legislation and executive action. In addition, mandatory funding levels and multi-year or block appropriations disbursed by a body independent of the executive and legislature should be considered to reduce the possibility of political interference with judicial authority through the budget process.

*Appointment of Judges*

Transparent and neutral approval procedures should be applied to probationary judges and applicants for promotion; the political acceptability of judges' opinions should play no part in determinations about tenure. In-court training periods for judge candidates should be extended, to reduce the felt need for probationary periods.

*Tenure*

Whenever possible, ordinary judges ought to have life tenure from their first appointment. Where judges are appointed for a fixed term, except possibly in the case of the constitutional court and probationary judges, a clear preference against re-election of judges following the expiry of their terms would seem in concert with European values.

Where probation is retained, it should be clearly understood that it is a mechanism to weed out incompetent judges, and cannot have any political content. Evaluating probation should be a non-political matter, and decisional authority should be vested in a commission of judges and legal professionals applying clear and neutral criteria.

At a minimum, renewal of judicial appointment must not be contingent on the political acceptability of the substantive conclusions the judge reached in any particular case.

*Retirement*

If a retirement age is specified, it should be mandatory; the political branches should not have the discretion to retain or release judges after they become eligible for retirement.

# Judicial Independence
in Bulgaria

# Table of Contents

Executive Summary ........................................................ 72

I. Introduction ..................................................... 75
    A. Areas of Persistent Political Branch Involvement in Core Judicial Affairs .......... 75
    B. Weak Political Commitment to Judicial Independence ............................................. 76
    C. The Judiciary and the Accession Process .... 78
    D. Organisation of the Judicial System ........... 79

II. Constitutional and Legal Foundations of Judicial Independence ................................... 82
    A. Separation of Powers and Guarantees of Independence ......................................... 82
    B. Representation of the Judiciary – the Supreme Judicial Council ................. 83
    C. Rules on Incompatibility ........................... 85
    D. Judges' Associations ................................... 87

III. Administration of the Court System and Judicial Independence ............................... 88
    A. Role of the Supreme Judicial Council ........ 88
    B. Involvement of the Ministry of Justice ....... 89
    C. Unclear Division of Authority .................... 91

IV. Financial Autonomy and Level of Funding ...... 92
    A. Budgeting Process ....................................... 92
    B. Work Conditions ......................................... 94
    C. Compensation ............................................. 95

V.  Judicial Office .................................................... 98
    A. The Selection Process ................................ 98
        1. Court Presidents ................................ 100
    B. Tenure, Retirement, Transfer
       and Removal ............................................ 100
        1. Tenure ................................................ 100
        2. Retirement ......................................... 101
        3. Transfer ............................................. 101
        4. Removal ............................................. 102
    C. Evaluation and Promotion ....................... 102
    D. Discipline ................................................. 103
        1. Liability ............................................. 103
        2. Disciplinary Procedures .................... 104

VI.  Intra-Judicial Relations ................................. 106
    A. Relations with Superior Courts ................ 106
    B. Case Management and Relations
       with Court Presidents .............................. 107

VII. Enforcement and Corruption ........................ 108
    A. Enforcement of Judgements ..................... 108
    B. Corruption ............................................... 108

# Judicial Independence in Bulgaria

## Executive Summary

Bulgaria has made important progress towards the creation of an independent judiciary, especially in the development of formal arrangements separating the judiciary from the other branches and giving it considerable administrative autonomy.

However, this formal consolidation of judicial independence has been seriously curtailed in its implementation. In particular, the continued involvement of the Ministry of Justice in administrative and supervisory matters, the executive's co-optation of the judicial budget, and the continued mixing of core judicial and non-judicial functions in the Supreme Judicial Council, limit judges' real independence.

More generally, these problems are symptomatic of the political branches' weakly held commitment to judges' independence. The executive and legislature demonstrate a persistent reluctance to concede the existence of a truly independent judicial branch.

The principal areas of concern identified in the Report are the following:

*Executive Involvement in Court Administration*
The Ministry of Justice continues to exercise extensive administrative powers, although in theory the Supreme Judicial Council should act as the administrator for the judiciary. In addition, the Ministry has extensive supervisory powers, which allow its Inspectorate to make intrusive investigations into the work of courts and individual judges.

*Co-optation of the Judiciary's Budget*
Although the Supreme Judicial Council formally drafts the judiciary's budget, in practice the executive prepares, and Parliament passes, a parallel budget, effectively excluding the courts from the process. Resource allocations are also controlled by the executive to some degree.

*Ineffective Supreme Judicial Council*
There are serious shortcomings in the Council's organisation. In particular, the Council's mixed composition – including numerous appointees of Parliament, the

Minister of Justice, and representatives of other magistrates – and its mandate to represent the whole magistracy (including judges, prosecutors and investigators) make it an ineffective representative of judges and their independence. The Council has too small a staff and meets too infrequently to be an effective administrator.

*Weak Political Commitment to Judicial Independence*

These particular problems are symptomatic of a political culture in which respect for independence in judges' decision-making processes is still not well developed. The actions of the political branches reflect widespread mistrust of or lack of confidence in the judiciary. Reportedly, some political actors still engage in practices such as "telephone justice". Courts' jurisdiction over some administrative acts have been curtailed in ways which – though technically within the law – inevitably have a punitive cast and affect judges' willingness to adjudicate based on the facts and law alone. The statutory composition of the Supreme Judicial Council, which represents and administers the judiciary, has been altered with changes of Government.

In addition to these general issues, the following issues of particular concern are discussed in the body of the Report:

*Mixed Judicial and Non-Judicial Roles in the Magistracy*

The formal guarantees of separation and independence provided in the Constitution refer to the judicial power as a whole – that is, to the magistracy – and not to the judiciary *per se* or to judges. As the magistracy includes prosecutorial and investigative functions outside the core judicial function, the formal separation of powers is blurred and the independence of judges is compromised. In addition, the conflation of three separate authorities in a single magistracy with a single formal administrative organ invites unnecessary involvement of the executive with the judiciary in a manner that limits judicial independence.

*Poor Working Conditions*

Courts suffer from chronic under-investment, and working conditions are unsatisfactory, especially concerning office space and equipment. While the situation is not uniformly bad throughout the country, in general courts and judges are overburdened. Court presidents are in a particularly vulnerable position in relation to the Supreme Judicial Council and the Ministry of Justice, which exercise control over needed resources.

*Pensions*

Salaries are generally satisfactory; however, pensions are quite low, which, when combined with discretionary rules on retirement, may endanger judges' decisional independence.

*Judicial Career*

There are very few clear or objective procedures to guide the Supreme Judicial Council in making personnel decisions. Particular problems of note include the provisions that judges are not tenured (and thus irremovable) until they have served three years in a position, that promotions are largely discretionary, and that in the absence of a mandatory retirement age older judges effectively serve at the pleasure of their court president and the Council.

*Case Assignment*

Case management lacks transparent and neutral standards for assignment.

*Enforcement*

Although judicial decisions are generally respected, there have been individual cases when high officials had to be fined for failing to fulfil obligations arising from court decisions. In addition, the enforcement of civil and commercial judgements poses significant problems.

*Corruption*

There is a widespread public perception that the courts are affected by corruption. Even absent conclusive documentation, such perceptions can negatively affect judicial independence. Concerns about corruption recently led to a proposal to limit magistrates' constitutional immunity. The proposal failed in the Parliament; however, it appears the issue may be revisited in the next Parliament.

## I. Introduction

Bulgaria has made important progress towards the creation of an independent judiciary, especially in the development of formal arrangements separating the judiciary from the other branches. The Constitution and major legislative acts provide explicit protections, and the judiciary has been given considerable administrative autonomy.

However, this formal consolidation of judicial independence has been seriously curtailed in its implementation. In particular, the continued involvement of the Ministry of Justice in administrative and supervisory matters, the executive's co-optation of the judicial budget, and the continued mixing of core judicial and non-judicial functions in the Supreme Judicial Council, the body responsible for representing and administering the judiciary, limit judges' real independence.

More generally, these problems are symptomatic of the political branches' weakly held commitment to judges' independence. The executive and legislature demonstrate a persistent tendency to intervene in the organisation and work of the judiciary both for short-term political gain and out of a reluctance to concede the existence of a truly independent judicial branch.

### A. Areas of Persistent Political Branch Involvement in Core Judicial Affairs

The real progress achieved in reform efforts to date has been limited and even undermined by significant and continued involvement of the executive in areas essential to the maintenance of an independent judiciary, in particular in administration, budgetary matters, and the organisation of the Supreme Judicial Council.

The Ministry of Justice continues to exercise extensive administrative powers, although in theory the Supreme Judicial Council should act as the administrator for the judiciary. The Council's powers are defined, but the Ministry's are not, allowing it in effect to operate without clear limits. In addition, the Ministry has extensive supervisory powers, which allow its Inspectorate to make intrusive investigations into the operations of courts and the actions of individual judges.

The Supreme Judicial Council formally has exclusive authority to prepare the judiciary's budget, but in practice the executive prepares a parallel budget which forms the basis of the budget passed by Parliament, and the judiciary is effectively excluded from the process. Because the Ministry of Justice continues to control building and infrastructure budgets, many of the resource needs of courts can only be met with its approval; in general the executive's budgetary control also augments its administrative authority.

The Supreme Judicial Council's own operations and composition reflect the continued influence of the political branches. The Supreme Judicial Council is supposed to represent and administer the judicial power, but it is composed of not only judges, but also prosecutors and investigators. The majority of its members are either appointed by Parliament or represent non-judicial functions, despite the fact that this body is formally responsible for the independence of the core judiciary, and actually exercises considerable discretionary authority over judges' career paths. The Council has too small a staff and meets too infrequently to be an effective administrator, leaving the door open for continued executive involvement in administration and supervision.

The judicial branch includes judges, prosecutors and investigators – commonly referred to as the magistracy.[1] The inclusion of three separate organs within the magistracy is a source of tension among them and can create conflicts of interest. For example, the Supreme Judicial Council, with its mixed composition, is supposed to represent and administer all three branches of the magistracy. Political actors, State institutions and society as a whole tend to treat the different bodies as equally responsible for, *inter alia*, the "fight against crime," without differentiating between their particular competencies, a situation especially problematic for the courts with their special guarantees of independence. Moreover, the different bodies have on occasion publicly criticised each other, thus adding to the pressure on the judiciary from the executive and the public at large.[2]

## B. Weak Political Commitment to Judicial Independence

The above problems are symptomatic of a political culture in which respect for the independence of judges' decision-making processes is still not well developed. The actions of the political branches suggest a posture of mistrust of or lack of confidence in the judiciary. Reportedly, political actors still routinely engage in practices such as "telephone justice" and other forms of direct and improper intervention, though such practices are difficult to document.

Issues fundamental to the independence of the judiciary have been the subject of continuing political controversy. Consecutive political majorities have attempted – with varying

---

[1] CONST. REP. BULGARIA, Art. 117(1).

[2] The Chief Public Prosecutor's office, for example, which wishes to regain competencies in the area of pre-trial detention, has accused courts of being lenient with respect to "proven" criminals.

success – to create their own majorities within the judicial branch. On two occasions (1991 and 1998), the composition of the Supreme Judicial Council has been altered by act of Parliament prior to the expiry of its members terms – formally a legal move, but one which seriously undermines the principles of independence which motivated the creation of the Council in the first place. These interventions by the legislature suggest that, in important ways, judicial reform has been subordinated to *ad hoc* political goals instead of consolidating judicial independence.[3]

Thus, concerns about corruption – reportedly endemic in the judiciary as well as in other branches – have brought (unsuccessful) calls in Parliament for judges' immunity to be revoked or curtailed, and courts' jurisdiction over some administrative acts (relating to privatisation and licensing of banks and insurance companies) has been curtailed in ways which – though technically within the law – inevitably have a punitive cast and affect judges' willingness to adjudicate based on the facts and law alone. In one recent instance, in 2000, Parliament adopted an interpretative law stripping the courts of competence in a case pending before the Supreme Administrative Court concerning the deportation of certain individuals on national security grounds, ordering that the proceedings be discontinued and past court judgements on the issue declared null and void. (The Constitutional Court repealed the final part of the interpretative law, holding that the legislature had acted as a judicial organ in breach of the constitutional principles of the rule of law, the separation of powers and independence of the judiciary.)[4] Parliament has also limited judges' right to appeal disciplinary rulings against them.[5]

---

[3] One commentator has noted: "[O]ne of the prerequisites of an independent court-system is the system being self-governing. It should have the requisite resources, managerial skills and necessary self-esteem to be self-governed. What are the obstacles for the realisation of this presently? First, the periodic influx of politics into the judicial system through the replacement of the Supreme Judicial Council which is not left to complete its term of office. In my opinion, this is a serious concern. The development of skills for self-government within the judiciary is a long and progressive process – it is related to building self-esteem and assurance that it can be self-governed. The periodic replacement of the supreme administrative body totally destroys the development of such skills. It destroys internal relations within the professional community, because it sends a clear signal that it is not keeping with the idea of an impartial and independent court... In my opinion, a serious responsibility for the system lies with the Constitutional Court, which a number of times has allowed for this frontal attack on the independence of the judiciary."

Statement of participant, OSI roundtable, 6 April 2001. *Explanatory Note: OSI held roundtable meetings in a number of candidate countries to invite critique of country reports in draft form. Experts present included representatives of the government, the Commission Delegations, Roma representatives, and civil society organisations. References to this meeting should not be understood as endorsement of any particular point of view by any one participant.*

[4] Judgement of 29 May 2001, State Gazette, No. 51/2001.

[5] See Section V.D.2.

The media generally regard the judicial system as insufficiently open or transparent. Certain media outlets do consistently voice support for judicial independence and protect individual representatives of the judiciary from being unduly discredited; others, however, promote or tolerate public attacks on magistrates, including distorted presentation of the circumstances of individual cases. Such attacks seem occasionally to be aligned with the stances of political actors outside the judiciary, giving the attacks a semi-official quality, although there is no clear evidence of any collusive practice between the media and other branches.

Public opinion polls suggest that popular confidence in the judiciary is low; polls reflect concerns about the considerable backlog of pending cases, the slow pace of proceedings, the poor quality of court decisions, deficiencies in the execution of court judgements, and corruption. Broad segments of the public have yet to voice substantial support for an independent judiciary, or to appreciate the connection between independence and effectiveness.

## C. The Judiciary and the Accession Process

The Commission's 2000 Regular Report notes that "significant further efforts and resources are needed if the judicial system is to become a strong, independent, effective and professional system able to guarantee a full respect for the rule of law."[6] The Regular Report specifically criticised the insufficient funding of judicial institutions, poor facilities and working conditions, cumbersome caseload management systems, non-transparent selection procedures, and the lack of training (especially training funded by the State).[7]

Following publication of the 2000 Regular Report, the executive has begun to take the issue of judicial reform more seriously. At the Prime Minister's request, a meeting with the Supreme Judicial Council on 29 November 2000 discussed the problems in the judicial system identified by the Commission and measures to address them. The meeting resolved to establish an informal commission including representatives of both the executive and the judiciary, to act on the European Commission's findings.

Although the judiciary is not directly involved in the EU accession negotiation process, in response to the Regular Report 2000 the Supreme Judicial Council adopted a Programme for the Development of the Judicial System in Bulgaria for the period 2001–2004. In

---

[6] European Commission, *2000 Regular Report on Bulgaria's Progress Towards Accession*, 8 November 2000 (hereafter *2000 Regular Report*), Section 2.

[7] *2000 Regular Report*, Section 2.

addition, on the initiative of the President of the Supreme Court of Cassation regional meetings of magistrates are being held, in which the chief government negotiator with the EU also takes part, to debate the conclusions and recommendations in the Regular Report.

## D. Organisation of the Judicial System

Prior to the Second World War, Bulgaria had a continental-style civil law system. With the introduction of the communist system, the civil law tradition's deference to the executive was greatly expanded, and legal institutions were viewed as instruments of unitary state-party control. The role of the prosecutor was expanded, and extra-legal interference with judicial decision making – so-called "telephone justice" – was common. The legacy of the communist re-organisation of the judiciary continues to have a profound impact.

Following the collapse of the Communist regime and the promulgation of the 1991 Constitution, the adoption of the Judicial System Act[8] put in place a legislative framework for making structural changes in the judicial system, a process which continued until 1998. 1998 amendments to the Code of Criminal Procedure and the Code of Civil Procedure established the existing four-level court structure containing three separate instances.

The current system includes 112 district courts (courts of first instance), 28 regional courts (of both first and second instance), five courts of appeal (which operate as courts of second instance with respect to the regional courts' judgements only), five regional military courts, one military court of appeal, a Supreme Court of Cassation and a Supreme Administrative Court.[9] Additional specialised courts may be established by law,[10] but the establishment of extraordinary courts is not allowed.[11]

At present there are 664 district court judges, 494 regional court judges (and 79 "junior judges"[12] serving at the regional courts), 27 judges at the military courts, and

---

[8] Judicial System Act, State Gazette No. 59/22.07, 1994 with twelve supervening amendments.

[9] In the absence of a separate system of administrative courts, the Supreme Administrative Court operates as court of cassation in the area of administrative jurisdiction carried out by "ordinary" courts and exercises original jurisdiction assigned to it by the Supreme Administrative Court Act.

[10] CONST. REP. BULGARIA, Art. 119(2).

[11] CONST. REP. BULGARIA, Art. 119(3).

[12] See Section V.A.

91 judges at the courts of appeal. There are 64 judges in the Supreme Court of Cassation and 54 in the Supreme Administrative Court.[13]

The number of judges has been increasing continuously, but still has not kept pace with the considerable extension of the courts' competencies and powers resulting from, among other things, the adoption of new economic and property legislation conferring new competencies upon the courts.

The Constitution unites judges, prosecutors, and investigators in a tri-partite body called "the judicial branch,"[14] also commonly referred to as the magistracy. Constitutional and legal provisions related to the institutional independence of the judicial branch and the independence of individual magistrates are applied to each of these bodies on an equal basis.[15] A Supreme Judicial Council administers the magistracy.[16]

Military courts have jurisdiction over a broad range of crimes and persons, including crimes committed by officers of the Ministry of Internal Affairs or civil servants of the Ministry of Internal Affairs or the Ministry of Defence in the course of their duties, as well as military personnel and military crimes.[17] Military court judges enjoy the full status of magistrates. They are appointed, promoted, demoted, reassigned and dismissed pursuant to a decision of the Supreme Judicial Council.[18] After being appointed as judges they are admitted to regular military service and an officer's rank is conferred on them.[19] In addition to the general grounds for imposing disciplinary punishments,

---

[13] In addition, there are also 208 execution judges and 97 registry judges. While the status of both categories is prescribed by the Judicial System Act, execution judges and registry judges are appointed by the Minister of Justice, and not by the Supreme Judicial Council. They must fulfill the general requirements for appointment to judicial office but do not enjoy the status of magistrates with regard to tenure, promotion, accountability and immunity from prosecution

[14] CONST. REP. BULGARIA, Chap. VI.

[15] This report is concerned with the independence of judges, even when discussing the "magistracy" as a whole. Generally, it should be clear from the context that a given rule discussed in connection with judges also applies to other magistrates. Where it is not, or where it is relevant to consider the position of the whole magistracy, reference is made to magistrates or to the other two organs by name. The term "the judiciary" is generally used with reference to the corps of judges, but without excluding the possibility that the issue under discussion may also affect magistrates in general.

[16] The Supreme Judicial Council is discussed at length in Section II.B.

[17] Judicial System Act, Art. 66, para. 1; Code of Criminal Procedure, Art. 388.

[18] Judicial System Act, Art, 124, para. 1.

[19] Judicial System Act, Art. 124, para. 2.

military judges are also responsible pursuant to the specific laws, regulations and procedures established with respect to servicemen.[20]

There is also a separate Constitutional Court, which principally rules on challenges to the constitutionality of laws and the acts of the State President, and provides binding interpretations of the Constitution.[21] The Constitutional Court is not a part of the regular judicial system. It is established under a separate chapter of the Constitution[22] and by its own ruling "is outside the three branches listed in Article 8 of the Constitution."[23]

---

[20] Judicial System Act, Art. 168, para. 2.
[21] CONST. REP. BULGARIA, Art. 150.
[22] CONST. REP. BULGARIA, Chapter 8.
[23] Judgement of the Constitutional Court of 21 December 1993.

## II. Constitutional and Legal Foundations of Judicial Independence

Formal guarantees of the separation of the various branches and the independence of the judiciary are undercut by the conflation of the three separate authorities – judges exercising core judicial functions, prosecutors, and investigators – in a single magistracy, inevitably allowing and inviting unnecessary involvement of the executive with the judiciary in a manner which limits judicial independence. In particular, the structure and composition of the Supreme Judicial Council, responsible for representing and administering the magistracy, is susceptible to this weakening of the barriers between the branches.

### A. Separation of Powers and Guarantees of Independence

The judicial branch as a whole is constitutionally separate from and independent of the other branches. The Constitution proclaims the principle of separation of powers by stating that "the power of the state shall be divided between a legislative, an executive and a judicial branch."[24] The judicial system is statutorily identified as the state authority administering justice,[25] suggesting an exclusive competence, and its rulings cannot be revoked or abolished by the other branches.[26] The judicial branch is also declared to be independent, and "in the performance of their functions, all judges, prosecutors and investigators shall be subservient only to the law."[27] The Constitution further provides that the judicial branch shall have an independent budget.[28]

However, the separation and independence provided in the Constitution refers to the judicial power as a whole – that is, to the magistracy – and not to the judiciary *per se* or to judges. As the magistracy includes prosecutorial and investigative functions outside the core judicial function, the formal separation of powers and discrete independence of judges and their branch is unnecessarily blurred.

---

[24] CONST. REP. BULGARIA, Art. 8.
[25] Judicial System Act, Art. 1(1).
[26] Judgement of 14 January 1999, State Gazette, No. 6, 22 January 1999.
[27] CONST. REP. BULGARIA, Art. 117, para. 2.
[28] CONST. REP. BULGARIA, Art. 117, para. 3.

## B. Representation of the Judiciary – the Supreme Judicial Council

Important representative functions (as well as broad powers over judicial administration and judges' career paths[29]) are vested in the Supreme Judicial Council. However, there are serious shortcomings in the Council's organisation; in particular, the Council's mixed composition – including numerous appointees of Parliament, the Minister of Justice, and representatives of other magistrates – and its mandate to represent the whole magistracy make it a less effective representative of judges and their independence.

The Supreme Judicial Council's members, duties, and competencies are regulated by the Judicial System Act, in accordance with the Constitution.[30] The Council is not, formally speaking, the constitutional representative of the magistracy, although in practice it does perform this function through its contacts with the executive and legislature. In addition, it has a broad range of administrative responsibilities,[31] which tend to also require it to engage in representation of the courts and magistrates it administers. It is also empowered to receive and review annual information from the three sections of the magistracy.[32]

*Composition:* The Supreme Judicial Council consists of 25 members, eleven of which are elected by Parliament and another eleven by the three bodies of the judicial branch.[33] The elected members of the Supreme Judicial Council serve single five-year terms and are not eligible for immediate re-election.[34] Sitting on the Council *ex officio* are the Presidents of the Supreme Court of Cassation and the Supreme Administrative Court and the Chief Public Prosecutor. In addition, the Minister of Justice serves as the chair, though without voting rights.[35] (In the absence of the Minister, the Presidents of the two Supreme Courts and the Chief Public Prosecutor take turns chairing meetings of the Council.)

---

[29] See Sections III. and V.

[30] CONST. REP. BULGARIA, Art. 133, providing for the regulation in law of the Supreme Judicial Council and the magistracy.

[31] See Sections III. and V.

[32] Judicial System Act, Art. 27.

[33] CONST. REP. BULGARIA, Art. 130(3). The corps of judges elects six, public prosecutors three and investigators two members of the Council. In practice, the parliamentary quota may and normally does include active members of the magistracy.

[34] CONST. REP. BULGARIA, Art. 130(4). See Constitutional Court judgement of 19 October 1999, State Gazette, No. 95, 2 November 1999.

[35] CONST. REP. BULGARIA, Art. 130(5).

While magistrates (and judges in particular) predominate in the composition of the Council, the parliamentary appointees have on occasion been regarded as representatives of the political majority in Parliament and the executive, rather than as neutral representatives. Individual members appointed by Parliament have rejected the suggestion that they are influenced by the manner of their appointment,[36] and there is no clear evidence to suggest that Council members vote along party lines or in accordance with the wishes of those who appointed them; rather, voting seems to be defined by personal or professional allegiances among members. Still, the legislature's two interventions altering the rules governing the Council's composition – and thereby also removing the individuals then sitting on the Council[37] – have seriously weakened the Council's ability to be an independent actor capable of defending judicial independence. Altering the rules by which Parliament elects members of the Council[38] – by requiring, for example, a qualified majority – could lessen the risk of legislative control of the body representing and administering the judiciary. Certainly, in the absence of clear procedures to govern the work of the Council, the opportunities for political interference are greater.

In addition, the involvement of the Minister of Justice in a double capacity as member of the Government and chair of the meetings of the Supreme Judicial Council may be seen as compromising the separation of powers and the independence of the judiciary. Moreover, since November 1998 the Minister of Justice has been authorised to initiate proposals before the Supreme Judicial Council and "to draw judges' attention to failures to observe the rules of handling cases and duly inform the Supreme Judicial Council."[39]

This arrangement is apparently meant to create a sort of "communications conduit" between the different branches, and the Constitutional Court has upheld the constitutionality of the Minister of Justice's extended competencies (with the exception of the competence to make proposals to the effect of lifting magistrates' immunity and suspend them).[40] The judgement held that the involvement of the Minister as a non-voting member of the Council does not violate the principle of separation of powers, and further that

---

[36] Information from conversations with Supreme Judicial Council members.

[37] See Section II.B.

[38] Any such alteration should properly only take effect after the scheduled termination of current Council members' terms.

[39] Judicial System Act, Arts. 30(2), 171(2), and 172. The Minister is not authorised to inform the Council of failures concerning Supreme Court judges.

[40] Judgement of 14 January 1999, State Gazette, No. 6, 22 January 1999.

that principle does not require the branches to avoid co-ordination of their actions.[41] Clearly, the Court's ruling does not move the Council towards less executive involvement or greater independent capacity.

*Representation of Non-Judges*: The Supreme Judicial Council represents all three kinds of magistrates, not only judges. Although in certain matters, the representatives of the three parts of the magistracy have separate competencies (such as in certain disciplinary matters[42]), for most matters the Council is a single corporate body; as a result, judges are represented and administered by a body composed of or appointed by non-judges.

It was the intention of the Constitution's drafters to break decisively with the communist legacy of a subordinated judiciary; this ambition apparently underlies the placement of the Prosecution and the Investigation Services within the judicial branch under a single Supreme Judicial Council competent to appoint and dismiss all magistrates. However, in practice this arrangement does not place the judiciary in a superior or equal position, but rather perpetuates problematic linkages between the executive and judges which can threaten judges' independence.

## C. Rules on Incompatibility

In general, judges are barred from improper relationships with other State entities or with private parties, in a manner which encourages their independence and impartiality. However, the safeguards unnecessarily allow the possibility of significant intermittent contact with the political branches over the course of a judge's career, in a manner that could jeopardise judicial independence.

The office of magistrate is incompatible with any other public office, which includes Member of Parliament, minister, deputy minister, mayor or municipal counsellor or any elected or appointed office in state, municipal and business organs.[43] Magistrates taking up such positions must therefore relinquish or suspend their judicial office.[44]

---

[41] Judgement of 14 January 1999, State Gazette, No. 6, 22 January 1999. It is noteworthy in this respect that by a judgement of the Constitutional Court of 3 April 1992 a provision of the then Supreme Judicial Council Act empowering the Minister of Justice to make proposals with respect of judges from district, regional and courts of appeal was repealed as being contrary to the principle of separation of powers. In a later judgement (of 3 October 1995) the Constitutional Court repealed a provision of the Judicial System Act stipulating that the administration of the Supreme Judicial Council is carried out by the Ministry of Justice.

[42] See Section V.D.2.

[43] Judicial System Act, Art. 132, paras. 1 and 3.

[44] Law on the Election of Members of Parliament, Art. 52.

The ban on engaging in political activity is interpreted as meaning that magistrates cannot be members of political parties or any other movements and coalitions with political aims while exercising their judicial functions.[45]

Upon completing their service in another public office or the Inspectorate of the Ministry of Justice, however, magistrates may be reinstated in their previous positions, and the time spent in public office is counted as legal experience in calculating eligibility for judicial office.[46] It is therefore permissible for a magistrate to move between the magistracy and the executive or legislature and back, which unnecessarily weakens the important distinction between the branches, to the detriment of judges' independence. More concretely, judges who have the opportunity to move into political or civil service positions at the discretion of a political official have incentives to rule in a manner which increases their chances of being selected for such assignments.

As a general rule, however, active judges cannot be appointed to positions in the executive, although judges are allowed to participate in certain specified bodies. For example, the President of the Supreme Court of Cassation may appoint some judges from the Court to serve on a non-permanent commission established to address access to former secret service documents. As members of this commission, the judges are paid a salary equal to the national minimum over and above their judicial salaries.[47] Magistrates also sit as members of electoral commissions. Only judges from the Supreme Administrative Court are prohibited from serving on the Central Electoral Commission.[48] As long as such appointments are limited to specified commissions and there are rules in place to ensure that these judges recuse themselves from any case relating to their commission work, they do not necessarily pose a threat to judicial independence. It would be preferable, as well, to limit the discretion the executive or senior judges exercise in selecting commission members, and to bar judges from receiving additional compensation, so that appointments cannot be used as a reward; appointing *ex officio* members can reduce this risk somewhat.

Judges are generally prohibited from engaging in most outside economic activity, including practicing law as advocates, or conducting activities pertaining to the legal profession.[49]

---

[45] Judicial System Act, Art. 132, para. 1. See also Law on the Election of Members of Parliament, Art. 52.

[46] Judicial System Act, Art. 132, para. 2, and Art. 36, para. 6, Art. 36a, para. 5, Art. 36b, para. 5, Art. 36c, para. 5 (concerning the Inspectorate of the Ministry of Justice). See Section V.A. concerning appointment to judicial office.

[47] Law on the Disclosure of the Documents of the Former Secret Services, Art. 4g.

[48] Law on the Election of Members of Parliament, Art. 10, para. 2. The rationale for this ban is the fact that an appeal against the decisions of this commission lies before the Supreme Administrative Court.

[49] Judicial System Act, Art. 132, para. 1(5).

Judges are banned from engaging in any commercial or other economic or profit-making activities; this includes membership in managerial or supervisory boards of commercial companies or co-operatives.[50] Scientific or teaching activities, and the exercise of authorial rights, constitute the only exceptions to the overall ban.

*Disclosure*: The members of the two Supreme Courts are obliged to make a public disclosure concerning their income and assets.[51] Lower judges have no such obligation. Moreover, the Supreme Court judges are only required to make a declaration, but there are no provisions for any legal consequences based upon their declarations. Given the widespread concerns about corruption in the judiciary, a requirement that judges disclose their assets would strengthen public confidence in the integrity of the judiciary, which in turn bolsters arguments for judges' independence.

## D. Judges' Associations

Judges are free to form and join organisations that protect their independence and professional interests and assist their professional qualifications.[52] The Union of Bulgarian Judges was founded in March 1997, and is gradually earning the confidence of the judicial community. The main objectives of the Union include consolidating judges into a common entity to protect their professional, intellectual, social and material interests, and conducting activities aimed at increasing the professional and social prestige of courts.[53] The Magistrates Training Centre was set up following an initiative by the Union. The Union has adopted a Code of Ethical Conduct of Judges, but it has no binding force.

In accordance with the principle of separation of powers, professional organisations representing judges or other magistrates cannot associate with trade union organisations representing other branches.[54]

---

[50] Judicial System Act, Art. 132, para. 1(4).
[51] Public Register Act.
[52] Judicial Systems Act, Art. 12(2).
[53] Statute of the Union of Bulgarian Judges.
[54] Judicial Systems Act, Art. 12.

## III. Administration of the Court System and Judicial Independence

The judiciary is supposed to be autonomous in its administration, and the Supreme Judicial Council is vested with extensive powers. At the same time, the Ministry of Justice retains important administrative and supervisory powers, and the relationships between the two, as well as the obligations placed on courts, are not clearly defined, creating room for non-transparent and arbitrary administrative decisions.

### A. Role of the Supreme Judicial Council

By law, the judicial branch is autonomous.[55] The Supreme Judicial Council, as an organ of the judicial branch,[56] administers the operations of the court system, and possesses decision-making competencies encompassing every aspect of the operation of courts.[57]

The Supreme Judicial Council exercises administrative and supervisory control over the performance and efficiency of the judiciary. It determines the number, seat, and geographic jurisdiction of courts, on the proposal of the Minister of Justice; determines the number of magistrates in each court, prosecutor's office, or investigating office; appoints, promotes, demotes, assigns and dismisses magistrates;[58] decides on their remuneration; decides on motions to lift magistrates' immunity; rules on disciplinary actions against magistrates; draws up the courts' budget and disburses allocated funds;[59] and requests and reviews information from magistrates.[60] In addition, the Council proposes to the State President candidates for Presidents of the two Supreme Courts, and may recommend their dismissal.[61]

---

[55] Judicial System Act, Art. 1.

[56] The Constitutional Court has clearly defined the Supreme Judicial Council as an organ of the judicial branch. At the same time, the Court held that the Council is not itself a judicial body but a high administrative organ carrying out the management of the bodies within the judicial branch. Judgement of the Constitutional Court, 15 September 1994, State Gazette, No. 78/1994.

[57] CONST. REP. BULGARIA, Art. 133, providing for the regulation in law of the Supreme Judicial Council and the magistracy.

[58] See Section V.

[59] See Section IV.

[60] Judicial System Act, Art. 27.

[61] Judicial System Act, Art. 27.

The Supreme Judicial Council determines numbers of judges and court staff. The Ministry of Justice exercises control over court space, facilities and maintenance through a Court Houses Fund.

The Supreme Judicial Council holds meetings every week; it must be convened at least every three months by the Minister or upon the request of at least one-fifth of its members at least once every three months.[62] However, the Council cannot sit per-manently,[63] and this is considered one of the principal sources of inefficiency in the Council's operations, since its occasional meetings are insufficient to address its varied functions with regard to the daily control of the judicial system's operations.

Day-to-day operations are overseen by court presidents. At present, court presidents carry out much of the work normally done by court registrars. A new position of secretary general is being introduced in some courts (and already exists at the Supreme Courts), to deal with some of these functions. Presidents of district, regional and appellate courts are obliged to submit to the Council an annual report on their courts' activities and the activities of lower courts under their jurisdiction.[64] Encouraging independent professional management can counter the frequent argument that courts are incapable of managing themselves, as well as reducing the administrative burden on court presidents and limiting the scope of their commercial and institutional contacts outside the court, which administration often entails.

## B. Involvement of the Ministry of Justice

Alongside the leading role of the Supreme Judicial Council, the Ministry of Justice retains significant areas of administrative and supervisory responsibility. In part because the Council has a small staff and meets only occasionally, the Ministry, with its larger staff and resources, is in practice much more involved than might appear from its formal legal position.

As noted elsewhere in this Report,[65] the Ministry of Justice, as part of the executive, exercises a far more important role in the development of the judiciary's budget than formal analysis of the constitutional and legal provisions would suggest. In addition,

---

[62] There has been one occasion so far in which upon the minister's refusal to call a meeting the Council was convened upon the request of a group of its members.

[63] Judgement of the Constitutional Court of 30 September 1994.

[64] Judicial System Act, Art. 56.1.2, 63.1.2, and 79.1.2.

[65] See Section IV.A.

the Ministry administers the courts building fund for the construction of new court facilities, which forms a separate part of the judicial branch's budget. In practice, requests for materiel go through the Ministry.

The Ministry of Justice issues regulations relating to court administration and certain personnel matters. For example, the functions of court personnel are determined by ministerial regulations.[66]

In addition to these extensive administrative responsibilities, the Ministry of Justice also has supervisory and information-gathering competencies which inevitably involve it in the routine administration of the courts. Although the Inspectorate of the Ministry has no direct decision-making competence over the judicial branch, it examines the organisation of administrative activities of district, regional, and appellate courts.[67] Its inspectors[68] carry out regular inspections of courts and judges' decisions in order to track civil and criminal cases and ensure that ministerial standards regulating the progression of cases through the courts have been met.[69] The Inspectorate submits to the Supreme Judicial Council information on its findings and assessments;[70] however, the Council is evidently not required to use the report for any particular purpose.

The Ministry of Justice also prepares an annual report on the activities of the courts (except for the Supreme Courts) which considers issues such as court caseloads, the progress of cases, and enforcement of judgements. The legal basis for drawing up this report is not clear, as it is not provided for in the Judicial System Act. The Ministry also holds annual meetings of presidents of district, regional and appellate courts to discuss the report. The Ministry also retains important functions with respect to the organisation of court records, which further involves it in supervisory activities in the courts.

---

[66] Judicial System Act, Art. 188.

[67] Judicial System Act, Chapter 3. The Inspectorate cannot monitor the two Supreme Courts. Judicial System Act, Art. 35(2).

[68] Inspectors are appointed by the Minister of Justice after the Supreme Judicial Council has expressed its opinion on the nominee. Inspectors must meet the qualifications for a position in the court of appeal, and they receive a salary equal to that of an appellate court president. Inspectors are often former judges, and may return to the bench after leaving the Inspectorate; they are generally thought of as akin to judges in their function. For example, inspectors have even been able to review the merits of court judgements, and it has been proposed that Supreme Court judges be commissioned as temporary inspectors while retaining their status as judges. At present, however, the Inspectorate is considered understaffed.

[69] Judicial System Act, Art. 35.2.

[70] Judicial System Act, Art. 35(1.3 and 1.6).

Presidents of district, regional and appellate courts are obliged to submit information on the manner cases are processed by judges to the Ministry of Justice every six months.[71]

## C. Unclear Division of Authority

There is neither a clear demarcation between the functions of the Supreme Judicial Council and the Ministry of Justice, nor of the areas in which they are supposed to co-operate; the competencies of the Supreme Judicial Council are clearly established, but those of the Ministry are not. Separation of power arguments do not explain when the Ministry is required to allocate its considerable resources to courts and court presidents, and the terms on which those resources are to be made available have not been established. The effect has been that court presidents often have no guidance concerning where to turn for material support. The Ministry's administrative role is even more prominent because the Supreme Judicial Council only meets periodically, allowing the Ministry greater scope of action.

---

[71] See Arts. 56.1.3, 63.1.2 and 79.1.3 of the Judicial System Act.

## IV. Financial Autonomy and Level of Funding

As one court president has noted, "[a] really independent judiciary is one that is self-governed, and sufficient funding is an indispensable condition to achieve this."[72] Judges and the courts do not have meaningful input into their own budgets, which are formally prepared by the Supreme Judicial Council, but in practice are prepared by the executive. Formal institutional arrangements cannot guarantee independence in the absence of meaningful financial autonomy.

### A. Budgeting Process

In theory, the Supreme Judicial Council drafts the budget for the whole judiciary.[73] However, the executive is legally allowed to prepare a parallel budget that in practice forms the real basis for Parliament's deliberations.

The Constitutional Court has held that since the judicial branch is constitutionally guaranteed an independent budget,[74] the executive may not be involved in its preparation but is obliged to incorporate the judicial branch budget *in toto* into the annual State budget proposal it submits to Parliament.[75] Accordingly, the annual State budget law contains a separate budget line for the judicial branch.

At the initial stage of preparation of each year's budget the Ministry of Finance proposes a general framework for budget planning including possible growth, and on this basis the Supreme Judicial Council makes its projections. It is only at this stage that some form of dialogue between the two branches takes place.

When drafting the judicial branch's budget the Supreme Judicial Council may collect initial figures from the three constituent bodies of the magistracy, it is not the practice, however, for each court to submit a request, and instead the previous year's figures serve as a basis for preparing the draft. As a result, individual courts' own estimates of

---

[72] OSI roundtable, Sofia, 6 April 2001.
[73] The Constitutional Court has its own budget. Constitutional Court Act, Art. 3.
[74] CONST. REP. BULGARIA, Art. 117(3).
[75] Judgement of 16 December 1993, State Gazette, No. 1., 4 January 1994. See also Organisation of the State Budget Act, Art. 20(2); Judicial System Act, Art. 196(3) (allowing the Government to raise objections and make proposals, but not allowing it to make changes in the judicial budget).

their needs differ sharply from the amounts actually disbursed to them through the budget process.[76]

Despite the clear constitutional provisions concerning the autonomy of the judicial budget, in practice the executive prepares its own parallel budget for the judiciary and submits it to Parliament along with the Supreme Judicial Council's budget.[77] Representatives of the Government are normally admitted to the meetings of the relevant parliamentary committees and are given the opportunity to defend their version.[78] Parliament has generally adopted the Government version in recent years.

The result is that the judiciary (and the magistracy as a whole) is almost completely isolated from the budget process, and in effect has no influence over its actual budget. There is no evidence that the Government or Parliament have made adequate funding for the judiciary conditional on some standard of productivity. At the same time, it seems clear that the executive's priorities in developing its budget version are different from those of the Supreme Judicial Council and are formulated in terms of productivity estimates, and in this sense the judiciary's own sense of its material needs may be discounted.

Apportionment of the budgeted funds – which are not specified in sub-lines – is still the responsibility of the Council. Until 1999 it was the practice to include sub-lines in the judicial branch budget for the Supreme Judicial Council, the two Supreme Courts, the rest of the courts in general, the Chief Prosecutor's office and the National Investigation Service. In the last three Annual Budget Acts, however, the budget line for the judiciary is not sub-lined, and the Supreme Judicial Council therefore determines the respective appropriations and distributes them among the different bodies of the judicial branch.[79]

---

[76] When preparing its version, the Supreme Judicial Council may collect some initial figures from the different organs but it is solely competent to assemble them and draw up the final draft. No specific methodology in this respect is in place. Requests from each particular court are not normally collected at the stage of drawing up the budget draft and only during the fiscal year such requests may be heard.

[77] The executive ostensibly does this in accordance with its right to make objections or proposals.

[78] Members of the Supreme Judicial Council may also attend hearings of the committee on budgetary matters and intervene.

[79] Organisation of the State Budget Act, Art. 23; Annual Budget Act for the Year 2001, Art. 2(7). There is a case currently pending before the Constitutional Court in which the constitutionality of the 2001 Annual Budget Act's failure to specify funding for the Supreme Judicial Council in particular is challenged. In 1995, the Court voided a budget provision that failed to specify the Council's funding. Two other sections of the same provision are also challenged. The first determines the amount of the subsidy appropriated to the judicial branch at 90 percent of the amount approved providing that the remaining ten percent are to be granted only on the condition that the established budget deficit is not exceeded. The second stipulates that any surplus revenues arising from the judicial branch's activities will be transferred to the account of the State budget.

(It is not possible to transfer funds from the judicial budget to other budgetary lines during the fiscal year, but any surplus revenues are transferred to the State budget.) The competition for limited resources exacerbates tension among the three components of the magistracy.

The 2000 budget contained no significant increase over 1999, despite the expansion of the courts' pre-trial detention supervision functions; the budget for 2001 marks an increase of roughly 14 percent over 2000. Approximately 0.9 percent of the total appropriations for 2001 go to the judiciary.

In this year's apportionment, the Supreme Judicial Council itself received 3.396 percent of the judiciary's portion of the budget, the Supreme Court of Cassation 5.501 percent, the Supreme Administrative Court 2.764 percent, all other courts 47.516 percent, the prosecutor's offices 23.218 percent, and the investigator's offices 9.867 percent,[80] with the distribution envisaging a budget deficit as compared with the subsidy from the state budget.[81]

## B. Work Conditions

Work conditions in the courts suffer from chronic under-investment. Between 70 and 80 percent of the budget allocation for the judicial branch goes to salaries for judges and staff, leaving only a relatively small amount for infrastructure and equipment. In addition, the expansion of courts' jurisdiction and functions over the past decade has intensified the workload of courts. While the situation is not uniformly bad throughout the country, in general courts and judges are overburdened, and the material conditions in which judges work are unsatisfactory, especially as regards shortages of office space, court rooms and equipment.[82] Court presidents are in a particularly vulnerable position in relation to the Supreme Judicial Council and the Ministry of Justice, which exercise control over needed resources.

There are no norms for allocation of office space or equipment, and in their absence it is more difficult to argue for better work conditions and modernisation of courts.

---

[80] Decision of the Supreme Judicial Council of 7 March 2001.

[81] In a cover letter of 13 April 2001 with which the distribution has been submitted to the Ministry of Finance, the Supreme Judicial Council points out the shortage of funding and states that it does not accept, as being inadequate, the amount allotted to the judicial branch by the Annual Budget Act.

[82] Normally three judges share an office in the Sofia district and city (regional) courts. Sometimes judges even have to queue up for courtrooms.

Information technology has been introduced in some courts, but not as part of a nationwide system. Indeed, it is largely due to the initiative of individual court presidents and to foreign assistance programs that some courts are better equipped than others. The judicial system as a whole still relies on donor assistance in setting up a uniform information system.[83]

Systems for court administration and organisation of court records, archives and statistics are extremely outdated. Methods for improvement through the introduction of a new information system have been discussed by the Supreme Judicial Council, but without any concrete outcome or agreement with the Ministry of Justice on proposed legislative changes.

Training of magistrates is formally organised by the Ministry of Justice, but the State does not fund or organise significant training, which is currently carried out by the Magistrates Training Centre, an NGO funded almost exclusively by foreign States. The European Commission recommends that "the training centre will need to become a public training institution in the medium term with adequate financial and human resources." In that event, its continued operation under the supervision of the Ministry of Justice could constitute an interference with the independence of the judiciary, as it would give the executive an unnecessarily intrusive opportunity to intervene in judges' professional development.

## C. Compensation

Salaries for judges are generally satisfactory, and do not pose any significant risk to judicial independence. However, discretionary rules on the provision of housing may make judges vulnerable to influence from local governments, and the disproportionately low pensions judges receive, when combined with discretionary rules on retirement, may also endanger their decisional independence.

Remuneration of members of the judiciary normally exceeds that of other public sector employees. The level of judicial salaries has increased the attractiveness of judicial posts, especially in light of the poor economic situation in the country as a whole, which has reduced the profitability of legal work in the private sector.

---

[83] A project aimed at setting up a uniform software program for the whole court system, supported by USAID, is currently in progress.

At the same time some judges maintain that their salaries are only slightly higher than those for the public administration, since rules on incompatibility[84] prohibit outside earnings for magistrates. In contrast to magistrates, public sector employees are allowed to earn additional income from, for example, participation in boards of state-owned companies.

The monthly remuneration for the lowest judicial position is fixed at double the minimum salary for employment in the public sector pursuant to data supplied by the National Institute of Statistics – currently about 470 BGL (c. € 243). A district court judge receives approximately 550 DEM (c. € 281), a regional court judge approximately 700 DEM (c. € 358), (roughly equal to the salary of a deputy minister), and Supreme Court judges about 1,000 DEM (c. € 511) per month. The Presidents of the two Supreme Courts each receive a monthly remuneration amounting to 90 percent of that received by the President of the Constitutional Court.[85]

Apart from salary, judges receive a yearly clothing allowance amounting to two average monthly salaries of an employee in the public sector, and life insurance. Judges may participate in national social security and health insurance schemes, but must pay 20 percent of the contribution themselves, whereas civil servants' contributions are paid out of the State budget. (Recently considered amendments to the Judicial System Act would have conferred on magistrates the same status as civil servants, but the proposals were not introduced into Parliament.)

In addition, under the Judicial System Act, a housing fund for the judiciary is supposed to be set up, although it is moribund for lack of resources. Instead, judges rely on local governments to supply housing, although such assistance is entirely discretionary. Usually it is the court president's duty to contact local authorities for housing allotments for judges. This reliance may affect judges' and court president's decisional independence.

A judge's compensation may not be reduced except for disciplinary reasons (either a direct reduction or as the result of demotion), on the decision of the Supreme Judicial Council.

Upon retirement, judges who have served in the judiciary for at least ten years are entitled to receive a one-time payment equal to twenty months' salary, in addition to their pension. However since pensions are very low at present,[86] it is impossible for

---

[84] See Section II.C.

[85] Judicial System Act, Art. 139(1). In the Constitutional Court Act remuneration is determined in correlation with the remuneration of the State President and the Speaker of Parliament.

[86] The maximum cannot exceed 160–170 BGL.

judges to maintain their standard of living after retirement on the income from their pensions alone which, combined with discretionary rules on retirement, may endanger older judges' decisional independence.[87]

---

[87] See Section V.B.2.

## V. Judicial Office

The principal decisions affecting a judge's career path – such as selection, promotion, assignment, and dismissal – are made by the Supreme Judicial Council.[88] There are very few clear or objective procedures to guide the Council, which acts with broad discretion. Particular problems of note include the provision that judges are not tenured (and thus are irremovable) until they have served three years in a position, that promotions are largely discretionary, and that in the absence of a mandatory retirement age older judges effectively serve at the pleasure of their court president and the Council.

### A. The Selection Process

Almost all judges and other magistrates[89] are selected by the Supreme Judicial Council[90] with considerable input from court presidents and the Ministry of Justice in a highly discretionary process. Apart from some minimal threshold requirements, there are no firmly established methods or criteria for selection of candidates for judicial office.[91]

There are no clearly defined national criteria or competitive examinations. Certain basic requirements for appointment to judicial office are regulated in the Judicial System Act;[92] in addition to citizenship and legal education, candidates must have "passed the required post-graduate training"[93] and have the "required moral and professional qualities."[94] Candidates must also have a requisite number of years of general legal

---

[88] CONST. REP. BULGARIA, Art. 129(1); Judicial System Act, Art. 27(1), Section 4.

[89] Except the Presidents of the two Supreme Courts and the Chief Public Prosecutor. See Section V.A.1.

[90] CONST. REP. BULGARIA, Art. 129, para. 1.

[91] The Commission's *2000 Regular Report* notes that "[j]udges are appointed to a particular court by the Supreme Judicial Council upon suggestion of the President of that Court. The criteria applied for their selection (except the purely formal criteria of University education and completion of a legal traineeship) are not always transparent and there is no national competition for recruitment." *2000 Regular Report*, Section 2.

[92] Judicial System Act, Art. 126.

[93] That is, a one-year practice at a regional court followed by a theoretical and practical exam. The trainees, or judicial candidates, receive a qualification certificate after taking the examination.

[94] Judicial System Act, Arts. 126(2) and (4).

experience: two years for district court, five years for regional court, eight years for courts of appeal, and twelve years for either of the Supreme Courts.[95]

In practice, selection of candidates for consideration by the Supreme Judicial Council is initiated by the court presidents at the local level, at their discretion and for the immediate needs of their courts. There is no law regulating the selection procedure, and different presidents adopt different practices for identifying candidates: some regional courts hold competitions for junior judges' positions, while others prefer personal interviews or an assessment based on documents only.

The Supreme Judicial Council makes no preliminary selection prior to considering candidates, who must be approved by majority vote in a secret ballot. The Council has no grounds upon which to judge the professional qualities of candidates for appointment besides the proposals for appointment and the assessment of the candidate made by the official submitting the proposal.

In some cases, junior judges are appointed by the Supreme Judicial Council at regional courts only for a term of two years which may be prolonged for another six months. They cannot sit alone as judges and may only sit in panel. After having served at least one year, junior judges may be commissioned to a district court to perform judicial duties.[96] Junior judgeship is generally perceived as a "first step" to a regular judicial career. However, during this period, the junior judge – who is adjudicating cases – does not have tenure or irremovability.

The Supreme Judicial Council and the Ministry of Justice have recognised the problems inherent in the current structure, and have initiated a discussion concerning introduction of a system for more accurate selection. A recently suggested amendment to the Judicial System Act would have introduced some form of competitive selection or a commission to review candidates prior to their approval by the Council, but the amendment – apparently the source of considerable disagreement between the Council and the Ministry – was not put before Parliament.

In the absence of a new legislative initiative, on 11 April 2001 the Supreme Judicial Council adopted a decision "in pursuance of the recommendations of the European

---

[95] The required legal experience may be acquired by serving as a judge, prosecutor, investigator, lawyer, junior judge, legal expert in the Ministry of Justice, or in a variety of other legally related positions. Judicial System Act, Art. 127(5). For courts of Appeal or the Supreme Courts, as an additional requirement, three or five years, respectively of the candidate's legal experience must have been as a magistrate. Judicial System Act, Art. 127(6).

[96] Judicial System Act, Arts. 147–148.

Commission," according to which appointment of junior judges and district courts judges is to be preceded by an examination of the candidates proposed by the presidents of regional courts. The examination is to be conducted by a commission composed of judges from the two Supreme Courts.

### 1. Court Presidents

Only the Presidents of the two Supreme Courts and the Chief Public Prosecutor are appointed and dismissed by the State President on a motion from the Supreme Judicial Council; moreover, the State President cannot refuse to appoint nominees whose candidacy is re-submitted by the Supreme Judicial Council.[97]

Court presidents are appointed by the Supreme Judicial Council.[98] There are no additional requirements for their appointment, which is not considered a matter of regular promotion and takes place upon the proposal of the officials authorised to make it – that is, the presidents of higher courts and the Ministry of Justice.

## B. Tenure, Retirement, Transfer and Removal

### 1. Tenure

Once tenured, judges are not removable from office without specific cause as specified in the Constitution and law. However, judges do not acquire tenure until they have completed their third year in office.[99] There is no formal review, and judges simply continue in office and acquire tenured irremovability if they are not removed by the Supreme Judicial Council, which acts, or does not act, at its discretion. The formal purpose of this rule is to ensure that new judges indeed have the qualities necessary for proper adjudication, but as a consequence, for the first three years they serve, judges have strong and immediate incentives not to rule in a manner that might displease the Council.

As an alternative to such a long period without tenure, increased training of judicial candidates or trainees could be introduced.

---

[97] CONST. REP. BULGARIA, Art. 129, para. 2.
[98] Judicial System Act, Art. 30.
[99] CONST. REP. BULGARIA, Art. 129(3); Judicial System Act, Art. 129.

## 2. Retirement

In the absence of a mandatory retiring age especially established for judges or other magistrates, the generally established statutory retirement age[100] is supposed to serve as a neutral limit on judges' tenure and thus a guarantee for judicial independence. In practice, retirement is not mandatory and judges serve past that age. However, the president of the judge's court or the Minister of Justice may propose to the Supreme Judicial Council – for any reason or no reason at all – that the judge be dismissed at any time after reaching retirement age. The Council has discretion in the matter.

The Council's practice to date has been to provide the judge concerned with an opportunity to make a presentation; it has tended to reject proposals for dismissal based on subjective reasons rather than on serious considerations, such as the merits of the respective judge and the availability of a suitable replacement in the respective region.[101] Nonetheless, the discretionary nature of the process introduces unnecessary threats to older judges' decisional independence, which a clear retirement date would eliminate.

## 3. Transfer

There are no provisions governing permanent, non-disciplinary transfer of judges. Transfer to another jurisdiction for up to three years, referred to as reassignment, may be imposed by the Supreme Judicial Council as a disciplinary action.[102] Short-term transfer within a given jurisdiction for up to three months within any given year is possible in cases in which a position is vacant or a judge is prevented from carrying out his or her duties and has to be substituted.[103] The decision is taken by the president of the respective court;[104] there are no explicit provisions requiring the judge's consent or laying out consequences for refusal. In the absence of clearer procedures or a requirement for the judge's consent, such short-term transfers – while often very useful for ensuring the efficient administration of justice – afford superior judges the opportunity unduly to interfere with lower judges' decisional independence.

---

[100] Fixed at 60 years and six months for men and 55 years and six months for women at present and to be gradually increased to 63 years for men and 60 years for women.

[101] The amendments to the Judicial System Act introduced in February 2001 contained also a proposal seeking to deprive the Supreme Judicial Council of the possibility to make any assessment in this respect and limit its competence to verifying the legal conditions for retirement.

[102] Judicial System Act, Art. 27(4) and Art. 169, para. 1.5.

[103] Judicial System Act, Art. 130.

[104] Judicial System Act, Art. 55(1), 62(1), 78(1), 83(1) and 94(1).

## 4. Removal

After judges acquire tenure, they cannot be removed from office, except "upon retirement, resignation, upon the enforcement of a prison sentence for a deliberate crime, or upon lasting actual disability to perform their functions over more than one year[,]"[105] or for an absence of professional merits for the performance of judicial duties, or as a disciplinary measure, as set forth below (See Section V.D).[106] In addition, judges may be removed if they have been serving in place of a judge temporarily or unlawfully removed from duty who then returns or is reinstated.[107]

## C. Evaluation and Promotion

In general, judges are progressively promoted in rank[108] and salary. Judges who demonstrate high professional qualification and exemplary performance of their duties are eligible for promotion within their current position[109] after at least three years in the post.[110] Promotion is not automatic, however, and there are no clear criteria for evaluating eligible judges.

The Supreme Judicial Council decides upon promotions, upon a proposal made by the respective court president or the Minister of Justice at either one's discretion.[111] A judge may also address the Supreme Judicial Council directly and request promotion.[112] The Supreme Judicial Council examines information concerning the judge's performance, which may include the rate of reversal, and which is provided by the president of the court or the Inspectorate of the Ministry.

There are no special procedures governing promotion to higher posts (as opposed to promotion in place), such as court president, or a seat on a higher court. Appointment

---

[105] CONST. REP. BULGARIA, Art. 129 (3).

[106] Judicial System Act, Art. 169(2) bars removal of tenured judges on disciplinary grounds.

[107] Judicial System Act, Art. 131.

[108] Ranks normally follow the structure of the court system. See Judicial System Act, Art. 143.

[109] That is to say, a so-called promotion in place, as opposed to a promotion to a higher position, such as court president, or to a higher court.

[110] Judicial System Act, Art. 142.

[111] Judicial System Act, Art. 30, paras. 1 and 2.

[112] In one particular case the Supreme Judicial Council appointed a commission to examine the relations between the respective judge and court president as to the existence of special reasons for the president's refusal to make a proposal.

to these positions is treated as a selection decided by the respective court's president or the Minister of Justice at their discretion (subject to the minimum requirement of a certain number of years of legal experience). This high level of discretion in promotions of all kinds increases the possibility for superior judges and the Ministry to exercise influence over the judges seeking career advancement.

## D. Discipline

In general, disciplinary measures work to ensure judges' impartiality, and do not appear to threaten their independence through improper or discretionary application. However, a proposed law would limit judges' right to appeal adverse disciplinary rulings. Also, a recent draft constitutional amendment would have lifted judges' immunity from prosecution; although the proposal failed, it suggests a less than firm consensus on fundamental commitments to judicial independence.

### 1. Liability

Judges are exempt from civil liability for acts and omissions in the exercise of their judicial functions unless they constitute a criminal offence.[113] Judges also enjoy the same degree of constitutional immunity as Members of Parliament,[114] which means that they cannot be held liable for their opinions or decisions[115] or be detained or prosecuted except for grave crimes.[116]

The Supreme Judicial Council can lift a judge's immunity from proscecution,[117] as well as from pre-trial detention for grave crimes.[118] The Chief Public Prosecutor must provide reasons before the Supreme Judicial Council to substantiate a request to lift a magistrate's immunity from prosecution or detention. (No such authorisation is required when a member of the judiciary is detained in the course of committing a grave harm, but the Supreme Judicial Council, or, in between its meetings, the Minister of Justice, must be notified forthwith.) The Council must decide on lifting immunity or suspending

---

[113] Judicial System Act, Art. 135.

[114] CONST. REP. BULGARIA, Art. 132(1).

[115] CONST. REP. BULGARIA, Art. 69.

[116] CONST. REP. BULGARIA, Art. 70. A crime is considered grave if punishable with imprisonment for more than five years. Criminal Code, Art. 93(7).

[117] Judicial System Act, Art. 134(1).

[118] Judicial System Act, Art. 134(2).

a magistrate within five days, by a two-thirds vote of all its members in a secret ballot, and after having considered oral or written explanations from the magistrate concerned.[119]

In February 2001, a proposal was made to limit magistrates' constitutional immunity, based on concerns about corruption. A draft amendment to the Constitution was introduced into Parliament, but failed on the first ballot. However, the issue remains to be resolved by the next Parliament, and has also been raised in the Commission's 2000 Regular Report, which noted that "judges' immunity needs to be clarified, notably as regards minor offences, for which they apparently cannot be charged, and offences not related to their work, where the Supreme Judicial Council determines whether or not judicial immunity should be lifted."[120]

## 2. Disciplinary Procedures

Judges are disciplinarily liable for breaches and omissions in the performance of their official duties, for undue delay, for acts that diminish the reputation of the judicial branch, and for failure to deliver judgements in the manner prescribed by law.[121] (An additional ground added in 1998 – violation of one's oath – was thrown out by the Constitutional Court as not comporting with the requirement that offences have clear and actual substance.)[122]

Various court presidents may initiate disciplinary proceedings against judges[123] beneath them: the President of the Supreme Court of Cassation against judges of that court and the courts of appeal; the President of the Supreme Administrative Court against judges of that court; the president of a court of appeal against judges of lower regional courts; and the president of a regional court against judges of lower district courts. In addition, since May 2000 the Minister of Justice may initiate proceedings against any magistrate.[124]

---

[119] Figures show that over the last two and a half years, i.e. during the tenure of the present Supreme Judicial Council, only two proposals for stripping members of the judiciary of their immunity have been made.

[120] *2000 Regular Report*, Section 2.

[121] Judicial System Act, Art. 168.

[122] Judgement of 14 January 1999.

[123] Since May 2000, judges, prosecutors and investigators have separate hierarchies for initiating disciplinary proceedings against their members. Between November 1998 and May 2000, any member of the Supreme Judicial Council had been competent to initiate disciplinary proceedings against any magistrate; the provision was altered when a judge on the Council announced her intention to bring proceedings against a prosecutor in the Chief Prosecutor's Office.

[124] Judicial System Act, Art. 171(1), (2).

Magistrates' conduct and professional performance are supervised by the Supreme Judicial Council. Disciplinary proceedings are held before a five-member disciplinary panel selected by lot from among the Council's members. The proposal for imposing a disciplinary proceeding is served to the magistrate concerned who may present a written reply within two weeks, attend the hearing of the panel and be represented by a lawyer. Written and oral evidence may be collected and heard.

The disciplinary punishments provided are: warning; reduction in salary equivalent to the minimum national salary for a period of two months; non-promotion in rank or in office for between one and three years; demotion either in rank or in office for six months to three years; reassignment to a different judicial region for three years; and dismissal from office.[125] The disciplinary panel may itself impose some of the disciplinary punishments – warning, salary reduction and non-promotion, or make a proposal for reassignment, demotion and dismissal to the Council. Decisions of the disciplinary panel and of the Council in disciplinary proceedings may be appealed to the Supreme Administrative Court.[126]

The current disciplinary procedure has been criticised by members of the judiciary, especially the three-year reassignment that is sometimes imposed with the intent of forcing the magistrate to resign (because a tenured magistrate cannot be dismissed). At the same time, some judges maintain the Supreme Judicial Council does not possess adequate resources to handle such factually and legally complex proceedings. It is not clear which procedural rules are to be followed when collecting and evaluating evidence, for example, and cases are often hastily decided on the basis of inadequate research into the circumstances. Problems of a procedural character are the main reason disciplinary decisions of the Council are repealed by the Supreme Administrative Court.[127]

In 2001, the Supreme Judicial Council adopted a decision in support of a Government draft law proposing elimination of judges' right to appeal decisions imposing disciplinary sanctions against them; this could marginally reduce judges' security from improperly imposed disciplinary measures.

---

[125] Judicial System Act, Art. 169. Dismissal as a form of disciplinary punishment may not be imposed on tenured judges.

[126] Constitutional Court judgement of 14 January 1999.

[127] Between 20 and 30 percent of appealed disciplinary cases have been repealed.

# VI. Intra-Judicial Relations

## A. Relations with Superior Courts

Judges of inferior instances generally possess sufficient independence in relation to superior judges when deciding cases.

The Constitution provides for "supreme judicial oversight" to be exercised by the Supreme Court of Cassation as to the precise and uniform application of the law by all courts[128] and by the Supreme Administrative Court in the sphere of administrative justice.[129] Both Supreme Courts, apart from being the highest judicial instances in their respective jurisdictions, have the competence to deliver interpretative judgements which are binding on the judiciary and the executive.[130] The Ministry of Justice is entitled to make proposals for interpretative ruling.[131]

Appellate instances may proceed with a full re-examination of the case after having heard new evidence and may deliver a new judgement on the merits; subsequently, a cassation appeal is limited to points of law and breaches of procedural rules. When an appealed judgement has been reversed by the Supreme Court of Cassation and the case remitted to the lower court, the Supreme Court of Cassation's instructions on the interpretation and application of substantive law are binding upon that court.[132]

There is no system of appointed supervisors or mentors from superior courts. Consultations with superior court judges in specific cases, where they occur, are carried out informally on the basis of personal relations and not on the basis of any administrative or teaching relationship. Such consultations can constitute improper interference with lower judges' decisional independence given higher court presidents' role in promotions to their courts and in temporary transfers.

---

[128] CONST. REP. BULGARIA, Art. 124.
[129] CONST. REP. BULGARIA, Art. 125.
[130] Judicial System Act, Art. 86, para. 2, and Art. 97, para. 2.
[131] Judicial System Act, Arts. 86 and 97.
[132] Code of Civil Procedure, Art. 218(h); Code of Criminal Procedure, Art. 358, para. 1(2).

## B. Case Management and Relations with Court Presidents

Judges are to a certain extent dependent on the court presidents. Case management in particular lacks transparent and neutral standards for assignment.

Cases are assigned to individual judges by the court presidents or by the heads of specialised civil or criminal sections, where those exist.[133] There are no specific, binding rules as to case distribution, and court presidents exercise discretion, often based on considerations connected with the complexity of the case and the capacity of the particular judge. (This apparently is one of the reasons why random distribution has not been introduced, although judges are familiar with the concept and its introduction is being considered by the Supreme Judicial Council.) Cases assigned to a particular judge can be revoked and reassigned to another judge if there are grounds for challenging a judge's impartiality or when it becomes impossible for a judge to perform his or her functions, such as for reasons of health or prolonged absence.

In addition to case assignment, court presidents may inform the Inspectorate of the Ministry of Justice as to the progress of cases dealt with by individual judges and to assess judges' performance in considering promotions or initiating disciplinary proceedings.

---

[133] Judicial System Act, Arts. 56, para. 1(4); 63, para. 1; and 79, para. 1.

## VII. Enforcement and Corruption

### A. Enforcement of Judgements

Although judicial decisions are generally respected by the Government and particular government agencies, there have been individual cases of non-compliance; for example, the Supreme Administrative Court has had to resort to imposing statutory fines on high officials – including regional governors and even cabinet ministers – following their failure to fulfil obligations arising from court decisions.

More broadly, the enforcement of judgements poses significant problems, especially with regard to civil and commercial disputes. Court bailiffs are appointed, and dismissed by the Ministry.[134] The 1999 annual report of the Ministry of Justice found a 12 percent increase in the number of judgements subject to execution and at the same time an approximately 12 percent decrease in the number of judgements that have been executed. Timely enforcement affects public confidence in the court system.

### B. Corruption

There is a widespread public perception that the courts, along with customs offices, the tax administration and the police, are affected by corruption.[135] The Commission's 2000 Regular Report similarly notes that "according to several surveys… customs, the police and the judiciary are considered to be the most corrupt professions in Bulgaria." At the same time, there are few demonstrated cases of corruption, and some judges maintain that the judiciary is wrongly identified as a locus for corruption, but is made a scapegoat by the executive and legislature for difficult economic and social situations.

As noted above,[136] concerns about corruption recently led to a proposal to limit magistrates' constitutional immunity. The proposal failed in the Parliament in February 2001; however, it appears the issue may be revisited in the next Parliament.

---

[134] Judicial System Act, Arts. 149(2) and 152.

[135] Coalition 2000, Corruption Assessment Report 2000. (Coalition 2000 is an initiative of Bulgarian non-governmental organisations).

[136] See Section V.D.1.

# Judicial Independence in the Czech Republic

# Table of Contents

Executive Summary ................................................. 112

I. Introduction ................................................. 115

   A. Shortcomings in Reforms to Date ............ 115
      1. Continuing Influence
         of the Ministry of Justice ................... 115
      2. Insufficient Material Conditions ........ 116

   B. Attitudes towards the Judiciary ................ 116
      1. Political, Public
         and Media Attitudes ......................... 116
      2. Judges' Attitudes ............................... 118
      3. The Judiciary and the
         EU Accession Process ......................... 118

   C. Reform Proposals ...................................... 120

   D. Organisation of the Judicial System ......... 121

II. Constitutional and Legal Foundations
    of Judicial Independence ................................ 123

    A. Separation of Powers and Guarantees
       of Judicial Independence .......................... 123

    B. Representation of the Judiciary ................ 124

    C. Rules on Incompatibility ......................... 124

    D. Judges' Associations ................................ 126

III. Administration of the Justice System
     and Judicial Independence ............................. 127

IV. Financial Autonomy and Level of Funding .... 129

    A. The Budget Process ................................. 129

    B. Work Conditions .................................... 130

    C. Compensation ......................................... 132

| | | |
|---|---|---|
| V. | Judicial Office .................................... 134 | |
| | A. The Selection Process ................ 134 | |
| | B. Tenure, Retirement, Transfer and Removal ........................... 136 | |
| |    1. Tenure and Retirement ...... 136 | |
| |    2. Transfer ............................ 136 | |
| |    3. Removal ........................... 138 | |
| | C. Evaluation and Promotion ........ 139 | |
| | D. Discipline ................................. 140 | |
| |    1. Liability ............................ 140 | |
| |    2. Disciplinary Proceedings ... 141 | |
| VI. | Intra-Judicial Independence ........... 143 | |
| | A. Relations with Superior Courts ... 143 | |
| | B. Case Management and Relations with Court Presidents .............. 144 | |
| VII. | Enforcement .................................. 145 | |

# Judicial Independence in the Czech Republic

## Executive Summary

The Czech Republic has made considerable progress in reforming its court system and guaranteeing the independence of the judiciary. Basic guarantees of judicial independence are enshrined in the constitutional order, while the role of judges has been appropriately expanded and their material situation has been improved.

However, a number of important problems still need to be addressed by the ongoing reform process, including the continuing influence of the executive on judicial administration and judges' career path, and the budgetary autonomy of courts. Underlying these particular problems are a lack of political will to complete the process of reform and a pervasive public mistrust of the judiciary.

*Continuing Influence of the Ministry*

The Ministry of Justice continues to exercise decisive influence over the administration of the courts and over important aspects of judges' careers, which are intertwined with those of Ministry officials in numerous ways troubling for judges' independence. The Ministry represents the judiciary in its relationship with the rest of the State. Considered as a whole, this continuing executive influence may seriously undermine the formal separations provided in the constitutional structure.

*Insufficient Material Conditions*

The courts are insufficiently funded, a reflection of the dependent relationship with the executive. The budget process is not transparent, and judges have little substantive involvement in it. The actual working conditions of judges are rather poor. Compensation for judges has improved significantly, however.

*Problematic Attitudes towards the Judiciary*

Underlying these specific problems are entrenched attitudes towards the judiciary which limit the prospects for successful reform aimed at strengthening the judiciary's independence. The political will to empower the judicial branch vis-à-vis the other branches, mainly the executive, has been lacking, and promised judicial reforms have stalled. Popular confidence in the judiciary is very low. Restoring the credibility of the judiciary and building public trust in the rule of law will require changes in both public and political perceptions of the judicial system. Perhaps most importantly, the success of the judicial reform depends upon judges accepting the responsibility and accountability that independence requires.

*Reform Efforts*

Several attempts have been mounted to introduce some form of judicial self-governance, but none have become law. At present a new set of proposals for judicial reform has been prepared by the Ministry of Justice and presented to Parliament. Some judges and the Czech Union of Judges have already voiced objections to the new proposals.

In addition to these general issues, the following issues are of particular concern and are discussed in the body of the Report:

*Representation of the Judiciary*

To date, judicial independence applies only to judges and courts, not to the judiciary as a whole, which consequently has no constitutional representative of its own.

*Judges Working at the Ministry of Justice*

The division of professional life between the judiciary and the Ministry of Justice is unclear in a manner that threatens judges' independence. Despite the fact that judges are not allowed to hold positions in the executive or legislative branches, judges routinely work as consultants or high-ranking officials at the Ministry of Justice.

*Ministry Administration of Courts*

Because the Ministry of Justice is the central administrator of courts, the possibility exists for the government to influence judges' substantive work. These problems are reinforced by the non-transparent, multi-level system of administration which assigns some tasks to the Ministry and others to court presidents. In this system responsibility is obscured. There is currently a proposal to share administration with new judicial councils. However, while the creation of judicial councils with some administrative authority is perhaps a positive step, this further dispersion of responsibility may prove problematic, absent more fundamental clarification of the division between the executive and the judiciary.

*Judicial Career*

As public officers, judges work within a bureaucratic career system which gives court presidents and the Ministry of Justice substantial influence. In particular areas, undue discretion is accorded to the executive in deciding on judges' tenure on the bench, the appointment and transfer of judges, the appointment and removal of court presidents, and the discretionary release of judges over age 65 – in ways which give judges direct and compelling incentives to tailor their decision-making to the executive's interests.

The powerful court presidents are appointed and removed entirely at the discretion of the Ministry of Justice. The Minister promotes judges to other courts and the Ministry, sometimes without their consent. Judges only have tenure until age 65, after which they may be released at the discretion of the Ministry, which creates particular incentives for compliant behaviour given the significantly lower pensions judges receive.

*Disciplinary Proceedings*

Court presidents both appoint judges to disciplinary panels and initiate disciplinary proceedings. Such accumulation of functions in a single person seems inappropriate. Current proposals would address this problem by providing that disciplinary panels be nominated by judicial councils.

*Enforcement*

While the majority of criminal law decisions are implemented effectively, the level of disrespect for civil judgements is growing, owing mainly to a highly inflexible enforcement procedure. A new Law on Court Executors has been passed and should help to improve the enforcement of judgements.

# I. Introduction

The Czech Republic has made considerable progress in reforming its court system and guaranteeing the independence of the judiciary. Basic guarantees of judicial independence and the rule of law are enshrined in the constitutional and legal order, while the role of judges has been appropriately expanded and their material situation has been improved.

However, a number of important problems still need to be addressed, including the continuing influence of the executive on judicial administration and judges' career path, budgetary autonomy and the level of funding for courts. These issues are the subject of ongoing reform initiatives which to date have not been successful. Underlying these particular problems are a lack of political will to complete genuine reform of the judiciary and a pervasive public mistrust of the judiciary.

## A. Shortcomings in Reforms to Date

Efforts at reform in recent years have not been successfully implemented in several major areas. Current law regulating the judiciary does not create a legal framework for the status of judges that secures their independence.

### 1. *Continuing Influence of the Ministry of Justice*

The Ministry of Justice continues to exercise decisive influence over the administration of the courts and over important aspects of judges' careers, which are intertwined with those of Ministry officials in numerous ways that are troubling for judges' independence.

The Ministry of Justice represents the judiciary in its relationship with the rest of the State, and it directly administers the judiciary's operations; to the degree court presidents – named by the Ministry – are involved in administrative matters, they do so in effect as members of the executive. Judges routinely work at the Ministry. In the selection of judges, the Ministry plays an important role, though it tends to defer to court presidents it has selected. The Ministry also decides on transfers (including promotions) and plays a role in initiating disciplinary proceedings; a current proposal would even expand the Ministry's power temporarily to transfer judges.

All these forms of involvement afford the Ministry opportunities to reward compliant judges, or to punish uncooperative ones. Considered as a whole, they may seriously undermine the formal separations provided for in the constitutional structure.

## 2. Insufficient Material Conditions

The courts are insufficiently funded, a reflection of the dependent relationship with the executive. The budget process is not transparent, and judges have little substantive involvement in it. The actual working conditions of judges – including facilities, equipment, and training – are, as a consequence, rather poor. Compensation for judges has improved significantly, however.

## B. Attitudes towards the Judiciary

Underlying these specific problems are important entrenched attitudes towards the judiciary which limit the prospects for successful reform aimed at strengthening the judiciary's independence.

### 1. Political, Public, and Media Attitudes

Certain obstacles to judicial reform will not be solved through legislation alone. Restoring the credibility of the judiciary and building public trust in the rule of law will require changes in both popular and political perceptions of the judicial system.

Throughout much of the 1990s the political will to empower the judicial branch vis-à-vis the other branches, mainly the executive, has been lacking. While politicians often declare the need for a strong and independent judiciary, they have failed to support decisive legislative and executive steps. The Government elected in 1998 announced that it would implement sweeping judicial reform; however, to date, judicial reform, at least with regard to the change in balance of powers between the government branches, has not yet found the necessary political support in Parliament.[1]

Popular confidence in the judiciary is also very low. A recent opinion poll showed that only about a quarter of the population had confidence in the Czech judiciary; the findings suggest that many citizens doubt courts' independence and many more criticise

---

[1] The Government approved the so-called Principles of Judicial Reform by its decision No. 325/1999, 14 April 1999. The Minister of Justice was subsequently authorised to prepare and submit a proposed "Concept of Judicial Reform", in accordance with the approved Principles. The various legislative proposals which comprised the Concept were variously rejected in the Spring and Autumn of 2000.

its low effectiveness. Some people also criticised light sentences for crimes or made critical comparisons between the effectiveness of judges and their salaries.[2]

There is a widespread perception that corruption is endemic in the judiciary – most commonly in the form of bribes to expedite commercial registration cases – although there is no clear evidence about the extent of the practice, and the perception of corruption is often based on unsubstantiated reports in the media. Only one case of bribery of a judge has been established, involving a judge who accepted a bribe in a criminal case. (Before the whole matter could be properly investigated, the judge committed suicide.) Transparency International, an organisation monitoring corruption in different countries, has suggested that corruption in the judiciary is not a systemic problem, due to the relatively high judicial salaries and the unpredictability of the results of the bribes.[3]

At the same time, the atmosphere of mistrust in the Czech judiciary is also encouraged, at least in part, by the unrealistically high expectations of both politicians and the general public regarding what the judicial system can provide. Courts are commonly expected to find solutions to problems whose nature is economic. Furthermore, the judiciary is blamed for failed efforts to control the levels of criminality and for the weakness of law enforcement. Additionally, the judiciary has been repeatedly criticised for its close ties to the former regime, in spite of the significant efforts taken to restore its credibility, such as the screening process which removed many judges who had served under the communist system.[4]

According to many judges, the media foster an unacceptably high level of mistrust and suspicion of the judiciary in the Czech Republic as frequent but unsubstantiated reports of corruption might indicate. The negative relationship between the media and the judiciary stems in part from journalists' inexperience with complex legal issues, but also from a weak tradition of journalistic objectivity and purposeful efforts to generate public controversy.

---

[2] STEM Agency, 2-10 January 2001, <http://www.stem.cz/scripts/vismo/tiskove_informace/index.asp>, in Czech, under TISKOVE INFORMACE ZA LEDEN 2001 – Policie a armada si ziskavaji duveru, soudy vsak podle lidi pracuji stale spatne (accessed 11 August 2001). Confidence in the judiciary was significantly lower than for the army or police.

[3] See 2000 Corruption Perception Indexes (CPI), < http://www.transparency.org> (accessed 20 August 2001) which placed the Czech Republic 42nd out of 90 countries (with a CPI score of 4.3). The CPI score relates to perceptions of the degree of corruption as seen by business people, risk analysts and the general public and ranges between 10 (highly clean) and 0 (highly corrupt).

[4] See Section V.B.2.

For example, in 1997, in response to a slowing economy, Parliament adopted a law abolishing the so-called fourteenth salary received by judges and some other functionaries; laws with similar impact were passed to affect salaries in 1998, 1999, and 2000. Because these laws also decreased judicial salaries that are guaranteed by law,[5] their constitutionality was challenged in the Constitutional Court.[6] The media reacted to the episode with numerous attacks on judges' relatively high salaries[7] and their efforts to defend them. While the media of course has a proper role in scrutinising public officials, attacks of the kind mounted in this effort can be dangerous to judicial independence when they undermine public respect for courts, which in turn reduces political actors' incentives to support courts' independence.

## 2. Judges' Attitudes

Perhaps most importantly, the success of the judicial reform depends also on how the reform will be accepted and supported by judges themselves. Many measures will be successful only if judges themselves accept and adopt certain principles for their functioning and if they understand that their main role – and the reason for their independence – is to provide a special service to other citizens.

It is not enough for the judicial branch to secure work conditions which support their independence and impartiality, especially as the judicial branch is currently not viewed by the citizens as an efficient means to protect their rights or to enforce the law. In addition to structural and legislative reform aimed at clarifying the relationship between judges and the other branches, an attitudinal change among judges is necessary. For this reason, it seems clear that if judges and other judicial professionals are to accept and internalise reform, they must be involved as much as possible in the conceptualisation of the reform. Only in this way a broad-base consensus can be built and only in this way the judges can feel treated as equal vis-à-vis the other branches.

## 3. The Judiciary and the EU Accession Process

Criticism of the state of judicial independence also comes from different international institutions. In its 2000 Regular Report, the Commission recognised that although some progress has been achieved, certain key elements of reform remain to be adopted.

---

[5] Law No. 236/1995 Coll.

[6] See e.g. Decision of the Constitutional Court, 15 May 1999, published under No. 233/1999 Coll.; Decision of the Constitutional Court, 3 July 2000, published under No. 320/2000 Coll.

[7] Judges are among the best-paid state employees, with salaries are between two and four times higher than the average Czech salary. See Section IV.C.

The Regular Report stated that "certain key parts of the reform remain to be adopted[,]"[8] including the failure to adopt a constitutional amendment concerning judicial self-administration; the undue length of judicial proceedings; the unsystematic training of judges and state prosecutors; and a poorly functioning administration, including inadequate staffing and technical support.[9]

The Regular Report also noted that "judges are appointed for life…and are independent, although the Minister of Justice can formally recall them (in practice, this has not happened)."[10] However, the conclusion that judges are independent is not supported by any defined evaluative criteria other than life tenure; as this Report notes in a variety of contexts, judges' independence may be seriously curtailed in other ways.

Judges are generally not involved in the accession process or negotiations for accession. The Ministry of Justice represents the Czech judiciary in the accession process, including negotiations for accession, harmonisation of national and EU law, and training in EU law. The Minister of Justice is a member of Governmental Committee for European Integration and the Head of the Ministry's Department of European Integration is a member of the inter-ministerial Working Committee for Integration of the Czech Republic into the European Union. In addition, the Ministry prepares all the relevant strategic documents in the area of European integration, such as the National programme, and collects data for preparation of the Commission's Regular Reports.

The Czech Union of Judges and the Supreme Court do have some regular contacts with the Commission to discuss persistent problems facing the judiciary. The Czech Union of Judges also provides members for most Phare programmes' teams, and there is also a special Phare project designed to communicate with the professional organisations of judges and state prosecutors.[11] However, the judiciary has no direct involvement in the Government-Union relationship or negotiations over accession.

---

[8] European Commission, *2000 Regular Report on the Czech Republic's Progress towards Accession*, November 2000 (hereafter *2000 Regular Report*), Section 2.

[9] *2000 Regular Report*, Section 2. In its 2000 National Programme of Preparation for Membership of the European Union, the Government evaluated the situation of the judiciary more optimistically, stating that "[T]he current state of justice corresponds in most of the areas to the European standards and also its weaknesses are similar to those in other European countries including Member States. … Substantial part of the Civil Judiciary Reform has been achieved by the…amendment to the Civil Proceedings Code. The state of the criminal justice is satisfactory, further important changes will be brought by amendments implementing the *acquis*." The fact that the Czech judiciary is currently undergoing a substantial reform does not mean that it is not prepared for accession to the EU and for the tasks stemming out of the membership before the completion of the reform.

[10] *2000 Regular Report*, Section 2.

[11] Phare project CZ 9810-03-01, "Support to the Association of Judges and to the Association of State Attorneys."

## C. Reform Proposals

Several attempts have been mounted to introduce some form of judicial self-governance. A Concept of Judicial Reform[12] was approved by the Government in February 2000, and the development of democratically established judicial representation – a Supreme Judicial Council – was one of the main goals of judicial reform proposals prepared in connection with the Concept. These proposals were rejected in 2000, however; this outcome suggests that the issue of self-governance is politically sensitive.

The major controversial parts of the reform remain unresolved. Indeed, although some progress has been achieved through legislation that fundamentally changes procedural laws, other proposals aiming at re-definition of status of judges, reorganisation of courts and introduction of judicial self-governance have been rejected in Parliament. Indeed, Parliament does not appear fully committed to introducing institutions that would enable self-governance. However, it does not necessarily follow that there is not enough political will to fortify the independence of the judiciary at least to the extent it is suggested by the Commission, Council of Europe or to the level its exists in European Union member countries.[13]

At present a new set of proposals for judicial reform has been presented to the Chamber of Deputies of the Parliament.[14] These proposals also follow to certain extent the goals of the Concept of Judicial Reform; some judges and the Czech Union of Judges have already voiced objections to the new proposals, however.[15]

---

[12] Concept of Judicial Reform, <http://www.justice.cz/cgi-bin/sqw1250.cgi/zresortu/koncepce1.html.>, in Czech (accessed 20 August 2001).

[13] In a television interview, when asked about the significance of the failure of the Concept of Judicial Reform, Deputy Prime Minister Pavel Rychetsky said: "I think that some positive role will be played here by the regular evaluative report of the European Commission, because the absence of the reform and the fact that it was rejected is viewed very negatively in Brussels. I suppose that the feeling of responsibility for the integration process of the Czech Republic will eventually prevail in the Chamber of Deputies of the Czech Parliament." 21 (program title), CT2, 2 October 2000, <http://www.vlada.cz/1250/aktuality.htm> in Czech (accessed 20 August 2001).

[14] The following constitute the package of draft amendments: (1) the Government proposal for a law on courts, judges, lay judges and state administration of courts (Chamber of Deputies Document No. 878); (2) the Government proposal for a law on state prosecution (Chamber of Deputies Document No. 879) and (3) the Government proposal for a law on proceedings in [disciplinary] matters of judges and state prosecutors (Chamber of Deputies Document No. 877). On 8 June 2001, these draft laws were submitted for a second reading in the Chamber of Deputies.

[15] The Union presented objections to the Legislative Council of the Government on 9 March 2001.

Any future reform should comprehensively and concretely stipulate who can become a judge and under what conditions, what rights and obligations are connected with judicial office, what consequences flow from the breach of a judge's duties. Furthermore, objective criteria should be specified for the appointment and recall of judges from managerial functions (as court presidents and vice-presidents, or presidents of judicial panels) and more detailed regulation should be outlined for management of judicial candidates, especially with regard to their training.

## D. Organisation of the Judicial System

Czech judicial doctrines date back to the system established in the late 19th century, although they underwent considerable alteration during the communist period. Significant changes in the judicial system followed the establishment of the non-communist state, and then of the Czech Republic on 1 January 1993, and the adoption of the Constitution, after which the court system was restructured.

Perhaps the most significant change came with the redefinition of the courts' role in light of steps taken to establish and to guarantee the functioning of the state and its institutions, including the judiciary, as a rule-of-law state. Following the enactment of the Charter of Fundamental Rights and Freedoms (Constitutional Law No. 23/1991 Coll.), guarantees of the rule of law were affirmed by the Law on Courts and Judges (No. 335/1991 Coll.), as well as by the relevant procedural laws. In 1993, the Czech Republic assumed all the obligations of the former Czechoslovak federation under the European Convention for the Protection of Human Rights and Fundamental Freedoms.[16]

After 1948, the procuracy, a new institution for general supervision of the law, was established, which, although conceptually part of the judicial structure, was in effect a separate power within the State. The procuracy was replaced in 1994 by the state prosecution.[17] State prosecution is, according to the Constitution, a part of executive power;[18] the organisation of its offices mirrors that of the courts.[19]

---

[16] The Czech and Slovak Federal Republic originally ratified the Convention in 1991. The Czech Republic assumed all obligations of the Czech and Slovak Federal Republic under the European Convention for the Protection of Human Rights and Fundamental Freedoms by the Constitutional Law No. 4/1993 Coll., Art. 5, para. 2.

[17] Law No. 283/1993 Coll.

[18] CONST. CZECH REP., Art. 80.

[19] Communication from the Ministry of Justice, April 2001.

The ordinary courts are organised into four levels: district, regional, two High Courts at Prague and Olomouc, and the Supreme Court. Military courts were abolished in 1994 and their jurisdiction over criminal matters was shifted to the regular civil courts. A separate Constitutional Court operates outside of the regular courts. In 2000, the regional commercial courts were abolished,[20] and their jurisdiction assumed partly by the district courts and partly by the regional courts.

As of 1 January 2001, there were a total of 2,577 judges, including 1,545 in the district courts and 841 in the regional courts, as well as 105 judges at the High Court in Prague, 34 judges at the High Court in Olomouc and 52 judges at the Supreme Court. Many judges who served during the communist period left office in the early 1990s,[21] and many new judges have entered the profession, so that the average age of a judge is relatively young. In spite of the steady increase in number of judges over the last decade, there are still more than 300 judicial vacancies.

In addition to the Constitution, the most important laws regulating the judiciary and state prosecution are: the Law on Courts and Judges (No. 335/1991 Coll.); Some Measures Regarding the Judiciary, Election of Lay Judges, and the Means of their Recall and the State Administration of Courts (No. 436/1991 Coll.[22]); and the Law on Judicial Discipline (No. 412/1991 Coll.). Court decision-making is regulated primarily by the Code of Civil Procedure (No. 99/1963 Coll.) and by the Code of Criminal Procedure (No. 141/1961 Coll.).

As noted above, the current Minister of Justice has prepared a number of proposals for legislative reform of the judicial system, which are considered at various points throughout this Report.

---

[20] Law No. 215/2000 Coll., amending Law No. 436/1991 Coll.
[21] See Section V.B.2.
[22] Hereafter "Law on State Administration of Courts".

## II. Constitutional and Legal Foundations of Judicial Independence

Judicial independence is recognised in the Constitution and the laws, though with significant limitations. It applies to judges and courts, not to the judiciary as a whole, which consequently has no constitutional representative of its own. Perhaps as a consequence, the division of professional life between the judiciary and its representative, the Ministry of Justice, is unclear in a manner that threatens judges' independence.

### A. Separation of Powers and Guarantees of Judicial Independence

The principle of separation and equality of powers is implicitly recognised by the systematic division of the Constitution[23] into separate chapters for legislative, executive, and judicial power. Various constitutional provisions[24] and the Charter of Fundamental Rights and Freedoms[25] establish the discrete role of the judicial power in this system of checks and balances and ensure judges and courts' independence and impartiality.[26] The judiciary as such is not explicitly recognised as a separate branch, however.

A qualified majority is required for the change of the constitution or constitutional laws. Much of the structure of courts, their administration, status and remuneration of judges and other matters are defined by statute, and thus can be amended by simple majority; they cannot be regulated by lower-level legislation, however, such as regulations of the Ministry of Justice.

---

[23] CONST. CZECH REP. (Constitutional Law No. 1/1993 Coll.).

[24] "Fundamental rights and freedoms are under the protection of judicial power." CONST. CZECH REP., Art. 4; "Judicial power is executed, in the name of the republic, by the independent courts." CONST. CZECH REP., Art. 81; "The main role of courts is to protect rights in a manner set by law. Only a court can decide about the guilt and punishment for crimes." CONST. CZECH REP., Art. 90.

[25] Constitutional Law No. 2/1993 Coll. Pursuant to the Constitution, the Charter is part of constitutional order. CONST. CZECH REP., Art. 3 and Art. 112, para. 1.

[26] "When executing their function, judges are independent. No one is allowed to threaten their impartiality." CONST. CZECH REP., Art. 82, para. 1.

## B. Representation of the Judiciary

Judicial independence is conceived of as referring to individual judges, rather than to the judiciary as a separate branch. As a result, the judiciary does not have its own representative body on national level. Instead, the judiciary is represented in its relations with other branches by the Ministry of Justice. (The President of the Supreme Court is, according to protocol, higher than the post of the Minister – although this does not mean the President has any representative function.)

There have been several proposals to reform this situation and to suggest some form of self-representation, including the Concept of Judicial Reform, proposed by the former Minister of Justice.[27] So far, however, no solution has been found which would be acceptable to judges and have the political support of Parliament. Some judges have argued that strengthening the independence of individual judges might eventually lead to the final, desired effect of strengthening the institutional independence of the judiciary as a whole.

## C. Rules on Incompatibility

Judges are public officers.[28] Judges are required "to refrain from anything that might discredit the dignity of the judicial office or threaten the trust of independent, impartial and fair judicial decision-making."[29] This is a general condition which judges must also observe with regard to their participation in civic activities, political debates and competitions, as well as other remunerative activities outside their judicial duties.

No specific ban on political activity is imposed on judges.[30] They are allowed to join political parties and the only limitation of their political activity comes from the aforesaid general condition that they must behave so as not to discredit the dignity of the judicial office. The only exception to this rule exists for the judges of the Constitutional Court, who are banned from joining political parties or movements.[31]

---

[27] Concept of Judicial Reform, <http://www.justice.cz/cgi-bin/sqw1250.cgi/zresortu/koncepce1.html.>, in Czech, (accessed 20 August 2001).

[28] Law on Courts and Judges (No. 335/1991 Coll.), Section 52, para. 1.

[29] Law on Courts and Judges (No. 335/1991 Coll.), Section 54.

[30] Judges do not have the right to strike. Law on Courts and Judges (No. 335/1991 Coll.), Section 54, para. 2; Charter of Fundamental Rights and Freedoms (Constitutional Law No. 23/1991 Coll.), Art. 27, para. 4.

[31] Law on Constitutional Court (No. 182/1993 Coll.) Section 4, para. 4.

Judges cannot hold high political office – such as State President or Member of Parliament – of any other positions in public administration.[32] Despite the fact that judges are not allowed to hold positions in the executive or legislative branches, judges can be temporarily appointed[33] as consultants to the Ministry of Justice, with their consent.[34] As consultants, they can be assigned any task regularly executed by the Ministry; at present, several active judges are temporarily appointed to the Ministry, and two serve as Deputy Ministers of Justice.[35] The judges appointed as consultants to the Ministry do not lose their status as active judges: although they do not exercise their judicial functions, they are still considered members of the judiciary and receive their judicial salary, although they are in effect working for the executive.[36]

Moreover, the possibility for a judge to work for, or rather to co-operate with, the Ministry of Justice is not limited to the appointment as a consultant. Some judges co-operate with the Ministry in a much looser co-operation scenario[37] which tends to blur the distinctions between the various branches. In one instance, Members of Parliament who received a lecture on a new law given by such a judge co-operating with the Ministry of Justice were under the impression that the judge was an employee of the Ministry and thus a part of the executive.[38] The distinction between the various powers is blurring.

In addition, the draft Law on Courts and Judges[39] would allow judges to be appointed to the Judicial Academy, where they would lecture, conduct examinations and execute other pedagogical functions while maintaining their active status.

---

[32] CONST. CZECH REP, Art. 82, para. 3; Law on Courts and Judges (No. 335/1991 Coll.), Section 52, para. 3.

[33] However, law does not limit the maximum time of their appointment to the Ministry of Justice. See Law on Courts and Judges (No. 335/1991 Coll.), Section 41, para. 3. In practice they are usually appointed to the positions of consultants for unlimited period of time.

[34] Law on Courts and Judges (No. 335/1991 Coll.), Section 41, para. 2(a).

[35] Currently both the president of the judicial panel of the Supreme Court and the president of the judicial panel of the High Court in Prague are working for the Ministry of Justice. One Ministry official was recently appointed a judge but did not leave the Ministry as she was immediately appointed to work for the Ministry.

[36] There is no legal obligation for a judge or the Ministry to consult the president of the relevant court. However, at least with respect to the presidents of the judicial panels, the president of the relevant court is usually consulted.

[37] For example, judges may co-operate with the Ministry in drafting new laws. The judge's participation may include attending the debate before the parliamentary committee. At the same time, because judges are usually not excused from executing their judicial functions, court presidents may determine whether or not judges may engage in such activities.

[38] Statement of participant, OSI meeting, Prague, 23 March 2001. *Explanatory Note: OSI held a roundtable meeting in Prague on 23 March to invite critique of the present report in draft form. Experts present included representatives of the government, the judiciary, and civil society organisations. References to this meeting should not be understood as endorsement of any particular point of view by any one participant,*

[39] Chamber of Deputies Document No. 878.

Entrepreneurial or other income-generating activities of judges are restricted to management of their own property, and "scientific, pedagogical, literary, journalistic and artistic activities."[40] Pedagogical activities are defined as "lecturing or other training activities conducted for the Ministry of Justice, courts and state prosecution offices or on their behalf, and similar activities at conducted at University faculties, secondary or elementary schools."[41] The economic effects of these activities must be reflected, by each individual judge, in his yearly income tax statement, as is required of every citizen of the Czech Republic; the returns are not public disclosure documents.

### D. Judges' Associations

Freedom of association is guaranteed for all citizens,[42] and judges are free to form and join associations of judges or similar organisations. The majority of judges are members of the Czech Union of Judges, a professional judicial association established over ten years ago. According to its bylaws, the Czech Union of Judges aims to: (1) help to improve the overall functioning of the judiciary; (2) represent their interests; (3) promote their professional training; and (4) protect their judicial independence. Judges are also allowed to join trade unions, and some judges are members of the Trade Union of State Employees.

---

[40] Law on Courts and Judges (No. 335/1991 Coll.), Section 52, paras. 4–5.
[41] Law on Courts and Judges (No. 335/1991 Coll.), Section 52, para. 4.
[42] Charter of Fundamental Rights and Freedoms, Art. 20; Law on Association (No. 83/1990 Coll.).

## III. Administration of the Justice System and Judicial Independence

The Ministry of Justice has a direct mandate centrally to administer the courts and state prosecution on the national level."[43] The political responsibility for state administration of courts therefore lies with the Minister; judges have little role in their own administration.

The Ministry of Justice has a number of separate departments responsible for various aspects of court administration, which includes responsibility for human resources, organisation, financial support and training, as well as supervision of court operations.[44] In addition, the Ministry regulates the establishment of new courts.[45]

The Organisation and Supervision Department directly oversees the operation of the court system. The Department has several sub-divisions: divisions of both civil and criminal law, organisation of courts and state prosecutions, and statistics. Its most noteworthy function is to collect and analyse the statistical data on the performance of individual courts, and to monitor the backlog. This Department also issues normative data showing the average number of cases decided by individual courts. The Ministry and the presidents of the respective courts tend to require judges to handle a caseload corresponding to at least the norm; in this way the Ministry controls the efficiency and productivity of the courts.

The Organisation and Supervision Department, together with the Human Resources Department, also supervises judges' behaviour and delays in proceedings; determines the number of judges in the courts and the need for new positions; organises the systems for court records, archives, and statistics; recruits court personnel. The Human Resources Department is separately responsible for judicial training through the Institute for Further Education of Judges and State Prosecutors and the School of Justice in Kromeriz.

The Department of the Director General (for Financial Matters), the Economic Department and Assets Administration Department are responsible for allocating budgetary resources to individual courts and controlling how they are spent by each court. They also execute control over court buildings and assets.

---

[43] Law on the Creation of Ministries (No. 2/1969 Coll.), Section 11, para. 1

[44] Law on State Administration of Courts (No. 436/1991 Coll.), Section 16.

[45] See Law on Courts and Judges (No. 335/1991 Coll.), Section 33, para. 5; Regulation of the Ministry of Justice No. 576/1991 Coll.

Besides the Ministry of Justice, various ranking judges – including the President and the Vice-President of the Supreme Court, presidents and vice-presidents of high courts, and presidents and vice-presidents of regional and district courts – act as institutions for state administration of the courts.[46]

Court presidents and vice-presidents supervise and administer the day-to-day operations of their courts. In this capacity they are guided by the directives and concrete instructions issued by the Ministry of Justice and superior courts' presidents. The directives of the Ministry are not binding for the Supreme Court.

Because the Ministry of Justice is the central administrator of courts, the possibility exists for the government to influence the substantive work of the courts (in addition to the indirect influence it might exercise through legislative initiative and control of the budget). At the same time, over the past decade a number of customary practices have developed by which the Minister of Justice defers to the wishes of higher court presidents concerning assignments, transfers and promotions of judges to be respected by the Minister of Justice, although such deference is not required by law.

At the level of day-to-day court administration, the dual status of court presidents as managers and judges, as well as the system of binding ministerial directives and instructions, poses some problems with regard to judicial independence. These problems are reinforced by the non-transparent, multi-level system of administration which assigns some responsibilities to the Ministry of Justice and others to court presidents.[47] In this system responsibility is obscured, information flow is disrupted and diverted; human, and financial and other resources are wasted. Some judges have suggested replacing this system with one identifying a clear connection between each court and the Ministry.

*Reform Proposals*: After previous reform proposals were rejected by Parliament in 2000, new reform proposals were submitted. The new proposals do not change the basic relations between the judiciary and the Ministry of Justice. The administration of the judiciary and career path of judges still basically remain in the hands of the Minister of Justice. The proposals would introduce judicial councils in each court; however, the councils would be only advisory.

The presidents and vice-presidents of courts, when executing their managerial powers, would be agents of the executive. This merger of functions seems to violate the principle of separation of powers as well as to threaten judicial independence.

---

[46] Law on State Administration of Courts (No. 436/1991 Coll.).

[47] The current law allows the Ministry of Justice to administer district courts either directly or through the regional courts. It is up to the Ministry to decide which approach to choose. In practice both approaches have been employed for different district courts.

# IV. Financial Autonomy and Level of Funding

Judges and courts have relatively little involvement in their own budget process, which is controlled by the Ministry. Perhaps as a consequence, material support for the judiciary has not been adequate, a shortcoming which can both indirectly place economic pressures on judges to the detriment of their decisional independence and impartiality, and erodes public support for the judiciary as its processes inevitably become less efficient. Evaluation procedures are not sufficiently transparent or objective.

## A. The Budget Process

Consistent with its institutional subordination to the Ministry of Justice, the judiciary does not prepare its own budget, and its input is limited to submitting initial figures to the Ministry, which in turn is responsible for drafting, submitting, and defending the budget. Moreover, even the practice of requesting initial figures from individual courts is reportedly being reconsidered.[48]

The overall State budget includes a separate line item or chapter for the Ministry of Justice, further divided into sub-line items for courts (including the Supreme Court) and state prosecution, the Prison Service, and the Ministry itself. The Ministry determines the allocation of funding for regional courts and state prosecution offices, which then distribute those funds within their regions. The allocation for the Supreme Court and the Supreme State Prosecution Offices, the high courts and the corresponding state prosecution offices is also performed by the Ministry of Justice.

The budget proposal is prepared by the Economic Department of the Director General for Financial Matters within the Ministry of Justice.[49] The draft proposal is then submitted by the Minister of Justice to the Ministry of Finance for discussions. The Ministry of Finance finalises an overall draft budget for approval in a plenary Government session. Subsequently, it is submitted to the Chamber of Deputies of the Parliament for final approval.

The judiciary's budget therefore depends both on the available resources and on the ability and willingness of the Minister of Justice to garner political support for allocating budgetary resources to Ministry.

---

[48] Statement of participant, OSI roundtable discussion, Prague, 23 March 2001.

[49] Law No. 218/2000 Coll.

The division of budgetary resources between individual courts is not transparent, and can act as an indirect threat to the judiciary's independence.[50] In some cases the personal relationships between the court president, vice-president or other managerial figure negotiating the budget resources allocation and the relevant employees of the Ministry of Justice plays an important role. Although the courts' productivity has never been made an explicit condition of budget approval, it is undoubtedly one of the criteria used to evaluate judicial performance. The Ministry's strong emphasis on productivity, combined with its dominant role in determining the budget and the lack of procedural safeguards, creates space for undue influence on the judiciary. Within any fiscal year, it is possible to transfer funds from one budget line of the overall budget to another sector, subject to the approval of the Ministry of Justice and in some cases also the Ministry of Finance.[51]

After 1989, some long-neglected investment needs were taken into account and substantial, though still insufficient, resources were allocated to the judiciary.[52] These budget allocations reflected, among other considerations, the costs of reconstructing court facilities and equipping courtrooms and judges' offices with computers, and the increased number of judges, clerks and personnel and their increased salaries.

In 2000, the budget for the Ministry of Justice was increased by 13 percent to over 13 billion CZK (c. € 379,481,743), or 2.05 percent of the overall budget. Of that, funds allocated to courts and state prosecution amounted to 7.5 billion CZK (c. € 218,925,368), representing some 1.19 percent of the overall budget. The budget for 2001 is similar to that for the year 2000, although it is still the subject of a dispute between the Ministries of Justice and Finance.

## B. Work Conditions

The working conditions of judges in the majority of courts remain unsatisfactory. At present, the majority of the courts are overburdened.[53] The worst situation is in the commercial sections of regional courts, where backlogs exist. Indeed, the length of

---

[50] Statement of participant, OSI roundtable discussion, Prague, 23 March 2001.

[51] Information from the Ministry of Justice, June 2001.

[52] The budgetary line item for Ministry of Justice is one of the few line items that have not been cut for several years.

[53] See Statistics of State Prosecution and Courts, <http://www.justice.cz/cgi-bin/sqw1250.cgi/zresortu/stati/st_vyber.sqw>, in Czech (accessed 20 August 2001). See also Time Sheets of Selected Nominators, <http://www.justice.cz/cgi-bin/sqw1250.cgi/zresortu/stati/st_vyber.sqw?s=R.>, in Czech (accessed 20 August 2001).

judicial proceedings and the generally low efficiency of the courts have generated the most criticism,[54] and raise concerns about the capacity of the judiciary as a whole to operate in an environment supportive of its independence.

Most court buildings are overcrowded and do not have enough capacity for the expanding role and additional tasks courts now perform. As of the beginning of 2000, the shortage of office space was about 45,000 square meters, and 255 additional courtrooms were needed but unavailable.[55] Although more current figures are not available, the trend of insufficient investment appears to be continuing.[56]

The level of computerisation and the availability of other technical equipment are quite low. Although it has been recognised that computerisation may bring higher efficiency and productivity, not all courts have been adequately computerised. However, there are positive efforts suggest that the political will exists to bring technology and more effective work procedures into the courts. In the year 2000, close to 900 computers and other IT equipment funded by an EU Phare project were allocated to different courts,[57] and the situation is also improving with regard to providing modem/internet access. Yet in some courts there are no modern stenographic machines and only a limited number of older machines. Courts have at their disposal a CD-ROM version of the national legal database, but on-line access to legislative databases is still very rare.

---

[54] See e.g., "Bez rychlejsich soudcu je pravo pouhou fikci" ("Without faster judges the law is just a fiction"), *Lidove Noviny*, 21 March 2001, p. 1 (discussing criticisms by the then acting Minister of Justice concerning extremely long delays in important criminal investigations).

[55] See "Resolution of the Czech Government of 7 July 1999, No. 688 With Regard To Evaluation of Technical Support For Functioning of Judiciary and Prison Service, which is a part of Proposal of Mid-term Investment Program Into the Resort of the Ministry of Justice", <http://www.justice.cz/cgi-bin/sqw1250.cgi/zresortu/navrhy/tezaju14.html>, in Czech (accessed 20 August 2001); Submission Report, <http://portal.justice.cz/justice/index.nsf/index?OpenPage>, in Czech (accessed 20 August 2001); "Summary Representing Capacity and Needs of Immovables In Judiciary – Courts", <http://www.justice.cz/cgi-bin/sqw1250.cgi/zresortu/navrhy/tezaju05.html>, in Czech (accessed 20 August 2001); "Mid-term Investment Program into the Judicial Sector of the Resort of the Ministry of Justice", <http://www.justice.cz/cgi-bin/sqw1250.cgi/zresortu/navrhy/tezaju06.html>, in Czech (accessed 20 August 2001); "Summary of Computerisation Projects in the Judicial Sector of the Resort of the Ministry of Justice", <http://portal.justice.cz/justice/index.nsf/index?OpenPage>, in Czech (accessed 20 August 2001).

[56] See *Hospodarske Noviny*, 24 May 2001, <http://portal.justice.cz/justice/index.nsf/index?OpenPage>, in Czech (accessed 20 August 2001), citing an official of the Economic Department of the Ministry of Justice concerning the insufficiency of current funding and the threat this poses to various projects.

[57] In the framework of Phare project CZ 9904-04-01, "Strengthening the Operation of Law Enforcement Institutions and Judiciary", 771 personal computers, 74 servers and 74 printers were delivered to district courts, allowing instalment of application software equipment and access to sector WAN, databases and Internet. The current Phare proposal envisons a larger allocation for expanding and updating court computer facilities.

To compensate for this deficit, a purpose-based fund in the amount of approximately € 54 per month has been allocated to judges for use in purchasing journals and books.

Court staff levels are not sufficient. The low number of court employees is caused primarily by the insufficient financial means available to individual courts for the purpose.[58] The Ministry of Justice is in the process of preparing a new law on judicial clerks, court secretaries and judicial execution officials, which may bring some desirable changes in this respect.

Funding from the state budget for the training of judges and state prosecutors is insufficient. A special need for judicial training has arisen in connection with the EU accession process and the requirement for harmonisation of national laws of the applicant countries with the *acquis communautaire*. Some funding has been allocated for judicial training over the past three years under such programs as Phare and TAIEX and under the auspices of MATRA (Dutch Ministry of Foreign Affairs); other funds have come from the educational assistance program of the Council of Europe, and bilateral assistance. Training for court employees needs to be addressed as well. Currently, judicial clerks are prepared for their jobs by the School for Judiciary in Kromeriz;[59] however, the capacity of this institution is insufficient compared to the needs of the Czech judiciary.

The new reform proposals envision the establishment of a permanent Judicial Academy. This proposition has been received critically by judges, as the Academy's administrative and academic affairs would be controlled by the Ministry of Justice.

## C. Compensation

Since 1995, salaries in the judicial sector have been steadily increasing and current salaries are sufficient to provide for a decent living standard; pension benefits are significantly lower than salaries, however, which raises issues of independence when combined with the executive's discretionary power to release judges over age 65.

---

[58] See e.g. Radioforum, CRo 1-Radiozurnal, 17 April 2001, <http://portal.justice.cz/justice/ms.nsf/Dokumenty/BB8F95E49CAF5BE5C1256A32001E5309>, in Czech (accessed 20 August 2001), information from, *inter alia*, Libor Vavra, President of the Czech Union of Judges, noting that the judiciary's human resources needs have been "heavily underfunded[,]" and further that the judiciary lacks "an adequate number of judicial employees inside or associated with the judicial offices, where these people would be capable to do lots of work instead of a judge, who could then be justifiably expected to judge more often and more intensively than today."

[59] See School for Judiciary in Kromeriz, <http://www.justice.cz/cgi-bin/sqw1250.cgi/zresortu/skola.html.>, in Czech (accessed 20 August 2001).

The remuneration of judges is comparable to that of Members of Parliament, and certainly judges are among the best paid public employees; salaries of state prosecutors are ten percent lower than those of judges. In certain cases private attorneys' income may exceed the level of judges' salaries, but with the increasing competition the existing gap may be narrowing.[60]

Judges' welfare and economic independence are guaranteed by law.[61] The level of judges' salaries can be changed only by law, not by executive regulation.[62] Salaries for judges vary between 35,000 CZK and 78,000 CZK gross (between € 1,022 and € 2,277),[63] depending on the number of years served and on the judge's position within the court system.[64] Higher remuneration is given to presidents and vice-presidents of the courts and the presidents of judicial panels of higher courts. Their remuneration is 10–15 percent higher than the salaries of regular judges.

The social benefits judges receive are somewhat more generous[65] than those of regular civil servants. This is mainly due to the fact that the law regulating the status, functioning and remuneration of civil servants has not yet been adopted.

The Czech Republic has not introduced any special retirement benefits for judges other than the standard governmental pension. The pension is significantly lower than the remuneration judges receive on the bench, which represents a potentially serious problem when combined with the executive's discretion in retaining judges on the bench after the retirement age of 65.[66]

---

[60] Statement of Participant, OSI Prague meeting, 23 March 2001.

[61] Law on Courts and Judges (No. 335/1991 Coll.); Law on Remuneration of the State President, Members of Government, Members of Parliament, Judges of the Constitutional Court and Judges (No. 236/1995 Coll.); Law on Remuneration and Other Matters Connected to the Execution of the Function of Government Functionaries, Certain State Institutions and Judges (No. 236/1995 Coll.).

[62] Law on Remuneration of the State President, Members of Government, Members of Parliament, Judges of the Constitutional Court and Judges (No. 236/1995 Coll.).

[63] According to the Czech Statistical Office's Compensation Survey in the Czech Republic 2000, the average monthly salary was CZK 12,684 (c. € 373) in July 2000. Judges' salaries are thus between two and four times higher than the average Czech salary. Corporate Policy on Remuneration and Employee Benefits in the Czech Republic (Joint Survey of PricewaterhouseCoopers and KNO Cesko), <http://www.pwcglobal.com/cz/eng/about/press-rm/>, accessed 20 August 2001.

[64] Law on Remuneration and Other Matters Connected to the Execution of the Function of Government Functionaries, Certain State Institutions and Judges (No. 236/1995 Coll.).

[65] For example, in case of illness, judges do not receive illness benefits only, as do other state employees; instead, they receive their full salary. Full salary can be paid to a judge who is ill or unfit for employment for a period not exceeding six months within one year.

[66] See Section V.B.

# V. Judicial Office

As public officers, judges work within a bureaucratic career system in which court presidents and the Ministry of Justice have substantial influence. In particular areas, undue discretion is accorded to the executive in deciding on judges' tenure on the bench – the appointment and transfer of judges, the appointment and removal of court presidents, and after judges reach age 65 – in ways which give judges direct and compelling incentives to tailor their decision-making to the executive's interests.

## A. The Selection Process[67]

Selection of candidates for district court judgeships is in practice a fairly bureaucratised process in which procedural requirements and the input of court presidents plays a substantial role, although formally the power of appointment rests with the State President. Introducing more specific and objective criteria could elevate the transparency of the appointment, resulting in greater credibility attaching to individual judges as well as the judiciary as a whole.

In addition to minimum requirements including a law degree, a candidate for judicial office must complete a judicial examination and must be "a person whose experience and moral qualities constitute a guarantee that he will exercise the judicial office properly."[68]

The selection process for judicial candidates is a four-round process.[69] The first two rounds consist of a review and evaluation of the received application, and a diagnostic psychological examination. The results of this examination and the evaluation of the personal characteristics of the applicant are then further evaluated by a five-member commission consisting of the representatives from the Ministry of Justice, courts and state prosecution and a psychologist. The commission decides which applicants enter the third selection round.

The third round consists of evaluating capabilities of the applicant by another commission composed of representatives from the Ministry, courts, state prosecutions, the Czech Union of Judges and the Association of State Prosecutors. The joint results of these three rounds

---

[67] Appointment of court presidents is discussed in Section V.C.

[68] Law on Courts and Judges (No. 335/1991 Coll.), Section 34.

[69] See Basic information about the selection process of judicial and legal candidates in the year 2000 and about the conditions of establishment of the employment and its contents, <http://www.justice.cz/cgi-bin/sqw1250.cgi/zresortu/po3.html>, in Czech (accessed 20 August 2001).

are complied in a point-based evaluation, which lists applicants from the most to the least capable.[70] In the fourth round, candidates are offered positions based on existing or planned vacancies in the relevant calendar year, with the candidates having the highest point totals receiving the first selection. Following his selection, the candidate is employed, by the Ministry of Justice, for a fixed period of time to complete an apprenticeship at the chosen district court.[71]

Upon completion of his apprenticeship, a candidate takes the judicial examination at the Institute for Further Education of Judges and State Prosecutors. Passing this exam is a condition for his judicial nomination. Another important factor is the candidate's performance during his apprenticeship, which is evaluated by the president of the district court where the candidate practised.[72]

Following the apprenticeship, examination, and evaluation by the court president, judges are appointed by the State President.[73] Although not required by law, the practice has developed throughout the years that the Minister of Justice nominates each judicial candidate, based on the recommendation of the president of the court to which the candidate shall be later assigned as well as the president of the regional court within whose jurisdiction the district court where the candidate practised sits. However, the decision about who to nominate belongs to the Minister, who can refuse to nominate a particular judicial candidate without cause, although, due to the existing customary practice, the requirements of the court presidents for assignment of a particular candidate to a particular court have been respected. The Minister's nomination is then submitted to the Government and then further submitted to the State President. The State President has the discretion to reject a nominated candidate without reason. Upon appointment, a judge takes a judicial oath. Subject to the consent of the judge, the Minister of Justice assigns the judge to a particular court, typically a district court.

The legislative branch stands outside the nomination and appointment process, with the exception that Members of Parliament may demand an explanation from the Minister

---

[70] See Ministry of Justice website, at <http://www.justice.cz/cgi-bin/sqw1250.cgi/zresortu/po3.html>, in Czech (accessed 20 August 2001).

[71] Law on Courts and Judges (No. 335/1991 Coll.), Section 61. The apprenticeship is regulated by internal rules of the Ministry of Justice – Instructions of Ministry of Justice issued on 11 December 1997, No. 314/97-pers., as amended by Instructions of Ministry of Justice issued on 22 December 1998, No. 973/98-pers.

[72] See Ministry of Justice website, <http://www.justice.cz/cgi-bin/sqw1250.cgi/zresortu/po3.html>, in Czech (accessed 20 August 2001).

[73] CONST. CZECH REP., Art. 93; Law on Courts and Judges (No. 335/1991 Coll.), Section 38, para. 1.

of Justice regarding his decision in this process. This right has rarely been invoked.[74] Local government authorities have no influence on the appointment or promotion of judges, except for lay judges.[75]

## B. Tenure, Retirement, Transfer and Removal

### 1. Tenure and Retirement

After judges are appointed by the State President, they are granted tenure until the age of 65. This does not represent a mandatory retirement age but only an opportunity for the Ministry of Justice to release the judge against his will.[76] There are no clear criteria governing the decision to release or retain a judge after that age, which means judges may feel pressured to adapt their decisions to please the executive, which can release them at any time at its discretion. In addition, given that judges' pensions are considerably lower than their salaries, there are financial incentives to adopt a compliant attitude towards the executive in order to stay on the bench.

### 2. Transfer

Judges cannot be transferred to another court without their consent, except for disciplinary purposes specified by law,[77] including temporary transfers for disciplinary reasons.[78] In 1995, the Parliament introduced an exception to this principle of non-transferability where the judiciary is not properly functioning and there has been a reorganisation provided for in law.[79] Transfers are determined by the Ministry of Justice and must

---

[74] In 1992, for example, due to the screening and reappointment process (See Section V.B.3.), certain judges were undergoing a re-appointment process; the then Minister of Justice refused to reappoint certain judges who were members of the Committee for Protection of the Unjustly Pursued. Subsequently certain Members of Parliament asked the Minister to explain and defend his decision.

[75] The councils of local municipalities elect the lay judges for both district and regional courts. Law No. 436/1991 Coll., Section 9. Lay judges are elected to four-year terms and participate in judicial decision-making and participate equally with regular judges in certain instances – See Law on Courts and Judges (No. 335/1991 Coll.), Sections 4, para. 2, and 12, para. 3.

[76] Law on Courts and Judges (No. 335/1991 Coll.), Section 46, para. 1(b).

[77] CONST. CZECH REP., Art. 82, para. 2.

[78] Law on Judicial Discipline (No. 412/1991 Coll.); Law on Courts and Judges (No. 335/1991 Coll.), Section 40, para. 8.

[79] Law No. 239/1995 Coll., amending the Law on Courts and Judges (No. 335/1991 Coll.).

be carried out within six months of the reorganisation. A judge who has been transferred without his consent may challenge the decision of the Minister of Justice in the Supreme Court.[80]

Some judges fear that the Ministry of Justice will use this power of transfer, originally developed to help the judiciary to adapt to the recent reorganisation of courts, to reassign judges to the regions less favoured by them and less often selected by judicial candidates.[81] The judges also charge that the law does not set out any specific conditions under which a judge can be transferred; the only condition appears to be a required consultation with the president of the court to which the judge was originally assigned. Neither do judges feel protected by the possibility of appeal to the Supreme Court, as the Supreme Court can review only the legality of the transfer,[82] not the merits of it. Since no specific conditions were set out for the transfer, the legality will hardly ever be in question.[83]

The Ministry of Justice, on the other hand, views the possibility to transfer a judge without his consent as an exceptional measure justified by the current need to implement some court reorganisation and institutional changes, such as bringing more judges into a particular specialisation. When the situation in the Czech judiciary is stabilised and no further need for this measure exists, the measure would be abolished;[84] the current Minister of Justice has proposed the abolition of this measure by the end of 2009.

However, the proposals for judicial reform prepared by the Minister of Justice would extend the exception to the principle of non-transferability even further by introducing non-consensual temporary transfer. A new institution, temporary assignment,[85] is introduced by those proposals. If used as proposed, such an extension seems to be in direct contradiction with the documents of the Council of Europe regarding judicial independence.

---

[80] Law on Courts and Judges (No. 335/1991 Coll.), Section 40, para. 7.

[81] Statements of participants at OSI meeting, Prague, 23 March 2001.

[82] The review is governed by the Code on Civil Procedure (No. 99/1963 Coll.), Section 250(1) and following.

[83] Statements of Participants at OSI meeting, Prague, 23 March 2001.

[84] Statement of Participant at OSI meeting, Prague, 23 March 2001.

[85] Section 68 of the Government proposal for a law on courts, judges, lay judges and state administration of courts would provide the following: "A judge assigned to a particular district or regional court...or transferred to the particular district or regional court...can be temporarily assigned, even without his consent but for the maximum period of one year, to another court of the same level, whose jurisdictional boundaries are neighbouring the jurisdictional boundaries to which the judge was assigned..., if it is not possible to guarantee the proper functioning of judiciary at this court."

## 3. Removal

Judges may be released or removed from office in accordance with a prescribed range of conditions.

Judges are released from office if they cease to meet the basic criteria for judgeships. Thus, a particular judge's office ceases upon the effective date of the judgement convicting him of an intentional criminal offence or upon the effective date of the decision on the loss or restriction of his legal capacity.[86] Furthermore, the loss of citizenship results in the termination of judicial office.[87] Another cause for release is the finding of a disciplinary panel establishing that health conditions prevent the judge from properly exercising his functions on a permanent basis.[88] Release is decided upon by the Minister of Justice.[89]

On his request a judge may resign from a managerial function as a court president or vice-president, or president of a judicial panel. Decisions about resignation belong to the institution that appointed the judge to the managerial function.[90] Only a person or an institution that appointed the judge to a managerial function may release a judge from that function. In practice this means that presidents and vice-presidents of high, regional and district courts can be released at the sole discretion of the Minister of Justice.

The grounds for the removal of a judge from his judicial office is a final decision of a disciplinary panel imposing removal as a sanction in disciplinary proceedings against the judge, if the judge seriously breached his fundamental responsibilities.[91] The removal is initiated by the Minister of Justice.[92] A president of the court can be recalled from his managerial function only based on a valid decision of the disciplinary court.[93] Resignation, release or recall of a judge from his managerial function does not result in the loss of judicial office.[94]

Disqualification in particular cases is governed by the Code of Civil Procedure and the Code of Criminal Procedure. As a general rule, a reason for a judge's disqualification or self-disqualification exists when doubts can be raised regarding his impartiality because

---

[86] Law on Courts and Judges (No. 335/1991 Coll.), Section 47.
[87] Law on Courts and Judges (No. 335/1991 Coll.), Section 48.
[88] Law on Courts and Judges (No. 335/1991 Coll.), Section 46, para. 1(a).
[89] Law on Courts and Judges (No. 335/1991 Coll.), Section 46, para. 3.
[90] Law on Courts and Judges (No. 335/1991 Coll.), Section 50, para. 1.
[91] Law on Courts and Judges (No. 335/1991 Coll.), Section 44, para. 1. See Section V.D.
[92] Law on Courts and Judges (No. 335/1991 Coll.), Section 44, para. 2.
[93] Law on Courts and Judges (No. 335/1991 Coll.), Section 50, para. 3.
[94] Law on Courts and Judges (No. 335/1991 Coll.), Section 50, para. 5.

of his relation towards the matter in dispute, the parties or their legal counsels, guardians, attorneys or representatives, or because of his involvement in a prior procedural stage or relation to another organ in the criminal prosecution.

*Lustration*: In an effort to deal with the legacy of the previous regime, the so-called Lustration Law (No. 451/1991 Coll.) was adopted, which prohibited active supporters of the previous regime from holding public office, including judicial office. As a result, all judges appointed prior to 1989 had to undergo a screening process, including hearings in front of a parliamentary committee, in order to maintain their posts. However, such hearings were held only if actions of a particular judge prior to 1989 were called into question.[95] The Lustration Law was to apply originally only through January 1996, but prior to this deadline the law's validity was extended through the end of 2000.

## C. Evaluation and Promotion

No statutory rules for appraisal of judges' performance have been established. In practice, the criteria sometimes used for the assessment of judge's performance are: (1) the number of cases decided by the judge per month; (2) evaluation by the regional court; and (3) delays caused by the judge or other well-founded complaints relating to his performance. While the rate of reversal is not an indicator for promotion, it may be a consideration for evaluation of a judge's performance. These criteria do not, however, influence the remuneration of judges with regard to the performance of a particular court or an individual judge.

The State President appoints the President and the Vice-President of the Supreme Court.[96] Presidents and vice-presidents of high, regional and district courts are appointed by the Minister of Justice from amongst the judges appointed to the courts in the Czech

---

[95] Under the Lustration Law, former agents of or collaborators with the secret police and communist officials were barred from holding positions in the state administration. Barred individuals included people who between 25 February 1948 and 17 November 1989 were: members of the State Security; registered with the secret police as agents; owners and occupants of conspiracy apartments used by the secret police; informers for the secret police; knowing collaborators with the secret police; Secretaries of the Communist Party of Czechoslovakia at the district level or higher; political officers in the Corps of National Security; or members of the People's militia; in addition, members of action committees of the National Front after 25 February 1948 or of committees that conducted party and other purges in 1948 and after 21 August 1968, as well as individuals who had studied at various Soviet internal affairs schools. Even before the screening process was completed, many judges decided to leave their posts. It is not clear whether their decisions were in any way motivated by the existence and procedures of the screening and re-appointment processes.

[96] CONST. CZECH REP., Art. 62, para. 1(f).

Republic.[97] The presidents of each section (*kolegium*) and judicial panel of the Supreme Court and the presidents of the judicial panels of the high courts are appointed by the presidents of those courts from amongst their judges.[98] Presidents of judicial panels for regional and district courts are appointed by the president of the relevant regional court from amongst the judges of that court or the district courts under its jurisdiction.[99]

No official criteria have been set out for the promotion of judges to courts of higher level, which properly is understood as a form of transfer. Transfer to a higher court depends solely on the decision of the Minister of Justice and the consent of the judge. This situation has been criticised in the Commission's Regular Reports ever since 1997 as an undesirable political influence on the judiciary. On the other hand, the customary practice has developed that the recommendation of the president of the court where the judge is serving as well as the consent of the president of the court to which the judge shall be promoted is solicited. In case of promotion of judges to the Supreme Court the consent of the President of the Court is required by law.[100] The current proposals would oblige the Minister to consult planned judicial councils concerning all personnel matters.[101]

## D. Discipline

While general liability protections and procedural guarantees for disciplinary hearings are in place, the current disciplinary system vests too many powers in the court presidents to appoint panels and initiate proceedings.

### 1. Liability

Judges are exempt, in law and in fact, from civil liability for acts or omissions in the exercise of their managerial functions or acting in their judicial capacity.[102] Where an omission or a breach of a judge' duties is found in disciplinary proceedings, a judge may be required to bear the burden of compensating, at least partially, the complainant in the regression proceedings. The limits for this compensation liability are equal to those limits applied to civil servants.

---

[97] Law on Courts and Judges (No. 335/1991 Coll.), Section 39, para. 3.

[98] Law on Courts and Judges (No. 335/1991 Coll.), Section 39, para. 2.

[99] Law on Courts and Judges (No. 335/1991 Coll.), Section 39, para. 4.

[100] Law on Courts and Judges (No. 335/1991 Coll.), Section 40, para. 9.

[101] According to the President of the Supreme Court, the obligation to consult the councils would not constitute an improvement upon the current practice, by which the Minister is encouraged to act according to the recommendations of the court president.

[102] Law on Judicial Discipline (No. 412/1991 Coll.).

Normally, a judge cannot be subjected to criminal prosecution for acts or omissions in the exercise of his functions. This immunity may be lifted by the authority that appointed a judge.[103] Should a judge's act be classified by law as a misdemeanour, judicial disciplinary proceedings are initiated, rather than misdemeanour proceedings.[104]

## 2. *Disciplinary Proceedings*

Considerable criticism has emerged concerning the current disciplinary rules. The main complaint is that the disciplinary system fails to rid the judiciary of those who, even though they might comply with the formal requirements for judicial office, are simply not suitable for office. At the same time, particular procedures – such as the practice of vesting authority to appoint disciplinary panels and to initiate proceedings in a single person – can threaten individual judges' decisional independence.

The authority for the supervision of judges' conduct lies with three different bodies: presidents and vice-presidents of each court; presidents of high courts (who therefore can also initiate proceedings against judges in courts below); and the Ministry of Justice. An individual complaint regarding a judge's conduct usually initiates disciplinary proceedings. However, proceedings can also be initiated *sua sponte*. About 20 disciplinary proceedings are initiated each year.

In general, judges are required to "exercise their duties with due care, increase their professional competence and respect judicial ethics both in the exercise of their judicial functions and private life and to refrain from anything that might discredit the dignity of the judicial office or threaten the trust in independent, impartial and fair judicial decision-making."[105]

Particular rules of conduct are not well defined, and the Law on Judicial Discipline formulates standards for judges' conduct only in a very general way. For example, delaying individual cases may be a cause for disciplinary proceedings, but what constitutes delay is not defined.[106]

---

[103] Law on Courts and Judges (No. 335/1991 Coll.), Section 55, para 1.

[104] Law on Judicial Discipline (No. 412/1991 Coll.), Section 10, para. 1(b).

[105] Law on Courts and Judges (No. 335/1991 Coll.), Section 54, para. 1.

[106] Since 1 January 2001, there are specified time limits for preliminary hearings in civil matters (seven days from filing), initiating actions in commercial registry (fifteen days), and issuing written decisions (30 days following oral issuance). Reforms to the Criminal Procedure Code, set to take effect on 1 January 2002, will also introduce some specific deadlines. However, the relationship of these deadlines to disciplinary actions for delay is not clear.

In addition, the Czech Union of Judges adopted a written code of judicial ethics in October 2000, though this does not have legal force. The Minister of Justice has proposed developing a more explicit code of conduct, a move some judges view with concern because it would convert ethical principles into legal obligations.

The Law on Judicial Discipline governs the procedure for disciplining and removing judges. A disciplinary panel consisting of five judges appointed to three-year terms by each court president hears proceedings. The parties to the hearing are the president of the court or the Minister of Justice and the accused judge, who may be represented by a colleague or an attorney.

Under the current system the same person – such as a president of a regional, high or Supreme court – both appoints judges to the disciplinary panel and submits proposals to initiate disciplinary proceedings. Although the appointment is for a period of three years, such accumulation of functions in a single person seems inappropriate. The current Minister of Justice's proposals would address this problem by providing that disciplinary panels be nominated by judicial councils as well as that the disciplinary proceedings be heard at high courts.[107]

The accused judge is granted all procedural guarantees accorded to a defendant in criminal proceedings. The disciplinary hearing is public and the decision is pronounced in open session. The highest sanction, namely the removal of a judge from the bench, can be imposed only if: (1) a proposal for the removal is submitted by the Minister of Justice, who can enter the proceedings even if they were initiated by another party; and (2) the removal is based on the disciplinary panel's finding that the judge has committed a "serious disciplinary offence" as stipulated in law.[108] Following proceedings, judges have the right to appeal, with the exception of decisions of the Supreme Court, which is final.

---

[107] According to the Minister's proposal, a five-member judicial council would sit at each of the high courts and would nominate representatives to disciplinary panels. It is unclear whether or not this system would constitute an improvement: the authority to nominate representatives to disciplinary panels would be shifted to a lower number of judges of the high courts. Moreover, unlike court presidents under the current system, judicial councils would not have a clear responsibility for the functioning of disciplinary panels assigned to them.

[108] Law on Judicial Discipline (No. 412/1991 Coll.), Section 3 par. 3. However, no specific definition of "serious disciplinary offence" is provided.

# VI. Intra-Judicial Independence

Judges are generally not subject to undue pressures through the supervision of their decisions or through the assignment of cases. However, as noted above, court presidents are representatives of state administration of courts, and in this capacity their task is to implement policies and specific regulations of the Ministry of Justice. Coupled with the fact that judges are largely dependent on their court presidents for material support and, to a certain extend, for the course of their career, this creates either real or perceived dependency on court presidents.

## A. Relations with Superior Courts

Supervision and enforcement of uniform jurisprudence is the task of the Supreme Court.[109] From 1 January 2001, the system of complete appeal in civil proceedings was replaced by a system of incomplete appeal. The new system has not been tested yet, as pending appeals are being completed under the previous system. Even under the new system the regional court will not be limited by the factual findings and interpretations of the lower court and will be able to require that certain additional evidence be gathered. However, the regional court will be prevented from taking into account such evidence that could have been presented to the lower court.

In civil proceedings the regional court can issue a binding legal opinion[110] which the lower court must follow.[111] The opinion can contain directions as to the extent and the manner in which the proceedings of lower courts have to be completed, including suggestions as to what evidentiary support shall be searched for. In criminal proceedings, the superior court may order a different judicial panel to review a case in which major faults were found.

There is no direct subordination between judges of different levels in their administrative or training relationships. There is no system of appointed judge-supervisors or mentors. Direct consultations with superior court judges in specific cases are not allowed. This, however, does not prevent general discussions of new legislation during training courses, in order to reach a common understanding. Lectures by judges of higher courts, and particularly the Supreme Court, at lower courts are also quite common.

---

[109] Statement of participant, OSI meeting, Prague, 23 March 2001.
[110] Civil Procedural Code, Section 221, para. 3.
[111] Civil Procedural Code, Section 226, para. 1.

## B. Case Management and Relations with Court Presidents

The system of courts is hierarchically organised. Judges are largely dependent on the court president for assignment of office space, and equipment. The court president assesses judges' performance and controls the court calendar.

Cases are assigned to judicial panels as well as to individual judges according to the work schedule prepared by the court president for each calendar year.[112] This schedule stipulates primarily the division of work between the individual specialisations of the court as well as which judges belong to each specialisation. The president of the individual court has no right to assign a specific case to a specific judge outside of the schedule of work. Similarly, after the particular case has been assigned, the president of the court cannot change this assignment, except for the situation when the judge can be disqualified because his impartiality is in question. Changes in this schedule, such as lowering of caseload of one judge (due to long-term illness or similar disability) and redistribution of cases to other judges, can be made within the calendar year.[113] Moreover, the schedule is public.[114] On 1 January 2001, a new distribution system for the allocation of civil (mostly commercial) cases among district and regional courts was implemented. In certain specialisations, such as commercial registry, software programs are used to assure the random assignment of cases.

There are unofficial monthly caseload norms set by the Ministry of Justice. Judges complain that the Ministry set these norms without any regard to the complexity of different specialisations or the complexity of different cases within each specialisation. Thus, the norms are not truly realistic in some cases and too relaxed in other cases. Whether the norms are observed depends more on the number of new cases, the existing backlog and the complexity of pending cases than on the effort and performance of an individual judge. There is no clear connection between the norms and evaluation.

With the exception of a limited number of time limits established in the civil procedure code,[115] judges may not be pressed to expedite cases, unless they fail to observe their caseload norms over the longer term. In this situation, they may be requested by the court president to manage their caseload more efficiently. Delaying individual cases may be a cause for disciplinary proceedings or cause for review of how well a particular judge executes his managerial function.

---

[112] Law on Courts and Judges (No. 335/1991 Coll.), Section 4(a).

[113] Law on Courts and Judges (No. 335/1991 Coll.), Section 4(a), para. 2.

[114] Law on Courts and Judges (No. 335/1991 Coll.), Section 4(a), para. 4.

[115] See Section V.D.2.

## VII. Enforcement

While the majority of criminal law decisions are implemented effectively, the level of disrespect for civil law decisions is growing, owing mainly to a highly inflexible enforcement procedure for those decisions.

Reform efforts have not responded to the changed economic and political circumstances; after the change of regime, the law continued to insist that priority be given to enforcement only through garnishment of the debtor's salary. The amended Code of Civil Procedure (No. 99/1963 Coll.) introduces new forms of the enforcement, such as execution or seizure of a debtor's shares or company. Besides the changes in civil proceedings introduced into the Code itself, a new Law on Court Executors/Judgement Enforcers (No. 120/2001 Coll.) has been passed and should help to improve the enforcement of judgements.

OPEN SOCIETY INSTITUTE 2001

# Judicial Independence in Estonia

MONITORING THE EU ACCESSION PROCESS: JUDICIAL INDEPENDENCE

# Table of Contents

Executive Summary ................................................ 150

I. Introduction .................................................. 153
    A. Ministry of Justice Administration of the Courts ............................................. 153
    B. Financial Autonomy ................................. 154
    C. Weakening Public and Political Support ... 154
    D. Reform Proposals – the Draft Courts Act ............................. 155
    E. The Judiciary and the EU Accession Process ............................... 157
    F. Organisation of the Judicial System ......... 158

II. Constitutional and Legal Foundations of Judicial Independence ............................... 160
    A. Guarantees of the Separation of Powers and Judicial Independence ....................... 160
    B. Representation of the Judiciary ................ 161
    C. Rules on Incompatibility ......................... 162
    D. Judges' Associations .................................. 163

III. Administration of the Court System and Judicial Independence ............................ 164

IV. Financial Autonomy and Level of Funding .... 167
    A. Budgeting Process ...................................... 167
    B. Work Conditions ....................................... 169
    C. Compensation ............................................ 169

| | | |
|---|---|---|
| V. | Judicial Office .................................................. 173 | |
| | A. The Selection Process ............................... 173 | |
| |     1. Court Presidents ................................. 174 | |
| |     2. Supreme Court ................................... 175 | |
| | B. Security of Tenure, Transfer, Retirement and Removal .......................... 175 | |
| |     1. Secure Tenure ..................................... 175 | |
| |     2. Transfer .............................................. 176 | |
| |     3. Retirement.......................................... 176 | |
| |     4. Removal ............................................. 177 | |
| |     5. Lustration .......................................... 177 | |
| | C. Evaluation and Promotion ....................... 178 | |
| | D. Discipline ................................................. 178 | |
| |     1. Liability .............................................. 178 | |
| |     2. Disciplinary Procedures ..................... 179 | |
| VI. | Intra-Judicial Relations................................... 181 | |
| | A. Relations with Superior Courts ................ 181 | |
| | B. Case Management and Relations with Court Presidents............................... 182 | |
| VII. | Enforcement .................................................. 184 | |

# Judicial Independence in Estonia

## Executive Summary

Estonia has made considerable progress in consolidating a truly independent judiciary, both by establishing formal arrangements and creating a spirit of respect for the principle of judicial independence. The Constitution and laws provide explicit protections; the independence of judges is generally acknowledged. The European Commission's Regular Reports have repeatedly noted that Estonia has stable institutions, including the court system, guaranteeing democracy and the rule of law.

There are some areas of concern, however, the most important of which are the continued involvement of the Ministry of Justice in administering the courts, courts' limited financial autonomy, and declining public support for an independent judiciary. The Draft Courts Act raises important issues as well.

*Ministry of Justice Administration of the Courts*

The Ministry of Justice continues to exercise a predominant influence on the administration of district and regional courts and supervision of court presidents, affording it opportunities indirectly to influence judges' deliberations.

Although the Supreme Court administers itself separately, the Ministry of Justice administers district and regional courts. This affords the executive opportunities indirectly to infringe upon the decisional independence of courts. Relations between the Ministry of Justice and the judiciary have been strained.

*Limited Financial Autonomy*

The courts have very limited involvement in the planning and administration of their own finances, which make them more susceptible to influence from the political branches. District and regional courts' involvement in the budget process is minimal.

*Declining Public and Political Support*

A more general problem concerns declining confidence in the judiciary, which may undermine support for further efforts to entrench its independent operation. Despite the progress that has been made, trust in the judiciary has decreased, which does not encourage politicians to adopt principled stands in favour of building upon the progress Estonia has made, rather than curtailing it. However, there have been no indications that political actors have attempted to pressure or improperly influence judges.

*Reform Proposals – the Draft Courts Act*

The most contentious issue in the debate over judicial reform in Estonia has been the institutional independence of the courts, a matter that has become especially sensitive with the drafting of a new Courts Act. The majority of Estonian judges believe that neither this draft nor current law guarantees the institutional independence of the courts to the extent necessary to ensure the independence of individual judges in their core decision-making activity.

Several other issues are discussed in the body of this Report – many of them related to the major themes noted above. Some of the most significant issues are the following:

*Representation*

The judiciary does not have a constitutionally identified independent representative in its dealings with other branches. There are ongoing discussions about whether to establish a National Judicial Council, but the Ministry of Justice has apparently agreed only to create a Council with consultative powers.

*Compensation*

Planned improvements to compensation in the draft Courts Act may create problematic linkages between increased pay and judges' quiescence about unpopular legislative changes.

*Selection*

The current selection process seems well balanced, but recent unsuccessful attempts by the Ministry of Justice to enlarge its role suggest that the executive has not fully accepted the logic and value of an independent selection process; indeed, the Draft Courts Act expands the Ministry's powers of appointment.

*Probationary Judges*

The probationary period for new judges includes no standardised or transparent norms of evaluation, allowing the Judges' Examination Commission discretionary removal power, giving judges strong incentives to please the Commission.

*Discipline*

The disciplinary rules allow the executive considerable discretion in initiating disciplinary proceedings – a system which would not be necessary if the executive's role in administration were more limited in general.

*The Judiciary and the EU Accession Process*

The main problems of the Estonian court system identified by the Commission have been the length of proceedings, the high percentage of repealed or amended court decisions and the continuously increasing backlog. The Commission has not publicly focused on problems concerning guarantees of judicial independence. The judiciary is not involved in any meaningful way in the accession process, and the status of the judiciary has not been raised in public discussions on accession.

## I. Introduction

Estonia has made considerable progress towards the consolidation of a truly independent judiciary, both by establishing formal arrangements and creating a spirit of respect for the principle of judicial independence. The Constitution provides explicit protections, and legislation likewise guarantees judges' independence in a variety of areas. More broadly, the independence of judges is generally acknowledged by political parties, the legislative and executive branches, the media, and the public. The European Commission's Regular Reports have repeatedly noted that Estonia has stable institutions, including the court system, guaranteeing democracy and the rule of law.[1]

There are some areas of concern, however, the most important of which are the continued involvement of the Ministry of Justice in administering the courts, courts' limited financial autonomy, and declining public support for an independent judiciary.

### A. Ministry of Justice Administration of the Courts

The continued administration of the district and regional courts by the Ministry of Justice to some extent limits the independence of the judiciary. Although the Supreme Court administers itself separately, there is no united national courts' administration, nor is there a separate and independent constitutional representative for the courts.

In general, the relations between the Ministry of Justice and the judiciary have been strained. The Ministry has proposed a new Courts Act to address the institutional position of the courts. The Draft Act contains a number of problematic provisions, and the majority of Estonian judges believe that neither current law nor the Draft Act guarantees the institutional independence of the courts to the extent necessary to ensure the independence of individual judges.[2]

Although Estonian judges are now generally well-paid, one current issue relating to compensation highlights the problems raised by continuing involvement of the executive in court administration: judges have been notified that their salaries will be increased after the new Draft Courts Act is adopted by Parliament – to a certain extent, this may curb criticism of the draft law by the judiciary.

---

[1] European Commission, *2000 Regular Report on Estonia's Progress Towards Accession*, 8 November 2000.

[2] Letter from the Estonian Association of Judges to the Ministry of Justice, 13 September 2000, <http://eky.just.ee/uudised.html>, in Estonian (accessed 11 June 2001).

## B. Financial Autonomy

The courts have very limited involvement in the planning and administration of their own finances, which may make them more susceptible to influence from the political branches. Apart from the Supreme Court, which has its own budget, the other courts of Estonia have no separate control over their own budgets or the budgeting process. The district and regional courts' involvement in the budget process is minimal. There are neither objective criteria for any stage of the budget process, nor any legislative or constitutional guarantees of funding levels.

The 1991 Legal Status of Judges Act substantially improved the material conditions and social security of the judiciary. Judges are now well paid, and courts do not suffer from severe under-investment as compared to other branches. Nevertheless, judges' physical working conditions require significant improvements.

## C. Weakening Public and Political Support

Another more general problem concerns declining confidence in the judiciary, which may undermine support for further entrenching its independent operation. Despite the progress that has been made, trust in the judiciary has decreased in the 1990s. In the beginning of the 1990s approximately 60 percent of the population reported that they trusted in the judicial system; by the end of 1990s the percentage had decreased to approximately 40 percent.[3] Both the public and media perceive the judiciary as slow and inefficient.

The State President has expressed his general disappointment with aspects of the judiciary's activities. In a speech on the 81st Anniversary of the Estonian Republic on 24 February 1999, the State President asserted that the thinking of the majority of judges indicates that they are holdovers from the old totalitarian system. In another speech on the 80th Anniversary of the Estonian Supreme Court on 14 January 2000, the State President declared that the credibility of the judicial system is in question because several court decisions have offended the citizenry's sense of justice.

Despite these general criticisms, the State President has never expressed dissatisfaction with any specific court decisions. Government officials have in some cases, however. For example, the Minister of Justice characterised the sentence imposed on a robber

---

[3] E. Soosaar, "Rahulolematuse kasvust ei ole meil paasu" ("No escape from increase of dissatisfaction"), *Aripaev*, 20 June 2000 (citing survey conducted by Saar Poll, May 2000).

in a highly publicised case as too severe.[4] There have been no indications that political actors have attempted to pressure or improperly influence judges. On a few occasions judicial independence has been publicly questioned, when court decisions ran contrary to public opinion. Government officials have not directed personal insults at judges.

## D. Reform Proposals – the Draft Courts Act

The most contentious issue in the debate over judicial reform in Estonia has been the institutional independence of the courts, a matter that has become especially sensitive with the drafting of a new Courts Act.

The institutional independence of the courts has been an important topic of discussion among the Estonian judiciary for years. As early as 1994, Estonian judges were discussing the need to reform the administration of the court system to increase judges' independence. Many judges felt that administration of the district and regional courts by the Ministry of Justice was in conflict with the independence of the courts.[5]

In 1995, the judges proposed a reform of the judicial system aimed at achieving its legal, organisational, and financial independence, following from the principle that the judiciary must decide for itself on all essential aspects of its activities and be independent of other State authorities. The plan's main feature, the creation of a Courts Administration under the Supreme Court or a National Judicial Council, was never implemented due to active resistance by the Ministry of Justice.

The Ministry has instead proposed a new Courts Act[6] to address the institutional position of the courts. Based on the opinions presented by the Estonian Association of Judges[7] as well as individual judges, it appears that the majority of Estonian judges believe that neither this draft nor current law guarantees the institutional independence of the courts

---

[4] "Siseminister ei poolda Ulo Voitkale armuandmist" ("Minister of Internal Affairs does not favor pardoning Ulo Voitka"), *Eesti Paevaleht*, 26 February 2001.

[5] This was not only because of the possibility of direct interference through the Ministry's discretionary adminstrative supervision, but also because the courts have the power to review the regulations and decisions of the Ministry, creating a conflict of interest which judges argued could harm the public's perception of the judiciary as an impartial and independent adjudicator. See R. Maruste, "Eesti Kohtususteemi korrastamise kava" ("The Plan for Reforming the Estonian Court System"), *Juridica*, 1995, No. 5, pp. 199–205.

[6] Draft dated 28 November 2000, http://www.riigikogu.ee/ems/plsql/ems.motions, in Estonian (accessed 11 June 2001).

[7] Letter to the Ministry of Justice, 13 September 2000.

to the extent necessary to ensure the independence of individual judges in their core decision-making activity.

The explanatory letter accompanying the Draft Courts Act[8] asserts that the independence of the courts shall be guaranteed at the level of individual judges. The Draft Act focuses, therefore, on such matters as ensuring that judges are not influenced by higher-ranking colleagues, that they are secure in their person against detention, and that criminal charges can be brought against them only with the authorisation of the State President on the proposal of the Supreme Court. The Draft Act does not, however, increase the institutional independence of the judiciary as a whole. Indeed, it seems that the working group, which drafted the new Courts Act, has adopted a very narrow definition of judicial independence.

This limited viewpoint may be due to the lack of a widespread, public debate focused on the institutional independence of the courts in a contemporary Estonian society based on the rule of law. Indeed, the relationship between the institutional independence of the courts and the independence of individual judges has mainly been debated in the legal literature and at judicial meetings, not in the media or in the political sphere. The weakening public support for the value of an independent judiciary does not encourage politicians to adopt principled stands in favour of building upon the progress Estonia has made to date in building an independent judiciary.

There seems to be a persistent belief that significant residual authority over the judiciary vested in the Ministry of Justice is appropriate. The Draft Courts Act reflects that attitude, assigning as it does greater powers to the Ministry and entrenching the idea that judges have only an individual, not a collective or institutional independence. Given the poor relationship between the Ministry and judges, however, as well as the recent legacy of the Soviet period during which the predecessor of the Ministry had an inappropriately intrusive role, such a belief seems misplaced. The progress Estonia has made will be consolidated, not by returning to a model of greater uni-directional executive and parliamentary control over judges, but by implementing fully the principles of separation and balance of powers and recognising the independence of the judiciary as a branch, with the organisational and administrative consequences that flow from that.

---

[8] *Riigikogu*, at <http://www.riigikogu.ee/englishindex.html>, in English (accessed 11 June 2001).

## E. The Judiciary and the EU Accession Process

Since 1998, the Commission has drawn up annual reports evaluating Estonia's progress on accession issues. The Regular Report on Estonia's progress Towards Accession 1999 stated that

> Inexperienced judges continue to pose major difficulties for the judicial system. Justice in lower level courts continues to be unsatisfactory, as there are many new, inexperienced and overburdened judges.[9]

The Regular Report for 2000 contained somewhat more positive, if still guarded findings, noting that

> Estonia has made some progress in addressing the concerns raised in last year's regular report in this area, in particular as regards training for judges. However, the workload of judges and backlog in the system has not registered noticeable improvements... Uncertainty by judges applying the law, in particular in the administrative and penal law field, continues to be a problem. The quality of court decisions varies considerably, although it remains unsatisfactory in the lowest-level courts.[10]

Thus, the main problems of the Estonian court system from the Commission's point of view are the length of proceedings, the high percentage of repealed or amended court decisions and the continuously increasing backlog. The Commission has not ever noted any problems concerning guarantees of judicial independence.

The judiciary is not involved in any meaningful way in the accession process. The status of the judiciary has not been raised in the public discussions on accession. The general public is not aware of what the Reports state about the Estonian judiciary, although the legislature, executive and judiciary are generally aware of the contents of the Reports. As EU support programs are administered through the executive, judges and judicial administrators have little familiarity with them or with opportunities for obtaining funding for different projects.

---

[9] See *1998 Regular Report From The Commission on Estonia's Progress Towards Accession,* November 1998 and *1999 Regular Report From The Commission on Estonia's Progress Towards Accession,* November 1999.

[10] See <http://europa.eu.int/comm/enlargement/dwn/report_11_00/zip/en/es_en.zip> (accessed 11 June 2001).

## F. Organisation of the Judicial System

Estonia has not had a very long history of independent courts. Before the First World War Estonia was a part of the Russian Empire, where the courts did not enjoy full independence. During the inter-war period, the Estonian Republic's civil law courts were independent, but Soviet rule introduced the principle of the unity of power and the subordination of the courts, with very negative consequences for judicial independence.

Reform of the Estonian judicial system was initiated before Estonia regained its independence from the Soviet Union in August 1991, as more open discussion of societal issues became possible in the late 1980s. In 1989, the first free elections took place and in October 1991, the first freely-elected Legislature adopted the Courts Act[11] and the Legal Status of Judges Act[12] regulating the functions of the judiciary. In June 1992, the new Estonian Constitution[13] was adopted by referendum. The Constitution further elaborated the structures introduced by the Acts of 1991, and the new judicial system became fully operational in 1993.

The mandate, organisation, and operation of the Estonian courts are regulated by various documents: (1) the Estonian Constitution of 1992; (2) the Courts Act of 1991; (3) the Legal Status of Judges Act of 1991; (4) the Statute of the Supreme Court adopted by the Supreme Court in 1999[14]; and (5) the Statutes of Circuit, City, County and Administrative Courts adopted by the Ministry of Justice in 1995.[15]

The Estonian judicial system consists of three levels: district courts, regional courts, and the Supreme Court (*Riigikohus*). At the district level, there are three city courts, fifteen county courts, and four administrative courts. Three regional courts share exclusive appellate jurisdiction. The Supreme Court is the court of last resort; it acts both as a cassation court and as a constitutional court.[16] There are no military courts in Estonia, and extraordinary courts are prohibited.[17] The Supreme Court and the regional courts are divided into Chambers according to types of case heard (Civil Chamber, Criminal Chamber, Administrative Law Chamber).

---

[11] *Riigi Teataja, Official Gazette* (hereafter: RT) 1991, 38, 472; *Official Gazette, Part I* (hereafter RTI) 2001, 21, 113.

[12] RT 1991, 38, 473; RTI 2000, 40, 251.

[13] RT 1992, 26, 349.

[14] See <http://www.nc.ee/riigikohus>, in Estonian.

[15] *Official Gazette, Supplement* (hereafter RTL) 1995, 78.

[16] CONST. REP. ESTONIA, Art. 152 (2), The Courts Act Art. 23 (3).

[17] CONST. REP. ESTONIA, Art. 148.

City and county (district) courts hear all civil and criminal cases; the majority of such courts have real estate, registration and probation supervision departments, which register real estate, companies, foundations and NGOs. Additional departments may be established within the framework of a county or city (district) court by the Ministry of Justice;[18] within Tallinn City Court, five specialised departments for different types of cases have been established.[19]

Since October 1996 there have been a total of 238 judgeships: 177 district, 44 regional, and 17 Supreme Court. As of April 2001 there were 14 vacancies, a figure which has remained roughly constant over the past three years. The number of cases has grown significantly while the number of judges has remained constant.[20] Consequently the caseload per judge has increased significantly. There will be extra 5 judgeships (3 district and 2 regional) from October 2001.[21]

During the 1990s, the courts' jurisdiction was significantly expanded to include registration of legal persons, both commercial and non-governmental organisations, registration of real estate and probation supervision. These additional functions have increased the overall workload of the district courts. The number of cases heard in the various courts has increased considerably over the 1990s: between 1994 and 2000, civil cases increased roughly 25 percent (from 17,612 to 22,413), criminal cases increased roughly 30 percent (from 6,199 to 9,224), and the relatively small number of administrative cases nearly doubled (from 1,118 to 2,018).[22] The average caseload has therefore increased considerably over this time.

---

[18] Courts Act Art. 16(6); Art. 18(7); Art. 20(5).

[19] The Tallinn City Court Statute, Arts. 11–13; RTL 1995, 78.

[20] See < http://www.just.ee/oldjust/JM/stat_kohtud2000.html>, in Estonian (accessed 11 June 2001).

[21] RTI 2000, 102, 678.

[22] See <http://www.just.ee>, in Estonian (accessed 11 June 2001).

## II. Constitutional and Legal Foundations of Judicial Independence

In general, guarantees of judicial independence are in place. However, there is no clear constitutional representative of the judiciary, and the executive's interpretation of independence focuses unduly on individual judges, to the detriment of the institutional independence of the judiciary. The Draft Courts Act fails to address existing problems, and even threatens to exacerbate them – allowing judges to work within the Ministry of Justice, for example.

### A. Guarantees of the Separation of Powers and Judicial Independence

The Constitution explicitly provides for the separation and balance of powers among the Parliament, the State President, the Government, and the courts.[23] Certain guarantees of judicial independence – such as life tenure and protections against removal from office – are also included in the Constitution.

The Constitution provides that "the courts shall be independent in their activities and shall administer justice in accordance with the Constitution and the laws."[24] There is some dispute as to what the term "courts" means. The Ministry of Justice interprets it as a collegium of judges deciding a particular case – thus emphasising a narrow and individualised focus for independence. Judges, however, interpret "courts" as institutions independent in all their activities, not only in delivering justice. The Ministry's view is problematic, as it reduces the scope of judicial independence at the collective or institutional level, which seems incompatible with the constitutional provisions for the separation and balance of powers among the various branches.

The Constitution also provides that guarantees for judges' independence shall be provided by law.[25] The Government has prepared a Draft Courts Act intended to replace both the current Courts Act and the Legal Status of Judges Act which regulate many issues integral to judicial independence, such as judges' career path, remuneration, discipline, and protections from prosecution. The Draft Act initially included several provisions

---

[23] CONST. REP. ESTONIA, Art. 4.
[24] CONST. REP. ESTONIA, Art. 146.
[25] CONST. REP. ESTONIA, Art. 147.

that could be detrimental to judicial independence and which were harshly criticised by the legal community. As a result, the current draft is more supportive of judicial independence; still, it includes a number of problematic provisions, which either harm judicial independence or fail to rectify existing problems. Various provisions of the Draft Courts Law are discussed in other sections of this report.

## B. Representation of the Judiciary

Although formally judges constitute a separate power equal with the legislative and executive branches, there are departures from this principle. The Estonian judiciary does not have a constitutional representative of its own, although the Supreme Court represents itself. There is no official body authorised to speak exclusively on behalf of the judiciary in its relations with the Parliament and the executive branch; instead, the Ministry of Justice acts as the spokesperson for the district and regional courts.[26]

There are ongoing discussions about establishing a National Judicial Council. This idea has been promoted by the judiciary, but has not been favoured by the executive branch. The idea to create the National Judicial Council was first proposed by the first President of the Supreme Court,[27] and today is advocated by the Supreme Court and the Estonian Judge's Association.[28]

Introducing a National Judicial Council would require changes in the Courts Act, although some officials of the Ministry of Justice have asserted that a constitutional amendment would be required to introduce such a Council.[29] Reportedly, the Ministry of Justice has agreed to create a Council with only consultative powers which would need no constitutional amendment.[30]

---

[26] 1995 Government of the Republic Act, Art. 59; RTI 1995, 94, 1628; RTI 2001, 7, 16.

[27] "Rait Maruste, Eesti kohtusüsteemi juhtimise korrastamise kava", *Juridica*, 1995, No. 5.

[28] Letter to the Ministry of Justice, 13 September 2000.

[29] The Constitution is silent about the management of the judicial system, but it does require that the State budget be submitted to Parliament by the Government, and proposals for a Council might affect that.

[30] There is already a General Conference of Judges, composed of all judges, although this body has no representational functions. The General Conference does have some indirect involvement in the selection of judges. See Section V.A.

## C. Rules on Incompatibility

The decisional independence and impartiality of judges is reinforced by limits on judges' cross-branch or outside activity. Judges may not be members of Parliament, municipal councils, or political parties. Judges may not hold any positions in the executive branch or elsewhere except in teaching and research.

Judges may not be members of the Board of Directors or founders of public or private limited liability companies;[31] participation in other entrepreneurial and commercial activity, such as partnerships, associations, and supervisory boards of companies is allowed. There are no rules limiting the employment of former judges after they retire.

Any other activity contrary to the oath of office taken by judges is also prohibited,[32] a provision which has been interpreted by judges as prohibiting them from participation in electoral campaigns (no cases of judges' involvement in electoral campaigns have been noted). No institution is authorised to waive these restrictions under any circumstances.

The Draft Courts Act would significantly alter the rules limiting judges' activity outside the judicial branch. It would allow a judge to work for the Ministry of Justice, during which time his judicial powers would be suspended, although his salary and social benefits would remain the same.[33] This proposed alteration would tend to increase the opportunities for the Ministry to exercise influence in the work of judges interested in coming to work for the Ministry, and would in practice blur the distinction between the constitutionally separate executive and courts.

The Draft Courts Act would also expand the ban on judges' participation in entrepreneurial activities to include the supervisory boards of all other types of companies, including partnerships, commercial associations, and subsidiaries of foreign companies. It would prohibit a judge from acting as a trustee in bankruptcy proceedings or as an arbitrator. However, the prohibition would not extend to holding or trading stock.[34]

---

[31] Legal Status of Judges Act, Art. 4.
[32] Legal Status of Judges Act, Art. 4.
[33] Draft Courts Act, Art. 60.
[34] Draft Courts Act, Art. 52.

## D. Judges' Associations

Judges enjoy freedom of association and the majority are members of the Association of Judges, which is an autonomous body financed mostly by the Ministry of Justice. The Association has been effective in protecting the interests of the judiciary and judicial independence. It has been involved in developing professional training programs for judges, but because the funds for judicial training are allocated to the Ministry of Justice, all decisions concerning judicial training are made by the Ministry. In making its decisions, the Ministry has often, but not always, taken into consideration the Judges' Association's remarks.

## III. Administration of the Court System and Judicial Independence

The Ministry of Justice continues to exercise a predominant influence on the administration of the judiciary and supervision of court presidents, affording it opportunities indirectly to influence judges' deliberations. The draft Courts Act does little to address executive involvement.

The Ministry of Justice supervises the organisation and management of the district and regional courts.[35] Arguably, this arrangement contradicts the separation of powers doctrine. As long as the district and regional courts are under the supervision of the Ministry of Justice, the Ministry will have opportunities to exert undue influence on the judges and especially the Presidents of the courts through its discretionary administrative decisions. For example, the Minister of Justice recently initiated disciplinary action against a judge for unduly prolonging administrative court proceedings in a highly publicised case in which the Government was a party.[36]

The Ministry of Justice has extensive administrative and oversight powers over the courts. For all district and regional courts, the Ministry determines the seats of courts, their territorial jurisdiction, and the number of judges and support staff at each court, with the approval of the Supreme Court,[37] as well as supervising court records and court facilities.[38] There is a Courts Department at the Ministry of Justice responsible for "management and financing of the [district and regional] courts; audits with regard to courts, judicial statistics, and settlement of complaints filed against the work of courts."[39]

The presidents of the courts administer the courts' day-to-day operations and supervise their performance and efficiency; for example, the district and regional court presidents are authorised to recruit court personnel.[40] However, the Ministry of Justice performs

---

[35] Statute of the Ministry of Justice, RTI 1997, 1, 7, RTI 2001, 8, 39; Sections 8, 12.

[36] Minister of Justice, Directive No. 514-k from 21 November, 2000. The Judges' Disciplinary Commission subsequently did not find any wrongdoing. Case No. 3-8-11-1. The case involved a land ownership dispute between the Ministry of Justice and a private party. See also Section V.D.

[37] Courts Act, Art. 16 (4). The overall number of judges on each level is determined by Parliament. Hence, the Minister of Justice can decide number of judges in a particular court only without exceeding the overall limit.

[38] Courts Act, Arts. 16–20; RT 1991, 38, 472; RTI 2001, 21, 113.

[39] Information from the Justice Ministry's web page, <http://www.just.ee>, in Estonian (accessed 11 June 2001).

[40] Statutes of Circuit, City, County and Administrative Courts adopted by the Ministry of Justice in 1995; RTL 1995, 78.

external supervision of the performance and efficiency of the district and regional courts. The Ministry prepares annual reports on the district and regional courts, including data about the number of cases filed and decided, the average duration of court proceedings, sentencing, and results on appeal. (The Ministry of Justice can not inspect a judge's activities in adjudicating particular cases; the reports do not affect directly judges' promotion and have not resulted in disciplinary actions.) This supervision can act as a limit on the administrative independence of the court presidents. Because the Ministry appoints district court presidents and recommends candidates for regional court president,[41] it is in a position to exercise influence upon them and through them on the administrative supervision of other judges.

In practice the Ministry of Justice has not abused these powers; however, in some cases judges have reported that the Ministry has informed them of its interest in speeding up proceedings. It would be preferable, therefore, to transfer the external supervisory function now vested in the Ministry to a more independent body such as a Judicial Council, a view favoured by the Association of Judges.[42]

The Draft Courts Act does not anticipate significant changes regarding the locus of judicial administration. It keeps the administration of district and regional courts within the competence of the Ministry of Justice. The Ministry would have the power to determine: the location and territorial jurisdiction of courts; the number of judges, lay assessors, and clerical staff; and the statutes of courts. The Ministry would also appoint and remove court presidents.

The Draft Act would introduce several bodies of judicial self-government, including a Council of Courts' Administration, though with only weak, mostly advisory powers. The Council would declare its position on the appointment of Justices of the Supreme Court and principles on changing the budgets of courts; in addition, its consent would be required before the Minister of Justice could determine the number of candidates in training for judicial posts. The Council would consist of: the President of the Supreme Court; five judges elected by the full assembly of judges; two Members of Parliament; a member of the Bar Association, appointed by the Bar; the Chief Public Prosecutor or his designee; and the Legal Chancellor or his designee.

In addition, each court would have a general assembly of judges to endorse rules for case assignment and to fill some consultative functions. The General Conference of Judges, comprising all sitting judges, would elect members of the Disciplinary Senate

---

[41] Under the Draft Courts Act, the Ministry will directly appoint regional court presidents as well.

[42] Letter to the Ministry of Justice, 13 September 2000.

and the Judicial Examination Commission[43] – matters currently in the purview of the general assembly of trial judges and general assembly of appellate court judges.

The Supreme Court is autonomous in administrative and organisational matters. The President of the Supreme Court supervises the Supreme Court,[44] which is consequently insulated from the Ministry of Justice. The State Audit Office has the authority to audit the efficiency of maintenance expenditures, the economic purposefulness of transactions, the use and preservation of state assets, the legality of financial transactions and the accuracy of accounting and reporting of all courts, including the Supreme Court.[45]

*Training*. The Ministry of Justice is also responsible for organising judicial training as well as the formulating the law curricula; thus, it is the executive that determines the subjects to be taught, the scope of training, and the lecturers. Judges are generally of the opinion that this is in conflict with the independence of the courts, because the executive determines which ideas and principles are disseminated among the judiciary.

The Ministry of Justice recently formulated a "Strategy for Training Judges and Prosecutors for the Years 2001–2004," adopted by the Government on 20 February 2001. As part of the Strategy a Training Council will be created, with representatives from the Association of Judges and the Public Prosecutors' Office, the Supreme Court, the Ministry of Justice, the Law Faculty of University of Tartu, and the Estonian Law Centre.[46] One of the most important tasks of the Training Council will be the elaboration of standards related to the competence of judges and prosecutors. The Ministry of Justice will still retain an important role in the training process, as the Council must report to it annually on implementation of the Strategy, and the Ministry will maintain certain accounting controls over the Strategy. The main source of finance for the implementation of the Strategy is the State Budget.[47]

---

[43] The primary contributor to this the Report is a member of the Commission.

[44] Statute of the Supreme Court, 39; Art. 8. See <http://www.nc.ee/riigikohus>, in Estonian (accessed 11 June 2001).

[45] State Audit Office Act Art. 6; RTI 1995, 11, 115; RTI 1999, 16, 271.

[46] The Estonian Law Centre was founded by the Government, the Supreme Court and Tartu University to organise judicial training. For several years it received substantial funding from the Ministry of Justice and from foreign donors. In recent years the Centre has less funding from both sources. Under the new Strategy, the Ministry has recognised the Centre as the main provider of training for judges and prosecutors and co-operation between the two is likely to improve.

[47] "Strategy for Training Judges and Prosecutors for the Years 2001–2004", adopted by the Government on 20 February 2001.

# IV. Financial Autonomy and Level of Funding

## A. Budgeting Process

The executive retains control of the budget process and the allocation of funds, with minimal involvement of judges. This arrangement unnecessarily allows the executive considerable leverage over the individual courts.

The district and regional courts of Estonia have no separate control over their own budgets or the budgeting process. In the State Budgets there is no separate general budget line for the courts, although the chapter devoted to the Ministry of Justice includes a separate budget line for district and regional courts.[48]

The district and regional courts' involvement in the budget process is minimal. The presidents of the district and regional courts submit a draft budget to the Ministry of Justice, which then submits its own draft to the Ministry of Finance. During the preparation of the final draft budget for the Government, the Finance Ministry has the right to change the draft budget line for the courts without the agreement of the Justice Ministry, with the Government settling unresolved disagreements between ministries. There is no requirement to inform the Parliament about the disagreements.[49] Thus, even when the Ministry of Justice is acting as an advocate for the judiciary, it may still not be able to ensure that the judiciary's needs are represented in governmental or parliamentary negotiations on the final budget; judges' or courts' perspectives need not be considered directly at any stage.

The Supreme Court drafts its own budget, which is submitted to the Ministry of Finance. The Ministry of Finance has the right to change the draft only with the agreement of the Supreme Court. The Government in turn has the right to make changes in the draft, but it is required to submit to the Parliament the exact content of, and the reasons for, the proposed changes.[50]

There are no objective criteria for any stage of the budget planning process, nor any legislative or constitutional guarantee of funding levels. The Supreme Court has only limited opportunities to defend its budgetary objectives throughout the budgeting process; Supreme Court justices maintain that the limits fixed by Ministry of Financial

---

[48] State Budget for the Year 2000 Act, Art. 1, Section 131, Subsection 21; RTI 2000, 1, 1; RTI 2000, 55, 364.

[49] State Budget Act, Arts. 11–17; RTI 1999, 55, 584; RTI 2000, 55, 360.

[50] State Budget Act, Arts. 11–17; RTI 1999, 55, 584; RTI 2000, 55, 360.

Affairs officials in the early stages of the budgeting process do not change. The budgeting procedure illustrates that problems lie not only in the political and legal culture, but also in legal and institutional limits to effective representation of the judiciary's interest.

The Draft Courts Act would not increase the involvement of the district and regional courts in the budgeting process. The working group responsible for the draft has asserted that involving the courts in the budgeting process would make courts party to a political negotiation.[51]

The Draft Act would empower a Council of Courts' Administration to develop budget principles; the Minister of Justice would then be authorised to change the budgets of courts only in accordance with the principles elaborated and declared by the Council. (It is not clear if this requirement extends to the original drafting of the budget and allocational decisions, or only to changes to the budget.)

Since the executive and legislative branches decide on the resources to be allocated to the judiciary, the priorities set in the State budget reflect their attitude towards the balance of powers in general and the judiciary in particular – another instance of the problems which a lack of independent representation creates.

For example, training – important in maintaining an efficient judiciary able to independently adjudicate disputes – is underfunded. The sums allocated in the Ministry of Justices' budget for training judges and prosecutors have been reduced from 4.34 million EEK (c. € 277,375) in 1999 to 2.66 million EEK (c. € 170,000) in 2001 – an amount clearly insufficient to ensure that judges are able to assimilate the fundamental changes in the legal system.

In general, the funds allocated to the judiciary have been decreasing from 1999 to 2001. This is not the result of a general budgetary cutback, as at the same time the total budget increased and the outlays for several individual ministries, including the Ministry of Justice, were higher in the 2001 budget than in 2000. The total budget for the judiciary constitutes 0.69 percent of the total State Budget for 2001 – a decline from the 0.76 percent in 2000 – or 0.22 percent of the expected GDP (0.24 percent in 2000).[52]

---

[51] Explanatory letter to the Bill No. 607; The Courts Act, 28 November 2000, <http://www.riigikogu.ee/otsimine.html>, in Estonian (accessed 11 June 2001).

[52] It may be more informative to compare the budget of the judiciary to the GDP than to the total national budget, because different budget and accounting practices can make the budget share appear to change. Up to 1999, Estonian budgets did not include social security and health care expenditures in the national budget and hence funds allocated to the judiciary as a percentage of the total budget were greater. See <http://www.seadus.ibs.ee/seadus/aktid/rk.s.19981229.133.20000109.html>, in Estonian (accessed 11 June 2001).

The Ministry of Justice is responsible for allocations of funds to individual courts and for supervising the spending of those funds. The Ministry can transfer funds among lines within the courts' overall budget line, within the framework established in the overall State Budget. Because there are no clear limits or safeguards on these discretionary allocative powers, they represent a threat to judges' independence.

## B. Work Conditions

The courts do not suffer from severe under-investment as compared to the other State branches. Nevertheless, judges' physical working conditions require significant improvements. Approximately half of all courthouses – including the Supreme Court's building – have been renovated, but some of the remaining courthouses are still in poor physical condition.[53]

The Ministry of Justice determines the number of judges and support staff in the district and regional courts based on the number of cases and the qualitative characteristics of the cases. However, no formal criteria, such as caseload per judge, have been established to determine the necessary number of staff. The courts' dramatically expanded jurisdiction during the 1990s has increased the workload on existing staff.[54]

There are no norms established for office space, standard equipment or technology. In general, however, courts are reasonably well equipped, and there is no indication that infrastructural or technological limits on judges' working conditions constitute a threat to their independent exercise of the judicial power. All courts are equipped with personal computers and connected to the Internet; every judge has a personal computer. The courts' offices are equipped with fax machines and the judges have Internet access to legislative databases. In most courts records and judgements are stored in computer archives. For the most part, however, legal information is still disseminated on paper, and every judge receives the Official Gazette and printed collections of new legislation.[55]

## C. Compensation

Since the early 1990s, new legislation has substantially improved the financial security of the judiciary – which is important to ensure judges are not subject to economic

---

[53] Information from Vice Chancellor of the Ministry of Justice, 9 April 2001.
[54] The situation is particularly difficult in the mostly Russian-speaking industrial north-east where a disproportionate number of judicial posts have gone unfilled, leaving judges extremely overburdened.
[55] Information from Vice Chancellor of the Ministry of Justice, 9 April 2001.

pressures which might encourage them to compromise their decision-making. However, planned improvements to compensation in the Draft Courts Acts seem to create problematic linkages between increased pay and judges' quiescence about unpopular legislative changes.

Compared to the situation of other public officials, an average judicial post is quite attractive financially; a judge's compensation is about 15 percent higher than the salary of a prosecutor of comparable level. If a judge's income is compared to the income of private lawyers, the judicial profession is tolerably attractive in some cities and counties, but not in the capital, Tallinn, or in some other regions.[56]

Judges' salaries now range from about € 985 per month for a district judge – approximately three times the average salary – to € 1,273 for justices of the Supreme Court and the presidents of the regional courts. The salary of the President of the Supreme Court is about € 1,540 per month. Judges receive extra compensation for experience, with bonuses ranging from ten percent after four years' service to 25 percent after 30 years. The pension for judges is 75 percent of their salary and is not taxable.[57]

The compensation package enjoyed by the most senior judges is comparable to, if somewhat lower than that of leading officials in the political branches which share State power. The salary of members of Parliament is slightly less than that of the Supreme Court justices (though considerably higher than an ordinary court judge's salary). Government ministers, the Chairman of the Parliament and the State President earn considerably more than any judge.[58]

Judges' salaries are established by Parliament. Although Parliament has the power to decrease judges' salaries, to date it has not done so. (Temporary reduction in pay up to a month's salary is possible in disciplinary cases.) Formally, judges' salaries are tied

---

[56] The disparity in income between judges and lawyers in private practice is the main reason behind the low number of applicants for judicial vacancies. In fact, some vacancies remain open either because there are no applicants at all, or, when there are applicants, their credentials are so low that they do not meet the legal requirements, according to the Judges' Examination Commission.

[57] The Legal Status of the Judges Act, Art. 33; RT 1991, 38, 473; RTI 2000, 40, 251.

[58] The State President, ministers, and Members of Parliament receive a non-taxable monthly supplement equal to 20 percent of their salary, to cover costs related to their post, which makes their compensation package even more attractive as compared to that enjoyed by judges. State Officials, Appointed by Parliament or the State President, Salaries Act, Art.12, RT1 1996, 81, 1448; RTI 2000, 55, 359; The State President of Estonia and Members of Parliament, Salaries, Pensions and Other Social Guarantees Act, Art. 9, RT 1992, 28, 381; RTI 2001, 21, 117. Of course, judges have life tenure, and politicians do not.

to those of other appointed public officials in the (non-political) civil service.[59] While this creates a neutral basis for setting judicial pay and decreases the likelihood that the political branches will engage in pay reductions as a form of punishment, there are nonetheless problems with this approach. Tying salaries to those of civil servants can effectively deflate the growth in judicial salaries, because the salaries of civil servants, while nominally flat in recent years, have been supplemented by additional payments based on workload. However, judges cannot receive additional payments for additional work. Accordingly, their salaries have been decreasing in relative terms.[60] Over time this will erode the valuable protection for judicial independence the increases in salary in the 1990s established.

Any Act regulating the salaries of judges should have more safeguards than ones regulating the remuneration of other public officials, and should consider the effects of the overall compensation scheme in setting rates. In addition, if linkage is considered, it would be more appropriate to link judicial salaries to those of members of the political branches, such as members of Parliament or the Government, with whom State power is shared.

Judges have a right to housing provided by their employer, if needed.[61] The Ministry of Justice allocates this housing for the time a judge spends in a certain court, after which the housing can be withdrawn with no obligation to provide alternative housing, unless the judge has served for more than 10 years, or has retired (or because of a reduction in the number of judgeships). In fact, so far the Ministry has not been able to provide housing to all judges who are eligible to receive this benefit.[62] As the Ministry allocates the benefit in the absence of any clear criteria, this benefit may not be compatible with the requirements of judicial independence.

Judicial salaries are scheduled to be increased after the Draft Courts Act is adopted. To a certain extent, this state of affairs may be used to curb criticism of the Draft Act by the

---

[59] Act on Salaries for State Officials Appointed by the Parliament or the State President, RTI 1996, 81, 1448; RTI 2000, 55, 359.

[60] For example, in 1998 the salary of a chancellor of a ministry – the equivalent of a permanent secretary – was 12,500 EEK (c. € 800) (the nominal highest salary of civil servants) and the district judge's salary was set at 1.15 times the chancellor's salary. In 2000 the salary of a chancellor of a ministry was the same 12,500 EEK (€ 800), but now the chancellor receives an additional work-related payment, bringing actual remuneration to 19,000 EEK (c. € 1,215). The judge's salary is still tied to the nominal salary of 12,500 EEK (c. € 800) and therefore judges receive the same salary as in 1998, that is less than 0.76 times the chancellor's actual salary in 2000.

[61] Legal Status of the Judges Act, Art. 36; RT 1991, 38, 473; RTI 2000, 40, 251. Judges pay state rent and utilities for the housing provided.

[62] Information from Acting President of the Estonian Judges Association, 9 March 2001.

judiciary, which is generally opposed to it; since judicial salaries will remain frozen until the Act is passed, judges may feel an incentive to limit their criticism in order to allow its passage. The Estonian Association of Judges has criticised the scheme to tie any increase of judges' remuneration to adoption of the Draft Act.[63]

*Court Employees:* The remuneration of civil servants employed in the judicial branch is poorer than that of similarly situated civil servants in any other branch or other constitutionally established institution. The salaries of civil servants employed in the courts are paid strictly in accordance with the salary scale of state public servants (their salary is approximately the average Estonian salary). Unlike the courts, other institutions have the opportunity to increase the salary of similarly situated employees by up to 50 percent.[64] These relatively lower salaries make employment in courts less attractive and may increase the susceptibility of court personnel to corruption.

---

[63] Letter from the Estonian Association of Judges to all members of the European Association of Judges, 14 February 2001. See <http://eky.just.ee/markel_eng.htm> (accessed 11 June 2001).

[64] Public Service Act, RTI 1999, 7, 112, Arts. 37–45.

## V. Judicial Office

### A. The Selection Process

The selection process for new judges includes significant representation from the judiciary as well as the executive. The current selection process seems well balanced, but recent unsuccessful attempts by the Ministry of Justice to enlarge its role suggest that the executive has not fully accepted the logic and value of an independent selection process; indeed, the Draft Courts Acts expands his powers of appointment.

Applicants[65] are required to successfully complete an examination before a commission composed of three district court judges and three regional court judges appointed by the General Conference of Judges, three Supreme Court justices appointed by the Supreme Court sitting *en banc*, a representative of the Ministry of Justice appointed by the Minister, and a representative of the University of Tartu Faculty of Law appointed by the Faculty Council.[66] The examination is graded on a pass/fail basis, and the results are presented to the Supreme Court.

The Supreme Court sitting *en banc* then selects the district and regional court judge candidates and proposes up to three candidates per vacancy to the State President. Almost invariably only one candidate is nominated to the State President, who then decides on appointments.

The State President is not required to provide any reasons for his decision about appointing – or not appointing – a nominee, and the current State President has never offered any. Until now, no major controversy has arisen over the State President's choices for the bench and no allegations that political parties influenced his decisions have been aired.[67]

In order to prepare for a judicial post, a qualified individual may, before taking the exam or after failing it, elect to participate in a training program organised by the Supreme Court lasting up to two years. No resources have been directly budgeted by the Supreme

---

[65] Legal Status of Judges Act enumerates the credentials required to qualify an individual for a judgeship: a university law degree, Estonian citizenship, and high moral standards; Legal Status of Judges Act, Art. 3; RT 1991, 38, 473; RTI 2000, 40, 251.

[66] Legal Status of Judges Act, Art. 10; RT 1991, 38, 473; RTI 2000, 40, 251.

[67] The State President is required to suspend his membership in political parties during his period in office. The current State President is not explicitly connected with any political party.

Court for the training and remuneration of the participants, but resources have been allocated to the Ministry of Justice for this purpose.[68]

In 1998, the Ministry of Justice attempted to arrogate to itself the power to select the candidates for judicial training and, by extension, the selection of future judges. The Ministry issued a regulation about how to select candidates for judicial training and according to that regulation selected candidates for judicial training. In discussions with the Ministry, the judiciary and legal scholars maintained that this action was unconstitutional, since there is no law authorising the Justice Ministry to regulate or perform such a selection. Ultimately, the Ministry of Justice annulled its regulation;[69] since then no new candidates for the training have been selected.[70] However, at the end of April 2001 the Supreme Court announced a competition for five new candidates for judicial training.[71]

## 1. *Court Presidents*

Presidents of district courts are appointed from among the judges of each court by the Minister of Justice with the approval of the Supreme Court.[72] Presidents of the regional courts are appointed from among the judges of a particular court by the Parliament on the proposal of the Minister of Justice and with the consent of the Supreme Court.[73] The presidents of both courts are appointed to unlimited terms; there are no regulations about procedures for their release.[74]

---

[68] State Budget Act for the Year 2001, RTI 2001, 4, 11. According to the Draft Courts Act, a trainee for the position of judge is to be appointed by the Minister of Justice on the recommendation of the Judge's Examination Commission. According to the draft law, the Judge's Examination Commission will be composed of one district judge, one regional court judge, two justices of the Supreme Court, one legal scholar, one representative of the Ministry of Justice and one member of the Bar Association; Bill No. 607; The Courts Act, 28 November 2000, Art. 70, <http://www.riigikogu.ee/otsimine.html>, in Estonian (accessed 11 June 2001).

[69] Regulation of the Minister of Justice, 06 May 1998, About the Rules of Selection of the Candidates for Judicial Training, RTL 1998, 165/166, 630, invalid since 18 July 1999; RTL 1999, 109, 1399.

[70] Information from Vice Chancellor of the Ministry of Justice, 9 April 2001.

[71] See <http://www.nc.ee/rkis/uudised/2001/05/#i105>, in Estonian (accessed 11 June 2001).

[72] Courts Act, Art. 16(4); RT 1991, 38, 472; RTI 2001, 21, 113.

[73] Courts Act, Art. 20(4); RT 1991, 38, 472; RTI 2001, 21, 113.

[74] "Release" is distinguished from "removal"; release is based on some objective criteria, but not on a culpable act of a judge that has to be proven in a special proceeding. In all likelihood the Courts Act would be interpreted to mean that the institution empowered to appoint a president is also empowered to release him.

The Draft Courts Act would empower the Minister of Justice to appoint both presidents of district courts, as now, and presidents of regional courts – expanding rather than limiting the executive's influence on the courts. District court presidents would be appointed to five-year terms and regional court presidents to seven-year terms; limiting presidents' terms, especially if there is a possibility of re-appointment, increases their vulnerability to influence from the executive.

## 2. Supreme Court

Candidates for posts on the Supreme Court are elected by the Parliament on the proposal of the President of the Supreme Court. The President himself is elected by Parliament on the proposal of the State President, without any consultation with the judiciary. There is no requirement that candidates for the Court must have served as judges prior to appointment.[75] These appointments are especially significant because the Parliament relies on the President of the Supreme Court's proposals in electing the other members of the Supreme Court, and the State President relies on the proposals of the plenary session of the Supreme Court in appointing all other judges.

The Parliament is, of course, an openly political body. In the process of appointing Supreme Court justices, members of Parliament have not volunteered any explicitly partisan explanations for their votes. However, the Parliament has in some cases not appointed candidates who have been associated with opposition political parties.

## B. Security of Tenure, Transfer, Retirement and Removal

Most rules regulating the judge's career path are well-designed to protect independence. However, the probationary period for new judges includes no standardised or transparent norms of evaluation, allowing the Judges' Examination Commission discretionary power to remove the judge, giving the judge strong incentives to please the Commission.

## 1. Secure Tenure

The Constitution provides that judges shall be appointed for life.[76] There are no provisions for appointing temporary judges. However, during the first three years of

---

[75] Legal Status of Judges Act, RT 1991, 38, 473; RTI 2000, 40, 251.
[76] CONST. REP. ESTONIA, Art. 147.

his appointment, a judge may be determined unfit for duty. Otherwise, probationary judges have the same status as other judges. There is no need for new appointment if this provision is not invoked. The Judges' Examination Commission provides opinion on the judge's fitness for the bench; however, there is no regulation governing complaints against release.

The rationale for the three-year probationary period is that it is not possible to determine whether individuals are fit for a judicial post before they have some years of experience. The period may arguably be unconstitutional, but to date the two judges who have been released on these grounds have not filed complaints. This in effect allows the Judges' Examination Commission to remove a judge at its discretion during the probationary period, which creates a strong incentive for new judges to make their rulings conform with the Judges' Examination Commission's expectations. If a probationary period is kept, evaluative criteria must be explicit and neutral, and should not be based on the substantive outcomes of decisions a judge has taken.

Supreme Court justices are appointed for life. They may also be elected to the Constitutional Review Chamber (which acts as the Constitutional Court) by the Supreme Court *en banc* for five-year terms, and can be re-elected. This creates an incentive for Review Chamber judges seeking re-election to rule in a manner that meets the expectations of their colleagues on the Supreme Court.

## 2. *Transfer*

There are no fixed criteria for the assignment or transfer of judges. However, judges cannot be transferred from one court to another without their consent, even for disciplinary reasons. The Supreme Court has the power to transfer a judge from one court to another of the same level with the consent of the judge and the Minister of Justice.[77] Presidents of regional courts and the Supreme Court are authorised to transfer a member of one Chamber to another Chamber within the same court for up to three months.[78]

## 3. *Retirement*

The mandatory retirement age is five years after the general retirement age. Upon reaching the mandatory retirement age, judges are released on the recommendation of the President of the Supreme Court.

---

[77] Legal Status of Judges Act, Art. 7(8); RT 1991, 38, 473; RTI 2000, 40, 251.

[78] Courts Act, Art. 22(2); RT 1991, 38, 472; RTI 2001, 21, 113.

## 4. Removal

The Constitution provides that judges may be released only on grounds and according to the procedures provided by law.[79] Judges may be released from office by the body that appointed them on the recommendation of the President of the Supreme Court only on certain specified grounds, including incapacity due to health, a reorganisation of the court system, or if circumstances arise which preclude the judge from continuing in office (such as loss of citizenship, conviction for an intentional crime,[80] or membership in a political party).[81]

Judges may be removed from office only by a court judgement.[82] In disciplinary cases, removal is possible if the Disciplinary Commission decides that the judge has to be removed and the Supreme Court sanctions the decision *en banc*.[83]

## 5. Lustration

There are no special lustration procedures for removal of judges active during the communist period, but certain provisions have served to discourage communist-era judges from remaining in office. All of the judges who had sat on the bench during the communist period and wished to continue serving had to re-apply for their positions and go through the ordinary appointment procedures (except the examination). The State President refused to appoint ten judges, that is, 15 percent of those communist-era judges who had applied for re-appointment.[84]

In addition, all judges are required to take an oath that they have not served, or been an agent of, a security organisation, intelligence or counterintelligence service of the armed forces of a State that has occupied Estonia, nor participated in the persecution or repression of persons because of their political beliefs, disloyalty, social class, or service in the civil or defence service of the Republic of Estonia.[85] Because Soviet rule in Estonia is legally

---

[79] CONST. REP. ESTONIA, Art. 147.

[80] Conviction for an intentional offence is a ground for release and and not removal because the offence has been already proven in separate criminal proceedings.

[81] Legal Status of Judges Act, Arts. 26–27, RT 1991, 38, 473; RTI 2000, 40, 251.

[82] CONST. REP. ESTONIA, Art. 147.

[83] See Section V.D.

[84] R Maruste, "Kohtureform – kas lopu alguses voi alguse lopus?" ("Court reform – in the beginning of the end or in the end of the beginning?"), *Juridica*, 1994, No. 5.

[85] Oath of Clear Conscience Act, RT 1992, 31, 408.

characterised as an occupation, any judge who co-operated with the security or military forces of the Soviet Union would be unable to take the oath in good faith. Some judges who felt that they could not take the oath did not apply for re-appointment. No data about how many judges refrained from applying for re-appointment on these grounds is available. No judges have been accused of having acted in a manner contrary to the oath; a judge believed to have so acted would be tried in an ordinary court, and if found guilty, would be released from service according to ordinary procedures.[86]

## C. Evaluation and Promotion

There are no provisions regulating the promotion of judges. Promotion of a judge to a higher court is possible only through the ordinary appointment process. In practice, the promotion of judges is based primarily on substantive criteria, such as professional ability, integrity, and experience, but there is no law codifying these informal criteria. The provisions for appointment to the regional courts and the Supreme Court – in effect, a form of promotion – are described in V.A. As a consequence, there are some limited political restraints to judicial independence in the selection and promotion process.

There are no pre-established rules for the appraisal of judges' performance. In practice, both the number of cases decided and the reversal rate on appeal are used to assess a judge's performance. The reversal rate is not a formal criterion for promotion, but the Supreme Court obviously considers it along with other criteria in proposing a candidate for a higher court position.[87]

## D. Discipline

The disciplinary rules allow the executive considerable discretion in initiating proceedings – a system which would not be necessary if the executive's role in administration were more limited in general.

### 1. Liability

Damages arising from a judgement issued contrary to law are paid by the State – thus judges are insulated against undue economic pressures stemming from the quality or acceptability of their decisions.

---

[86] Oath of Clear Conscience Act. RT 1992, 31, 408; Art. 9.

[87] Data from discussions in the Judges' Examination Commission.

Judges can be charged with a criminal offence and arrested only on the order of the State President acting on a proposal of the Supreme Court.[88] Supreme Court justices and the President of the Supreme Court can be charged with a criminal offence and arrested on a proposal by the Legal Chancellor[89] to which a majority of the members of the Parliament must give their assent.[90] Thus judges are institutionally insulated against direct interventions by the executive in the form of trumped-up criminal charges.

## 2. Disciplinary Procedures

Court presidents and the Ministry of Justice supervise the conduct and behaviour of district and regional judges. Disciplinary proceedings may be initiated against any judge or justice by the President of the Supreme Court, against judges of district and regional courts by the Minister of Justice, and against the President of the Supreme Court by the Supreme Court *en banc*. Disciplinary cases are then heard by the Disciplinary Commission, to which the district courts, regional courts, and the Supreme Court each elect three of their members.[91] The Disciplinary Commission hears cases sitting in panels of three to five judges.

The Disciplinary Commission may apply various sanctions: warning, reprimand, fine of up to a month's salary and removal from office. Removal from office has to be sanctioned by the Supreme Court *en banc*. The Statute of the Disciplinary Commission regulating the Commission's procedures is adopted by the Supreme Court.[92] A judge whose behaviour is examined by the Disciplinary Commission has the right to be heard and may have legal assistance. Decisions of the Disciplinary Commission may be appealed to the Supreme Court where appeals are heard by the Court *en banc*.[93]

There are three grounds for disciplinary action: 1) breach of rules of procedure;[94] 2) behaviour which brings discredit upon the judicial system; or 3) other transgressions in office. Only the first two grounds have been used bring disciplinary charges; out of

---

[88] Legal Status of Judges Act, Art.18 (1), RT 1991, 38, 473; RTI 2000, 40, 251.

[89] The Legal Chancellor is an independent public official, appointed by the Parliament, whose main functions are: 1) to examine concordance of adopted legal acts to the Constitution, and 2) to act as an ombudsman.

[90] Legal Status of Judges Act, Art.18 (2), RT 1991, 38, 473; RTI 2000, 40, 251.

[91] Legal Status of Judges Act, Arts. 19-23, RT 1991, 38, 473; RTI 2000, 40, 251.

[92] See <http://www.nc.ee/riigikohus>, in Estonian (accessed 11 June 2001).

[93] Statute of the Disciplinary Commission.

[94] Insignificant breaches of the rules of procedure are not grounds for disciplinary proceedings.

seven cases heard between 1999 and 2001, five were initiated on the grounds of a breach of procedural rules and two on the grounds of behaviour discrediting the judicial system.

As was noted above,[95] the Ministry of Justice's authority to initiate disciplinary proceedings against a judge may hinder judicial independence, especially considering the Ministry's various other forms of involvement with and influence over the judiciary. However, the fact that proceedings are actually heard by the Disciplinary Commission, whose members are selected only by the courts, mitigates this potential harm to some degree.

The Association of Judges has adopted Judges' Rules of Behaviour. Although judges customarily obey them, the Rules have no official standing since the Association is a non-governmental organisation and there has been no delegation of power to the Association to adopt any generally binding rules.

---

[95] See Section III.

# VI. Intra-Judicial Relations

## A. Relations with Superior Courts

District court judges enjoy full discretion in deciding cases brought before them within the framework provided by law; higher court judges have no opportunity to dictate the outcome of a case, outside the normal process of appellate review.

At higher instances, cases are reviewed strictly within the boundaries of the regulations governing appeal and cassation. A superior court can proceed beyond the appeal or cassation stage only if statutorily defined defects in the judgement or the composition of the original court are found.[96] A superior court is authorised to amend or annul a lower court's judgement in full or in part and issue a new judgement without referring the matter for a new hearing, or to annul the judgement in full or in part and refer the matter to the court of first instance for a new hearing.[97] However, a higher court does not have authority to give a lower court binding instructions on what has to be rectified on retrial.

The Supreme Court does not issue compulsory clarifications of laws binding for the courts of general jurisdiction. Rather, the lower courts recognise the authority of higher courts by citing the judgements of higher courts; it is extraordinary for a lower court to disagree consciously with a prior judgement of a higher court in a similar case, but it is not forbidden and does sometimes happen in practice.

There is no subordination between judges on different levels in terms of the substantive administration of justice outside of the appeals process. There are no appointed supervisors in higher courts to act as mentors to or inspectors of lower court judges. Higher court judges are occasionally consulted on legal matters by the judges of lower courts, but there is no information from which to conclude that such consultations have involved specific pending cases. (A large proportion of higher court judgements are published on the Internet, a task fully managed by the courts; inevitably, publication of these judgements influences lower court judgements, but this influence cannot be regarded as improper.)

---

[96] Such a defect may be found if: (1) the matter was adjudicated by an unlawful panel of the court; (2) the decision of the court concerns a person who was not summoned to court pursuant to the requirements of law; or (3) the court issued a decision concerning the rights and obligations of a person who was not involved in the matter under consideration. See Code of Criminal Appeal and Cassation Procedure, Arts. 39, 49; RT1 1993, 50, 695; RTI 2000, 86, 542.

[97] Code of Criminal Appeal and Cassation Procedure, Arts. 32, 63; RT1 1993, 50, 695; RTI 2000, 86, 542.

Of course, the various administrative powers of appointment and supervision noted elsewhere in this Report may unduly affect lower court judges' decision-making. Superior court judges are informally consulted before a person is nominated for a position on their court;[98] the fact that a lower court judge knows that these consultations will take place when he/she applies for a position on a higher court may influence that judge's judgements. However, this influence appears to be minor, and moreover, making nominations without such consultations would involve perhaps even more serious incursions on judicial independence, as it would reduce higher court judges' ability to influence the promotion process, leaving it in the hands of the executive.

Because Constitutional Review Chamber judges are elected – and re-elected – by other Supreme Court judges, those interested in re-election may seek to rule in a manner that meets the expectations of their colleagues on the Supreme Court.[99]

## B. Case Management and Relations with Court Presidents

District judges are not dependent on the court president for obtaining the benefits to which they are entitled. There are no circumstances in which the court president's assessment of a judge's performance is legally required. Court presidents do assess district judges' performance in practice, however, and occasionally they are asked to provide their assessment in matters concerning promotion, disciplinary proceedings or removal from office. In general, presidents are consulted before proposals for appointment are made. This may create a risk to the internal independence of judges, but as there have to be some procedures for assessment and someone has to be contacted to give information about a judge's performance, court presidents are one of the sources of information least dangerous to judicial independence, especially as their assessment is not binding.

Court presidents cannot control individual judges' trial calendar, although they do determine the dates that trial judges can take their vacation,[100] and they submit proposals to the Minister of Justice for extraordinary unpaid leave.[101]

Court presidents do have some influence on the assignment of judges within their courts. Presidents of regional courts present proposals to the Supreme Court about

---

[98] Data from discussions in the Judges' Examinations Commission.
[99] See Section V.B.1.
[100] The Legal Status of Judges Act regulates the length of vacation.
[101] Statute of the County, City and Administrative Courts, Subsection 6.8; RTL 1995, 78.

assignment of regional judges to Chambers and appointment of the presidents of the Chambers; presidents of regional courts and the Supreme Court are authorised to transfer a member of one Chamber to another Chamber for up to three months.[102]

Since March 2000 cases are assigned to judges in a random order,[103] and in a number of courts cases are assigned by computers running special software. If some judges are specialists in certain fields of law, all specialised cases are distributed among these judges randomly.[104] Hence, "judge shopping" is almost unknown; there have been some indications, though, that prosecutors' applications to place a suspect into custody are filed taking into account which judge is on duty.

Once assigned, a case can be re-assigned to another judge only if the first judge is excused or recuses himself.[105] If a judge is removed or released from office, or is unable to perform his duties for an extended period of time due to illness, his cases are assigned anew to some other judge according to case-assignment rules.

Otherwise, there are no other formal rules regulating caseloads of individual judges. As a result the caseload of judges differs greatly from court to court; there are no rules to reassign cases to alleviate a judge's caseload simply on the grounds of overload. The only rule pertaining to case flow management is that cases have to be assigned at random.

---

[102] Courts Act, Art. 22(2) ; RT 1991, 38, 472; RTI 2001, 21, 113.

[103] Courts Act, Art. 71; RT 1991, 38, 472; RTI 2001, 21, 113.

[104] Earlier the assignment of cases was not regulated and very often cases were assigned by the court president.

[105] See e.g. Code of Criminal Procedure, Arts. 20, 26; RTI 2000, 56, 369; RTI 2001, 3, 9.

## VII. Enforcement

Judicial decisions are quite often criticised in the media, but despite the criticism judicial decisions are respected. There have been no cases in which the Government has failed to comply with a court decision; criminal court judgements are unequivocally executed. Judges' jurisdiction to oversee execution of civil and administrative judgements was revoked in April 2001, and private execution, by individuals appointed by the Minister of Justice but receiving their income from the liable party, was introduced.[106]

---

[106] Civil Execution Officer Act. RTI 2001, 16, 69.

OPEN SOCIETY INSTITUTE 2001

# Judicial Independence in Hungary

MONITORING THE EU ACCESSION PROCESS: JUDICIAL INDEPENDENCE

# Table of Contents

Executive Summary ................................................. 188

I. Introduction .................................................. 191

    A. Politicisation of the Commitment
to Judicial Reform ..................................... 191
        1. Public Criticism
by Government Officials ..................... 191
        2. The 1999 Amendments and Delayed
Creation of the Appeals Courts .......... 192
        3. Extension of the Lustration Law ........ 193
        4. Executive Control
of the Budget Process ........................ 194

    B. Outlines of the Judicial System ................. 194

II. Constitutional and Legal Foundations
of Judicial Independence ................................ 197

    A. Guarantees of the Separation
of Powers and Judicial Independence ....... 197

    B. Representation of the Judiciary ................ 198

    C. Rules on Incompatibility ......................... 199

    D. Judges' Associations ................................. 200

III. Administration of the Court System
and Judicial Independence ............................ 202

IV. Financial Autonomy and Level of Funding .... 205

    A. Budgeting Process .................................... 205

    B. Work Conditions ...................................... 206

    C. Compensation .......................................... 207

| V. | Judicial Office | 211 |
|---|---|---|
| | A. Selection | 211 |
| | B. Tenure, Retirement, Transfer and Removal | 213 |
| |    1. Tenure | 213 |
| |    2. Retirement | 213 |
| |    3. Transfer | 214 |
| |    4. Removal | 214 |
| | C. Evaluation and Promotion | 215 |
| | D. Discipline | 217 |
| |    1. Liability | 217 |
| |    2. Disciplinary Procedures | 218 |
| VI. | Intra-Judicial Relations | 220 |
| | A. Relations with Superior Courts | 220 |
| | B. Case Management and Relations with Court Presidents | 221 |
| VII. | Enforcement | 223 |

# Judicial Independence in Hungary

## Executive Summary

Hungary has made very significant progress in creating a truly independent judiciary. Basic guarantees of independence and the functional separation of powers among the branches are firmly established in constitutional jurisprudence; broad powers of administration have been located in an autonomous National Council of Justice. In general, respect for the principles of judicial independence and the role of judges in a free society are accepted by politicians and the public.

However, the positive changes initiated in the early 1990s and advanced by the reforms of 1997 are not yet finished, or have even been partly reversed. There is concern that the Government has unduly politicised judicial reform in a manner that undermines its commitment to judicial independence. In particular, public criticism of the judiciary by Government officials, the delays in establishing appellate courts and the extension of lustration laws to the judiciary give cause for concern, as does the executive's continued control of the budget process.

*Politicisation of the Commitment to Judicial Reform*

Judicial reform appears to be increasingly politicised, threatening the social and political consensus necessary to protect the judiciary's separate and independent status.

Since passage of the 1997 reforms, Government officials have increasingly complained that this separation of the judiciary from the political branches has not been effective in practice. Members of the executive have criticised judges' decisions for their leniency, blaming them for an increase in crime, and have bemoaned publicly the fact that the reforms cut ties between the judiciary and the executive. While criticism by officials of other branches is perfectly reasonable in a free society, in the context of reasserted executive influence in areas affecting the judiciary, such comments raise questions about the Government's commitment to the judiciary's independence.

*Delayed Establishment of Appeals Courts*

In 1999 Parliament amended the 1997 reforms, delaying and scaling back the establishment of the appellate courts – a decision whose constitutionality has been questioned. Such delay and backtracking in institutional reform increase the uncertainty the judiciary faces in its relations with the other branches, and can threaten the judiciary's fundamental independence.

*Extension of the Lustration Law*

Lustration screening rules introduced during the transition from communism have recently been extended to the judiciary. Coming at such a remove in time from the fundamental social and political changes which normally justify such interventions, and in light of the increasing criticisms of judges made by political figures, these new lustration rules may undermine the independence of long-serving individual judges; more generally, they may be seen as an improper attempt by the political branches to signal disapproval of the judiciary.

*Control of the Budget Process*

The executive retains strong influence over the financing of the judiciary through its effective control of the budget process. Despite the National Council of Justice's formal right to prepare a draft budget, it is the Government that submits a draft courts budget to Parliament and that has the power to provide supplementary funds to the courts from State reserves when needed.

In addition to these issues, the following issues of particular concern are discussed in the body of the Report:

*Problems with the Power of the National Council of Justice*

Court administration has been removed from the executive and placed in the National Council of Justice, an independent body in which judges have strong representation. This has reduced the threat of executive interference, although problems of intra-judicial independence are consequently greater, and the administrative burdens on judges have not decreased.

A number of judges have criticised the fact that the President of the Supreme Court is at the same time the President of the National Council of Justice. The President of the Supreme Court has an obligation to maintain a posture of neutrality towards the legislative and executive branches, while the President of the Council cannot avoid being drawn into political conflicts.

Since the National Council of Justice meets only once a month, the Office of the National Council of Justice runs many of its operations. Some observers assert that the real power rests with this office, which has inherited many staff members from the now defunct courts department within the Ministry of Justice.

*Working Conditions*

Investment in court infrastructure has not been sufficient, and working conditions are sub-standard. The number of court personnel has not kept pace with the increase in the courts' caseload, and judges are overburdened.

*Probationary Period*

Judges' tenure is insufficiently protected at the start of their careers, when they serve a three-year probationary period and are not granted irremovability.

*Performance-Based Awards*

Certain pay increases are linked to evaluation in a manner that may compromise judges' decisional independence.

*Enforcement*

Enforcement of judgements is unsatisfactory. Public criticism of the judiciary is linked to difficulties in executing property rights decisions, while judges complain that the police often fail to implement orders to find defendants. Inadequate enforcement reduces public support for and reliance on judicial processes, which in turn can weaken political support for maintaining an independent judiciary.

## I. Introduction

Hungary has made very significant progress in creating a truly independent judiciary. Basic guarantees of independence and the functional separation of powers among the branches are firmly established in the constitutional jurisprudence, as are clear rules concerning the careers of judges; broad powers of administration have been located in an autonomous National Council of Justice. In general, respect for the principles of judicial independence and the role of judges in a free society are accepted by politicians and the public.

However, the changes initiated in the early 1990s and advanced by the reforms of 1997 are, in many respects, not yet finished, or have even been partly reversed. There is some concern that the Government has unduly politicised judicial reform in a manner that undermines its commitment to judicial independence. In particular, the unfinished creation of appellate courts, and the extension of lustration laws to the judiciary give cause for concern, as does the executive's continued control of the budget process.

### A. Politicisation of the Commitment to Judicial Reform

The subject of judicial reform appears to be increasingly politicised, weakening the social and political consensus necessary to protect the judiciary's separate and independent status. In the past few years, several different factors – public criticism of the judiciary by government officials, delays in the creation of appeals courts, the extension of lustration screening laws, and continuing executive control of the judiciary's budget – have combined to threaten the progress made in establishing truly independent courts.

#### 1. *Public Criticism by Government Officials*

The judicial reforms of the early 1990s and 1997[1] resulted in more clearly defined relationships among the branches, strong judicial autonomy, and significant improvement in judges' social status. However, since passage of the 1997 reforms Government officials have increasingly complained that this separation of the judiciary from the political branches has not been effective in practice. Members of the executive have criticised

---

[1] In 1997, Act LXVI on the Organisation and Administration of Courts and Act LXVII on the Legal Status and Remuneration of Judges were passed, instituting major reforms in the organisation of the judiciary. They are discussed further in Section I.B; mention in the text of the 1997 reforms refers to these laws.

judges' decisions for their leniency,[2] blaming them for an increase in crime, and have bemoaned publicly the fact that the reforms cut ties between the judiciary and the executive.[3] While criticism by officials of other branches is perfectly reasonable in a free society, in the context of continued or reasserted executive influence in certain areas affecting the judiciary, such comments have raised questions about the Government's commitment to the judiciary's basic independence.

## 2. The 1999 Amendments and Delayed Creation of the Appeals Courts

The appeals courts provided for by the Constitution and Act LXVI of 1997 on the Organisation and Administration of the Courts have not been established yet. Three appeals courts were to have been created by 1 January 1999 and an additional two by 1 January 2001. In 1999, the Government introduced and Parliament passed amendments to the laws regulating the judiciary, and as a result, a single appeals court with country-wide competence is to be established only by 1 January 2003.[4] Some question the constitutionality of the decision, given the Constitution's apparent requirement that there be several such courts.[5] While the principles of judicial independence do not require any given number of court instances, delay and backtracking in institutional reforms themselves can be harmful to the judiciary's fundamental independence, as they increase the uncertainty the judiciary faces in its relations with other branches.

According to the Government, the 1997 reforms had not attached enough importance to the need to ease the workload of district courts.[6] However, rather than address the district courts' workload, the 1999 amendments postponed and limited the planned creation of appellate courts.

---

[2] See e.g. P. Nagy, "Az osszetort tablak felett" ("Above the broken tablets"), Nepszabadsag (Weekend Section), 30 September 2000, p. 22 (citing the Minister of Justice's criticisms of court decisions, her suggestions that the courts had purposefully delayed a criminal case, and her statement that "[j]udicial independence cannot serve as a screen.").

[3] For example, the current Prime Minister's chief advisor described the existence of the National Council of Justice as an "absurdity, because in Hungary there is not judicial autonomy, but a judicial monopoly." P. Nagy, "Az osszetort tablak felett" ("Above the Broken Tablets"), Nepszabadsag (Weekend Section), 30 September 2000, p. 22.

[4] Act CX, 1999.

[5] The Constitution refers to appeals *courts*: "In the Republic of Hungary justice is administered by the Supreme Court, appeals courts…" CONST. REP. HUNGARY, 1949, Act No. XX, Art. 45(1).

[6] See the Report of the Minister of Justice on Act CX of 1999, p. 1.

Certainly, a new Government and Parliament have the right to revise laws passed by their predecessors. Still, some legal professionals have expressed concern that the apparent backtracking on some of the basic elements of the 1997 reform may signal a troubling Government readiness to change judicial structures for inappropriate reasons. Together with the other factors outlined here, such an inconsistent policy concerning the organisation of the judiciary may generate a sense of insecurity among judges that can have a negative impact on their independence.

## 3. Extension of the Lustration Law

Lustration screening rules introduced during the initial stages of the transition from communism have recently been extended to the judiciary. Coming at such a remove in time from the fundamental social and political changes which normally justify such interventions, and in light of the increasing criticisms of judges made by political figures, these new lustration rules may undermine the tenure, and therefore the independence, of individual judges long serving under the current order; more generally, they may be seen as an improper attempt by the political branches to signal disapproval of the judiciary.

Only very limited measures were introduced after the fall of the communist regime to force judges to leave office because of decisions they handed down during the communist era; a number of judges retired without any official sanctions or public denunciations. Some measures were introduced – such as acts of nullification declaring null and void any judgements imposed as retribution on the participants in the 1956 Revolution[7] and convictions for political crimes[8] as well as laws providing compensation – but none of these measures directly affected judges.

Ten years after the return to democracy, however, Parliament modified the Law on the Screening of Individuals in Important State Positions."[9] Under the original 1994 Act, only the President of the Supreme Court was subject to screening; in 2000, amendments extended the screening to all judges, public prosecuting attorneys, and those holding leading positions in the media.[10]

Under the Act, a special committee of judges investigates whether an individual served as a political agent (such as an informer for the security service) under the communist

---

[7] See Act XXXVI of 1989.
[8] See Act XXVI of 1990 and Act XI of 1992.
[9] Act XXIII on the Screening of Individuals in Important State Positions, 1994.
[10] Act XCIII, 2000, Art. 2(3).

regime. If evidence indicates that the individual did serve, the committee calls upon the individual to resign. Only individuals who refuse to resign have their names and the cause for the petition to resign published. There is no compulsory removal procedure.[11] All investigation procedures must be completed by 2004.

There can certainly be no objection, on independence principles, to the removal of a judge found to have committed specific serious crimes, or even to the removal of a judge under lustration rules after many years' service if the grounds for dismissal have only recently been uncovered. However, lustration is, by its nature, an extraordinary intervention against individuals who might normally not be removable, and is justified by exigent political circumstances, such as the political transition immediately after 1989. More than ten years after the event, the introduction of such rules at the least raises reasonable concerns that the motivations are more immediate and narrowly political. Because the initiative for expanding lustration at such a late date lay with the Government and Parliament, it may also be seen as an extension of political control over the judiciary, contrary to the spirit of the reform process.

### 4. Executive Control of the Budget Process

The executive retains strong influence over the financing of the judiciary through its effective control of the budget process. Under the current system, despite the National Council of Justice's formal right to prepare a draft budget, in practice it is the Government that submits the draft budget for the courts to Parliament and that has the power to provide supplementary funds to the courts from State reserves when needed.

## B. Outlines of the Judicial System

The reform of the court system and introduction of guarantees of judicial independence over the past decade have been a protracted process. Although courts were not used for political purposes during the decade immediately preceding 1989, the entire political system was based on the principle of unity of power and supremacy of the Communist Party. As a consequence, courts were dependent on political centres of power, with the Ministry of Justice acting as an intermediary and the locus of administrative power over the courts. Initial steps towards dismantling the monopoly of the Party and establishing the rule of law were taken in 1989, prior to the first free elections in 1990.

---

[11] Inasmuch as judges will suffer no penalty save publicity of their past actions, there is no direct compulsion which might impinge upon their decisional independence. However, the stigma attaching to an official investigation and the consequent publicity would presumably be considerable, practically compelling judges to resign.

Since 1990 reforms have gradually eliminated most attributes inherited from the past regime that did not meet the requirements of an independent judiciary. During the early period of Hungary's transformation, however, lingering distrust, lack of institutional safeguards for judicial independence, and relatively low salaries all contributed to the judiciary's low standing in the eyes of the public. Of comparatively lesser priority than other demands of the democratic transition, comprehensive reform of the judiciary only took place in 1997, with the passage of the Act on the Organisation and Administration of Courts,[12] and the Act on the Legal Status and Remuneration of Judges.[13]

Justice is administered by a four-tier system of courts: the Supreme Court, the appeal courts, the regional courts including the Budapest Municipal Court, and the district courts.[14] In addition, there are labour courts and military tribunals.

District courts are courts of first instance. Regional courts, including the Budapest Municipal Court,[15] function both as first instance courts and as appeals instance for cases arising in the district courts. Appeal courts – which have yet to be established – will have no first instance jurisdiction, but instead will adjudicate appeals against decisions of the regional courts.

The Supreme Court reviews decisions handed down by the regional and appellate courts. In addition, it reviews final decisions if these are challenged through an extraordinary remedy and adopts "uniformity decisions" and publishes decisions on issues of principle.[16] The Supreme Court is the highest judicial body but it has no central administrative functions; however, the president of the Supreme Court also serves as the President of the National Council of Justice.

Labour courts and military tribunals are part of the ordinary court system on the district and regional level.[17] Military panels have only very limited jurisdiction over civilians or the police, which does not appear to present any serious concerns for the independence or competence of the ordinary courts.[18]

---

[12] Act LXVI on the Organisation and Administration of Courts, 1997.

[13] Act LXVII on the Legal Status and Remuneration of Judges, 1997.

[14] CONST. REP. HUNGARY, Art. 45(1).

[15] The Budapest Municipal Court has the status of a regional court.

[16] See Act LXVI on the Organisation and Administration of Courts, 1997, Arts. 27–29.

[17] See Act LXVI on the Organisation and Administration of Courts, 1997, Art. 19(3); Art. 20(5); Art. 23(2).

[18] Civilians are only tried in military courts when they are co-accused with a member of the military, and the offences cannot be severed. Military courts may try policemen only for offences of a so-called "military" nature, such as refusal to obey orders.

The number of judges increased steadily between 1990 and 2000, from 1,611 to 2,512.[19] The number of new cases reaching the courts of first instance also increased from 1991 to 2000,[20] primarily as a result of the courts' broadened competence. However, because of the increase in the number of judges, the average caseload has not changed significantly since 1992, and the courts are expected to catch up with the existing backlog of cases by 2002.[21]

*The Constitutional Court*: The Constitutional Court is not part of the ordinary court system. The Court's decisions reviewing the constitutionality of norms have *erga omnes* effect and cannot be appealed. Its jurisdiction includes *ex ante* review of bills of Parliament forwarded to it by the State President.[22] The procedure for *ex post* review of constitutionality of laws can be initiated by anyone.[23] Ordinary judges may also initiate *ex post* review and suspend procedures before them if they think that the law to be applied in a specific case is unconstitutional.[24] The Constitutional Court may also review whether a law violates an international treaty,[25] review unconstitutional omission of statutory regulation,[26] and decide conflicts of competence among state agencies and municipalities.[27] The Court has 11 members, elected by Parliament.[28]

---

[19] See information given at the plenary session of the Parliament by the President of the National Council of Justice, 1999, 2000.

[20] See information given at the plenary session of the Parliament by the President of the National Council of Justice, 1999, 2000.

[21] See information given at the plenary session of the Parliament by the President of the National Council of Justice, 2000.

[22] CONST. REP. HUNGARY, Art. 26(4).

[23] CONST. REP. HUNGARY, Art. 32/A(3); Act XXXII of 1989 on the Constitutional Court, Art. 48; Decision 66/1997 (XII. 29.) of the Constitutional Court.

[24] Act XXXII of 1989 on the Constitutional Court, Art. 38.

[25] Act XXXII of 1989 on the Constitutional Court, Arts. 44–47.

[26] Act XXXII of 1989 on the Constitutional Court, Art. 49.

[27] Act XXXII of 1989 on the Constitutional Court, Art. 50.

[28] CONST. REP. HUNGARY, Art. 32/A(4).

## II. Constitutional and Legal Foundations of Judicial Independence

Constitutional and legislative guarantees of judicial independence are well established. The judiciary has a clearly identified representative, and rules separating its functions and its officials from those of the political branches are clearly defined.

### A. Guarantees of the Separation of Powers and Judicial Independence

The judiciary is a separate branch of State power. The Constitutional Court has ruled that there can be no political connection between other branches of the State and the judiciary as there is between the executive and Parliament.[29] Everyone, including other branches, has to obey the judgements of the courts and no one may change, annul or supervise them.[30]

The Constitution declares that "Judges are independent and answer only to the law."[31] A judge's right to make decisions free from all external constraints enjoys an effectively absolute constitutional protection, subject to very limited exceptions.[32] "Judges are independent; they shall render their decisions based on the law, in accordance with their convictions. Judges may not be influenced or instructed in relation to their activities in the administration of justice."[33]

The Constitution also defines the functions of the judiciary – to protect and uphold the constitutional order and the rights and lawful interests of citizens, to impose criminal sanctions, and to review the legality of the decisions of public administration[34] – in such a way as to further define its separateness from the other branches. Statutory law further provides that administration of justice is exclusively the responsibility of the courts.[35]

---

[29] Decision 51/1992 (X. 23) of the Constitutional Court.

[30] Jozsef Petretei, Magyar Alkotmanyjog II. Allamszervezet. (Hungarian Constitutional Law II. Institutions.). Dialog-Campus, Pecs, 2000. p. 206.

[31] CONST. REP. HUNGARY, Art. 50(3).

[32] Decision 17/1994 of the Constitutional Court, relying on CONST. REP. HUNGARY, Art. 50(3). The Constitutional Court has noted two exceptions of external control: the European Court of Human Rights, and the institution of constitutional complaint.

[33] Act LXVI of 1997 on the Organisation and Administration of Courts.

[34] CONST. REP. HUNGARY, Chap. X.

[35] Act LXVI of 1997 on the Organisation and Administration of Courts.

Below the Constitution, the Act on the Organisation and Administration of Courts,[36] and the Act on the Legal Status and Remuneration of Judges, both passed in 1997, incorporate basic guarantees of judicial independence.[37] A two-thirds parliamentary majority is required for the enactment and amendment of these two basic Acts,[38] providing some additional protection against short-term political intrusion on the guarantees they contain.

## B. Representation of the Judiciary

The National Council of Justice is the supreme representative of judicial power and is responsible for the administration of the courts.[39] In addition, self-governing judicial councils representing judges also participate in the administration of the courts.[40]

The National Council of Justice, constitutionally established as the organ responsible for the administration of the judiciary, conducts a number of representative activities: it proposes legislation; gives its opinion on bills relating to the judiciary; and represents the courts in legal proceedings. The President of the National Council of Justice is obligated to inform Parliament on an annual basis regarding the general state of the courts and the administrative activities of the Council.[41] The president may not be questioned, however. The Council also submits to the Government a budget proposal for the following year and also provides the Government with an accounting of the funds allocated to the judiciary in the previous year's budget.[42]

The National Council of Justice is composed of fifteen members, including four *ex officio* members, two Members of Parliament, and nine judges. The four *ex officio* members are the Minister of Justice, the Prosecutor General, the President of the National Bar Association, and the President of the Supreme Court, who acts as President of the Council.[43] Two

---

[36] Act LXVI on the Organisation and Administration of Courts, 1997.

[37] Act LXVII on the Legal Status and Remuneration of Judges, 1997.

[38] CONST. REP. HUNGARY, Art. 50(5).

[39] CONST. REP. HUNGARY, Art. 50(4).

[40] Judicial councils are consultative bodies, created at different levels of the court system, providing opinions on personnel matters, such as appointments to judgeships, dismissals, and appointments of judges to judicial leadership positions. See Act LXVI on the Organisation and Administration of Courts, 1997, Art. 77C; Art. 50(4). See also Section III.

[41] Act LXVI on the Organisation and Administration of Courts, 1997, Art. 47.

[42] Act LXVI on the Organisation and Administration of Courts, 1997, Art. 39(b). See Section IV.A.

[43] There is no judicial representation on the highest body administering the prosecutorial service.

Members of Parliament[44] are designated by the Constitutional and Justice Committee and the Budget and Finance Committee, respectively.[45] The nine judges are elected by delegates chosen by all ordinary court judges from among themselves at plenary sessions, with one delegate chosen for every 40 judges.[46] Under this scheme, the nine elected judges and the President of the Council constitute a two-thirds majority on the Council.

A number of judges have criticised the fact that the President of the Supreme Court is at the same time the President of the National Council of Justice. The President of the Supreme Court has an obligation to maintain a posture of neutrality towards the legislative and executive branches. Yet the President of the Council cannot avoid being drawn into political conflicts.[47]

## C. Rules on Incompatibility

The extra-judicial activities of judges are restricted, especially involvement with other branches of the State; such restrictions tend to support the decisional independence and impartiality of judges.

Judges may not be members of political parties or engage in any other political activity. Judges cannot be Members of Parliament[48] or of any national or local legislative organ.[49] A judge may not hold any leading executive position at the national or local level.[50] A judge who is a nominee to a political, state, or local administrative position must suspend judicial activities.[51] Judges are required to inform their employers[52] if they intend to submit their name for nomination.[53] Judges who are elected to such posts have their judgeships terminated *ex lege*.[54] Judges may not be members of arbitration courts.[55]

---

[44] Act LXVI, 1997, Art. 35.
[45] Act LXV, 1997, Art. 35.
[46] Act LXVI on the Organisation and Administration of Courts, 1997, Art. 36(2), (6).
[47] See *Nepszabadsag*, 30 September 2000, pp. 22–23.
[48] CONST. REP. HUNGARY, Art. 20(5).
[49] Act LXVII on the Legal Status and Remuneration of Judges, 1997.
[50] Act LXVII on the Legal Status and Remuneration of Judges, 1997.
[51] Act LXVII on the Legal Status and Remuneration of Judges, Art. 56/A(1).
[52] Act LXVII on the Legal Status and Remuneration of Judges, Art. 57(1).
[53] Act LXVII on the Legal Status and Remuneration of Judges, 1997, Art. 56/A(1).
[54] Act LXVII on the Legal Status and Remuneration of Judges, Art. 57(1).
[55] Act LXVII on the Legal Status and Remuneration of Judges, 1997.

A judge may not hold any position in any entrepreneurial organisation.[56] A judge cannot be a senior officer or member of the supervisory committee of a business company or co-operative, nor can judges be members of a business company with unlimited liability or personally engage in the business operations of the company.[57] Scientific, artistic, literary, educational and technical or creative work is allowed unless it jeopardises a judge's impartiality and independence or creates the appearance of such bias.[58]

Relatives of the president, deputy president, or the head of judicial council or judicial college of a court cannot work as judges at the same court, council or college concerned. A judge concerned must disclose the occurrence of any such conflict of interest without delay.[59]

Further restrictions on judges' conduct help to bolster their impartiality. Judges may not publicly express their opinion on any matter that has been or is being heard in the courts, nor may they inform the media about any matters heard by them. Only the court president or a designee[60] may provide information to the media;[61] regional courts have established press departments that are authorised to provide information to the media. Judges are prohibited from disclosing any state or judicial secrets either during their tenure in the judiciary or after their retirement. Only a legally authorised body[62] can grant exemption from this obligation.

There are no regulations restricting judges' employment after they retire. Judges may not act as an attorney before the court in which they served for two years following their retirement. This restriction does not harm judges' decisional independence, and in fact contributes to the maintenance of serving judges' impartiality.[63]

## D. Judges' Associations

There are a number of voluntary judges' associations, including the Hungarian Association of Judges and separate Associations for judges adjudicating administrative, labour, and

---

[56] Act LXVII on the Legal Status and Remuneration of Judges, 1997.
[57] Act LXVII on the Legal Status and Remuneration of Judges, 1997, Art. 23(2).
[58] Act LXVII on the Legal Status and Remuneration of Judges, Art. 23(1).
[59] Act LXVII on the Legal Status and Remuneration of Judges, Art. 24(3).
[60] See National Council of Justice Resolution, 7/1999.
[61] Act LXVII on the Legal Status and Remuneration of Judges, 1997, Arts. 28(2), 29(1), (2), 24(1), and 27.
[62] Act LXV of 1995 on State and Official Secrets, Art. 18(2).
[63] Act XI of 1998 on Attorneys, Art. 7.

economic matters, and the registration of companies. Their task is primarily to represent the interests of their members. There are very few restrictions on their formation or membership.[64] The primary function of the Hungarian Association of Judges, which was established prior to the political changes in Hungary, is to promote judicial independence and reform of the court system.

Many judges also belong to trade unions. The Trade Union of Judicial Employees represents the interests of judges as well as court staff. The Trade Union of Judicial Employees advocates higher salaries and pensions for judicial employees.

---

[64] However, they cannot engage in political activities. CONST. REP. HUNGARY, Art. 50(3).

## III. Administration of the Court System and Judicial Independence

Administration has largely been removed from the hands of the executive and placed in an independent body in which judges have strong representation. This has largely removed concerns of executive interference, although problems of intra-judicial independence are consequently greater, and the administrative burdens on judges have not decreased.

The National Council of Justice is the central administrative body for the courts; it has decision-making authority over all administrative matters and supervises the administrative activities of the presidents of appellate and regional courts.[65] The Council has the authority to issue regulations, make recommendations and take decisions that are binding on the courts and monitors implementation of its decisions.[66] From its inception in December 1997 the Council has been quite active, adopting numerous rules, regulations, and recommendations.[67] Rulings and regulations issued by the Council pertain mostly to employment issues, such as appointments, dismissals, and transfers, but a number of decisions have dealt with financial questions, budgetary approval, allocation of funds, investments, rewards, and the training of judges. One of the Council's most important rulings to date dealt with the evaluation of judges' performance and the detailed provisions of judicial assessment.

The National Council of Justice is also responsible for all other matters relating to self-governance of courts. The Council gives its consent to the internal administrative regulations of the courts, is responsible for the recruitment of personnel and the training of judges,[68] and also has the right to pass binding regulations for court staff on personnel and budgetary matters, as well as to take decisions for their implementation.

The National Council of Justice also has supervisory competence over the efficiency of courts, and oversees the administrative activity of all court presidents except for the President of the Supreme Court.[69] The Council also has competence to monitor court compliance with administrative rules and observance of procedural deadlines.[70]

---

[65] Act LXVI on the Organisation and Administration of Courts, 1997, Art. 41(2).

[66] Act LXVII on the Legal Status and Remuneration of Judges, 1997, Art. 39(q).

[67] Recommendations and Rulings of the National Council of Justice, published by the Office of the National Council of Justice, Budapest, 2000.

[68] Act LXVI on the Organisation and Administration of Courts, 1997, Arts. 38–41.

[69] Act LXVI on the Organisation and Administration of Courts, 1997, Art. 39(a).

[70] Act LXVII on the Legal Status and Remuneration of Judges, 1997.

*The Office of the National Council of Justice*: Since the National Council of Justice meets only once a month, the Office of the National Council of Justice was established to assist the Council in fulfilling its various functions.[71] The Office of the Council prepares the meetings of the Council, arranges for the implementation of its resolutions and performs administrative duties related to its operation.[72] Critics assert that the real power rests with this office, because the Council is extremely overburdened and relies on the permanent staff at the Office of the Council to prepare draft decisions that it generally adopts. There is a kind of bureaucratic continuity between the now defunct department within the Ministry of Justice responsible for court matters and the Office of the Council that replaced it.

The administration of the judicial system is quite centralised. The large judicial administration on the national level produces numerous regulations and instructions. Combined with the quite time-consuming participation of judges in the extensive system of self-administrative structures (including plenary sessions, judicial councils, and judicial colleges, discussed immediately below), this unnecessarily takes time from judges' core adjudicative duties.

*Other Loci of Administrative Power*: There are also other judicial bodies involved in the administration of the courts.[73] The largest official body of judges is the Plenary Session of judges. The Plenary exists in the Supreme Court, and the appellate and regional courts.[74] The Plenary elects delegates, who in turn elect the members of the National Council of Justice. The Plenary also issues opinions on applications for leading judicial posts at courts where the nomination is within the competence of the Council, and may initiate the dismissal of court leaders.

Judicial councils[75] are elected for six years by the plenary sessions of judges. Judicial councils give opinions on case distribution as well as on all issues related to judges' status (such as appointment, transfer, and removal) as well as on appointments of judicial leaders by

---

[71] Act LXVII on the Legal Status and Remuneration of Judges, 1997, Art. 34(3).

[72] Act LXVII on the Legal Status and Remuneration of Judges, 1997, Art. 55.

[73] See Act on the Organisation and Administration of the Courts.

[74] The members of the Plenary Session of the Supreme Court are judges of the Supreme Court; members of the Plenary Session of Appeal courts are members of the particular appeal court; members of the Plenary session of Judges on a regional level are all judges who hold judicial office in the particular court region either at the regional court or district court of the region. Act LXVI on the Organisation and Administration of Courts of 1997, Art. 78.

[75] Act LXVI on the Organisation and Administration of Courts, 1997, Arts. 82–88.

the President of the Supreme Court, Presidents of appeal and regional courts,[76] and may initiate dismissals of appointees. Judicial councils also give opinions on regulations relating to the internal organisation of courts, and make proposals on drafts of the budget and on allocations.

Judicial colleges are organisations of judges at the Supreme Court, appellate court and regional court level who specialise in specific areas of law.[77] Judicial colleges make proposals and issue opinions on judges' appointments, and make proposals for the appointment of heads and deputy heads of judicial colleges as well as chairmen of the chambers.[78] Judicial colleges also participate in the evaluation of judges.[79]

Regular consultation between the presidents of the regional courts takes place through an informal forum at which questions of judicial administration and practice are discussed. The informal fora facilitate co-ordination among regions.

The day-to-day operations of individual courts are managed by the court presidents together with the National Council of Justice and its Office.

---

[76] Judicial leaders are: presidents and vice-presidents of courts; presidents and vice-presidents of judicial colleges; heads of judicial councils; presidents and vice-presidents of judicial groups. Act LXVI on the Organisation and Administration of Courts, 1997, Art. 62.

[77] Act LXVI on the Organisation and Administration of Courts, 1997, Art. 89.

[78] Court divisions consist of judges specialising in the same area of law on regional, appeal and Supreme Court levels. At county courts there are economic, criminal, administrative and civil divisions. At regional courts there are administrative, civil and criminal divisions, while on the Supreme Court there are administrative, civil and criminal divisions. Act LXVI on the Organisation and Administration of Courts, 1997, Arts. 20, 23, 26.

[79] Act LXVI on the Organisation and Administration of Courts, 1997, Art. 90.

## IV. Financial Autonomy and Level of Funding

The extensive administrative autonomy of the judiciary is somewhat undermined by its continued dependence, in practice, on the executive's control of the budget process. Although the National Council of Justice prepares its own budget, the executive is legally allowed to sidestep this by introducing its own, considerably lower budget. Perhaps as a consequence, investment in court infrastructure has not been sufficient, and working conditions are sub-standard.

### A. Budgeting Process

The National Council of Justice prepares a court budget proposal and submits it to the Government. According to a ruling of the Council,[80] the Office of the National Council of Justice prepares the budget proposal in co-operation with court presidents and conducts negotiations with the Ministry of Finance. The outcome of these negotiations is submitted to the Council, which approves the proposal before submitting it to the Government.

By law, the budget for the courts is presented in a separate chapter of the State budget.[81] If there is any difference between the proposal of the National Council of Justice and the budget bill submitted by the Government to Parliament, the Government is obliged to make a detailed note of the original proposal and state the reason for the difference.[82]

In practice, however, the Government confines itself to presenting its own parallel budget without comments on the judiciary's version; Parliament, in turn, has always passed budgets quite close to the Government version. The draft budget submitted by the Government to Parliament for 1999, 2000, 2001 and 2002 were substantially lower than the proposal put forward by the National Council of Justice; Parliament has passed a budget with roughly the same or only slightly higher allocations than those

---

[80] National Council of Justice Ruling, 4/1998.
[81] Act LXVI on the Organisation and Administration of Courts, 1997, Art. 6.
[82] Act LXVI on the Organisation and Administration of Courts, 1997, Art. 39(b).

contained in the Government version.[83] 0.89 percent of the State budget was allocated for the judiciary in 2000.

Many judges feel that the repeated curtailments of the National Council of Justice's budget proposals is a signal from the Government of dissatisfaction with the judiciary for delays in handling cases, and for allegedly meting out lenient sentences. (By contrast the Public Prosecutor's Service was granted considerable financial appropriations during the same period.)

The Budget Department and the President of the Office of the National Council of Justice monitor court expenditures. In order to cope with "operational disturbances" the President of the Office of the Council may re-allocate money from one court to another. However, the President's discretion is limited by the fact that he or she may only allocate funds that are distinct from court-staff-related expenditures.[84]

The Constitutional Court prepares its own annual budget and submits it directly to Parliament.[85] Although the final decision on the budget remains in the hands of the Parliament, many believe that it would be beneficial if the budgetary process for the judiciary were closer to that of the Constitutional Court.

## B. Work Conditions

The conditions in which judges work are sub-standard. Over the last few decades, insufficient resources have been dedicated to the maintenance of court facilities, and the capacity of most courts is jeopardised as a result. Though significant funds have been spent in recent years on improving court infrastructure,[86] most court buildings are

---

[83] In each of the last three budgets for example, the expenditures budget proposed by the Council and the Government, and approved by Parliament were:

| Year | Council | | Government | | Parliament | |
|---|---|---|---|---|---|---|
| | HUF | € | HUF | € | HUF | € |
| 2000 | 44,122,300 | 175,895 | 34,243,500 | 136,513 | 34,081,600 | 135,867 |
| 2001 | 59,167,100 | 235,872 | 35,586,200 | 141,866 | 36,348,800 | 144,906 |
| 2002 | 57,420,300 | 228,908 | 36,130,400 | 144,035 | 37,636,500 | 150,039 |

The higher figures approved by Parliament in 2001 and 2002 represented the re-instatement of a proposed judicial salary rise not included in the Government proposal.

[84] National Council of Justice Resolution of 4/1998, Art. 8(3).

[85] Act XXXII of 1989 on the Constitutional Court, Art. 2.

[86] In 1999, almost 400 million HUF (c. € 1,564,533) were spent for technical equipment, such as dictaphones, photocopiers and fax machines.

very old and require extensive repair and remodelling. In some courthouses, particularly in Budapest, judges have to cope with a severe shortage of space. There are significant differences in material conditions among regions. There is no norm for minimal logistical conditions, but a proposal is being drafted.

There has been insufficient funding for new judicial and support posts in the last few budgetary cycles, and as a result the number of court personnel (and to a much lesser extent, of judges) has not kept pace with the increase in the courts' caseload during the same period. As a result, in general judges are overburdened. This seriously hampers the work of judges, who have considerable administrative burdens.

The National Council of Justice is authorised to decide on the number of judges and support staff,[87] which it does in consultation with the regional court presidents in order to assess the needs in individual regions. There are no minimal requirements concerning the number of administrative staff, although a proposal is reportedly being drafted by the Office of the National Council of Justice. On average, there are approximately 1.75 staff members for each judge.[88] Since January 2000, an attempt has been made to reduce judges' workload by expanding the authority of judicial clerks.[89]

## C. Compensation

Judges' salaries are satisfactory when compared to those of civil servants, although generally lower than those of legal professionals in the private sector.

A crucial element in the 1997 reforms was the establishment of an adequate base salary for judges, in hopes of attracting new candidates to the bench. Two years after the enactment of these reforms, it seems that the financial disincentives that kept individuals from considering a career on the bench have been removed, and judgeships have become increasingly attractive to lawyers.

The level of compensation of judges is similar to that of state prosecutors. The basic salary of judges is between that of a Member of Parliament and a Government

---

[87] Act LXVI on the Organisation and Administration of Courts, 1997.

[88] Draft annual report of the President of the Office of the National Council of Justice to Parliament, Appendix No. 4.

[89] Draft annual report of the President of the Office of the National Council of Justice to Parliament, Appendix No. 3.

Minister.[90] It should be noted, however, that MPs are entitled to a wider spectrum of additional compensation and benefits, and they have fewer restrictions on their extra-legislative activities than judges. In addition, judges' extra-judicial work (and remuneration) is limited to the scientific, literary, educational, and artistic realms. Overall, judges' salaries are competitive compared to the salaries of public officials, but not when compared to the salaries of lawyers employed in the private sector.

Judges are guaranteed a level of compensation that ensures their independence and is commensurate with the level of responsibility and dignity of judicial office,[91] outlined in detailed rules.[92] The amount of the first salary grade is determined every year in the Act on the Budget.[93] It cannot be lower than it was in the previous year,[94] and the basic salary of a judge must be increased every three years according to a pre-established multiplication factor ranging from one to 1.55.

Court presidents and other leading officials are entitled to additional compensation, which is a fixed percentage of the first salary grade.[95]

In addition to their basic salary, judges receive some guaranteed rewards or bonuses, benefits, and compensation for various expenses. Every judge is entitled to a customary bonus, calculated according to the different levels of the judiciary, and ranging from ten percent for district judges to 40 percent for appellate and Supreme Court judges. One month's additional salary is guaranteed yearly,[96] and anniversary rewards are given to judges at twenty-five, thirty, and forty years of service.[97]

---

[90] In 2000, for example, the first grade basic salary of a judge was 173,200 HUF (c. € 680); a minister's base salary was 183,000 HUF (c. € 717), and a parliamentarian's salary was 140,750 HUF (c. € 552). The amount of a first grade basic salary for a judge in 2001 is 188,350 HUF (c. € 738).

[91] Law on the Legal Status and Remuneration of Judges.

[92] Act LXVII on the Legal Status and Remuneration of Judges, 1997, Arts. 101–121.

[93] There are ten grades altogether. See Act LXVII on the Legal Status and Remuneration of Judges, 1997, Appendix 2.

[94] Act LXVII on the Legal Status and Remuneration of Judges, 1997, Art. 103(2).

[95] Act LXVII on the Legal Status and Remuneration of Judges, 1997, Art. 108, Appendix 3.

[96] Act LXVII on the Legal Status and Remuneration of Judges, 1997, Art. 112(1).

[97] Act LXVII on the Legal Status and Remuneration of Judges 1997, Art. 114.

Supplementary funds are also provided for clothing, meals,[98] and foreign language proficiency training.[99] Other forms of financial support depend on the financial situation of the courts. Housing support,[100] social and recreational support, public transport support and language scholarships fall into this category,[101] which can be dispensed from court funds. The travel costs of judges living outside the city limits are at least partly covered.[102] Resources for these forms of financial support are financed from the savings of the respective courts, and granted variously by the presidents of Supreme Court and regional courts and head of Office of the National Council of Justice.[103]

In 1999, the National Council of Justice provided 70 million HUF (c. € 273,757) worth of loans for judges' housing. Criteria include the interests of the justice system, and the financial and housing situation of the petitioner.[104] The level of such loans depends on the amount the Parliament sets aside in the budget for the courts. There are complaints that local court judges are prevented from applying for promotion to regional courts because the additional financial resources that would be required for such promotions are lacking; in addition, the "interests of the justice system" is an in-sufficiently clear criterion, and could be an avenue for preferential distribution of housing benefits.

The basic compensation system is augmented by a number of rewards based on evaluation of judges' performance, which allow the evaluating authority to favour individual judges in a way that can affect their decisional independence.[105]

---

[98] This allowance may not exceed two percent of the first grade salary. Act LXVII on the Legal Status and Remuneration of Judges, 1997, Art. 118.

[99] For an intermediate level exam four percent, for an advanced level exam eight percent of the first grade salary. Act LXVII on the Legal Status and Remuneration of Judges, 1997, Art. 110.

[100] National Council of Justice Ruling, 1/1998.

[101] According to Act LXVII on the Legal Status and Remuneration of Judges, 1997, Art. 118, it is the National Council of Justice that determines the distribution of these resources. See Ruling 4/1999 of National Council of Justice.

[102] Ruling 4/1999 of the National Council of Justice.

[103] Ruling 4/1999 of National Council of Justice, Art. 1.

[104] National Council of Justice Ruling, 1/1998, Arts. 2 and 5. Loan-requirements not exceeding 300,000 HUF are decided by the Head of the Office of the National Council of Justice; others are decided by a committee of the Council. National Council of Justice Ruling, 1/1998, Art. 4.

[105] See Section IV.C.

There are no special pension schemes for judges.[106] The amount of a judge's pension is roughly one-third of the salary received during the last years of service. In addition, the real value of pensions after years of retirement depends on the inflation rate, which was relatively high throughout the 1990s, and on whether adjustments of pensions to the inflation rate takes place regularly. The National Council of Justice may make contributions to judges' private pension funds.[107]

A reduction in a judge's compensation may only be imposed as a disciplinary punishment arrived at through the established procedures.[108]

---

[106] Act LXXX of 1997 on Social Security and Private Pensions (or Private Pension Funding).

[107] Ruling 4/1999, Art. 5 stipulates that the presidents of the Supreme, appeal and regional courts, in cooperation with the head of ONJC, decide upon the financial support of private pension of judges from the court's budget.

[108] Act LXVII on the Legal Status and Remuneration of Judges, 1997, Art. 79(1); Art. 81.

# V. Judicial Office

## A. Selection

The increase in judicial salaries, the guarantees of judicial independence, and the rising prestige of a judgeship have made a judicial career more attractive than in the past. There are now more candidates than available judicial vacancies. Initial selection procedures for new judges are generally in accord with the requirements of judicial independence. There is some criticism of the National Council of Justice's broad discretion in naming court presidents.

Judicial vacancies are filled through an open application process.[109] Appointment to the bench is a multi-step process, including a clerkship, examinations, secretaryship, probationary judicial appointment, and final appointment.

Law school graduates may be appointed as junior clerks by the president of a regional court for a three-year apprenticeship period;[110] their training is regulated by the Ministry of Justice.[111] After the three-year clerkship, candidates who pass the state professional exam and a vocational exam[112] may be appointed as court secretaries,[113] where they must serve for at least one year, after which they are eligible for nomination. (Candidates who were previously a prosecutor, prosecutorial secretary, attorney, notary public or constitutional court judge, may be directly appointed.[114])

There are no clearly fixed criteria for selection. Supreme, appeal and regional court[115] presidents select candidates for the bench on the basis of a personal interview with the applicant and non-binding opinions provided by the relevant judicial council.[116] Having

---

[109] Act LXVII on the Legal Status and Remuneration of Judges, 1997, Art. 6(1).

[110] Act LXVIII of 1997 on the Justice System Servants, Arts. 3(3), 8(1.e), and 13(1).

[111] Act LXVII on the Justice System Servants, Art. 3(3); Decree of the Ministry of Justice, No. 11, 1999.

[112] The vocational exam measures the physical as well as psychological capabilities of the individual and in general assesses the character and intelligence of the candidate. It consists of an interview and a standardised psychological test. Decree on the Vocational Selection of Judges and Court Clerks, No. 1, 1999 (I.18.).

[113] Act LXVII on the Justice System Servants, Art. 13(1).

[114] Act LXVII on the Legal Status and Remuneration of Judges, 1997, Art. 11.

[115] Presidents of regional courts decide on the selection of district court judges.

[116] Act LXVII on the Legal Status and Remuneration of Judges, 1997, Art. 8.

selected the candidates, the court president recommends them to the National Council of Justice,[117] which in turn forwards its own nominations to the State President.

Judges are first appointed by the State President[118] for three years, after which they may be appointed (again by the State President) for an "indefinite time".[119] The pro-bationary period and the partly discretionary determination about final appointment means that new judges' possibility for securing a permanent position could be conditional on their being politically acceptable.[120]

*Court Presidents*: Special rules and regulations govern selection of the leadership of the judiciary. The President of the Supreme Court is elected by a two-thirds majority vote in Parliament upon the nomination of the State President.[121] Deputy Presidents of the Supreme Court are appointed by the State President on recommendation of the President of the Supreme Court.[122]

The National Council of Justice appoints presidents and deputy presidents of the regional courts and heads of the judicial colleges[123] for six-year terms. (Judicial colleges are established at Supreme Court, appeal, and regional court level and consist of judges practising in the same area of the law, such as criminal, civil, economic, or administrative law.) Regional court presidents appoint the president and deputy president of district and labour courts, and appoint judges to some other positions within the regional and local courts.[124]

Only certain judicial bodies have the right to express opinions on the appointment of court leaders: the plenary session of judges of regional, appeal and the Supreme Court in case of leaders appointed by National Council of Justice; the judicial college in case of the head and deputy head of the college; and the judicial council at each respective level in case of other appointments to leading positions. Moreover, these opinions are not binding;[125] as a result, court presidents and the National Council of Justice have broad discretionary powers over appointments. Some judges have criticised the appointment

---

[117] Act LXVII on the Legal Status and Remuneration of Judges, 1997, Art. 8.

[118] Act LXVII on the Legal Status and Remuneration of Judges, 1997, Art. 2(2).

[119] Act LXVII on the Legal Status and Remuneration of Judges, 1997, Arts. 11–12.

[120] See Section V.B.1.

[121] CONST. REP. HUNGARY, Art. 48 (1).

[122] CONST. REP. HUNGARY, Art. 48 (1).

[123] Act LXVI on the Organisation and Administration of Courts, 1997, Arts. 69–70.

[124] Act LXVI on the Organisation and Administration of Courts, 1997, Art. 70(5).

[125] Act LXVI on the Organisation and Administration of Courts, 1997, Arts. 72(1), and (2).

powers of the Council as excessively discretionary; a number of judges believe that the Council should be required to solicit the consent of other judicial bodies, instead of mere advice.

## B.  Tenure, Retirement, Transfer and Removal

Judges' tenure is insufficiently protected at the beginning of their careers, when they serve a three-year probationary period and are not granted irremovability. The expansion of lustration screening procedures, more than ten years after the transition from communism, represents an unnecessarily political intervention into judges' normal irremovability.

### 1.  *Tenure*

Judges are initially appointed to a fixed three-year term, and do not receive tenure until they are re-appointed by the State President. This system places new judges in a position of considerable insecurity, and can discourage them from issuing decisions which they suppose could be offensive to the entities within and without the judiciary which must approve their continued service.

At the end of the first three years on the bench, a judge's overall performance is evaluated.[126] (Judges who actually perform a judge's functions for less than 18 months during this term can be re-appointed to a second three-year term.)[127] The professional evaluation of judges' performance is regulated by the Law on the Legal Status and Remuneration of Judges[128] and by a ruling of the National Council of Justice,[129] and has the stated purpose of filtering out those who are unable to perform a judge's tasks satisfactorily.

### 2.  *Retirement*

The compulsory retirement age for judges is 70,[130] but judges may choose retirement after they reach age 62, which is the general age of retirement.[131]

---

[126] Act LXVII on the Legal Status and Remuneration of Judges, 1997, Arts. 11–12.
[127] Act CVI, 2000.
[128] Act LXVII on the Legal Status and Remuneration of Judges, 1997, Arts. 47–56.
[129] National Council of Justice Ruling, 5/1998.
[130] Act LXVII on the Legal Status and Remuneration of Judges, 1997, Art. 57(1).
[131] Act XXXIII of 2000.

## 3. Transfer

A judge's consent is necessary for assignment or transfer to a particular court.[132] However, a judge may be temporarily posted without consent to a different court in the interest of the administration of justice once every three years and for a maximum period of one year.[133] The presidents of the regional courts can decide transfers within their region, while the National Council of Justice decides on transfer outside the jurisdiction of a given regional court,[134] but in exercising this prerogative both are obliged to treat all judges equitably.[135] If a judge is to be transferred to a post outside the region he or she is serving in, the Council has to obtain the opinion of the presidents of the affected regional courts.[136]

It is not clear what consequences would follow if a judge refused to be transferred. It is possible, however, that it would constitute a breach of judicial duty and could trigger a disciplinary procedure.[137] Some judicial leaders consider the establishment of a mobile group of judges at the National Council of Justice's disposal as the solution to the uneven caseload distribution in different jurisdictions.[138]

## 4. Removal

The Constitution specifically prohibits the unlawful removal of judges.[139] A judge's tenure may legally be terminated in the following cases: voluntary resignation, permanent inability to perform judicial functions, final conviction for a criminal offence, disciplinary penalty, mandatory or voluntary retirement, loss of citizenship, and election or appointment to a political or administrative post incompatible with the judicial function.[140]

---

[132] Act LXVII on the Legal Status and Remuneration of Judges, 1997, Art. 14(4).

[133] Act LXVII on the Legal Status and Remuneration of Judges, 1997, Art. 17.

[134] Act LXVII on the Legal Status and Remuneration of Judges, 1997, Art. 20.

[135] LXVII on the Legal Status and Remuneration of Judges, 1997, Art. 17(3).

[136] Act LXVII on the Legal Status and Remuneration of Judges, 1997, Art. 17(2).

[137] See Act LXVII on the Legal Status and Remuneration of Judges, 1997, Art. 63.

[138] In 1999 the National Council of Justice assigned judges to two district courts to cope with the caseloads at these courts.

[139] CONST. REP. HUNGARY, Art. 48(3): "Judges may only be removed from office on the grounds and in accordance with the procedures specified by law."

[140] Act LXVII on the Legal Status and Remuneration of Judges, 1997, Art. 57.

Even though a judge may legally be dismissed on the grounds of inadequate performance on the bench,[141] there is no record of such dismissals taking place. In practice, the present provisions allow under-performing judges to leave the judiciary of their own accord. If the president of a court asks a judge to resign, but that judge refuses to do so voluntarily, an extraordinary evaluation of the judge's work is compulsory.[142]

The National Council of Justice may remove presidents and deputy presidents of the regional courts and heads of the judicial colleges[143] of district and regional courts and the Supreme Court.[144]

Lustration laws designed to screen individuals who were involved with the communist-era security services were recently expanded to include all members of the judiciary.[145]

## C. Evaluation and Promotion

Judges are evaluated on a regular basis. Some pay increases are linked to performance-based evaluation in a manner that may compromise judges' intra-judicial independence.

There are two types of judicial evaluation processes: ordinary and extraordinary.[146] An extraordinary evaluation of a judge's performance must be held either when a judge requests it or in cases in which a judge is declared[147] unable to perform his or her tasks.[148] An extraordinary evaluation is ordered by the president of the judge's court (except for district courts, where the relevant regional court president has the authority).[149]

Ordinary evaluation of a judge's performance is performed three times during a judge's career: prior to indefinite appointment to the bench[150] and again six and twelve years

---

[141] This refers rather to the "permanent inability to perform judicial functions", which could be both professional and health-related. Act LXVII on the Legal Status and Remuneration of Judges, 1997, Art. 54.

[142] Act LXVII on the Legal Status and Remuneration of Judges, 1997, Art. 50.

[143] Act LXVI on the Organisation and Administration of Courts, 1997, Arts. 69–70.

[144] Act LXVI on the Organisation and Administration of Courts, 1997, Art. 40(2).

[145] See Section I.

[146] Act LXVII on the Legal Status and Remuneration of Judges, 1997, Art. 50.

[147] Act LXVII on the Legal Status and Remuneration of Judges, 1997, Art. 54 Seems to indicate that the president of the court receives a piece of information pertaining to the inability of the judge.

[148] Act LXVII on the Legal Status and Remuneration of Judges, 1997, Art. 50(2).

[149] Act LXVII on the Legal Status and Remuneration of Judges, 1997, Art. 49(1).

[150] See Sections V.A. and V.B.1.

following the initial evaluation. The court president or a designee conducts the evaluation,[151] and the judge's performance is evaluated on both substantive and procedural terms. Judges may receive evaluations of outstanding, suitable, or non-suitable. Judges who are assessed as non-suitable have the right to challenge the result before a court of law.[152]

In 1998, the National Council of Justice issued a set of regulations detailing the procedures and criteria for evaluating judges' performance. An evaluation must include a review of at least fifty cases the judge presided over and rendered final verdicts in. A detailed performance evaluation must take into consideration all aspects of a judge's work, but the timeliness with which judges handle their work is heavily stressed.[153] The evaluator's opinion must be based on the suitability of the judge on three different grounds: the judge's disposition and skills; quantitative measures; and quality of work.[154]

Judges in leadership positions are subject to additional evaluations. The president's administrative activities may be examined by the authority that appoints a court president or other leading official at any time.[155] In addition, judicial bodies – the Plenary Sessions, the judicial councils, and the judicial colleges – may conduct evaluations.[156]

*Performance-Based Awards*: The National Council of Justice may award the title of honorary regional, appellate, or Supreme Court judge to a judge one level below the respective title after six years of outstanding service.[157] The titles carry bonuses of between 20 and 50 percent of the first grade salary. (From the time one of the above titles is awarded, the judge is no longer entitled to receive a customary bonus,[158] thus partly offsetting the monetary value of the honour.)

---

[151] Act LXVII on the Legal Status and Remuneration of Judges, 1997, Art. 49(1), provides that the procedure is either conducted by the president of the respective court (regional, appeal or Supreme) or a designee.

[152] Act LXVII on the Legal Status and Remuneration of Judges, 1997, Art. 53(4).

[153] Ruling of the National Council of Justice, No. 5, 1998, Art. 11.

[154] The following criteria must be assessed: the judge's ability to discern the essence of the subject matter and to render decisions, the judge's thoroughness, diligence, working capacity, work, organisational skills, involvement in professional forums; case and time management skills, trial preparation skills, adeptness in managing and conducting hearings and trials, relationship to the parties; clarity of recording, timeliness in handing down written decisions, along with the quality of the judge's decision making, the extent to which the reasoning of the decisions complies with the laws, and the clarity of instructions the judge has given to office staff. Ruling 5/1998 of National Council of Justice, Arts. 10–13.

[155] Act LXVI on the Organisation and Administration of Courts, 1997, Art. 74(1).

[156] Act LXVI on the Organisation and Administration of Courts, 1997, Arts. 74, 77.

[157] Act LXVII on the Legal Status and Remuneration of Judges, 1997, Art. 107(3).

[158] Act LXVII on the Legal Status and Remuneration of Judges, 1997, Art. 107(4).

In 1994 the Constitutional Court annulled a law granting rewards to members of the judiciary,[159] holding that it was incompatible with the requirements of judicial independence because it enabled the Government to award honours to judges without the judicial bodies being directly involved in the procedure.[160] The current system of performance-based rewards is administered by judicial bodies; however, it appears to raise analogous concerns about judges' internal independence.[161]

The National Council of Justice may also elevate judges one level on the salary scale twice during their career, on the proposal of the relevant judicial college; "outstanding work" is the only condition set forth in the Law on the Legal Status and Remuneration of Judges for pay promotion.[162]

*Promotion*: There are no standardised, formal criteria governing promotions to a higher court, which as a form of appointment is done by the State President. A higher court president generally invites applications for vacant posts. The judicial college issues a non-binding opinion on the application before nomination by the president of a regional court or the Supreme Court. In practice, the court president generally follows the opinion of the judicial college.

## D. Discipline

### 1. *Liability*

Criminal proceedings, proceedings for petty offences and coercive measures (such as detention[163]) may be initiated against a judge only with the approval of the State President, except for *delicti in flagranto*. Lay judges' immunity extends only to crimes and petty offences committed in the course of their participation in the administration of justice.

---

[159] Decree No. 8/1992 of the Minister of Justice, Art. 8.

[160] Decision of the Constitutional Court of the Republic of Hungary, No. 45, 1994, AB hat.

[161] In the same Constitutional Court decision (No. 45, 1994, AB hat), three judges of the Constitutional Court issued a separate opinion asserting that even performance-based rewards issued by judicial bodies would unconstitutionally violate judges' internal independence.

[162] Act LXVII on the Legal Status and Remuneration of Judges, 1997, Art. 105.

[163] The term "coercive measures" under Art. 5 of Act LXVI on the Organisation and Administration of Courts, 1997, includes detention, search and the like. The terms and conditions of applicability of coercive measures is defined in Arts. 91–108 of Act I of 1973 on Criminal Procedure and in Arts. 76–81 of Act LXIX of 1999 on Administrative Offences.

Both professional judges and lay judges may waive their immunity in relation to proceedings for petty offences.[164]

Judges are exempt from civil liability for acts undertaken in the performance of their duties. In suits for damages caused by members of the judiciary, the National Council of Justice acts on behalf of the defendants,[165] and regional courts are authorised to provide compensation for damages caused by judicial officers.

## 2. Disciplinary Procedures

There are two categories of judicial disciplinary misconduct: breach of the inherent duties of judicial office, and behaviour or lifestyle that harms or endangers the prestige and reputation of the judiciary.[166]

Disciplinary proceedings may be initiated: by the National Council of Justice against judicial leaders appointed by the Council; by the President of the Supreme Court against judges of that Court; and by the presidents of regional and appeal courts in all other cases.[167]

First instance disciplinary courts have been established at the regional courts and the Supreme Court, and second instance disciplinary courts at the Supreme Court.[168] The Plenary Session elects the disciplinary court judges to six-year terms. Judges with more than five years' experience are eligible; members of the National Council of Justice and court presidents – who are authorised to initiate disciplinary procedures – are ineligible to serve on disciplinary courts.[169]

Decisions of the disciplinary court may be appealed. Disciplinary proceedings are not public.[170] Judges subjected to disciplinary proceedings have a right to a hearing and may appoint other judges or attorneys to defend them.[171]

---

[164] Act LXVI on the Organisation and Administration of Courts, 1997, Art. 5.
[165] See Act IV of 1959 on the Civil Code, Art. 349.
[166] Act LXVII on the Legal Status and Remuneration of Judges, 1997, Art. 63.
[167] Act LXVII on the Legal Status and Remuneration of Judges, 1997, Art. 64(1).
[168] Act LXVII on the Legal Status and Remuneration of Judges, 1997, Art. 68(1).
[169] Act LXVII on the Legal Status and Remuneration of Judges, 1997, Art. 69(2).
[170] Act LXVII on the Legal Status and Remuneration of Judges, 1997, Art. 74.
[171] Act LXVII on the Legal Status and Remuneration of Judges, 1997, Art. 76(2).

Possible disciplinary sanctions include reprimand, admonition, demotion to a lower salary grade, dismissal from leadership posts and initiation of dismissal proceedings.[172] The majority of disciplinary cases were instituted for breach of judicial duty. Only a single dismissal has been initiated to date.

A written code of ethics is currently being prepared in consultation with judges.

---

[172] Act LXVII on the Legal Status and Remuneration of Judges, 1997, Art. 79(1).

# VI. Intra-Judicial Relations

## A. Relations with Superior Courts

Second instance courts – which may be regional courts and the Supreme Court – have full authority in reviewing cases; an appeals court may affirm, amend, or annul (quash) the decisions of the first instance courts.[173] In criminal cases, the second instance court has a limited competence to hear evidence and verify the facts established in the first instance adjudication of the case. If a judgement is annulled, the second instance court remands the case to the first instance court for re-trial, or it may order that a different panel retry the case. The second instance court may indicate deficiencies in the first instance judgement, and the reasoning of the appellate decision serves as a guide for any new trial; in addition, it may give explicit instructions on how to proceed in the retrial.

The opinions of higher courts are an important factor in the evaluation of judges' performance and it is one of the criteria used in a judge's evaluation. In light of the procedures used in the promotion of judges, it is clear that conformity with the practices advocated by higher courts is important.

The Supreme Court ensures the uniformity of judicial practice,[174] by adopting uniformity decisions[175] and decisions on issues of principle.[176] Uniformity decisions are issued if required for the development of or to ensure the uniformity of judicial practice, or if a chamber of the Supreme Court intends to deviate from the case law established by another chamber of the Supreme Court. The officially published selection of the Court's judicial practices has substantial influence on the judicial practices of lower courts. Presidents of lower courts are obligated to continuously monitor judicial practice in their courts in order to ensure that it is indeed uniform and to inform higher-level court presidents on deviations from accepted practice.[177]

Recently, a selective compilation of regional court decisions was published, provoking fierce opposition from the Supreme Court, which was concerned that such collections

---

[173] Act I on Criminal Procedure, 1973, Arts. 346, 348, 352, 354, 372. Act III on Civil Procedure, 1952, Arts. 253, 251.

[174] Act LXIV on the Organisation and Administration of Courts, 1997, Art. 27.

[175] Act LXIV on the Organisation and Administration of Courts, 1997, Arts. 30–32.

[176] Act LXVI on the Organisation and Administration of Courts, 1997, Art. 27.

[177] Act LXVI on the Organisation and Administration of Courts, 1997, Art. 28(2).

would undermine the Supreme Court's power to orient the practice of lower courts. The Office of the National Council of Justice has taken the position that publication of regional court decisions does not change the fact that the Supreme Court is responsible for ensuring the uniformity of judicial practice.[178]

Representatives of the judiciary have strongly criticised the Ministry of Justice for proposing a Government bill to allow the Constitutional Court to review decisions of the Supreme Court aimed at ensuring uniform interpretation.

There is no official subordination between judges on different levels. Informally, lower court judges often contact higher court judges for consultation concerning difficult legal problems or application of law.

## B. Case Management and Relations with Court Presidents

Court presidents supervise the work of individual judges serving in their courts and their supervision extends to a broad range of judges' activities.

According to a National Council of Justice ruling,[179] court presidents determine the order of case assignment; in district courts, the president or the head of the relevant judicial college performs this task. In regional courts, the president or a designee assigns new cases. There is no national system of automatic case assignment. There are reportedly some regional courts using a system of automatic case assignment, and the National Council of Justice is considering the establishment of such a system nationwide.[180]

Cases must be heard in the order they reach the courts, except when an extraordinary out-of-turn procedure is ordered,[181] when the National Council of Justice "may exceptionally, at the proposal of any of its members, order the prompt hearing and disposal of cases affecting a wide circle of society or cases of outstanding importance for the "public interest".[182] (The Minister of Justice, as a member of the Council, has used this extraordinary procedure clause to expedite the court proceedings in certain types of cases, such as organised crime or corruption cases. Decisions in such matters are taken by a majority vote; in some cases, the Minister's proposals have been accepted, but not always.)

---

[178] Statement of Office of the National Council of Justice, 29 March 2001, p. 5.

[179] National Council of Justice Ruling, 3/1999.

[180] Information from the Office of the National Council of Justice.

[181] National Council of Justice Ruling on the Administration of Justice, 9/1999.

[182] Act LXVI on the Organisation and Administration of Courts, 1997, Art. 41.

Cases in which the defendant is in pre-trial detention shall be given priority.[183] Once a case is assigned it may not be withdrawn and arbitrarily reassigned to a different judge.[184] The court leader authorised to allocate cases may in exceptional circumstances reassign a case to another judge[185] if the designated judge is absent from the bench for more than 45 days, or is already carrying a disproportionate workload.

The National Council of Justice determines caseload norms and fixes the number of trial days. The Council issued a ruling that judges shall hear cases at least two trial days per week and a minimum of 80 trial days per year.

---

[183] Act I of 1973 on Criminal Procedure, Art. 96(1).

[184] Act LXVI on the Organisation and Administration of Courts, 1997, Art. 11(1).

[185] National Council of Justice Ruling, 3/1999.

## VII. Enforcement

The system for enforcing judgements – involving two categories of bailiff[186] – is unsatisfactory. The first category, regional court bailiffs, ensures the execution of judgements taken in respect of State organs and public authorities, and constitutes part of the judicial organisation. The secondary category of bailiffs is independent from the judicial organisation, and ensures the execution of all other claims.[187] Most public criticism directed at the judiciary is linked to difficulties in executing decisions concerning property rights, while judges complain that the police frequently fail to implement their orders to find defendants who fail to appear in court. Inadequate enforcement reduces public support for and reliance on judicial processes, which in turn can weaken political support for maintaining an independent judiciary.

---

[186] Act LII of 1994 on the Execution of Judgements, Art. 225(1).

[187] Act LII of 1994 on the Execution of Judgements, Art. 225(2).

# Judicial Independence
# in Latvia

# Table of Contents

Executive Summary ................................................. 228

I. Introduction ..................................................... 231
    A. Unfavourable Political Environment ........ 231
    B. Undue Executive and Legislative Involvement in the Judiciary ..................... 232
        1. Insufficient Separation of Powers and Independence ............................. 232
        2. Insufficient Funding and Work Conditions ........................... 233
    C. The Judiciary and the EU Accession Process ............................... 233
    D. Organisation of the Judicial System ......... 234

II. Constitutional and Legal Foundations of Judicial Independence ................................. 237
    A. Separation of Powers and Guarantees of Independence ............. 237
    B. Representation of the Judiciary ................ 238
    C. Rules on Incompatibility .......................... 239
    D. Judges' Associations ................................. 240

III. Administration of the Justice System and Judicial Independence ............................. 242

IV. Financial Autonomy and Level of Funding .... 245
    A. Budget Process .......................................... 245
    B. Work Conditions ...................................... 247
    C. Compensation ......................................... 249

V. Judicial Office .................................................. 252
   A. Selection Process ......................................... 252
   B. Tenure, Retirement, Transfer
      and Removal ................................................ 253
      1. Non-Tenured Appointment ............... 254
      2. Retirement .......................................... 255
      3. Transfer ............................................... 256
      4. Removal ............................................... 256
   C. Evaluation and Promotion ........................ 258
   D. Discipline .................................................... 259
      1. Liability ................................................ 259
      2. Disciplinary Proceedings .................... 260

VI. Intra-Judicial Relations ................................... 262
   A. Relations with Superior Courts ................ 262
   B. Case Management and Relations
      with Court Presidents ................................ 263

VII. Enforcement and Corruption ........................... 264
   A. Enforcement of Judgements ..................... 264
   B. Corruption .................................................. 265

# Judicial Independence in Latvia

## Executive Summary

Latvia has made important progress towards the creation of an independent judiciary. Many of the formal guarantees of judicial independence are in place, partly as a result of progressive reforms in the early 1990s.

However, reform has not remained a priority, and major problems persist. In particular, the political and social environment is unfavourable to the development of an independent judiciary, over which the executive continues to exercise unduly intrusive administrative, supervisory, and financial powers.

*Unfavourable Political Environment*

The judiciary has failed to evolve into a fully effective, independent, and authoritative branch, due in part to a lack of political and public support for the principle of a strong and independent judiciary.

*Insufficient Separation of Powers*

As a consequence of these attitudes towards judicial independence, insufficient efforts have been made fully to develop and implement the structural framework of separate powers on which judicial independence relies. Important elements of the separation of powers are poorly defined in the constitutional structure, or are based only on ordinary legislation. Parliament has attempted to pre-empt the courts' jurisdiction on important cases.

*Undue Executive Involvement*

The executive – in particular the Ministry of Justice – has retained extensive authority over judicial administration, finances and career paths, exercising broad discretionary powers with numerous opportunities for improper influence on judges' decision-making. The concentration of so many regulatory, administrative, information-gathering, and supervisory functions in the Ministry inevitably places courts and individual judges in a subordinate position. In addition, political actors have occasionally attempted to circumvent formal procedures to intervene directly in cases.

*Insufficient Funding and Work Conditions*

The judiciary has little legal or practical control over or input into its own financing, which is determined by the Ministry of Justice. The judiciary is poorly funded. Unsatisfactory working conditions and a lack of technology contribute to other problems, including serious inefficiencies, backlogs, lack of enforcement, and corruption, all of which further erode public support for the judiciary.

In addition to these general issues, the following issues of particular concern are discussed in the body of the Report:

*Parliamentary Committees*

Parliamentary committees have investigated pending court cases, threatening to pre-empt the courts' jurisdiction. No specific Law on Parliamentary Investigation Committees has been adopted, while the Constitution and the Rules of Procedure of the Parliament provide only limited guidance.

*Representation*

There is no independent institution representing the judiciary in its relations with other branches, to speak on its behalf or ensure the independence of the judicial system.

*Training*

Training of judges in particular is poorly funded.

*Supplemental Pay*

Supplemental payment levels are established in law; however, some judges have not received their supplemental payments in full and in 2000 the promotion of some 100 judges was blocked as it would have necessitated additional remuneration. Discretionary refusal to pay promised and legally established benefits can be used by the executive as a form of improper leverage against judges.

*Non-Tenured Appointment*

Judges are initially appointed to a three-year term, after which they may be confirmed by Parliament for an unlimited term in office or re-appointed for an additional two-year term. The Minister of Justice proposes candidates for reappointment based on assessments provided by the Judicial Qualification Board. There are no additional criteria for deciding whether to nominate a judge for an additional two-year term or for an unlimited term of office. Such a system of largely discretionary vesting of tenure inevitably has a chilling effect on judges' willingness to adjudicate without concern for their job safety.

*Discretionary Extension beyond Retirement*

Discretionary extension of service beyond the mandatory retirement age – over which the Minister of Justice and senior judges have effective vetoes – gives judges an incentive to curry favour with the executive or their judicial superiors.

*Supreme Court Binding Clarifications*

The Plenum of the Supreme Court issues compulsory clarifications on the application of laws, which are binding for the courts of general jurisdiction. Many judges feel this practice effectively subordinates them to another court's interpretations, in violation of the constitutional provision that "judges shall be independent and subject only to the law."

*Case Assignment*

The system of case-assignment is outdated and unnecessarily allows court presidents too much discretion.

*Enforcement*

Enforcement of civil judgements is particularly problematic; seventy percent of all civil judgements are not enforced. Such low levels of enforcement undermine public confidence in and respect for the judiciary. Court bailiffs are hampered by meagre resources, a lack of legal training and equipment, and poor salaries that encourage corruption.

*Corruption*

Corruption is generally perceived to be widespread in the judiciary, as in other segments of public life.

## I. Introduction

Latvia has made important progress towards the creation of an independent judiciary. Many of the formal guarantees of judicial independence are in place, partly as a result of progressive reforms in the early 1990s.

However, reform has not remained a priority, and several major problems persist. In particular, the political and social environment is unfavourable to the development of an independent judiciary, over which the executive continues to exercise unduly intrusive administrative, supervisory, and financial powers.

### A. Unfavourable Political Environment

The judiciary has failed to evolve into a fully effective, independent, and authoritative branch of the State. This is due in part to a lack of political and public support for the principle of a strong and independent judiciary, and as a result the judiciary operates in a generally unfavourable environment.

There have been no reports of public denunciation of judges by government officials or personal insults directed at judges. However, politicians have publicly voiced opinions to influence judicial decisions in pending cases, and individual judges have been exposed to severe criticism, with frequent accusations of corruption and bias raised in the mass media. Media criticism in particular is often superficial and polemical, and not founded on a thorough examination of the case.

Public scepticism and suspicion regarding the judicial system persists, despite the introduction of reforms. In one recent survey, almost one quarter of Latvian firms surveyed indicated a lack of confidence that the justice system would uphold their contract and property rights.[1] The lack of public confidence in the protection of property rights is closely connected to more general dissatisfaction with the judiciary; according to the same survey, many individuals believe that courts are unfair, corrupt, inconsistent, costly, and slow, and that their decisions are poorly enforced.[2] Without public trust in judges, there is little incentive for politicians to support policies that would entrench real judicial independence.

---

[1] World Bank and the European Bank for Reconstruction and Development, Monitoring Performance of the Latvian Judiciary, Danish Trust Fund, 2001 (in English).

[2] World Bank and the European Bank for Reconstruction and Development, Monitoring Performance of the Latvian Judiciary, Danish Trust Fund, 2001 (in English).

## B. Undue Executive and Legislative Involvement in the Judiciary

### 1. Insufficient Separation of Powers and Independence

Neither political actors nor Latvian society as a whole appreciates the importance of the separation of powers and institutional independence of the judiciary. As a consequence of these attitudes, insufficient efforts have been made fully to develop and implement the structural framework of separate powers on which judicial independence relies. Instead, the executive has retained extensive and intrusive authority over judicial administration and finances.

In particular, the executive, through the Ministry of Justice, is responsible for representing and administering the judiciary, and for preparing and allocating its budget. The Ministry also plays a decisive role in determining judges' career paths. In all these areas, the Ministry exercises broad discretionary powers, which create numerous opportunities for it improperly to influence court presidents and individual judges' decision-making. In a number of areas, Parliament also has unnecessarily broad discretion in areas of judicial administration which could more properly be conducted by judges themselves; for example, judges may only be granted tenure by a vote of Parliament after three to five years of service.

In addition, political actors have occasionally attempted to circumvent formal procedures in favour of more direct intervention in cases. For example, eight Parliamentary deputies submitted a petition to the Riga Central District Court in March 1999, requesting the discharge of a journalist from prison; this action was widely considered to be an attempt to interfere with the activities of the court and the prosecutor's office.[3]

In 2000, two Members of Parliament (MPs) publicly expressed their views on a pending case involving another MP accused of co-operating with the KGB. The Judges' Association considered these actions as undue pressure on the court, because in 2001 the judge hearing the case was to be considered for lifetime tenure before Parliament. Parliament has also attempted to pre-empt the courts' jurisdiction on important cases. More problematic is the fact that Parliament is in a position to pass on a judge's tenure in the first instance.

---

[3] The announcement on 26 March 1999 of the general meeting of the Latvian Judges' Association. See also *Diena*, 27 March 1999.

## 2. Insufficient Funding and Work Conditions

As a consequence of the poorly developed separation of powers and persistent executive interference, the judiciary has little legal or practical control over or input into its own financing. The regional and district courts have no say in the process of drafting their budgets; they are represented by the Ministry of Justice, acting on a discretionary basis.

The judiciary is poorly funded. Working conditions in courts are inadequate and contribute to serious inefficiencies, backlogs, lack of enforcement, and corruption, which in turn further erode public support for the judiciary. The most important short-term challenges facing the judiciary are working conditions, fighting corruption, and improvement of the legal qualification of judges – all of which can be attributed to insufficient funding.

Apparently in response to criticisms from the Commission's 2000 Regular Report the Minister of Justice declared that the judiciary should be a priority for the 2002 State budget, and acknowledged that funding for the judiciary to date has been insufficient for the judiciary to fulfil its responsibilities.[4] The Program for Developing the Judicial System in 2002–2006 identifies increasing judicial salaries as a priority.[5]

## C. The Judiciary and the EU Accession Process

The EU has consistently highlighted various areas in need of improvement over the past several years. The Commission's 1998 Regular Report identified the need to improve the status of judges in order to attract qualified individuals and to increase public confidence in the court system. The 1999 Regular Report noted that the court system still required improvements, including training for court bailiffs.[6] The 2000 Regular Report stressed the need to complete the legal framework, expand and intensify the training of judges, and to make further improvements to the infrastructure of court buildings.[7] Most recently, during his visit to Latvia in July 2001, EU Enlargement Commissioner Guenter Verheugen raised the issue of improving Latvia's judicial system.[8]

---

[4] I. Klinsane-Berzina, "Judicial power in the tether of the budget", *Neatkariga rita avize*, 23 April 2001.

[5] The Program was adopted by the government on 12 December 2000, protocol No. 58.

[6] See <http://www.mfa.gov.lv/eframe.htm>, in Latvian (accessed 20 August 2001).

[7] European Commission, *2000 Regular Report on Latvia's Progress towards Accession*, November 2000, <http://europa.eu.int/comm/enlargement/dwn/report_11_00/pdf/en/lv_en.pdf> (accessed 20 August 2001), p. 17, (hereafter *2000 Regular Report*).

[8] RFE/RL Newsline, Vol. 5. No. 137, Part II, 23 July 2001.

In general, political actors, State officials and judges are aware of Commission recommendations, but there has been little debate on the issues raised, or on accession in general.

## D. Organisation of the Judicial System

Prior to the Second World War, Latvia had a civil law system. With the introduction of the Soviet system, the executive powers were greatly expanded, and legal institutions were viewed as instruments of unitary state-party control. The role of the prosecutor was expanded and given a significant measure of authority over the judiciary. Extra-legal interference with judicial decision making – "telephone justice" – was common. The legacy from the communist re-organisation of the legal system continues to have a profound impact on the judiciary.

Latvia's independence was re-established *de facto* in 1991. The Constitution, first adopted in 1922, was fully restored in 1993. In 1992, the Law on Judicial Power was adopted, with the purpose of reforming the judicial system by establishing a modern, efficient court system based on the continental European model.

The Constitution and the Law on Judicial Power establish a three-tier court system, consisting of district courts, regional courts and the Supreme Court, collectively considered the courts of general jurisdiction.[9] District courts are courts of first instance for all civil, criminal, and administrative cases, unless otherwise provided by law.[10] There are thirty-four district courts. Civil and administrative cases are reviewed by one professional judge; criminal cases are reviewed by a panel consisting of one professional judge and two lay judges. District court decisions may be appealed to a regional court or, under the cassation procedure, to the Supreme Court.

There are five regional courts.[11] Regional courts are courts of first instance for criminal cases concerning grievous crimes and for civil cases as established by law. Regional courts also act as courts of appeal for district court decisions. Each regional court has two sections: one for civil matters and another for criminal matters. Panels of three judges review regional court cases. When reviewing a case in the first instance the

---

[9] Constitution of the Republic of Latvia, adopted 15 February 1922, *State Gazette*, 1 July 1993, No. 43 (hereafter CONST. REP. LATVIA). Law on Judicial Power, adopted 15 December 1992, Art. 82. *"Augstakas Padomes un Ministru Padomes Zinotajs"*, 14 January 1993, No. 1, Art. 1.

[10] Law on Judicial Power, Arts. 29–33.

[11] Law on Judicial Power, Arts. 35–42.

panel consists of one professional judge and two lay judges. When reviewing a case as an appellate court the panel consists of three professional judges.

Land Registry Offices are attached to the regional courts.[12] Land Registry Office judges have the status of district judges.

The Supreme Court consists of a Senate and two Divisions for civil and criminal matters.[13] The Divisions hear appeals against regional court decisions in which the regional courts have acted as the court of first instance. The Senate reviews appeals under the procedure of cassation. There are three Departments in the Senate: the Civil Matters Department, the Criminal Matters Department, and the Administrative Matters Department. A panel of three judges of the Court hears Supreme Court cases.

All judges of the Supreme Court constitute the Plenum. The Plenum issues instructions concerning the application of laws which are binding for the lower courts, establishes the Divisions and Departments of the Senate of the Court, and provides an opinion as to whether there is a basis for the removal of the President of the Supreme Court or the dismissal of the Prosecutor General from office.[14] The Plenum functions in accordance with the Law on Judicial Power as well as the Statute of the Plenum.

There are no military courts in Latvia. The Constitution provides that any military courts should function on the basis of a separate law,[15] but no such law has been adopted since the restoration of independence.

A separate Constitutional Court reviews laws for compliance with the Constitution.[16] The Court can declare laws or other enactments invalid. Its judges are appointed by Parliament.[17] The Constitutional Court is considered an independent institution of judicial power;[18] consequently, the Constitutional Court is detached from the general court system both jurisdictionally and organisationally.

---

[12] Law on Judicial Power, Arts. 42(1), 98(1), and 98(2).
[13] Law on Judicial Power, Arts. 43–50.
[14] Law on Judicial Power, Arts. 49.
[15] CONST. REP. LATVIA, Art. 86.
[16] CONST. REP. LATVIA, Art. 85.
[17] CONST. REP. LATVIA, Art. 85.
[18] Constitutional Court Law, 11 September 1997, Art. 1(1).

As of March 2001, there were 423 professional judges in Latvia: 219 district court judges, 88 regional court judges, 38 Supreme Court justices and 78 Land Registry Offices judges.[19] The ratio of judges to the total Latvian population (2,431,000)[20] is one judge for about 5,750 people.

Most current judges joined the bench in the 1990s. In the first few years following the restoration of Latvia's independence, 60 to 70 percent of all judges (including 30 percent of Supreme Court judges) retired from office on their own initiative. Some retired because of legal restrictions introduced to remove members of the former Soviet military and secret service from the judiciary.[21] Judges retired for other reasons as well, including lack of necessary qualifications, refusal or inability to study new laws, and involvement as a judge in earlier political cases. This law is still in force, and every judicial candidate must undergo compulsory screening. In practice, no judicial application has been rejected due to screening.

---

[19] Information from the Deputy State Secretary of the Ministry of Justice, 19 March 2001.

[20] The Data of the Central Statistical Bureau on 10 August 1999, <http://www.csb.lv/>, in Latvian (accessed 20 August 2001).

[21] Persons who are or were in the past salaried or contracted employees of the former USSR or Latvian SSR KGB, the USSR Ministry of Defense, the Security Service of the Army, the intelligence or counterintelligence services of Russia or other countries, and the owners and inhabitants of apartments used for secret meetings, may not be candidates for the office of judge (or lay judge). Furthermore, persons who are or were in the past members of organisations whose activities are restricted by the laws or judgements of the courts of the Republic of Latvia may not be judges. Law on Judicial Power, Art. 55.

## II. Constitutional and Legal Foundations of Judicial Independence

### A. Separation of Powers and Guarantees of Independence

The principle of the separation of powers is not explicitly stated in the Constitution. The clearest expression of a separation of powers is found in the Law on Judicial Power, which declares that "[a]n independent judicial power[22] exists in the Republic of Latvia, alongside the legislative and the executive power"[23] and that "only a court shall deliver justice."[24]

In order to change constitutional guarantees a two-thirds majority is necessary, as well as other procedural guarantees.[25] Statutes regulating the judicial power can be changed by ordinary procedure which makes them more susceptible to political swings. Therefore, the fact that the separation of powers is only established in law and not clearly in the Constitution, despite the Constitutional Court's rulings, weakens the certainty and protection the separation can provide.

However, the principle may be implied in the division of the Constitution into Chapters addressing "The Parliament", "The State President", "The Government", and "Courts".[26] Moreover, the Constitutional Court has made clear its opinion that the Latvian system is based on the separation of powers, although it is also clear from the Court's rulings that the other branches have violated that principle. For example, in a 24 March 2000 decision[27] the Constitutional Court stated that the Cabinet of Ministers ignored the principle of separation of powers and infringed upon the competence of the judiciary by adopting a resolution which authorised the Privatisation Agency to settle a dispute between two companies by ensuring that one of the parties, a State stock company, signed a contract with the opposing party. The Constitutional Court held that according to

---

[22] There is no accepted interpretation of what either a judicial power or an independent judicial power means.

[23] Law on Judicial Power, Art. 1(1).

[24] Law on Judicial Power, Art. 1(2).

[25] CONST. REP. LATVIA, Art. 76.

[26] See CONST. REP. LATVIA, Chapter VI, on the courts.

[27] Decision of the Constitutional Court, Case No. 04–07(99), *State Gazette*, 29 March 2000, No. 113.

the Constitution and the Law on Judicial Power, civil disputes should be reviewed exclusively by the courts, and that the Constitution obligates all State institutions to observe the rule of law, the principle of the separation of powers, and the principle of checks and balances. In pre-empting the courts' jurisdiction, the executive violated those principles.

The Constitution does enshrine the independence of individual judges and courts, establishing that "[j]udges shall be independent and subject only to the law"[28] and that judgements shall be made only by the courts.[29]

*Parliamentary Committees*: There have been instances of a parliamentary committee investigating pending court cases. No specific Law on Parliamentary Investigation Committees has been adopted, while the Constitution and the Rules of Procedure of the Parliament regulate this issue only minimally.

The draft Law on Parliamentary Investigation Committees now before Parliament has raised certain doubts as well. The main concern is that the draft law may interfere in the judicial domain by ignoring the principle of separation of powers, since the committees would be authorised to request information from "public institutions," which could be construed to include courts.

## B. Representation of the Judiciary

There is no independent institution to speak on behalf of the judiciary and represent it in its relations with other branches. In practice, the Ministry of Justice and the President of the Supreme Court act as representatives; the Ministry's involvement raises concerns about conflicts of interest and also weakens the separation between the branches.

The Conference of Judges is a self-governing organisation of the judiciary.[30] All judges participate and vote in the Conference, which has, however, quite limited powers, and is perceived as a vetting device for decisions made in other fora. The Conference examines current issues of court practice; submits requests to the Supreme Court Plenum to issue explanations on the application of laws and discusses financial, social security, and other significant matters integrally related to the work of judges. The Conference

---

[28] CONST. REP. LATVIA, Art. 83.

[29] CONST. REP. LATVIA, Arts. 82 and 86.

[30] Law on Judicial Power, Art. 92.

also elects the Judicial Qualification Board[31] and its chairman and elects the Judicial Disciplinary Board.[32] Except for election of the Boards, the powers of the Conference are purely advisory.

In practice, the Minister of Justice, or the Ministry's State Secretary, and the President of the Supreme Court speak on behalf of judiciary and represent it in its relation with the other branches of government. There is no legal basis for their role, but rather a common perception among judges and political actors that the President of the Supreme Court is the senior ranking judge and that the Minister is the chief of the judiciary and has administrative and supervisory responsibilities over it.

Many judges believe that introduction of an independent Judicial Council would enhance representation of the judiciary *vis-a-vis* the other branches and help consolidate the judiciary's control over its own affairs, including finances.[33] To date, however, there has been no widespread public discussion of the question.

## C. Rules on Incompatibility

Judges in courts of general jurisdiction are prohibited from membership in any political party or movement and cannot hold political office. A judge who is nominated as a candidate for Parliament must resign from judicial service when the list of candidates is registered.[34] In municipal elections, judges need only relinquish their judicial posts upon being elected – that is, they may participate in political campaigns while still sitting on the bench.

---

[31] The Judicial Qualification Board consists of ten judges. The Supreme Court Senate, the Plenum of the Supreme Court, the regional courts, the district courts and the Land Registry Offices are each represented on the board by two judges. The Head of Parliament's Legal Committee, the Minister of Justice, the Prosecutor General, the President of the Supreme Court, the Dean of the Faculty of Law of the Latvian University, the Rector of the Latvian Police Academy and the representative of the Latvian Judges' Association may attend the meetings of the Judicial Qualification Board. The Chairman of the Board is elected by the Conference of Judges. The Board acts in compliance with the Law on Judicial Power, Regulations On the Judicial Qualification Board and Rules for Attestation of Judges.

[32] See V.D.2.

[33] Information from a Justice of the Constitutional Court, 18 May 2001.

[34] *Saeima* (Parliament) Election Law, adopted 25 May 1995, *State Gazette*, 6 June 1995, No. 86, Art.6; and the Election Law on City and Town Councils, District Councils and *Pagasts* (Councils), adopted 13 January 1994, *State Gazette*, 25 January 1994, No. 10, Art. 10.

Generally, judges cannot serve in the executive branch. However, judges may hold specific positions prescribed by other laws and international agreements.[35] For example, by law one of the nine members of the independent Central Election Commission is a judge elected by the Plenum of the Supreme Court.[36] A judge of the Supreme Court was employed as a consultant to the independent State Human Rights Bureau. As long as clear procedures allow such judges to recuse themselves in the event a case related to their commission work comes before them, such limited work on independent commissions may not present a serious threat to judicial independence.

However, the draft amendment to the Law on Judicial Power would allow the Minister of Justice to second judges to other state institutions or international organisations.[37] Having in mind the executive's traditional dominance over the judiciary, this provision would seem to give the Ministry undue leverage over judges' external career options, as well as unnecessarily introducing opportunities for compromising contacts between judges and other State actors.

Limitations on other professional activities of judges are established by the Anticorruption Law, which covers not only judges but all State officials.[38] Judges are prohibited from holding any other position or engaging in any other professional or commercial activity, with the exception of educational, scientific, and creative activities.[39] Judges are not allowed to strike.[40]

## D. Judges' Associations

Judges are free to form or join professional associations. The Latvian Judges' Association is the only registered judges' association at present. The Association was originally founded in 1929 and its charter was renewed in 1992.[41] The Association is an independent, voluntary, professional organisation, which, according to its statute, promotes the "intellectual, social and material interests of judges" and strengthens judicial power

---

[35] Anticorruption Law. Art. 19, adopted 21 September 1995, *State Gazette*, 11 October 1995, No. 156, Art. 15.

[36] Law on the Central Election Commission, adopted 13 January 1994. *State Gazette*, 20 January 1994, No. 8, Art. 2.

[37] Information from the Deputy State Secretary of the Ministry of Justice, May 2001.

[38] Anticorruption Law, Art. 15.

[39] Anticorruption Law, Art. 19.

[40] Law on Judicial Power, Art. 86.

[41] Information from the President of the Latvian Judges' Association, August 2000.

and its prestige within the State. More than fifty percent of all Latvian judges are currently members of the Association, which is the largest public organisation of lawyers. The Association has not been particularly influential, however, or successful in petitioning the executive on issues it considers important.[42]

---

[42] For example, the Association lodged complaints with the Government concerning its December 1999 decision to transfer ownership of certain court buildings from the Ministry of Justice to a stock company – an action which the Association believed harmed judges' independence – but has never received a reply.

## III. Administration of the Justice System and Judicial Independence

The system of court administration has perpetuated the judiciary's dependence on the Ministry of Justice, a phenomenon that has also been noted by international observers.[43] This subordination creates conditions for the executive improperly to influence judges and especially court presidents.

There is no independent court administration on the national level. The Ministry of Justice manages regional and district courts through a special Department of Courts[44] and through the court presidents, who are responsible for day-to-day administration. The Supreme Court administers itself autonomously.

The Department of Courts consists of two sections: the Section of Court Operations and Statistics and the Section of Legal Professionals and Qualification.[45] The Section of Court Operations and Statistics prepares rules and issues regulations concerning court management and the handling of documents in regional and district courts; gives instructions on administrative issues to presidents of regional and district courts; supervises the organisation of regional and district courts' work (including case allocation, statistics, and internships); and supplies courts with legislative and other materials. In addition, it may request information and clarifications from officials of district and regional courts.[46]

The Section of Courts Operation and Statistics also indirectly monitors the performance and efficiency of the judiciary through its collection of statistics and assessments of individual judges' performance.[47] This data can be used, for example, by the Judicial Qualification Board in deciding whether to grant a judge a higher qualification or by the Ministry of Justice in deciding whether to ask the Parliament to increase the number of judges in the country. The Department of Courts prepares annual reports on the work of courts for the Minister of Justice, which form part of the Minister's annual report to the Prime Minister.[48]

---

[43] World Bank, Functional and Organisational Review of the Ministry of Justice, 2000; Swedish Court Administration (SIDA), Development of the Court administration in Latvia, 2000.

[44] Law on Judicial Power, Arts. 33 and 40.

[45] Statute of the Department of Courts of the Ministry of Justice, adopted 2 April 1996.

[46] Statute of the Department of Courts of the Ministry of Justice.

[47] Statute of the Department of Courts of the Ministry of Justice.

[48] Information from the Director of the Department of Courts of the Ministry of Justice, May 2001.

The Ministry of Justice organises inspections of the district and regional courts, using either Ministry employees or judges from the Supreme Court and regional courts.[49] There is no formal system for selecting judges for this task. In practice, the presidents of regional courts and the Supreme Court have discretion in this matter. In practice, however, judges are not normally involved in inspections, which are conducted entirely by Ministry employees.[50] Such inspections, even though they are not directed at the core decision-making acts of judges, often serve as a tool to restrain judges and, in effect, to subordinate them to the Ministry.

The Ministry of Justice is also responsible for training and improving the qualifications of judges and court employees.[51] In 1999, the Ministry of Justice delegated this competence to the Latvian Judicial Training Centre, a non-profit organisation established by the Latvian Judges' Association, and several international organisations. The Centre is funded partly by the Ministry of Justice and partly by its founders.[52]

There are few clear rules with regard to the Ministry's exercise of its administrative functions. The concentration of so many regulatory, administrative, information-gathering, and supervisory functions in the Ministry of Justice – an organ of the executive – inevitably places courts and individual judges in a subordinate position. Without staffing, financial resources, access to information, and involvement in the rule-making process, judges are dependent on the executive for almost all their needs and may be vulnerable to pressure if they fail to satisfy the executive's expectations.

In March 2000, the then Minister of Justice announced that the Ministry supported the introduction of expanded administrative autonomy for the courts;[53] no practical steps followed, however. Currently, following a study carried out by the Swedish Court Administration project "Development of the Court administration in Latvia", the Ministry of Justice has been developing a concept paper on the transformation of

---

[49] Law on Judicial Power. Art. 108.

[50] Information from the Director of the Department of Courts of the Ministry of Justice, May 2001. The Ministry of Finance may also ask the State Audit Office to perform an audit. Such audits are requested after a financial evaluation of issues under the Ministry's competence. The State Audit Office monitors the condition of State property and the finances of all State organisations, including courts. Law on the State Audit Office, adopted 28 October 1993, *State Gazette*, 4 November 1994, No. 101, Art. 1.

[51] Law on Judicial Power.

[52] See Section IV.A.

[53] The Minister also stated that "it is important for society to recognize authoritative judicial power." *State Gazette*, 7 March 2000, No. 76/77.

court administration. The original deadline for the preparation of the Concept of 1 March 2001 has been superseded, and work on the Concept Paper is still in progress.[54]

*Other Administrative Provisions*

District and regional court presidents have a broad management role at the court level. They oversee case allocation and management;[55] legal training for lay judges and court personnel; court schedules;[56] the compilation of court statistics; and the execution of court decisions. Many of these management functions require close contact with and reliance upon the personnel and resources of the Ministry of Justice. The position of a manager also places court presidents in a situation of frequent contacts with various agencies and individuals in order to ensure smooth operations of a court. This can compromise their independence and impartiality as they are also judges hearing cases.

The number of judges in district and regional courts is determined by Parliament based on the Minister of Justice's recommendation; each individual court recruits its own staff. There are no formal rules regulating staffing levels; in practice, the Ministry determines the required number of judges and court personnel based on its calculation of the average caseload in each court.[57]

As noted, the Supreme Court has an autonomous administration. The total number of judges in the Supreme Court as well as the number of judges in the Court's Senate and Divisions are determined by Parliament based on the recommendation of the President of the Supreme Court.[58] The Court has its own internal inspection system.

---

[54] Information from the Assistant to the Deputy State Secretary of the Ministry of Justice, June 2001.
[55] See Section VI.B.
[56] Law on Judicial Power, Art. 33.
[57] Information from the Director of the Department of Courts of the Ministry of Justice, May 2001.
[58] Law on Judicial Power. Arts. 32, 39, and 44.

## IV. Financial Autonomy and Level of Funding

By law, the Ministry of Justice manages the financial resources for the operation of regional and district courts,[59] including preparation of the budget and the subsequent distribution of funds.[60] The judiciary is effectively excluded from the budget process, and has little involvement in the allocation of funding. The Ministry's broad discretion in financial matters and in supervising resource allocation introduces opportunities for indirect influence on court presidents and individual judges.

### A. Budget Process

The Ministry of Justice effectively controls the budget drafting process for the regional and district courts. The financial position of the Supreme Court is also weak. As a whole, the judicial branch suffers from severe under-funding.

The State Budget Law does not provide for separate budget lines for the district and regional courts. Rather, their budget is incorporated into the budget line of the Ministry of Justice, and the Ministry is responsible for deciding upon allocations to these courts. District and regional court officials' budgetary requests do not bind the Ministry, and at no other stage in the budgetary process do the district and regional courts have input as to their budget allocation.

The Ministry of Justice prepares the draft budget request for regional and district courts and submits it to the Ministry of Finance. The Ministry of Justice does not follow any formal regulations with regard to the determination of funds for the district and regional courts, but the established practice is to base calculations on the number of positions and bills for infrastructure work.[61]

In practice there are no criteria for determining the amount allocated for each court; it appears that personal relationships between court presidents and Ministry officials are particularly important. There is a separate budget line in the State Budget Law for the Supreme Court, which prepares its own budget request and submits it directly to the Ministry of Finance.

---

[59] Law on Judicial Power, Art. 107.

[60] Information from the Directors of the Departments of Courts and Accountancy of the Ministry of Justice, May 2001.

[61] Information from the Director of the Department of Accountancy of the Ministry of Justice, May 2001.

The Ministry of Finance is responsible for drafting the overall State budget,[62] and negotiates with the Ministry of Justice and the President of the Supreme Court over their respective sections. Disagreements are forwarded to the Cabinet of Ministers, although it appears that in practice State institutions' objections are not given much weight in the intra-governmental discussions.[63]

While reviewing the draft budget, the Government may, at its discretion, invite the President of the Supreme Court to participate in the review, and such an invitation has been issued occasionally; however, reportedly these opinions are not given serious consideration in the deliberations.[64] After the Government has given its approval, the budget is sent to Parliament, which adopts the annual State Budget Law.[65] The judiciary does not participate in the parliamentary debates over the budget.

The courts are therefore almost entirely dependent on the executive branch for their funding. The discretionary elements of the budgeting and allocation processes create opportunities for the executive to exercise undue influence over dependent court presidents.

The consequence is that courts remain under-funded. Court funding for 2001 was 7,316,892 Ls (c. € 13,193,053) representing approximately 0.50 percent of the overall State budget.[66] In 2000, the budget for the judiciary amounted to 8,102,231[67] – somewhat more than in 2001. The Government has already established spending limits for all State institutions, including the courts, until 2003. In setting these limits, proposals for increased funding of the courts were not taken into account.[68]

Training in particular is poorly funded.[69] In 1999, the Judicial Training Centre had insufficient funds to conduct courses and was in crisis. The Centre received 40,000

---

[62] Law on the Budget and Management of Finances, adopted 24 March 1994, *State Gazette*, 6 April 1994, No. 41. Arts. 19 and 20.

[63] Information from the President of the Supreme Court, August 2000; Information from the Director of the Department of Courts of the Ministry of Justice, May 2001.

[64] Information from the Assistant of the President of the Supreme Court, May 2001.

[65] Law on the Budget and Management of Finances, Arts. 20–22.

[66] Information from the Director of the Department of the Accountancy of the Ministry of Justice, June 2001.

[67] Information from the Ministry of Finance, July 2000.

[68] The Resolution of the Cabinet of Ministers No. 30, Art. 24. On top state basic budget expenses of ministries and central state institutions and on key financial indicators in the special state budget for 2001–2003 years, adopted 5 June 2000. *State Gazette*, 7 July 2000, No. 252/254.

[69] Information from the Latvian Judicial Training Center, July 2000. The Commission's *2000 Regular Report* notes that the training of judges is insufficient.

Ls from the Ministry of Justice's 2000 and 2001 budgets, as well as donations from non-governmental organisations.[70] The Government has reportedly promised an equivalent sum for the Centre in the 2002 budget.[71]

## B. Work Conditions

As a consequence of inadequate funding, the judiciary suffers from shortages of space, necessary equipment, legal information and human resources, resulting in slow adjudication and large backlogs that undermine efforts to consolidate support for an independent judiciary.

Many court buildings do not meet basic requirements.[72] There are not enough courtrooms, and often there are no storage rooms for documents and no premises where lawyers and prosecutors can gather to review a case.[73] The most pressing shortages are in Riga Regional Court, where as of January 2001 there were ten courtrooms for 36 judges; some judges hold court hearings in their offices although there is no legal provision for doing so.[74]

In many courts, technical equipment, such as printers, copying machines, and safes are in short supply and of poor quality.[75] There are no tape recorders or stenographic machines in courtrooms for recording statements of witnesses;[76] court secretaries record session minutes by hand, which significantly reduces the efficiency of proceedings. Some progress has been made, however, with regard to computerisation. All Supreme Court judges have computers and in several district and regional courts each judge of

---

[70] Information from the Assistant to the Executive Director of the Latvian Judicial Training Center, May 2001.

[71] Information from the Assistant to the Executive Director of the Latvian Judicial Training Center, May 2001.

[72] Ministry of Justice instruction No. 1 "The Guidelines for the Courthouses Project" of 20 March 2000 provides that the number of courtrooms should be the same as the number of judges in the first instance court (in exceptional circumstances two courtrooms for three judges) and one courtroom for three judges in the second instance court. The Development Program of the Judicial System of the Republic of Latvia 2002–2006. Courthouse Agency, January 2001.

[73] According to one estimate, as of January 2001, there was a shortfall of 173 courtrooms, 75 judges' offices, 168 offices for assistants, and 78 rooms for other court personnel. The Development Program of the Judicial System of the Republic of Latvia 2002–2006, Courthouse Agency, January 2001.

[74] Information from the Director of the Department of Courts of the Ministry of Justice, May 2001.

[75] The Development Program of the Judicial System of the Republic of Latvia 2002–2006. Courthouse Agency, January 2001.

[76] C. Sandgren, D. Iljanova, United Nations Development Program, "Needs Assessment of the Judicial System of Latvia", September 2000 (in English).

the court has a computer.[77] A unified computer network has been established in several courts, a unified database is being organised, and all regional courts and 16 district courts have been connected to the State data transmission network.[78] However, some district courts have a single computer for the entire court.[79]

Legal research resources are insufficient. Most courts, including the Supreme Court, have no law library.[80] There is no electronic database for case law or legal writing in Latvia, although the case law of the Senate of the Supreme Court is published annually and one or two paper copies are provided to each court. One paper copy of the official gazette, which contains current legislation adopted by the Parliament, is provided to each court. In addition, the gazette is also available in electronic version to all Supreme Court judges, regional court judges, and judges in twenty of the thirty-four district courts. There are plans to extend these services to the remaining courts within two to three years.

The shortage of technical staff contributes to large case backlogs and promotes superficial review of cases. Each judge is supposed to have a secretary and a legal assistant. However, since the wages of the court staff are low and there is a lack of space to accommodate them, many judges do not have assistants.[81] The court docket is so congested that cases are scheduled several years in advance. The worst situation is in Riga Regional court,[82] which is currently scheduling hearings for late 2003,[83] and has been compelled to disregard the one-month time limit for beginning review of filed cases.[84] Appeals in criminal cases are sometimes reviewed after the appellants have served their sentence and have been released.[85] Under these circumstances, the right of appeal is rendered

---

[77] Information from the President of the Supreme Court, July 2000.

[78] See <http://www.mfa.gov.lv/eframe.htm>, in Latvian (accessed 20 August 2001).

[79] The Development Program of the Judicial System of the Republic of Latvia 2002–2006. Courthouse Agency, January 2001.

[80] C. Sandgren, D. Iljanova, United Nations Development Program, "Needs Assessment of the Judicial System of Latvia", September 2000 (in English).

[81] See "Development Program of the Judicial System of the Republic of Latvia 2002–2006", Courthouse Agency, January 2001, which acknowledges the problem.

[82] A. Gulans, President of the Supreme Court, "The political will for strengthening of the Judicial power is necessary", *State Gazette*, 7 March 2000, No. 76/77.

[83] *The Baltic Times*, 12 July 2001.

[84] See Criminal Procedure Code, adopted 6 January 1961, Art. 241.

[85] For example, in March 2000, the Minister of Justice reported that one convicted individual had already served a term of three years and been released without his appeal having been reviewed by a regional court. V. Birkavs, "It is important for society to realize authoritative judicial power", State Gazette, 7 March 2000, No. 76/77.

meaningless.[86] Extended delays in civil cases similarly undermine confidence in the judicial process.

## C. Compensation

Compensation for judges may be considered sufficient from the point of view of ensuring their independence and impartiality.

Judges' incomes have improved considerably during the 1990s, and are comparable to that of civil servants, but lower than that of high political officials, such as Members of Parliament. Their earnings are considerably above the national average of 149.30 Ls/month (c. € 269/month).[87]

The salaries of judges are fixed by law in relation to the salaries in the civil service. Compensation for judges consists of a base salary and supplemental payments. The President and Vice-Presidents of the Supreme Court, the judges of the Supreme Court, and the presidents of the regional courts receive salaries equal to the maximum salary of a civil servant of the first qualification class,[88] which includes the State Secretaries of the Ministries and the Head of the Prime Minister's Office. The salary of a civil servant of the first class varies from 286 to 372 Ls (approximately € 516 to € 671), averaging 329 Ls (approximately € 593).[89]

The salary of a regional court vice-president, and those of regional court judges and district court presidents equal 90 and 85 percent, respectively, of the salary of a first class civil servant. The salaries of vice-president and judges of district courts equal 90 percent and 85 percent, respectively, of the salary of presidents of district courts.[90]

---

[86] On 12 July 2001, *The Baltic Times* reported that in April 2001 the State President Vaira Vike-Freiberga visited Brasas, a prison for men, which at the time housed 192 boys aged 14–18. Of the 192, 160 had been waiting for trials or appeal hearings more than six months and 31 more than two years. The situation was described by the State President as a "shameful violation of human rights."

[87] Information from the Central Statistical Bureau of Latvia, July–September 2000.

[88] Law on Judicial Power, Art. 119

[89] Regulations of the Cabinet of Ministers, No. 380, Regulations on positions of civil service and wages for civil servant candidates in the transitional period, adopted 8 October 1996, *State Gazette*, 11 October 1996, No. 172.

[90] Law on Judicial Power, Art. 119.

Judges receive monthly supplemental payments in addition to their base salary, based on their qualification class,[91] ranging from 20 to 100 percent of the base salary.[92] The President of the Supreme Court receives an additional 50 percent supplemental payment, while a Vice-President of the Supreme Court receives an additional 25 percent supplemental payment.

Supplemental payment levels are established by law. However, State budgets consistently do not allocate sufficient funds to cover supplemental payments for judges. This opens the opportunity for manipulation: in 2000, some judges received their supplemental payments, and others did not and the promotion of some 100 judges was blocked as it would have necessitated additional remuneration.[93] Failure to allocate funding sufficient to guarantee legally established payments opens channels for improper leverage against the judiciary. In addition, it demonstrates the low regard in which the judiciary is held by the government.

Similarly, although judges are entitled to an extensive list of benefits,[94] which should equal the social benefits of civil servants,[95] in practice few judges receive these benefits; however, there is no evidence that payments are being made selectively to individual judges on any improper preferential basis. One of the most important of these benefits is the paid vacation benefit equal to up to one month's salary; no vacation benefits were paid to judges of district and regional courts in 1999 and 2000.[96] By law, other social benefits which should be provided to judges include a residence benefit for judges serving away from their permanent residence; transfer benefits for moving posts; benefits for special occasions (such as an accident, death of a family member, birth of a child); a family allowance; foreign language proficiency allowance; insurance upon being appointed to office; and insurance in case of injury or death.[97] However, special occasion benefits, family allowances, foreign language allowances, and transfer benefits have not been paid to judges.[98]

---

[91] See Section V.C.

[92] Law on Judicial Power, Art. 120

[93] D. Ankipane, "Finances for legislation in budget are not provided", *Neatkariga rita avize*, 17 August 2000.

[94] See Law on Judicial Power, Art. 125 (providing that the benefits outlined in the Law on Public Civil Service apply to judges as well).

[95] Law on Public Civil Service, Arts. 32–37, 49 and 50.

[96] Information of the President of the Latvian Judges' Association, September 2000.

[97] Law on Public Civil Service, Arts. 32–37, 49 and 50.

[98] Nor, in some cases, to civil servants also entitled to them.

Within six months of the date of appointment, a judge is supposed to be provided with an apartment or house upon the recommendation of the Minister of Justice or the President of the Supreme Court.[99] However, in reality, judges encounter difficulties in the process of obtaining an apartment from local authorities.

Judges' pensions are calculated on the same basis as pensions for all other pensioners, by a formula taking into account contributions to the State Social Insurance Fund and length of service. Therefore, pension amounts vary from judge to judge, but on average the amount of pensions is about 40 percent less than the last income earned.[100] These relatively lower pensions create disincentives for judges to leave the bench which may make them susceptible to pressure from the executive, especially when combined with discretionary retirement ages.[101]

Reduction in salary may only be used as a disciplinary sanction. In appropriate cases, the Judicial Disciplinary Board may reduce up to 20 percent of a judge's salary for up to one year.[102]

*Staff Compensation*: The compensation of the technical staff is very low – about 100 Ls before taxes,[103] which is approximately two thirds of the national average salary. Such low salaries make it difficult to maintain full staffing support for judges, and also encourage corruption.

---

[99] Law on Judicial Power, Art. 124.

[100] Information from the Deputy State Secretary of the Ministry of Justice, May 2000.

[101] See Section V.B.2.

[102] Judicial Disciplinary Liability Law, Art. 7. See Section V.B.2, concerning judges' pensions and possible pressures for them to remain on the bench after retirement.

[103] Information from the Head of the Courts' Department of the Ministry Of Justice, 17 May 2001.

## V. Judicial Office

The executive exercises considerable influence over the career path of judges with relatively few clearly established rules to restrain its discretion, such that it is in a position to hinder judicial independence. Particularly problematic are the removability of judges for their first three to five years in office and discretionary decisions to extend judges' terms beyond the mandatory retirement age.

### A. Selection Process[104]

*Selection:* Apart from the threshold legal requirements,[105] there are no clear rules for identifying candidates for a judgeship. Court presidents invite individuals to submit an application or the Ministry of Justice may advertise a competition for candidates. Candidates who comply with the legal requirements are invited to discussions with the State Secretary of the Ministry and with the president of the court with the vacancy, after which they may be selected for an apprenticeship.[106]

The apprenticeship period varies from one to six months, based on the decision of the State Secretary of the Ministry of Justice and the candidate's professional qualifications. The main responsibility of apprentices is to familiarise themselves with the work of a judge by analysing cases and helping the judge in legal research.[107] Apprentices do not adjudicate cases. Following the apprenticeship, candidates must complete an examination before the Judicial Qualification Board elected by the Conference of Judges of Latvia.[108] At this point, they are eligible for appointment.

*Appointment:* District court judges are nominated by the Minister of Justice and appointed by the Parliament.[109] Apart from confirming the threshold legal eligibility requirements, there are no other standards limiting Parliament's discretion to approve or reject a candidate. Judges are initially appointed only for a term of three to five years.[110]

---

[104] Appointment of court presidents is discussed at Section V.C.

[105] In order to qualify as a candidate for district court judge, an individual must be a citizen at least 25 years old, have a legal education and have completed two years of service in a legal field.

[106] Law on Judicial Power, Art. 52; Information from the Director of the Department of Courts of the Ministry of Justice, May 2001.

[107] Information from the Director of the Department of Courts of the Ministry of Justice May 2001.

[108] Law on Judicial Power, Arts. 52 and 93.

[109] CONST. REP. LATVIA, Art. 84; Law on Judicial Power. Arts. 51–52, 55, 57, and 60.

[110] See Section V.B.1.

The Minister of Justice makes nominations based on an assessment issued by the Judicial Qualification Board following review of a candidate's examination results and an evaluation of performance during the apprenticeship. The law is unclear as to whether an assessment of the Board is binding or merely a recommendation.[111] In practice, however, the Ministry has not deviated from the Board's assessments to date.

*Higher Court Judges*: Regional court judges are also nominated by the Minister of Justice on the basis of the opinion of the Judicial Qualification Board, and appointed by the Parliament for unlimited terms.[112] This system applies to both the judges elevated from the district court (who must have at least two years' experience) and to initial nomination (for individuals who have at least three years' experience as an attorney or public prosecutor). For judges elevated from the district court, appointment is treated as an entirely new process, not a promotion.

Candidates for the Supreme Court judgeship are nominated by the President of the Supreme Court on the basis of the opinion of the Judicial Qualification Board, and appointed by Parliament to unlimited terms. District court judges (with at least four years' experience), regional court judges (with at least two years' experience) and certain legal professionals (attorneys, prosecutors and law lecturers with six years of experience) are eligible.[113]

Lay judges for the district and regional courts are elected by the local municipality for five years. A lower legal threshold applies to candidates for lay judgeship, who must be citizens of Latvia at least twenty-five years old.[114]

## B. Tenure, Retirement, Transfer and Removal

Discretionary political involvement in judges' careers remains a problem. Parliament's power to delay the vesting of tenure and irremovability– up to five years after appointment – threatens judges' decisional independence for that period. Discretionary extension of retirement – over which the Minister of Justice and senior judges have effective vetoes – gives judges incentives to be co-operative with the executive or their judicial superiors.

---

[111] Law on Judicial Power, Art. 57.

[112] Law on Judicial Power, Arts. 51, 53, 55, 57, and 61.

[113] Law on Judicial Power, Arts. 51, 54, 55, 59, and 62.

[114] Law on Judicial Power, Arts. 56 and 64.

## 1. Non-Tenured Appointment

According to the Constitution, judicial appointments are irrevocable.[115] Once appointed to an unlimited term, judges are guaranteed tenure until a mandatory retirement age. However, judges are not given tenure until three to five years into their service, and the final decision to grant them tenure is based, in part, on their performance in office and in part on the Ministry of Justice's and Parliament's discretion, which inevitably creates incentives for judges to avoid adjudicating in ways which might displease the executive.

Judges are initially appointed to a three-year term.[116] On completion of the initial term, a judge may be confirmed by Parliament for an unlimited term in office or re-appointed for an additional two-year term. In one instance, in 1998 Parliament refused to re-appoint two probationary judges who were to hear a politically sensitive case concerning the mayor of Daugavpils. When one of the rejected candidates was re-nominated, the Parliament appointed him; the other judge was re-nominated to the Land Registry Office and was also appointed by the Parliament, which provided no explanations for either the initial rejection or subsequent appointment of either candidate. In general, however, the Parliament rarely rejects a nominee for the bench.

The Minister of Justice proposes candidates for reappointment based on assessments provided by the Judicial Qualification Board; the Minister may refuse to re-nominate a judge.[117] There are no additional formal criteria for deciding whether to nominate a judge for an additional two-year term or for an unlimited term of office. There is no possibility provided in any rules to appeal a decision of the Board or the Ministry, although the Ministry is reportedly planning a proposed amendment to provide for the possibility of appeals.[118]

Informally, the judge's performance on the bench, litigants' complaints concerning the judge's performance, the number of cases decided by the judge, and the percentage of the judge's decisions overturned on appeal are taken into account by the Board.[119] Usually, after the initial three-year term, judges are appointed to unlimited terms of office. In 2000, for example, only one judge, and in 2001 two judges, were given two-year re-appointments; there were no instances reported of the Minister refusing a re-

---

[115] CONST. REP. LATVIA, Art. 84.

[116] CONST. REP. LATVIA, Art. 84; Law on Judicial Power. Arts. 51–52, 55, 57, and 60.

[117] Law on Judicial Power, Art. 60.

[118] Information from the Director of the Department of Courts of the Ministry of Justice, 17 May 2001.

[119] Information from the Director of the Department of Courts of the Ministry of Justice, 17 May 2001.

nomination altogether, nor of Parliament refusing to appoint a candidate nominated by the Minister. Nonetheless, such a system of largely discretionary vesting of tenure inevitably introduces chilling effects on judges' willingness to adjudicate without concern for their job safety.

For example, in 2000, two Members of Parliament made public statements to the press concerning the pending court case of another Member accused of co-operating with the KGB. The presiding judge, in the final year of his three-year probationary term, was to be considered for lifetime tenure by Parliament in 2001. The Latvian Judges' Association opined that the Parliament members' actions constituted an attempt to indirectly influence the decision of the court.

What is most relevant from this case is the fact that Parliament is in a position to rule on a serving judge's tenure. Although using the media to make inflammatory attacks on the judiciary or to create a hostile atmosphere against judges is improper, there is nothing necessarily improper in Members of Parliament publicly criticising a judicial decision, or even the conduct of a pending case. The Members' statements are potentially troublesome only because they are in a position actually to affect the outcome of the case, because the law bests power to grant or withhold judicial tenure.

In 2001, a major opposition political party recently proposed a constitutional amendment abolishing life tenure in favour of direct popular elections of judges to four-year terms; the amendment would also allow the State President to appoint the President of the Supreme Court to a four-year term as well.

## 2. Retirement

The mandatory retirement age is sixty-five for district and regional court judges and seventy for Supreme Court justices.[120] Judges receive a pension after leaving office.

A judge's term of office may be extended beyond the mandatory retirement age. The Minister of Justice and the President of the Supreme Court, upon receiving a favourable opinion from the Judicial Qualification Board, may extend, with a joint decision, the office of a district or regional court judge for up to five years. The President of the Supreme Court alone has the same power with regard to the Supreme Court judges.[121] This discretionary power may give judges approaching retirement improper incentives

---

[120] Law on Judicial Power, Art. 63.

[121] Law on Judicial Power, Art. 63.

to ensure that their rulings do not jeopardise their chances for extension, especially as judges' pensions are considerably lower than their salaries. The authority for this decision is dispersed, but at the same time, as all three bodies – the Ministry, the President of the Supreme Court, and the Board – must give their consent, any one can also veto a judge's request to remain on the bench.

The Minister of Justice may assign emeritus judges, with their consent, to fill vacancies for up to two years, an arrangement which could potentially compromise the independence of those judges, especially if they are available for multiple substitute assignments.

## 3. Transfer

Parliament assigns judges to specific district or regional courts. Supreme Court justices are all assigned to Riga, the seat of the Court. Judges may not be permanently transferred without their consent. Judges may be temporarily transferred to substitute for another judge.[122] Whenever a vacancy develops in a district or regional court, the Minister of Justice may assign an emeritus judge or a serving judge of the same or a higher level (i.e., regional court judges may be assigned to district courts) to act as a substitute for a maximum period of two years, with the judge's consent. Lay judges may also be assigned as substitute judges at district courts. A serving or emeritus judge of the Supreme Court or a regional judge assigned by the President of the Supreme Court may substitute for a judge of the Supreme Court.

## 4. Removal

Judges may be dismissed or removed[123] only on grounds and by procedures established by law;[124] the executive's involvement, though it is unnecessary and perhaps increases marginally the possibility for undue influence, is not a particular threat to independence, as the power to remove or dismiss is divided among several powers.

---

[122] Law on Judicial Power, Arts. 74–80.

[123] Procedures for dismissal and removal differ only in that dismissal is recommended by the Judicial Qualification Board (and dismissal of the President of the Supreme Court requires, in addition, the opinion of the Plenary session of the Supreme Court), while removal is recommended by the Minister of Justice for district and regional court judges, by the President of the Supreme Court for Supreme Court judges, and by the Cabinet for the President of the Supreme Court.

[124] See Law on Judicial Power.

Judges may be removed by Parliament in the following circumstances: at their own request; if they are elected or appointed to another post; for health reasons; or if they have reached the mandatory retirement age.[125] A judge convicted and sentenced in a criminal case must be dismissed by Parliament after the judgement has entered into force. In addition, a judge may be dismissed on the basis of the Judicial Disciplinary Board's decision to dismiss in a disciplinary procedure.[126] In all cases Parliament has final discretion in the matter.[127]

If a disciplinary action is initiated against a district or regional court judge, the Minister of Justice can suspend the judge's activities until a final decision is reached. If a judge is charged with a criminal offence, the Minister suspends the judge's activities pending a final decision in the case. Judges of the Supreme Court can be suspended by a decision of the President of the Supreme Court under the same conditions.[128]

District court presidents can be removed by the Minister of Justice on the basis of a decision of the Judicial Disciplinary Board. Regional court presidents can be removed by Parliament on the proposal of the Minister or the President of the Supreme Court acting on the basis of the decision by the Board.[129]

A lay judge may be much more easily dismissed. A local government may dismiss a lay judge upon the request of a district or regional court.[130] Lay judges must be dismissed if they have been sentenced for a crime, are guilty of an intentional violation of the law in connection with the issuance of judgements, or if their conduct is deemed incompatible with the status of a lay judge's office.

A proposed constitutional amendment would make repeated and clearly unfounded decisions grounds for removing a judge. Even if cabined within careful procedural protections, such a rule risks chilling the very core of judicial decision-making.

---

[125] Law on Judicial Power, Arts. 81–83.

[126] Law on Judicial Power, Art. 83. See Section V.D.

[127] Law on Judicial Power, Art. 81.

[128] Law on Judicial Power, Art. 84.

[129] Law on Judicial Power, Arts. 33 and 40.

[130] Law on Judicial Power, Art. 85.

## C. Evaluation and Promotion

*Promotion in Class*: There are six qualification categories for judges.[131] The Judicial Qualification Board decides about granting a particular qualification class,[132] which carries a pay rise with it.

The Minister of Justice makes recommendations on assigning district and regional court judges to a particular class, which must be submitted no later than two months after the judge has become eligible for the next class.[133] The President of the Supreme Court makes the recommendation for judges of that Court. (Judges themselves cannot directly request a promotion in class.)

Placement in a specific qualification class depends on seniority. New judge appointees are usually awarded the lowest, fifth qualification class, but if a new appointee is highly qualified and has extensive legal experience, he or she may be placed in a higher qualification class. However, class promotion is not connected with promotion to a higher court; some district court judges have the highest qualification class.[134] A higher qualification class entitles the judge to higher supplementary payments, ranging from 20 percent to 100 percent of the base salary.[135]

In deciding to grant a particular qualification class, the Judicial Qualification Board reviews the judge's personnel file, maintained by the Personnel Department of the Ministry of Justice, as well as references from the State Secretary of the Ministry, the presidents of courts in which the judge has served.[136] However, there are no clearly formulated assessment criteria, nor do there appear to be any clearly established informal rules. There is no complaint procedure against a refusal to grant the next qualification; however the Ministry reportedly supports the introduction of such a procedure.[137]

---

[131] Regulation on the Judicial Qualification Board and Rules for Attestation of Judges, adopted 23 April 1999 by the Judicial Qualification Board.

[132] Law on Judicial Power, Arts. 93 and 94.

[133] Regulation On the Judicial Qualification Board and Rules for Attestation of Judges, Art. 4(3). Promotion to a higher qualification class requires a (progressively longer) period of service in the class immediately preceding it, so that a judge must serve two years in the lowest class to be eligible for promotion to the next class, while to be promoted to the highest class, he or she must have served seven years in the preceding class.

[134] Information from the Director of the Department of Courts of the Ministry of Justice, May 2001.

[135] See Section IV.C.

[136] Information from the Director of the Department of Courts of the Ministry of Justice, May 2001.

[137] Information from the Director of the Department of Courts of the Ministry of Justice, May 2001.

The absence of clearly formulated criteria may allow the Judicial Qualification Board to abuse its discretion. To date, however, no controversy has been reported; judges are granted the next qualification class more or less automatically once they have completed the minimum service requirement in their current class.

*Appointment as Court President*: Court presidents are all appointed by the Ministry of Justice or the Parliament for limited, renewable terms, which unnecessarily allows the political branches a regular opportunity to intervene in the organisation of court supervision.

A nominee for court president must meet all the criteria for appointment as a judge to that same court, and in addition the Board, in forming its opinion, takes into account a poll among the judges of the court.[138]

Parliament appoints the presidents of regional courts for a five-year period based on the joint recommendation of the Minister of Justice and the President of the Supreme Court.[139] Their joint recommendation is based on the opinion of the Judicial Qualification Board. Although the law does not clarify whether the Board's opinion is binding, its opinion has not been rejected to date. Parliament appoints the President of the Supreme Court on the recommendation of the Cabinet of Ministers from among appointed judges of the Supreme Court for a period of seven years.[140]

Judges' irremovability is not affected by their appointment to or removal from positions as court presidents; however, the regular opportunity for the Ministry and Parliament to determine the court president unnecessarily provides the political branches opportunities to intervene in the organisation of the courts, and through them with the work of individual judges.

## D. Discipline

### 1. Liability

Judges (including lay judges) have immunity "during the period he fulfils his duties in relation to adjudication in a court."[141] Judges are exempt from civil liability for

---

[138] Information from the Director of the Department of Courts of the Ministry of Justice, May 2001.

[139] Law on Judicial Power, Art. 40.

[140] Law on Judicial Power, Art. 50.

[141] Law on Judicial Power, Art.13.

actions carried out during the performance of their functions. A judge's property is not subject to forfeiture for damages suffered by a litigant resulting from an unlawful judgement;[142] in such cases, as specified by law, damages are paid by the State, but no indemnification of the judge is allowed.[143]

A judge can be arrested or prosecuted only with the consent of the Parliament. Criminal cases against judges may be initiated only by the Prosecutor General, and decisions concerning a judge's arrest, forced appearance before a court, detention or subjection to search are made by a specially authorised judge of the Supreme Court.[144] A lay judge cannot be arrested or prosecuted while executing judicial duties without the consent of the local government that elected that judge. However, a lay judge is subject to disciplinary proceedings for administrative violations.[145]

## 2. Disciplinary Proceedings

The Judicial Disciplinary Liability Law establishes the grounds and procedures for disciplinary proceedings against judges.[146] The process does not appear to present any particular risks to judges' decisional independence.

A judge may be charged with misconduct for intentional violation of the law during review of a case; failure to perform professional duties; dishonourable actions; administrative violations; or refusal to discontinue membership in a party or political organisation.[147] The most common cause for disciplinary procedure is intentional breach of the law during hearings.[148]

All disciplinary cases are reviewed by the Judicial Disciplinary Board.[149] The Board consists of the President and Vice-President of the Supreme Court, as well as three

---

[142] Law on Judicial Power, Art. 13.

[143] Law on Compensation for the Damages Suffered as a Result of the Unlawful or Ungrounded Action of an Investigator, Prosecutor or Judge, adopted 28 May 1998, *State Gazette*, 16 June 1998, No. 176.

[144] Law on Judicial Power, Art. 13.

[145] Law on Judicial Power, Art. 13.

[146] Judicial Disciplinary Liability Law, adopted 27 October 1994, *State Gazette*, 10 November 1994, No. 132.

[147] Judicial Disciplinary Liability Law, Art. 1.

[148] Information from the Director of the Department of Courts of the Ministry of Justice, May 2001.

[149] Judicial Disciplinary Liability Law, Art. 2.; Law on Judicial Power, Art. 90.

judges of the Supreme Court, two regional court chairmen, two district court chairmen and the two heads of Land Registry Offices elected by the Conference of Judges.[150]

The President of the Supreme Court, the Minister of Justice, presidents of regional and district courts, or heads of the Land Registry Offices may initiate a disciplinary procedure against judges beneath them.[151] Any judge against whom a disciplinary case has been initiated has the right to review the case materials, furnish explanations, and participate in the meetings of the Judicial Disciplinary Board.

The Judicial Disciplinary Board may take the following actions: dismiss the disciplinary case; impose disciplinary sanctions, such as a reprimand or reduction of base salary; forward the case to the Prosecutor's Office for criminal proceedings; recommend to the Parliament that the judge be removed from office; or forward the case to the Judicial Qualification Board for a review of the judge's qualification class.[152] Decisions of the Board are not subject to appeal.

The Latvian Judges' Association adopted a Code of Judicial Ethics in 1995 but the Code is not applied in practice. The principle that a judge may be subject to liability for dishonourable actions is interpreted narrowly, and violations of the Code of Ethics do not constitute grounds for disciplinary liability.[153]

---

[150] Judicial Disciplinary Liability Law, Art.2.
[151] Judicial Disciplinary Liability Law, Art. 3.
[152] Judicial Disciplinary Liability Law, Art. 7.
[153] Judicial Disciplinary Liability Law, Art. 1.

# VI. Intra-Judicial Relations

## A. Relations with Superior Courts

The Plenum of the Supreme Court issues clarifications on the application of laws, which are binding for the courts of general jurisdiction,[154] a practice which many judges feel effectively subordinates them to another court's interpretations as if they were legislative acts, in violation of the constitutional provision that "judges shall be independent and subject only to the law."[155] The Plenum has issued clarifications on the application of laws in many highly contested and notorious civil and criminal cases.[156]

The regular appeals processes provide opportunities for superior court judges to alter the outcome of lower court judges' decisions, but according to procedures that do not affect individual judges' legitimate independence. Generally speaking, appeals of first instance claims may be reviewed on both factual and legal grounds as to the whole judgement or any part of it; the appellate court reviews the case on its merits *de novo*. The appellate instance court may affirm the judgement of the court of the first instance; vacate the judgement of the first instance court in whole or in part; or direct further investigation or a new review at the court of first instance.

Decisions of the appellate instance court may be further appealed under a cassation procedure. (Direct cassation review of a first instance decision is also possible.) The cassation court may affirm the decision, vacate it, or modify it. If the court of cassation instance vacates a decision it may return the case for pre-trial investigation (in criminal cases) or for retrial, or may terminate the proceedings.

There is no official system in Latvia of appointed supervisors acting as mentors, but in practice lower court judges often consult with superior court judges in specific cases. The Supreme Court organises an annual seminar for regional court judges to discuss

---

[154] Law on Judicial Power, Art. 49.

[155] Constitution of the Republic of Latvia, Art. 83.

[156] The Plenum's clarifications concerning interpretation of the Civil Code include On Court Practice in Cases Concerning Defamation, On Court Practice in Cases Concerning Establishment of Facts Having Legal Significance (1993); On Application of the Law in Inheritance Cases (1995); On Application of the Law Reviewing Cases of Family Law (1996); On Application of the Law Reviewing Liability Conflicts (1997); and On Application of Article 1635 of the Civil Code when Reviewing Cases Concerning Moral Damages (1999).

topical issues of legal practice.[157] In addition, judges of the Supreme Court deliver lectures to judges of regional courts at the Judicial Training Centre.

## B. Case Management and Relations with Court Presidents

The system of case-assignment is outdated and unnecessarily allows court presidents discretion in assignment of cases. In district courts, the president of the court assigns cases to judges, while in regional courts, the Presidents of the Civil and Criminal Divisions assign cases; in the Supreme Court, cases are assigned by the President of the Senate and by the presidents of the Divisions.[158]

In January 2001, the Ministry of Justice's instruction on case assignment took effect for district and regional courts.[159] The Ministry allows cases to be assigned by date of submission, to judges specialised in the relevant area of law, or alphabetically by the defendant or other respondent's name; each court president selects one of these three methods to distribute cases.[160] Judges' workload and specialisation are taken into consideration.

According to the January 2001 instruction, the Ministry of Justice intends to establish a new computer-based system of random case assignment by the year 2006.[161] However, the allocative principles of the system will not differ in substance from those employed now.

Although the law does not contain any provisions for transferring a case from one judge to another, in practice a case may be transferred to another judge if the original judge must take a long absence due to illness or pregnancy, for example, or if the original judge opts for recusal.

---

[157] Information from the President of the Supreme Court, September 2000.

[158] Information from the President of the Supreme Court, September 2000.

[159] Instruction from the Ministry of Justice, No. 1–2/4, "On appointment of a judge to review a case", adopted 27 March 2000.

[160] Instruction from the Ministry of Justice, No. 1–2/4, "On appointment of a judge to review a case".

[161] Information from the Computerisation Expert of the Courthouse Agency, May 2001.

# VII. Enforcement and Corruption

## A. Enforcement of Judgements

State institutions generally fulfil their obligations arising from court decisions. Enforcement of civil judgements is particularly low, however; 70 percent of all civil judgements are not enforced, in part due to the difficult working circumstances of the court bailiffs responsible for enforcement as well as the difficult socio-economic situation in the country.[162] Such low levels of enforcement can lead to a decline in public support for the judiciary and calls for firmer control which will curtail judges' independence.

Court bailiffs are employees of the Court Bailiffs' Department of the Ministry of Justice.[163] Court bailiffs are in perhaps the most difficult material position of any of the legal professions. The profession is hampered by meagre resources and a lack of legal training and equipment. Basic salaries are minimal – 89 Ls (€ 162) per month for a junior bailiff and 112 Ls (approximately € 203) for a senior bailiff, both well under the national average – and corruption is reportedly widespread. The prestige of the profession is very low, and there are insufficient numbers of bailiffs to enforce outstanding judgements effectively.[164]

In response to these problems, the privatisation of the profession has been planned. A draft Law on Sworn Court bailiffs was prepared in 1999,[165] and the Cabinet of Ministers submitted it to Parliament at the end of April 2001.[166] The law would create an Institute of Independent Sworn Court Bailiffs as a body of legal professionals responsible for providing themselves with all necessary means to perform their duties, with compensation dependent on the number of executed court decisions. Bailiffs would also be required to have more legal qualifications.

---

[162] C. Sandgren, D. Iljanova, UNDP "Needs Assessment of the Judicial System of Latvia", September 2000.

[163] Law on Judicial Power, Art. 109.

[164] See Information from Concept Paper: "Proposal on UNDP/Multi-Donor Assistance for Judicial Reform", October 2000.

[165] Information from "Latvian National Program for Integration in the European Union", *State Gazette*, 7 July 2000, No. 252/254.

[166] Information from the Head of the Legal Bureau of Parliament, 14 May 2001.

## B. Corruption

Corruption is generally perceived to be widespread in the judiciary, as in other segments of public life. Latvia ranked 57th out of 90 States in the Transparency International Corruption Perceptions Index of 2000.[167] According to one poll, citizens listed the courts as the seventh most dishonest institution in the country.[168]

The actual level of corruption – as opposed to measurements of public perception about the issue – is difficult to determine. Allegations of widespread corruption in the judicial system are seldom substantiated. It seems likely that corruption in the judiciary is no more widespread – and perhaps less so – than in segments of the police, customs and municipal governments, although this is only a relative standard.[169] Nonetheless, even limited levels of corruption – or persistent, uncontradicted perceptions of corruption – can seriously weaken public support for the judiciary's special measure of independence.

---

[167] See <http://www.delna.lv/english/index.htm.> (accessed 20 August 2001).

[168] See Delna (Latvian branch of Transparency International), <http://www.delna.lv/> (accessed 20 August 2001).

[169] C. Sandgren, D. Iljanova, UNDP "Needs Assessment of the Judicial System of Latvia", September 2000 (in English).

OPEN SOCIETY INSTITUTE 2001

# Judicial Independence
# in Lithuania

MONITORING THE EU ACCESSION PROCESS: JUDICIAL INDEPENDENCE

# Table of Contents

Executive Summary ..................................................... 270

I. Introduction ...................................................... 273

    A. Judicial System in Transition – the 1999 Constitutional Court Ruling ................... 273
       1. The 1999 Ruling ............................... 273
       2. Post-ruling Developments .................. 274

    B. Political and Public Attitudes towards the Judiciary ............................. 276

    C. The Judiciary and the Accession Process ... 278

    D. Organisation of the Judicial System ......... 279

II. Constitutional and Legal Foundations of Judicial Independence ................................. 281

    A. Separation of Powers and Guarantees of Independence ........................................ 281

    B. Representation of the Judiciary ............... 282

    C. Rules on Incompatibility .......................... 284

    D. Judges' Associations ................................. 285

III. Administration of the Court System and Judicial Independence .............................. 286

IV. Financial Autonomy and Level of Funding .... 289

    A. Budgeting Process ..................................... 289

    B. Work Conditions ....................................... 291

    C. Compensation ........................................... 293

V. Judicial Office .................................................. 295
   A. Selection Process ........................................ 295
   B. Tenure, Retirement, Transfer
      and Removal ............................................. 296
      1. Tenure and Retirement ........................ 296
      2. Transfer ................................................ 298
      3. Removal ............................................... 298
   C. Evaluation and Promotion ......................... 299
   D. Discipline .................................................. 300
      1. Liability ............................................... 300
      2. Disciplinary Proceedings .................... 301

VI. Intra-Judicial Relations .................................. 303
   A. Relations with Superior Courts ................. 303
   B. Case Management and Relations
      with Court Presidents ............................... 305

VII. Enforcement .................................................. 306

# Judicial Independence in Lithuania

## Executive Summary

Lithuania has made progress in developing a judiciary founded on respect for the rule of law. Fundamental guarantees of judicial independence and separation of powers are entrenched in constitutional jurisprudence, and a landmark ruling by the Constitutional Court in 1999 mandated major restructuring which, when it is completed, will likely reduce the executive's undue influence over judges.

However, despite these achievements, Lithuania still has not completed structural reforms important to ensuring the independence of the judiciary. The same 1999 Constitutional Court ruling has created an institutional and legal vacuum, and it is not yet clear who exercises authority over core judicial administrative issues; in some important areas, the executive retains unnecessarily broad authority. Funding for the judiciary is inadequate, working conditions inadequate, and the basic economic independence of judges has been threatened by salary reductions. Many of these problems are rooted in a political culture that is suspicious of the judiciary and still insufficiently committed to the principle of judicial independence.

*Judicial System in Transition*

The judicial system is in flux. Since the Constitutional Court's 1999 ruling, no sanctioned system has been instituted to replace the voided provisions of the Law on Courts, and instead, a number of *ad hoc* solutions have been employed. The immediate effect has been a significant reduction in the executive's influence over the judiciary, but the uncertainty has allowed continued undue executive interference in some areas. A new Law on Courts is being drafted.

*Political and Public Attitudes*

The judiciary operates in an inhospitable environment and is mistrusted and not respected by politicians, the general public, and media. Political actors across the spectrum evince an insufficient level of respect for the separate position of the courts and the systemic importance of judges' independence; in some cases, they have tried improperly to influence judges' decisions. The effect of such actions is to jeopardise the actual independence of courts. Public and media attitudes towards the judiciary are also fairly negative.

*Funding for the Judiciary*

Notwithstanding the Constitutional Court's 1999 ruling, courts still do not have effective control of their budgets. The executive's involvement in the budgeting process and the allocation of funds is still significant, and the budget process itself remains insufficiently transparent. In part as a consequence, courts remain seriously under-funded; funding has decreased in absolute terms, despite an increase in the number of judges and the workload of the courts. Working conditions in courts are poor to the point that that they may well interfere with judges' ability to carry out their duties, create unnecessary reliance on the executive's ability to provide support, and place pressures on judicial impartiality.

In addition to these general issues, the following issues of particular concern are discussed in the body of the Report:

*Representation*

The judiciary does not have a separate constitutional representative. The lack of such a representative tends to undercut other constitutional and legislative guarantees of independence, especially during the current period of flux. This is particularly problematic in the budget process, in which the judiciary's participation is limited.

*Administration*

Perhaps no section of the judiciary's organisation has been more affected by the 1999 ruling than its administration. Under the previous system, the Ministry of Justice exercised extensive administrative control over the courts. The draft Law on Courts would transfer administrative control of courts to the Council of Judges and the National Court Administration, which should substantially reduce executive influence.

*Pensions*

Judges are awarded pensions far lower than many other State officials involved in law enforcement receive. The draft Law on Courts would extend comparable benefits to judges.

*Executive Involvement in Judges' Careers*

Despite the changes mandated by the 1999 ruling, the executive still retains undue influence over the careers of judges, especially during their initial probationary appointment. New district court judges are appointed for a probationary term of five years, only after which they are eligible for life tenure. This places younger judges in a position of reliance on executive discretion, which places their decisional independence at risk.

*Enforcement*

As a rule, judicial decisions are respected by political authorities, although civil judgements often go unenforced. This can lead to decreased respect for or reliance on legal processes, and a concomitant decline in support for the judges who issue decisions.

*Corruption*

Corruption appears to be a serious problem; there have been several cases in which judges, particularly those of the district courts who receive the lowest salaries, have been sentenced for corruption.

## I. Introduction

Less than a decade after the restoration of its independence, Lithuania has made progress in developing a judiciary founded on general respect for the rule of law. Fundamental guarantees of judicial independence and the separation of powers are entrenched in constitutional jurisprudence, and a landmark ruling by the Constitutional Court in 1999 has mandated a major restructuring of the courts' administration which, when it is completed, will likely reduce the executive's influence over judges.

However, despite these achievements, a number of problems remain, and Lithuania still has not completed structural reforms important to ensuring the independence of the judiciary. The same 1999 Constitutional Court ruling has in effect created an institutional and legal vacuum, in which it is not at all clear who exercises authority over core judicial administrative issues. In some important areas, the executive retains unnecessarily broad authority, either legitimately or in the absence of new legislation redistributing its former powers.

In addition, and partly as a consequence of the incomplete transition, funding for the judiciary is inadequate, working conditions inadequate, and the basic economic independence of judges has been threatened by salary reductions. Many of these problems are rooted in a political culture that is suspicious of the judiciary and still insufficiently committed to the principle of judicial independence.

### A. Judicial System in Transition – the 1999 Constitutional Court Ruling

The judicial system is in flux. A major constitutional ruling in 1999 effectively voided large areas of established law and practice relating to administration of the judiciary on the grounds that it gave the executive undue influence in violation of the constitutionally mandated separation of powers. To date, however, no constitutionally sanctioned replacement has been instituted, and instead, a number of *ad hoc* solutions have been employed. The immediate effect has been a significant reduction in the executive's influence over the judiciary, but in some areas the uncertainty has allowed executive influence to remain entrenched.

#### 1. *The 1999 Ruling*

In 1999 a group of Members of Parliament applied to the Constitutional Court to review the constitutionality of certain articles of the Law on Courts dealing with the

Ministry of Justice. The petitioners argued that the provisions created direct and indirect opportunities for the Ministry to interfere with the activities of courts and thereby contradicted the principles of separation of powers and judicial independence enshrined in the Constitution.[1] The Court's 21 December 1999 ruling found 16 provisions of the Law on Courts unconstitutional.[2]

The Court's ruling has established a conceptual basis for judicial independence, but it has also created what many observers have called a "legal vacuum". According to the Constitution, a legal act is not applicable from the day a Constitutional Court ruling finding the act in contravention of the Constitution is published; thus the unconstitutional articles are not applicable any more. However, a new law on courts is still being drafted, and as a result, lines of administrative authority are presently unregulated. In some cases, the Council of Judges has taken over functions of the Ministry of Justice, but in others – as, for example, when court division presidents' terms expire[3] – there is no authority clearly competent to act.

## 2. Post-ruling Developments

The new draft law has been delayed by difficulties in developing a unified concept acceptable to both judicial and non-judicial actors. A draft law prepared by a working group formed by the Council of Judges, and finalised by the Supreme Court, was forwarded to Parliament in summer 2001. Parliament's Committee for Legal Affairs has established a broadly representative working group to discuss the numerous objections and additional proposals to the initial draft. The different provisions of the draft law as of May 2001 are considered in relevant sections of this report.

The stalled process of institutional and legal reform has contributed to the persistence of both financial and administrative problems in the legal infrastructure underlying the judiciary's independence.

Thus, although the Constitutional Court's 1999 ruling was supposed to ensure that courts have meaningful economic independence, they still do not have effective control

---

[1] The concept of judicial independence had been progressively developed by the Constitutional Court. The Court's ruling of 6 of February 1995, dealing with safeguards of judicial independence, was of great importance in developing the concept.

[2] Ruling of the Constitutional Court adopted on 21 December (*Valstybes Zinios*, hereafter "Official Gazette", 1999, No. 109–3192).

[3] Under the system before 1999, presidents of court divisions (criminal and civil) were appointed by the Minister of Justice. The terms of office of a number of them have since expired.

of their budgets, and the executive's involvement in the budgeting process and the allocation of funds is still significant. In part as a consequence, courts remain seriously underfunded, leading to a lack of infrastructure investment and economic pressures throughout the system. Working conditions in courts are so poor that they may well interfere with judges' ability to carry out their duties, create unnecessary reliance on the executive's ability to provide support, and place pressures on judges to accept assistance from private actors which would compromise their impartiality.

The Law on Wages of Politicians, Judges and Government Officials, passed in August 2000,[4] would significantly reduce the salaries of judges, despite rulings of the Constitutional Court suggesting that any such reduction would be an obvious infringement on the economic independence of the judiciary.[5] The Constitutional Court has ruled the decreases unconstitutional, but it as yet unclear what will happen with judges' salaries, and in any event the effort by the political branches to reduce the salaries unnecessarily sends a worrisome message to judges.

Moreover, since the 1999 ruling, it has not been clear which institution or officials may legitimately represent the judiciary in its relations with the other branches or who has decisional power over a range of administrative matters.

The new draft Law on Courts would give bodies connected to the judiciary substantial authority over administrative matters. Under the law, the Council of Judges would have broad powers to: approve the budgets of courts and the National Court Administration and submit them to the Government; represent the courts on budgetary matters before the Government and other State institutions; approve the framework for administration of the courts; supervise the activities of the National Court Administration and receive its reports; advise the State President on matters related to judicial selection and careers; and convene the General Meeting of Judges.[6] A National Court Administration would be responsible for day-to-day administration of the court system on a national level.[7] However, these reforms have not been completed.

---

[4] Law on Wages of Politicians, Judges and Government Officials No. VIII–1904, (Official Gazette 2000, No. 75–2271).

[5] The Law on Wages of Politicians, Judges and Government Officials has not itself been the subject of a Constitutional Court ruling, and therefore it is possible that its provisions would be found consistent with the Constitution, the guidance of the earlier cases notwithstanding.

[6] Draft Law on Courts, Art. 121.

[7] Draft Law on Courts, Arts. 124–126.

## B. Political and Public Attitudes towards the Judiciary

The judiciary operates in an environment which is not always hospitable. Courts and judges are, on the whole, mistrusted and not fully respected by a number of politicians, as well as substantial segments of the general public and media. Weak political and public support for the judiciary not only encourages incursions on judges' decisional independence, but also reduces the willingness and/or ability of other actors to bolster judicial independence indirectly, including through sufficient resource allocation. This in turn further weakens courts' claim to social and political support.

*Political Attitudes*: Political actors across the spectrum evince an insufficient level of public respect for the separate position of the courts and for the fundamental importance to democratic government of judges' independence.

Although there is no evidence of political actors attempting to blackmail judges, over the past decade some public officials have approached, and others have crossed, the line between appropriate criticism of specific decisions and improper defiance of the legitimate authority of the courts. Last year, certain Members of Parliament ignored repeated summons to appear as witnesses in a case before the district court in Svencioniai, leading the judge to fine them.[8] While criticism by political actors of the court system or of individual decisions is acceptable in a free society, sustained attacks and disregard can undermine support for the independence of judges.

The political branches have also sought improperly to control courts' activities. In 1997, for example, the Government issued a decree instructing the Ministry of Justice to control certain criminal cases.[9] In 1999 the President of Parliament appealed to the Minister of Justice to consider disciplinary actions against certain judges who had issued judgements in highly publicised cases that were subsequently overturned on appeal.[10] Particularly in matters that have attracted media attention, public officials have on occasion pressed judges to avoid acquittals in criminal cases or to reach decisions favourable to specific parties in civil cases. In one instance, for example, the then President of Parliament forwarded to the President of the Supreme Court the complaint of the plaintiff in a pending civil

---

[8] "Defendants and witnesses ignore the courts", *Lietuvos Rytas*, 7 August 2000.

[9] Decree of the Government of the Republic of Lithuania, 4 February 1997, No. 92. Official Gazette 1997, No. 13–267.

[10] Chronicles of *Seimas* (Parliament), 1999, No. 7(112).

dispute, indicating how the case should be resolved, and underlining his official right to initiate disciplinary action against judges.[11]

The cumulative effect of these intrusions has been to place in jeopardy the actual independence of the courts, and of individual judges.

*Public and Media Attitudes*: Public attitudes towards the judiciary as reflected in public opinion polls and in the media are generally negative. According to two recent surveys, a high percentage of the population mistrusts the judiciary[12] and believes them to be corrupt.[13] Indeed, there have been several cases in which judges of the district courts have been sentenced for corruption.[14] At the same time, another poll reported that 86.1 percent of those polled supported reductions in judicial salaries.[15]

The media is also generally critical of State institutions, including the courts, and frequently airs allegations of corruption. Periodically, individual judges are criticised in the media for allegedly unfair, partial, or biased decisions, and for being highly paid.[16] As with politicians, such criticisms are acceptable in a free society – and particularly welcome when they expose real incidents of corruption or malfeasance. However, intemperate criticism can weaken the public support necessary for sustaining the independence of the judiciary.[17] Indeed, lack of respect for courts manifested by statements of politicians and journalists was seen as one of the main reasons for the lack of public confidence in the judiciary.[18]

---

[11] The defendant in the case, considering such an action to be a direct influence on the activities of court, has requested that the Prosecutor General initiate criminal proceedings. "The threat of penitentiary service to V. Landsbergis", *Lietuvos Rytas*, 1 March 2001.

[12] Baltijos Tyrimai survey, see <http://www.5ci.lt/ratings/lit/frameset.htm>, in Lithuanian (accessed 22 August 2001).

[13] Transparency International survey "Lithuanian Residents about the Corruption in Lithuania", <http://www.transparency.lt/En/TILS_projects.htm> (accessed 22 August 2001).

[14] See "Judges' solidarity with regard to compensation makes one wonder", *Lietuvos Rytas*, 2 August 2001.

[15] See, generally, for polls on public opinion, <http://www.press.lt/DefaultL.htm>, in Lithuanian (accessed 22 August 2001).

[16] "Greedy judges covet millions", *Vakaro Zinios*, 13 March 2001.

[17] After the case concerning the Chairman of Parliament's attempt to influence a pending case, one paper criticised the courts' lack of independence; one paper commented that it is difficult to believe that the courts are really independent if the mere request of a politician is enough to change the course of a case. See *Lietuvos Rytas*, 2 March 2001.

[18] A. Sakalas, "Why do we mistrust courts?" *Lietuvos Zinios*, 8 December 1998.

There have been some efforts to bridge the gap between the media and the judiciary. In 2000, the Lithuanian Association of Judges and the Union of Journalists of Lithuania organised five regional meetings of judges with journalists in different regions of the country.[19] In 2001, three such meetings have taken place, with preparatory work for two more underway.[20]

## C. The Judiciary and the Accession Process

The Commission's 1999 Regular Report called for continued reform of the judiciary. The 2000 Regular Report concluded that there had been only limited concrete progress since the previous year, which was due to especially stringent budgetary constraints. The Report underlined several problems related to appointment of judges, adequate remuneration, working conditions and equipment.[21]

In general, the judiciary is not involved in the accession process.[22] Moreover, the public and representatives of the political branches are not aware of the Commission's comments about the judiciary. No national plan for implementing the Commission's recommendations has been developed, either by the judiciary itself or the executive.

Judges are largely unfamiliar with existing EU support programs and do not know where or how to apply for funds.[23] Certain co-operative training and development projects have been supported though the EU Phare programme, including a "Twinning" programme which brings German and Swedish court officials together with Lithuanian colleagues. However, the content of these projects, and others providing training in EU law, have not been developed in consultation with local judges, and to date little attempt has been made to multiply the effects of training over longer periods of time.[24]

---

[19] G. Ambrasaite, "Judicial independence and public trust", *Justitia*, 2000 No. 6. The event was also described in EAJ newsletter *Euroiustitia*.

[20] Information provided by the President of Lithuanian Association of Judges, August 2001.

[21] See *1999 Regular Report on Lithuania's Progress Towards Accession*, November 1999; and *2000 Regular Report on Lithuania's Progress towards Accession,* November 2000, <http://europa.eu.int/comm/enlargement/dwn/report_11_00/pdf/en/lt_en.pdf> (accessed 10 August 2001).

[22] Statements of participants, OSI Roundtable, Vilnius, 1 March 2001.

[23] Statements of participants, OSI Roundtable, Vilnius, 1 March 2001.

[24] Statements of participants, OSI Roundtable, Vilnius, 1 March 2001.

## D. Organisation of the Judicial System

Lithuania has not had a very long history of independent courts. Before the First World War Lithuania was a part of the Russian Empire, where the courts did not enjoy full independence. During the inter-war period, Lithuania's civil law system courts were fairly independent. Soviet rule introduced the principle of the unity of power and the subordination of the courts, with very negative consequences for judicial independence.

After regaining independence in March 1990, Lithuania embarked upon a major restructuring of its legal system. The foundation of this new legal system was put into place when a new Constitution based on the rule of law was adopted by referendum on 25 October 1992. In 1994 Parliament adopted the Outline for Reform of the Legal System,[25] which articulated the most important objectives for judicial reform, emphasising conformity with EU standards, and set a timeline for reform. An updated edition of the Outline was approved by Parliament in 1998.[26]

The 1994 Law on Courts[27] established a four-tiered court system with 54 district courts, five regional courts, the Court of Appeal and the Supreme Court. In addition, a special administrative court system hears cases pertaining to the activities of public officials,[28] with five administrative regional courts, and, since 1 January 2001, a Head Administrative Court,[29] which is the appellate instance for administrative cases. There is no cassation within the administrative courts. (Currently, the Supreme Court is the only institution responsible for cassation review.) As of August 2001, there are 675 judges in the ordinary court system.[30]

---

[25] The Resolution of Parliament "Concerning the Outline of Reform of Legal System and Its Implementation", adopted on 14 December 1994.

[26] The new edition of the Outline of Reform of Legal System had been approved on the basis of the Resolution of Parliament No. VIII–810, 25 June 1998.

[27] The Law on Courts of the Republic of Lithuania No. I–480, adopted 31 May 1994 (Official Gazette No. 46–851).

[28] Law on the Establishment of Administrative Courts (Official Gazette 1999, No. 13–309). The administrative courts were created in line with Art. 111 of the Constitution, which stipulates that the solving of problems of an administrative nature, problems related to employment, family and other relationships could be made within a specialised court.

[29] Law on the Amendment of the Law on the Proceedings of Administrative Cases (Official Gazette 2000, No. 85–2566).

[30] Information provided by the Director of Department of Legal Institutions of the Ministry of Justice on 9 August 2001.

In 1998 the law was amended to abolish the old economic court, whose functions were transferred to district and regional courts or to commercial arbitrators.[31] There are no military courts in Lithuania, and extraordinary courts are prohibited in times of peace.[32]

Prosecutors are considered an integral part of judicial authority;[33] however, the Constitutional Court has held that prosecutors may not perform judicial functions assigned to courts.

*Constitutional Court*: The Constitutional Court operates as an independent institution alongside the regular court system.[34] The Court reviews the constitutionality of acts of Parliament and the legality and constitutionality of acts of the State President and Government. The decisions of the Court on issues assigned to its jurisdiction by the Constitution are final and may not be appealed. The Court has played an important role in mandating the current restructuring of the judiciary.

As provided in the Constitution,[35] the status of the Constitutional Court is regulated by a separate law[36] from that governing the regular courts. The Court consists of nine judges appointed for non-renewable nine-year terms, with one-third of the Court being appointed every three years. Parliament appoints all judges, selecting three each from the nominees put forth by the State President, the Chairman of Parliament, and the President of the Supreme Court respectively. The Constitutional Court is financed directly from the State budget and has a separate budget line.

---

[31] Law on the Abolition of Economic Court (Official Gazette "Valstybes Zinios", 1998, No. 26-672)

[32] CONST. REP. LITHUANIA, Art. 111.

[33] See CONST. REP. LITHUANIA, Chap. IX (on "the Court").

[34] CONST. REP. LITHUANIA, Chap. VIII.

[35] CONST. REP. LITHUANIA, Art. 102.

[36] Law on the Constitutional Court of the Republic of Lithuania (Official Gazette, 1993, No. 6–120).

## II. Constitutional and Legal Foundations of Judicial Independence

The basic constitutional guarantees of judicial independence and separation of powers have been bolstered by the Constitutional Court's 1999 ruling giving those principles a broad scope which covers even more indirect, economic levels of independence. However, the legal framework which the Court invalidated in its ruling has not been replaced, and as a consequence many of the legislative provisions affecting judges' independence – both for good and ill – are in suspension. Other problems persist, such as the lack of a clearly identified representative for the judiciary and the national administration for courts.

### A. Separation of Powers and Guarantees of Independence

The judiciary is constitutionally recognised as a separate power equal with the legislative and executive branches: State power is exercised by Parliament, the State President and Government, and by the courts,[37] which have the exclusive right to administer justice.[38] The Constitution,[39] the Law on Courts,[40] and other legal acts provide a set of rules to prevent interference with the actions of judges when administering justice in order to guarantee the rendering of impartial and fair judgements. The Constitution declares: "When administering justice, judges and courts shall be independent. While investigating cases, judges shall obey only the law."[41] Interfering with the work of a judge by government authorities and institutions, Members of Parliament and other officers, political parties and public organisations or individuals is prohibited and incurs liability provided by law.[42]

---

[37] CONST. REP. LITHUANIA, Art. 5. The term "courts" is understood as both the panel of judges hearing a case and as a system of institutions independend from two other branches. Ruling of the Constitutional Court adopted on 21 December 1999 (Official Gazette 1999, No. 109-3192).

[38] CONST. REP. LITHUANIA, Art. 109.

[39] CONST. REP. LITHUANIA, Arts. 109–117.

[40] Law on Courts, Art. 46.

[41] CONST. REP. LITHUANIA, Art. 109.

[42] Art. 298 of the Criminal Code currently in force envisages a criminal liability for the interference into activity of judges. The Criminal Code of the Republic of Lithuania, adopted on 26 June 1961, "State News", 1961, No. 18–147, with subsequent amendments and supplements.

The concept of an independent judiciary has been developed in the rulings of the Constitutional Court. In its ruling on 6 December 1995, the Constitutional Court held that "the following three groups of safeguards may be conditionally identified among the safeguards guaranteeing the independence of judges: a) those guaranteeing the security of tenure, b) guaranteeing personal immunity of a judge, and c) those securing social (material) guarantees of judges."[43]

In its 1999 ruling, the Constitutional Court further developed the concept of judicial independence by identifying two aspects of the principle: the decisional independence of judges and courts in the administration of justice, and the organisational independence of judicial institutions. Only an independent and self-governing institutional system can guarantee the organisational independence of courts and procedural independence of judges;[44] under the Constitution, therefore, the activity of courts may not be administered by the executive, which may only retain sufficient powers to create conditions for the independent work of courts through, for example, building construction.

Although constitutional guarantees of judicial independence cannot be changed without qualified majority votes and other procedural protections,[45] the protections contained in legislative acts such as the Law on Courts are subject to change by majority vote. A party in the governing coalition has proposed a draft law which would include the new Law on Courts and the Law on the Constitutional Court on a list of constitutional laws which require a qualified majority to be changed.[46]

## B. Representation of the Judiciary

Although it is a constitutionally recognised branch of State power, the judiciary does not have a separate constitutional representative. The lack of such a representative tends to undercut other constitutional and legislative guarantees of independence, especially during the current period of flux; this is particularly problematic in the budget process, in which the judiciary's participation is limited.[47]

---

[43] Ruling of the Constitutional Court adopted on 6 December 1995 (Official Gazette, 1995, No. 101–2264).

[44] Ruling of the Constitutional Court adopted on 21 December 1999 (Official Gazette, 1999, No. 109–3192).

[45] CONST. REP. LITHUANIA, Art. 148.

[46] See proposed draft Law on List of Constitutional Laws, Art. 3, <http://www.lrs.lt>, in Lithuanian (accessed 22 August 2001). See also CONST. REP. LITHUANIA, Art. 69(2).

[47] See Section IV.A.

In practice, the President of the Supreme Court represents the judiciary in communications with the other branches, although there is no constitutional or legislative authorisation for such a function; the President of the Association of Judges often speaks on behalf of the judiciary as well. The only other body that fulfils any representational functions is the Council of Judges. The Council currently has a very limited advisory role, but would have a much broader representative and administrative mandate under the new draft Law on Courts.

In accordance with the Constitution,[48] the Council of Judges advises the State President on matters relating to the judiciary.[49] The Council advises the State President on the appointment, promotion, transfer and dismissal from office of judges; assesses whether investigations of activities of a judge (usually following complaints by a party in a case) or court did not violate independence of judge or court; elects members to the Judges' Examination Commission; approves the Statute of the Court of Honour of Judges; comments on issues related to the organisation of operations of courts and judges when requested by the State President, Parliament, Minister of Justice or General Meeting of Judges; and receives the annual report of the Director of the Department of Courts on the activity of courts.

The Council consists of 14 members:[50] five judges elected by the General Meeting of Judges;[51] one judge elected by the Lithuanian Association of Judges; two judges appointed by the State President, and two judges appointed by the Minister of Justice, as well as the President of the Supreme Court, the chairmen of the two divisions of the Supreme Court, and the President of the Court of Appeal sitting *ex officio*.

The draft Law on Courts would broaden the competence of the Council of Judges.[52] The Council would approve the budgets of courts and the National Court Administration and submit them to the Government; represent the courts on budgetary matters before the Government and other State institutions; approve the framework for administration of the courts; supervise the activities of the National Court administration and receive its reports; and call the General Meeting of Judges as necessary.[53]

---

[48] CONST. REP. LITHUANIA, Art. 112(5).

[49] Law on Courts, Art. 30.

[50] Draft Law on Courts, Art. 120, stipulates that the Council of Judges will consist of 22 persons.

[51] The General Meeting of Judges is the highest self-governing institution of courts, convened by the President of the Council of Judges at least once every two years (Law on Courts, Art. 32); it is not in a position to represent the judiciary in an ongoing capacity, but does have some other administrative responsibilities. See also Section III.

[52] Draft Law on Courts, Art. 121.

[53] Draft Law on Courts, Art. 121.

Under the draft Law, the Council of Judges would consist of 22 members, with 11 members elected by the General Meeting of Judges and one by the most numerous professional association of judges, and ten *ex officio* members (the Presidents of the Supreme Court, High Administrative Court, Court of Appeal and five regional courts as well as the Presidents of Civil and Penal Divisions of the Supreme Court). The chairmen of the parliamentary legal and budget committees, a representative of the State President, and the Minister of Justice would participate in meetings of the Council of judges in an advisory capacity.[54] This model would be more independent of the other branches and more authoritative than the current 14-member Council. On the other hand, the Council consisting exclusively of judges might be perceived, and indeed may prove to become, a closed corporate body that would have problems in securing public support and collaborating with other branches. In addition, it may lack certain expertise in non-judicial matters such as budgeting and public administration.

## C. Rules on Incompatibility

Judges are prohibited from taking part in the activities of political parties or other political organisations.[55] Judges may not hold any other elected or appointed post. And in general, judges may not work in other branches of the State. Prior to the 1999 ruling, judges of a district or regional court, with their consent, could be suspended from office by presidential decree and transferred to a division of the Ministry of Justice directly associated with the organisation and operational control of the courts. During such employment, judges retained their judicial salary and tenure, and after finishing their employment could be reinstated without having to take examinations.[56] In the 1999 ruling, the Constitutional Court prohibited this suspension-and-transfer procedure, noting that it effectively makes the judge a civil servant and therefore violates the separation of power between the judiciary and the executive.[57]

The draft Law on Courts would permit a judge to be delegated to the National Administration of Courts,[58] while retaining judicial status and privileges.[59]

---

[54] Draft Law on Courts, Art. 120.
[55] Law on Courts, Art. 50.
[56] Law on Courts, Art. 50(3).
[57] Ruling of the Constitutional Court, adopted 21 December 1999 (Official Gazette, 1999, No. 109–3192).
[58] See Section III.
[59] Draft Law on Courts, Arts. 47 and 126.

Judges may not be employed in any business, commercial, or other private enterprise or institution. Judges are not permitted to receive any remuneration other than their judicial salary, although they may receive payments for educational, academic, or creative activities.[60]

Rules on impartiality may also limit a judge's scope of participation in a case. Judges are required to recuse themselves if they have participated in a previous phase of the same case; if they are a relative of a party or other person participating in the case; if they or their relatives are directly or indirectly interested in the outcome of the case; or if there are other circumstances raising doubts concerning their impartiality.[61]

*Disclosure.* Judges and their family members must make an annual declaration of their income and property.[62] The information is published in a special annex of the Official Gazette.[63]

## D. Judges' Associations

To represent their interests judges may unite into a professional association.[64] 87 percent of judges have joined the Lithuanian Association of Judges,[65] established in 1993. The objectives of the Association are: to protect the professional and social rights of judges; to co-operate with lawyers' organisations; to increase the prestige of the profession of judges and to retain the traditions of the judges' corps; and to provide assistance in organising professional training for judges, and by co-operating in the activities of the Lithuanian Judicial Training Centre.[66]

---

[60] CONST. REP. LITHUANIA, Art. 113.

[61] Code of Civil Procedure, Art. 19; Law on the Proceedings of Administrative Cases, Art. 47; Code of Criminal Procedure, Art. 29.

[62] Law on Declaration of Income and Property of Residents No. I–1338, adopted 16 May 1996, with subsequent amendments and supplements.

[63] Law on Declaration of Income and Property of Residents, Art. 10(2).

[64] Law on Courts, Art. 51(2); Draft Law on Courts, Art. 43(3).

[65] Annual Report of the President of the Lithuanian Association of Judges, 6 October 2000, *Justitia*, No. 4, 2000.

[66] Regulations of the Lithuanian Association of Judges, adopted 4 July 1997, Art. 4.

## III. Administration of the Court System and Judicial Independence

Perhaps no section of the judiciary's organisation has been more affected by the 1999 ruling than its administration. The 1999 ruling held that permitting the Minister of Justice to control the administrative activities of courts created the pre-conditions for institutions of the executive or its officials to exert undue influence on courts, thus contradicting the constitutional principle of the independence of judges.[67]

Since this section of the Law on Courts has been declared unconstitutional, a legal and institutional vacuum exists concerning the courts' administration. The draft Law on Courts would transfer competence for administrative support for and control of courts from the Ministry of Justice to the Council of Judges and the National Court Administration,[68] which should substantially reduce the influence of the executive.

Prior to the 1999 ruling, the Ministry of Justice was responsible for directing and controlling the administrative work of courts and judges (with the exception of the Supreme Court[69]). The Ministry exercised its control through the Department of Courts or through the court presidents or their authorised deputies, and issued regulations.[70]

The Department of Courts,[71] operating under the Ministry of Justice, was responsible for determining the number of judges in each court, providing material and technical support to courts, and controlling the administration and auditing of courts (with the exception of the Supreme Court).

The General Meeting of Judges, the highest self-governing institution of courts, has some administrative functions as well. Under the current Law, the General Meeting of Judges approves and elects members of the Council of Judges (other than *ex officio*

---

[67] Ruling of the Constitutional Court, adopted 21 December 1999 (Official Gazette, 1999, No. 109–3192).

[68] Draft Law on Courts, Chaps. 3–4.

[69] Law on Courts, Art. 73(2).

[70] "The Rules for the Control of Administrative Activity of Courts (Judges), except the Supreme Court", were approved on the basis of the Order of the Minister of Justice No. 190, 19 November 1998.

[71] Established on 1 August 1998 by the Decree of the Government of the Republic of Lithuania No. 717, adopted on 15 June 1998, authorised the Ministry of Justice to act as a founder of the Department of Courts.

members); elects the Court of Honour of Judges and its Chairman; and approves the regulations of the Court of Honour of Judges.[72]

Under the current Law on Courts, court presidents are responsible for the proper functioning of their courts. Their responsibilities include controlling the administrative activities of judges; dealing with complaints against judges; monitoring compliance with the rules of judicial ethics; organising the work of court personnel; and hiring and dismissing court personnel. Vice-presidents and division presidents of courts are responsible for the organisational matters of courts, assigned to them by the president of the respective court.[73]

There is no clear division between the decisional and administrative activities of the court president; while hearing cases the president acts as an ordinary judge, alongside certain administrative and economic functions. This combination of responsibilities creates unnecessary risks to the court president's impartiality. For example, under current practice, responsibility for repairs or construction of court facilities falls on the court president, thus bringing judges and private companies into contact in a commercial context; in some cases, a court president has been accused by other parties of being biased in the organisation of a tender for construction projects. Such cases may influence the impartiality of the court as well as its image in society. There have been some discussions about introducing professional management positions in courts. In general, however, the court presidents (except at the Supreme Court), do not seem willing to relinquish their administrative authority.

The Supreme Court has a separate position of Chancellor to handle administrative and economic matters; thus its President does not confront the same potential conflicts of interests that lower court presidents do. Financial, material, and technical support for the Supreme Court is provided by the Government, while a commission formed by Parliament inspects the financial activities of the Supreme Court.[74]

Under the draft Law on Courts, the Council of Judges would approve regulations relating to court administration, standard court structures, numbers of court staff and descriptions of their functions. It would also receive reports and control the activities of the National Court Administration.[75]

---

[72] Law on Courts, Art. 32.
[73] Law on Courts, Art. 39.
[74] Law on Courts, Art. 73.
[75] Draft Law on Courts, Art. 121.

The National Court Administration in turn would be responsible for the day-to-day operations of courts. Its tasks would include preparation of the meetings of the Council of Judges and the General Meeting of Judges; preparation and implementation of regulations approved by the Council and decisions adopted by the General Meeting; analysis of courts' activities (apart from the administration of justice); collection and analysis of statistics; and inspection of operational activities of all courts (except the Supreme Court).[76]

The General Meeting of Judges would retain some administrative functions as well under the draft Law on Courts. Under the draft Law, the General Meeting of Judges would approve the regulations of the General Meeting; approve the rules of judicial ethics; elect and recall members of the Council of Judges (other than *ex officio* members) and the Court of Honour of Judges; and receive the reports of the Court of Honour of Judges and the Council of Judges.[77]

Judicial training is organised through the Lithuanian Judicial Training Centre. The Training Centre is a non-governmental and non-profit organisation founded jointly by various State institutions and domestic and international organisations.[78] Under the draft law, responsibility for judicial training would fall under the competence of the National Court Administration.[79]

---

[76] Draft Law on Courts, Art. 125.

[77] Draft Law on Courts, Art. 118.

[78] The founders of the Training Centre are the Ministry of Justice, the Supreme Court, the Lithuanian Judges Association, the United Nations Development Programme, the American Bar Association-Central and East European Law Initiative, and the Open Society Foundation-Lithuania.

[79] Draft Law on Courts, Art. 124.

# IV. Financial Autonomy and Level of Funding

## A. Budgeting Process

In its 1999 ruling, the Constitutional Court stressed that the principle of judicial independence required that courts be financially independent from the executive.[80] In order to satisfy this principle, the Court required that funds be assigned to each court directly, instead of being allocating through the Ministry of Justice, as had previously been the case. In addition, the Ministry can no longer act as an administrator determining the end use of allocated funds.

However, the Ministry of Justice retains the right to draft and defend parts of the State budget allocating funding for special programs to benefit the whole judicial system, such as supply programmes, although the Ministry could not then administer the finances of any such programme once allocated to individual courts.[81] To ensure that the draft budget allocates sufficient finances, the Ministry has the right to gather data about the needs of courts from court presidents.[82]

Two days after the 1999 ruling Parliament approved the 2000 budget, which contained separate budget lines for each court.[83] For the 2001 budget every court presented an estimate directly to the Ministry of Finance, which included it in the overall budget estimate. There are no objective or transparent methodologies for determining the initial funding requests or responding to them, and the courts did not take part in the subsequent preparation of or negotiations over the budget. In previous years, the Ministry of Justice had represented the judiciary's interests in the budget negotiations, but in response to the 1999 ruling, withdrew its representative support.[84] The absence of any designated representative unnecessarily broadens the scope the executive enjoys in preparing the budget and limits the legislature's access to important input in exercising its legitimate discretion to set funding for the courts.

---

[80] Ruling of the Constitutional Court of 21 December 1999, Official Gazette, 1999, No. 109–3192.

[81] Decision of the Constitutional Court Concerning the Interpretation of the Ruling of the Constitutional Court of 21 December 1999, of 12 January 2000, Sec. 4.3 ff.

[82] Decision of the Constitutional Court Concerning the Interpretation of the Ruling of the Constitutional Court of 21 December 1999, of 12 January 2000.

[83] The state budget for the year 2000 had been approved by the Law on Approval of Financial Indices of Budgets of Municipalities and State Budget, No. VIII–1503, 23 December 1999.

[84] Information provided by Parliament Law Department official who wished to remain anonymous.

The draft Law on Courts would revise the process of drafting and submitting the budget of the judicial branch in line with the 1999 ruling's requirements.[85] Each court as well as the National Court Administration would prepare its own budget,[86] which would then be submitted to the Council of Judges for consideration and approval, and then submitted to the Government and through it to Parliament. During the preparation and adoption of the Law on State Budget, the courts (with the exception of the Supreme Court) would be represented by the National Court Administration.[87]

Both under current practice and the draft Law, the Supreme Court submits its budget directly to the Government; there is no clear argument as to why other courts must necessarily have a different procedure from this Court. The Constitutional Court has its own budget, which will be unaffected by the draft Law on Courts.

Funding for the courts has decreased in absolute litas since 1998, despite of the significant increase of the number of judges, cases heard, and overall increase of the role of courts in the state life. The relative share of the State budget going to the courts has remained fairly constant, even increasing slightly over 1998.[88] Funding for training has been decreasing in absolute Litas since 1999,[89] and the financial stability of the Lithuanian

---

[85] Draft Law on Courts, Arts. 129–32.

[86] Draft Law on Courts, Art. 130(1).

[87] Draft Law on Courts, Art. 130(4).

[88] Funding of the Judiciary, 1998–2001:

| | 1998 | 1999 | 2000 | 2001 |
|---|---|---|---|---|
| State budget, in Litas | 7,406,962,000<br>€ 1,981,267,263 | 6,760,832,000<br>€ 1,808,435,781 | 6,851,088,000<br>€ 1,832,578,103 | 6,161,834,000<br>€ 1,648,211,505 |
| Projected funds for courts, except the Supreme Court, in the State Budget, in Litas | 112,446,200<br>€ 30,077,915 | 108,577,000<br>€ 29,042,954 | 106,557,500<br>€ 28,502,764 | 95,637,000<br>€ 25,581,670 |
| Actually received funds for courts, in Litas | 111,600,600<br>€ 31,189,164 | 99,616,100<br>€ 26,646,028 | 106,218,903<br>€ 28,412,193 | — |
| Percentage of the State Budget spent on the judiciary, except the Supreme Court | 1.5066 | 1.4734 | 1.5544 | 1.5521 |

[89] Information provided by the Director of the Judicial Training Center, March 2001.

Judicial Training Centre is in question.[90] The draft Law on Courts would require that judicial training be directly financed by the State budget.[91]

There have been no instances reported in which the Government or Parliament has made the approval of the judiciary's budget conditional on greater efficiency, productivity or other aspects of the courts' activities. At the same time, no legal safeguards exist to prevent such manipulation or reduction of resources for political ends. Currently, the judiciary is almost entirely excluded from the budgetary process. Court presidents submit their requests directly to the Ministry of Finance and no representatives of the judiciary participate in further deliberations.

## B. Work Conditions

The physical infrastructure of courts and the conditions in which judges work are unsatisfactory, to the point where they may materially interfere with judges' independence and create unacceptable pressures on their impartiality.

The creation of a multi-layer court system with expanded responsibilities has significantly increased the need for financial, material and human resources; during the last ten years the competence of courts, their public role, responsibility and workload has been expanding, and the number of judges increased by 35 percent between 1996 and 2001.[92] Yet allocations have not kept pace. Despite the increase in the number of judges, the dramatic increases in the number of cases[93] has increased the average workload considerably, and there is a shortage of judges, especially in the district courts.[94] Judges of the district courts have the heaviest workloads, which have been increasing: 40.48 cases per month in 1997, 45.77 in 1998, 55.34 in 1999, and 52.68 in 2000.[95]

---

[90] The operation of the Training Centre for the year 2001 was ensured only because the Government of Finland and UNDP extended financial support for 2001. Information provided by the assistant to the President of the Lithuanian Association of Judges, 19 April 2001.

[91] Draft Law on Courts, Art. 93.

[92] In 1996 there were 456 judges, while the number of judges in August 2001 was 675.

[93] See generally Department of Courts website, <http://www.teismai.lt.>, in Lithuanian (accessed 22 August 2001).

[94] The number of vacancies for judgeships has been gradually decreasing: there were 126 vacancies in 1998, 103 in 1999, and 64 in June 2000. The planned deadline to fill all court vacancies was 30 December 2000. However, as of August 2001 the number of vacancies had increased to 71. Information provided by the Director of the Department of Legal Institutions, the Ministry of Justice, August 2001.

[95] Information from the Director of the Department of Legal Institutions of the Ministry of Justice, August 2001.

Budget allocations for construction have lagged considerably behind the amounts required. Although some courthouses have been built or renovated, others remain in very poor condition. The building housing the Vilnius Second District Court, Vilnius Regional Court and the Court of Appeal is in dire condition. Provincial courts are in particularly poor condition. In district courts about 40 percent of cases are tried in judge's offices.[96]

The efficient functioning of courts is still hampered by the lack of necessary technical equipment, such as computers, typewriters, and copying machines. Some district courts even lack basic furniture and writing supplies. The lack of proper financing leads to conditions in which judges of some courts covered the costs of office supplies and court mailing expenses themselves.[97]

Computerisation of the courts is gradually progressing, but very slowly; the installation of a common network is in a fairly elementary stage. However, over the last two years the percentage of courts with Internet connections has increased from 20 percent[98] to 85 percent.[99] Starting from 1 July 2000, all decisions and judgements of regional courts and the Court of Appeal are to be published on the website of the Ministry of Justice, and decisions of the Supreme Court on its website.[100] The Legal Information Centre[101] has already initiated a programme called LITEKO, which aims to prepare courts for computerisation. Yet, progress in the execution of this project is hindered by the lack of funding,[102] and implementation of the computerisation programme will probably not begin until 2003.

Access to information is inadequate. Judges do not all receive the official gazette, although most have access to printed codes.[103] Legal information can be accessed by computer in courts that have installed LITLEX (a legislative databank) or are connected to the database

---

[96] Information from the Director of the Department of Finances and Accounting, Ministry of Justice, July 2000.

[97] Information from the Presidents of Vilnius 1st and 2nd District Courts, February 2001.

[98] Activities Report 1999, Department of Courts, <http://www.teismai.lt>, in Lithuanian (accessed 22 August 2001).

[99] Information from the Department of Courts, 6 March, 2001.

[100] Law on Courts, Art. 8.

[101] The Legal Information Centre is a non-profit organisation, which was established on 5 May 1993. In 1998, it was reorganised into a State enterprise.

[102] Information from the Director of Legal Information Centre, June 2000, and Director of the Department of Legal Institutions of the Ministry of Justice, August 2001.

[103] Information from the Head of the Division of the Organisation of Work of Courts, Department of Courts, 5 March 2001.

via the Internet. LITLEX is available to the great majority of judges in the regional and appellate courts and the Supreme Court, but some district court judges do not have access to it.

## C. Compensation

The Law on Courts required that salaries of judges be established by law.[104] However, from 1993 until 2000, under an interim arrangement[105] judges' salaries were fixed by governmental decree, and during this time, judges' salaries were increased twice and then reduced by over 30 percent in response to economic hardship and public criticism of the pay rises.[106]

Parliament finally adopted a law regulating judicial salaries in August 2000,[107] which aims to harmonise the compensation policies for government officials and judges established by previous governments.[108] The common salary system is based on a coefficient called the Minimal Monthly Salary.[109] Under the law, salaries of judges as well as government officials and politicians will be increased or decreased gradually between 2001 and 2006.[110] Judges' salaries will gradually be reduced by between 500 to 5000 litas (c. € 137 to € 1,368) depending on the category of the judge; all judges will continue to earn salaries well above the national average, however.[111]

---

[104]  Law on Courts, Art. 55.

[105]  Law on the Official Salaries of Judges of the Courts of the Republic of Lithuania, Officers of the Prosecutor's Office, the State Arbiters, and Officers of the Department of State Control, adopted 3 February 1993, <http://www.lrs.lt>, in Lithuanian (accessed 22 August 2001). See also Ruling of the Constitutional Court of 6 December 1995, <http://www.lrs.lt.>, in Lithuanian (accessed 22 August 2001).

[106]  Decree of the Government of the Republic of Lithuania No. 942, 27 August 1999; Decree of the Government of the Republic of Lithuania No. 1494, 28 December 1999; information from the Ministry of Justice to the Parliamentary Committee on Public Administration and Municipalities. See also Conclusion of the Principal Committee Concerning the draft Law on Compensation of Government Officials Not Reckoned as Public Servants (No. P–2351) No. 16, 10 April 2000.

[107]  Law on Wages of Politicians, Judges, and Government Officials.

[108]  L.Cesniene, "The Government Took Care of the Salaries of Successors: the Cabinet of Ministers Suggests to Increase Salaries of the Members of Parliament of the Next Term of Office", *Respublika*, 11 May 2000.

[109]  Minimum Monthly Salary was 430 Litas (c. € 118) on 13 April 2001.

[110]  L.Cesniene, "The Government Took Care of the Salaries of Successors: the Cabinet of Ministers Suggests to Increase Salaries of the Members of Parliament of the Next Term of Office", *Respublika*, 11 May 2000.

[111]  The average remuneration in the fourth quarter of 2000 was 1073 Lt. Supplement to Official Gazette, *Informaciniai prabesimai*, 2001, No. 20.

The decreases were challenged by about one-third of all judges as contravening the Constitutional Court's ruling of 6 December 1995, which stated that "any attempts to reduce the salary of judges or other social guarantees or restrictions of funding of courts should be treated as an infringement of independence of judges and courts."[112] These cases reached the Constitutional Court and on 12 July 2001 the Court declared the projected decrease unconstitutional[113]

Judges salaries will be comparable to those in other branches, with district court judges earning less than Members of Parliament, for example, but all other judges earning more, and the highest judges earning salaries equal to those of top officials in other branches. (For example, the President of the Supreme Court will earn as much as the Chairman of Parliament or the Prime Minister.) At present, prosecutors enjoy almost the same level of compensation as judges, while the compensation of private lawyers is quite varied and often higher. However, pay raises during the 1990's have attracted to the judicial corps a number of well-qualified practitioners and legal scholars, and the proposed decreases could reverse that trend.

Pensions remain one of the most serious concerns of the judiciary. Judges are awarded pensions pursuant to the general Law on State Pensions.[114] Other members of law enforcement institutions are governed by a separate law[115] which ensures them far higher pensions than judges receive – in the case of policemen or prosecutors, the pension is roughly three times as high. The draft Law on Courts would extend the provisions of that separate law to judges as well.[116] Judges do not receive housing from the Government or local entities.

*Other Employees*: The work compensation of court employees, such as secretaries and registrars, is very low, which can be an inducement to corruption in the administration of the courts and in the processing of claims and cases.

---

[112] The same principle was repeated in the Ruling of the Constitutional Court of 21 December 1999 (Official Gazette 1999, No. 109–3192).

[113] Decision of the Constitutional Court of 12 July 2001 (Official Gazette 2001, No. 62–2276).

[114] Law on Courts, Art. 52.

[115] Law on State Pensions of Internal Service Officers, Officers of National Security, Officers of Military Service, Prosecutors, Judges, Officers of Prisons Department, and Officers of State Enterprises.

[116] Draft Law on Courts, Art. 100.

# V. Judicial Office

The Ministry of Justice has traditionally had significant powers over judges' career paths. However, following the 1999 ruling the Ministry lost a number of functions, such as the power to nominate candidates for judgeships or positions as court presidents; to propose their dismissal; to dismiss division presidents; to appoint court division presidents; and to nominate judges for full tenure after their probationary period.[117] The situation is still in transition, but courts and judges have increased involvement in their own career paths, and the executive's role has diminished somewhat.

## A. Selection Process

*Preliminary Selection*: Before the 1999 ruling, preliminary judicial selection had been greatly influenced by the Ministry of Justice. The Ministry's Department of Courts advertised the selection process, organised the official competition,[118] and formed a reserve of judges for district and regional courts and the Court of Appeal.

According the draft Law on Courts, the selection of judges would be conducted according to regulations for selection adopted by both the Minister of Justice and the President of the Council of Judges.[119] The regulations should set forth the main methods and criteria for selection, including merits of preference, order of verification of qualities of candidates, and criteria of assessment.

Apart from general threshold requirements concerning citizenship, age, and education, the principal criterion for selection as a judge is an examination. (There is also an undefined requirement that the candidate have an impeccable reputation.) The current examination commission was appointed by the Minister of Justice for a three-year term. The commission consists of five members – three Justices of the Supreme Court, one judge of the Court of Appeal, and one representative of Vilnius University Law Faculty. The President of the commission is the President of the Civil Division of the Supreme Court. Under the draft Law on Courts, the Council of Judges would appoint the examination commission for three years. The commission would consist of seven members, at least five of whom must be judges. Three members (2 judges and one legal scholar) would be selected by

---

[117] Ruling of the Constitutional Court of 21 December 1999.

[118] Order Concerning Announcement of Official Competition for the Positions of Judge of Regional Court and Court of Appeal No. 190, 19 November 1998.

[119] Draft Law on Courts, Art. 55.

the President of the Council of Judges; three members (2 judges and one legal scholar) by the Minister of Justice; and one by the professional association of judges from among its own members.[120] The proposed commission therefore would have a majority of judges, appointed by judges.

*Appointment*: The State President appoints district and regional court judges; judges of the Court of Appeal are appointed by the State President with the consent of Parliament; and Supreme Court judges are appointed by Parliament upon the recommendation of the State President.[121] Decisions concerning the appointment or rejection of a candidate are not subject to appeal.

Court presidents are chosen from among the judges of the relevant court and appointed in the same manner as the judges: district and regional court presidents are appointed by the State President; the President of the Court of Appeal is appointed by the State President with the consent of Parliament; and President of the Supreme Court is appointed by Parliament upon the recommendation of the State President. The term of office for a court president varies from five years for a district court to nine for the Supreme Court or a division of the Supreme Court.[122] Under the pre-1999 system, the president of a division of the court was assigned by the Minister of Justice upon the proposal of the court president; however, the Minister has lost this power and there is no clear authority at this time to assign the presidents of court divisions. Court presidents can be re-appointed, which increases the appointing power's influence over them.

## B. Tenure, Retirement, Transfer and Removal

Despite the changes mandated by the 1999 ruling, the executive still retains undue influence over the careers of judges, especially during their initial probationary appointment and in the evaluation process.

### 1. Tenure and Retirement

District court judges are initially appointed for a probationary term of five years, after which they are eligible for life tenure. This probationary period places younger judges

---

[120] Draft Law on Courts, Art. 53.

[121] CONST. REP. LITHUANIA, Art. 112.

[122] Law on Courts, Arts. 33–35.

in a position of reliance on the discretion of the executive, both under the system prevailing before the 1999 ruling and under the proposed system – which inevitably introduces incentives for those judges to limit their own decisional independence where it might depart from the wishes of those on whose decision their career depends.

Judges can start work at age 25 and with little experience, and in light of this a probationary term might be seen as a compromise between individual judges' independence and the need to ensure that the members of the judiciary are highly qualified and capable. However, less intrusive means – such as more extensive training or apprenticeships – are available. At a minimum, the probationary period should be reduced, and clear criteria for determining which judges do not receive tenure must be established.

Until the 1999 ruling, the Minister of Justice made proposals to the State President regarding judges who had finished their probationary period. The Minister had absolute discretion concerning such proposals, against which there was no right of appeal. In practice, the Minister never refused to recommend a judge for tenure.

The State President consulted with the Council of Judges, which evaluated the performance of probationary judges based on data submitted by the regional court under which they served as well as their personnel file and complaints or disciplinary actions against them.[123] The State President would sometimes meet with a judge prior to taking a final decision.[124] Only at this point was a judge granted tenure, with its guarantee of irremovability.

The draft Law on Courts would provide that at the expiration of the five-year probationary term, a district court judge could be appointed by the State President upon the recommendation of the Council of Judges. The Minister of Justice therefore would no longer have any role.

Retirement at age 65 is mandatory. A judge reaching the age of 65 while a case is being heard continues to serve until the case is settled or the hearing is suspended.[125]

---

[123] Personnel files of judges are kept and updated by the Department of Courts.

[124] Information from the Head of the Division of the Organisation of Work of Courts, Department of Courts, 18 September 2000.

[125] Law on Courts, Art. 36.

## 2. Transfer

Under the system until 1999, judges could not be transferred from one court to another without their consent. Judges of district and regional courts could be transferred, with their consent, to another court of the same type by the State President upon the proposal of the Minister of Justice, acting on the recommendation of the Council of Judges.[126] In exceptional cases, the court president has the right to transfer a judge from one division to another within the same court for a specific case.

If a district court judge was ill or absent for an extended period, the State President, upon the proposal of the Minister of Justice, could assign that judge's duties to another judge of the same court for up to six months.[127] The 1999 ruling eliminated the role of the Minister of Justice in this process.

Under the draft Law on Courts it would still be possible to transfer a judge from one court to another court of the same level for up to six months without that judge's consent, if necessary to ensure the functioning of the court. Transfers would be decided by the State President on the advice of the Council of Judges. However, it is not clear how often such a transfer could occur.[128] Unless procedural limitations are in place, the Council and State President could use this power to move judges with few limitations, which could, in effect, amount to a permanent transfer without a judge's consent.

## 3. Removal

Once re-appointed after their probationary period judges are irremovable. A judge cannot be dismissed from office except for reasons determined by law – at that judge's request or after reaching retirement age, upon appointment to another office, or for reasons of health.[129] There are two additional grounds for dismissal of a judge from office: behaviour discrediting the position of a judge, or when a court judgement against that judge enters into force.[130] Parliament may impeach judges of the Supreme Court or Court of Appeal for gross violations of the Constitution, breaches of oath, or criminal acts.[131]

---

[126] Law on Courts, Art. 37.

[127] Law on Courts, Art. 38.

[128] Draft Law on Courts, Art. 63.

[129] CONST. REP. LITHUANIA, Art. 115.

[130] CONST. REP. LITHUANIA, Art. 115.

[131] Law on Courts, Art. 57. See Section V.D.1.

Since 1998, judges have been subject to the lustration law, which prohibits persons who served in the Soviet Union State Security from working in certain public service jobs, including that of a judge, for a period of ten years.[132] If a former staff member conceals a past connection to USSR State Security structures, he or she must be dismissed no later than the next day.[133] Removing individual judges who have committed crimes or behaved improperly is an appropriate function for State organs or legislation. However, the fact that the lustration law was only extended to judges nearly eight years after independence may raise concerns that screening is designed to put limits on individual judges' decisional freedom rather than to serve a legitimate re-organisational purpose. However, there have been no cases involving judges reported to date.

## C. Evaluation and Promotion

There are no legal provisions to ensure that the advancement of judges[134] is based on objective or unbiased factors. The Department of Courts uses special forms to assess the performance of district court judges.[135] The forms, which are usually collected twice a year, include information on the number, kind and disposition of cases each judge has presided over.[136] The data are used for statistical purposes as well as to compile comprehensive data about individual judges' quantitative accomplishments. The rate of reversal is also a factor in evaluating a judge's qualifications for advancement. The focus on quantitative criteria, especially the completion of cases, has been strongly criticized by the Lithuanian Association of Judges, arguing that such a method produces incentives for judges to adjudicate cases quickly rather than well and places judges under pressures which effectively hamper their decisional independence.

---

[132] Law Concerning Evaluation of the Committee of USSR State Security (NKVD, NKGB, MGB, KGB) and Current Activity of Regular Staff of This Organisation, Art. 2, adopted 16 July 1998 (Official Gazette, 1998, No. 65–1877). Those who were exclusively investigating criminal cases or who left the Security Service before 11 March 1990 (the date of Lithuania's formal declaration of independence from the USSR) are exempted from the Law's provisions.

[133] The Law on Implementation of the Law Concerning Evaluation of the Committee of USSR State Security (NKVD, NKGB, MGB, KGB) and Current Activity of Regular Staff of This Organisation No. VIII–859, 16 July 1998, Art. 2.

[134] There is no concept of promotion *per se*; instead, judges are appointed separately to each position at each instance (although a judge moving to a higher position need not repeat the examinations that candidates for initial appointments must take). There are also no ranks, although there are salary promotions.

[135] The form of the Report on Work of Judges is approved by the Order of the Minister of Justice No. 52 on 6 March 1999.

[136] Information from the Head of the Division of the Organisation of Work of Courts, Department of Courts, July 2000.

There are no criteria to evaluate managerial skills or professional performance of candidates to be appointed as court and division presidents, as well as presidents of divisions of courts.

## D. Discipline

### 1. Liability

A judge is not liable for any material damage incurred by a party as a result of an erroneous decision by the courts or the judge. Any such damages must be reimbursed by the State according to procedures provided by law.[137] Allocations for compensation are incorporated into the State budget and managed by the Ministry of Justice. The State has the right to recover any damages paid by indemnifying the judge;[138] however, there has no been such case yet.

Judges may not be arrested or detained, nor may legal actions be initiated against them, without the consent of Parliament, or of the State President between parliamentary sessions.[139] Only the Prosecutor General may institute criminal proceedings against a judge. If criminal proceedings are instituted against a judge, that judge's powers are suspended by Parliament, or by the State President between parliamentary sessions, pending final judgement in the case.

In accordance with impeachment proceedings, Parliament may remove a judge of the Supreme Court and Court of Appeal from office in cases of gross violation of the Constitution, breach of oath, or the commission of an offence such as a criminal act.[140]

However, less serious administrative actions may not be brought against a judge. If a judge commits an administrative violation of law, the evidence must be transferred to the President of the Supreme Court in order to bring a disciplinary action against a judge.[141]

---

[137] The Law on Compensation of Damage Caused by Unlawful Actions of Office of Investigators, Interrogators, Prosecutors and Courts No. VIII–484, adopted 4 November 1997.

[138] Law on Courts, Art. 48; Law on Compensation of Damage Caused by Unlawful Actions of Office of Investigators, Interrogators, Prosecutors and Courts, Art. 1.

[139] CONST. REP. LITHUANIA, Art. 114, para. 2; Law on Courts, Art. 47.

[140] Law on Courts, Art. 57.

[141] Law on Courts, Art. 47.

## 2. Disciplinary Proceedings

Disciplinary action may be instituted against a judge for negligence at work, malfeasance discrediting the court, or behaviour discrediting the judicial office.[142]

Prior to the 1999 ruling, disciplinary action against the judges of district and regional courts and the Court of Appeal could be initiated by the President of the Supreme Court or the Minister of Justice, upon the motion of the Director of the Department of Courts or on their own initiative. A judge subject to disciplinary proceedings could be suspended by the State President, upon proposal of the Minister of Justice, until the completion of the case.[143] In its 1999 ruling, the Constitutional Court ruled that the Minister of Justice's powers to recommend judges to the Court of Honour of Judges, to propose a suspension in office and to initiate disciplinary proceedings against a judge were unconstitutional.[144]

There are two Courts of Honour that hear disciplinary actions. The Court of Honour of Judges hears actions brought against judges below the Supreme Court.[145] The State President appoints all five members to two-year terms – three members were appointed upon the recommendation of the Minister of Justice, and two with the advice of the Council of Judges. The Court of Honour of Supreme Court Judges hears cases against Supreme Court judges under rules approved by the Supreme Court Senate.[146] The Court of Honour of Supreme Court Judges is composed of three judges; the Supreme Court Senate appoints three judges as members for five-year terms.

Judges against whom a disciplinary action has been brought have the right to participate in the court session, and may retain counsel.[147]

Upon hearing a case, the Court of Honour of Judges may: acquit the judge or dismiss the case on procedural grounds; confine itself to a hearing on the case without taking action; issue various levels of reprimand or reproof; recommend to the State President that the judge be dismissed; suggest to the State President that the judge be transferred

---

[142] Law on Courts, Art. 59, para.1.

[143] Law on Courts, Art. 59, para. 4.

[144] Official Gazette, 1999, No. 109–3192.

[145] "The Regulations of the Court of Honour" were approved by the Council of Judges in the meeting of 8 January 2000.

[146] Law on Courts, Art. 58.

[147] The Regulations of the Court of Honour, Art. 17 (1). The same rule applies to the Court of Honour of Supreme Court Judges.

to another court of the same level or lower; or prohibit the judge's promotion for up to three years. The Court may also recommend that Parliament initiate impeachment proceedings against a judge of the Supreme Court or the Court of Appeal. Decisions of the Court of Honour of Judges may be appealed to the Supreme Court Senate.[148]

Under the draft Law on Courts the Minister of Justice, a judge's court president and higher court presidents would be able to initiate disciplinary action.[149] The official initiating a disciplinary action would have to apply to the special Commission of Judicial Discipline and Ethics, which would decide whether or not to start a disciplinary action. The Commission of Judicial Discipline and Ethics would consist of five members, appointed by the Council of Judges for a four-year term. The President of the Supreme Court would propose three candidates; the President of the Court of Appeals one, and the President of the Head Administrative Court one.

In 1999, 30 disciplinary cases were initiated: two judges were acquitted, ten were reproved, two were issued reprimands, six were issued severe reprimands, and in nine cases the Court confined itself to hearing the proceedings without taking action. Disciplinary action was initiated against approximately 5.5 percent of all judges.[150] Twenty-eight disciplinary cases were initiated in 2000, and, as of April, two cases in 2001.[151]

The "Rules of Ethics of Judges", regulating issues such as judges' independence, and their judicial and extra-judicial activities, were approved by the General Meeting of Judges on 18 December 1998.[152] The Rules do not have legal force, but may be taken into account in interpreting disciplinary liability under the law.

---

[148] Law on Courts, Art. 60.

[149] Draft Law on Courts, Art. 84(3).

[150] R. Blauzdaius, "Honor habet onus", *Justitia*, Nos. 5–6, 1999.

[151] Information from a judge of the Court of Honour of Judges, 23 April 2001.

[152] Published in "Judicial Practice" No. 10, the Bulletin of the Supreme Court, Vilnius 1998.

# VI. Intra-Judicial Relations

## A. Relations with Superior Courts

The Supreme Court ensures the uniform application of the laws by courts.[153] Judgements of the Supreme Court, its panels, or plenary session that are passed by the cassation procedure[154] must be taken into account by courts and other State institutions when applying the same laws. The Supreme Court also issues summary reviews of judicial practice pertaining to the application of laws and provides consultations to judges on the same issue during its visits to regional courts and the Court of Appeal.

There is discussion among judges and lawyers concerning the impact of the Supreme Court's consultations on the independence of individual judges of lower courts. The consultations – and the Court's judgements and summary reviews – undoubtedly contribute to the uniformity of legal practice, but inasmuch as the Court's consultations are seen as rendering statutes, they take on a legislative quality which some believe improperly restricts the individual judge's scope of decisional independence.

The President and the Chairmen of the Civil and Criminal Divisions of the Supreme Court may submit cassation petitions concerning lower court judgements. Though such a practice does contribute to the uniformity of justice, the European Court of Human Rights decided that this practice may be incompatible with the principle of the impartiality of the judiciary.[155]

---

[153] The Statute of the Supreme Court, Law No. I–856, 18 April 1995.

[154] The Supreme Court is the only cassation instance; cases may be heard by either a panel of three judges, an enlarged panel of seven judges, or by a plenary session of the Supreme Court. Code of Criminal Procedure, adopted on 26 June 1961 (Official Gazette, 1961, No. 18-148) with subsequent amendments and supplements; Code of Civil Procedure, adopted 7 July 1964 (Official Gazette, 1964, No. 19–139) with subsequent amendments and supplements.

[155] European Court of Human Rights, *Daktaras v. Lithuania*, 42095/98 (2000). In this case, the President of the Criminal Division of the Supreme Court lodged a cassation petition (at the request of the first instance judge who was dissatisfied with the judgement of the Court of Appeal amending his original decision). The same President of the Criminal Division appointed the Judge Rapporteur and convened the Chamber, which was to examine the case. The Chamber of the Supreme Court granted the cassation petition. The European Court of Human Rights stressed that in addition to subjective impartiality, a tribunal must also be impartial from an objective viewpoint – that is, it must offer sufficient guarantees to exclude any legitimate doubt as to its impartiality. When the President of the Criminal Division not only took up the prosecution case but also convened the Chamber, there were not sufficient guarantees to exclude a legitimate doubt as to the absence of inappropriate pressure. The Court therefore held that the applicant's doubts as to the impartiality of the Supreme Court were objectively justified and, consequently, a breach of Art. 6, para. 1 of the Convention had occurred.

The system of appeal allows a case to be reviewed by a higher court that may affirm, change, or cancel the decision of the first instance court, cancel the decision of the first instance court and return the case to that court to be reviewed *de novo*, or dismiss the case.[156] When a lower-court decision is cancelled by a higher court, there are no binding instructions to lower courts on what must be rectified upon retrial, although the lower courts are required to take into account the arguments of the superior court when retrying the case.

There is no official system of appointing supervisors or mentors for lower judges. Nevertheless, the practice of consultations with more experienced judges occurs informally and is widespread. In most courts, judges have regular consultative meetings to discuss issues related to their performance, such as application and interpretation of the law, assessment of evidence, and decisions of higher courts.[157] Inasmuch as such consultations are strictly informational, they do not necessarily pose any threat to an individual judge's independence; however, they do not contribute to the transparency of judicial decision-making.

Higher court judges may conduct inspections in lower courts, usually following a complaint lodged against a particular judge. There are no clear rules governing the procedure or scope of such visits, which can therefore be a means of interfering with judges' intra-judicial independence.

---

[156] Criminal Procedure Code, Art. 380, para. 1.

[157] Information from the Head of the Division of the Organisation of Work of Courts, Department of Courts, July 2000.

## B. Case Management and Relations with Court Presidents

Court presidents, their deputies and division presidents have no right to exert influence upon other judges when the latter administer justice, or in any other manner that compromises judicial independence.[158] Instructions that would contradict the order established by law and exert influence on a decision are considered "gross interference in case processing,"[159] and are subject to disciplinary sanctions. There had been no reports of such interference.

In general, judges are not overly dependent on their court presidents. Judges do not depend on court presidents for performance assessments, which are conducted by the Department of Courts, nor for any benefits or promotions. A court president in a first instance court cannot control the calendar of a judge, as judges set their own calendar. Nevertheless, informal requests by a court president that judges work more effectively are widespread.[160]

Cases in first instance courts are assigned by the court president according to one of three methods: alphabetically according to name of the defendant; numerically according to the case number; or a combination of the alphabetical and numerical distribution also taking into account judges' specialisation.[161] The court president is obliged to follow one of these three methods, but can change procedures for the next year if a chosen method proves ineffective. The court president's order on the method for annual case assignments is distributed to judges by the president of the court or division of the court not later than 20 December each year, and deviations from these rules may be made only in exceptional cases, for instance in case of the long absence of a judge. Although there is no formal legal prohibition, in practice court presidents cannot reassign a case except under exceptional circumstances, such as illness, a business trip, or other objective reason. Consequently, the phenomenon of "judge shopping" is rather limited.[162]

---

[158] Law on Courts, Art. 39.

[159] Rules of Ethics of Judges, Rule 5.

[160] Information provided by the Senior Specialist of the Division of the Organisation of Work of Courts, Department of Courts, September 2000.

[161] Rules on Assignment of Cases for Judges of the Court of Appeal, Regional and District Courts were approved on the basis of the Order of the Minister of Justice No. 190, 19 November 1998.

[162] This point of view was expressed by a public relations officer of the Department of Courts, 5 July 2000.

## VII. Enforcement

As a rule, judicial decisions are respected. There have been no reports of governmental institutions refusing to comply with a judicial decision. At the same time, civil judgements often go unenforced, which can lead to decreased respect for or reliance on legal processes, and a concomitant decline in support for the judges who issue decisions; indeed, the ineffective system of enforcement is often mentioned as one of the main reasons for public mistrust in courts.

Problems related to enforcement of judgements stem from the combined effects of the significant increase in the number of cases and the system of poorly qualified court bailiffs with insufficient resources. Between 1994 and 1999, for example, the number of cases subject to execution increased more than 200 percent, while the number of court bailiffs increased only by 30 percent.

To modernise the system of court bailiffs, the Government announced that it is going to introduce a system of enforcement by private persons empowered by the State to execute court decisions and provide other legal services for a fee.[163] In addition, in a draft Code of Civil Procedure, reportedly to be adopted by July 2001, the procedures for enforcing court judgements are revised, redressing the imbalance in rights and duties between creditors and debtors.

---

[163] R.Budbergyte, Vice-minister of Justice, "Directions of Institutional Reform of Court Bailiffs Office", presentation at the conference "Reform of Legal System: Problems of Institutions", 29 June 2000.

# Judicial Independence
# in Poland

# Table of Contents

|  |  |  |
|---|---|---|
| Executive Summary | | 310 |
| I. | Introduction | 313 |
| | A. Executive Involvement in the Affairs of the Judiciary and Budget Issues | 313 |
| | 1. Undue Executive Involvement | 313 |
| | 2. Budget | 314 |
| | B. Intra-Judicial and Public Attitudinal Problems | 314 |
| | 1. Uncertainty among Judges about Their Role | 314 |
| | 2. Uneven Public and Political Support for the Judiciary | 315 |
| | C. The Judiciary and the EU Accession Process | 315 |
| | D. Outline of the Court System | 316 |
| | 1. The Communist Legacy | 316 |
| | 2. The Transitional Period | 317 |
| | 3. The Contemporary System | 318 |
| II. | Constitutional and Legal Foundations of Judicial Independence | 320 |
| | A. Guarantees of the Separation of Powers, or Independence | 320 |
| | B. Representation of the Judiciary | 321 |
| | 1. The National Council of the Judiciary | 321 |
| | C. Rules on Incompatibility | 323 |
| | D. Judges' Associations | 326 |
| III. | Administration of the Court System and Judicial Independence | 327 |

| IV. | Financial Autonomy and Level of Funding .... 330 |
|---|---|
| | A. Budgeting Process ....................................... 330 |
| | B. Work Conditions ....................................... 332 |
| | C. Compensation ............................................ 333 |
| |    1. Constitutional and Court Challenges ......................... 335 |
| |    2. Other Court Employees ..................... 336 |
| V. | Judicial Office ................................................. 337 |
| | A. Selection .................................................... 337 |
| |    1. Court Presidents ............................... 338 |
| |    2. Military Judges ................................. 339 |
| | B. Tenure, Retirement, Transfer and Removal ............................................. 339 |
| |    1. Tenure ............................................... 339 |
| |    2. Retirement ........................................ 339 |
| |    3. Transfer ............................................ 340 |
| |    4. Removal ........................................... 341 |
| | C. Evaluation and Promotion ....................... 343 |
| | D. Discipline ................................................... 343 |
| |    1. Liability ............................................ 344 |
| |    2. Discipline ......................................... 344 |
| VI. | Intra-Judicial Relations ................................... 346 |
| | A. Relations with Superior Courts ................ 346 |
| | B. Case Management and Relations with Court Presidents .............................. 347 |
| VII. | Enforcement ................................................... 348 |

# Judicial Independence in Poland

## Executive Summary

Poland has made considerable progress towards the creation of a truly independent judiciary as a third branch. Many guarantees of independence have been elevated to the constitutional level. For the most part, the boundary between the judiciary and the political branches has been clearly defined and accepted.

There are significant remaining areas of concern, however. The most important of these are the continuing involvement of the executive in the administration of the judiciary and the budget process; and the problematic attitude of many judges, politicians, and members of the public towards judicial independence, which threatens to undermine the progress made in creating an independent judiciary.

*Undue Executive Involvement*

The executive – and the Ministry of Justice in particular – retains considerable administrative and supervisory authority over the organisation and affairs of the judiciary. Judges frequently work for the Ministry of Justice while adjudicating cases, which inevitably compromises their independence. Current draft legislation would actually exacerbate this problem.

*Budget*

The judiciary has almost no input into the budgeting process. Compensation is lower than for the political branches, which undercuts the separation and equality of the branches. These problems are in part a function of the executive's continued control of the budget process and the allocation of funding. Two draft laws may address these concerns.

*Uncertain Attitudes among Judges*

Judges are not in agreement about their proper relationship to each other, the political branches, and society. Many judges, trained in a passive professional culture, have an excessively deferential approach towards higher court judges, while others believe that any form of accountability is an attack on their independence. The result, in either case, is a corps of judges deciding cases not independently, but in isolation, and unable collectively to defend its interests.

### Uneven Public and Political Support

Public and political support for the institutions of judicial independence has been uneven. In recent years, judges and courts have come under fire from the media and politicians, and allegations of corruption have been raised. Such criticism and investigations of corruption have led to a drop in the public approval ratings enjoyed by judges. In its 2000 report, the Commission expressed concern over delays and reports of corruption, which contribute to negative perceptions of the justice system.

In addition, several other issues are discussed in the body of this Report – many of them related to the major themes noted above. Some of the most significant are the following:

### National Council of the Judiciary

The status of the National Council as a representative of the judiciary as a whole is not clear, which limits its effectiveness in negotiations among the branches. Further clarification of its role would be welcome.

### Compensation

The constitutional principle concerning judges' remuneration raises important questions about the proper level of compensation, especially in light of judges' concerns that their lower compensation is inappropriate in a system of separated and equal branches.

### Constitutional Tribunal

Clarification of the proper relationship between the Constitutional Tribunal and the ordinary courts is needed.

### Tenure Issues

The institution of court assessor – effectively a probationary judge – allows the Ministry of Justice and senior court officials to exercise undue influence on those new judges whose future employment is insecure. At the other end of a judge's career, the grant of an extension before retirement is discretionary, which gives rise to concern that extensions may be based on inappropriate considerations.

*Lustration*

Two separate acts limit the right of judges to serve based on their actions under the regime prior to 1989; neither appears to violate norms on judicial independence, although they have generated controversy within Poland.

*Case Allocation*

The current rules do not provide sufficiently transparent and neutral criteria for allocating cases. Although court presidents are fairly powerful and have broad supervisory responsibility over administrative matters, there is no evidence of their attempting to influence or supervise judges' adjudication directly.

*Accession*

Social expectations and the requirements promulgated by the EU demand changes in the performance of the judiciary. However, judges are not directly involved in the accession process.

# I. Introduction

Poland has made considerable progress towards the creation of a truly independent judiciary. One of the priorities in the Polish transformation was to ensure that the judiciary is a fully independent third power, and this has largely been achieved. Many guarantees of independence have been elevated to the constitutional level, and the National Council of the Judiciary has acquired a constitutional mandate to safeguard judges' and courts' independence. For the most part, the boundary between the judiciary and the political branches has been clearly defined and accepted.

There are significant remaining areas of concern, however, the most important of which are the continuing involvement of the executive in judicial administration and the budget process, which results in low levels of funding; and two attitudinal problems: many judges' continuing posture of excessive deference to the political branches and higher judges; and uneven public support for the judiciary, which ultimately threatens its independence.

## A. Executive Involvement in the Affairs of the Judiciary and Budget Issues

### 1. Undue Executive Involvement

Despite the establishment of constitutional guarantees of independence, the executive, in particular the Ministry of Justice, retains considerable administrative and supervisory authority over the organisation and affairs of the judiciary. There is still no clear constitutional authority representing the judiciary as a whole – although the National Council of the Judiciary fulfils some important representative functions for judges – which tends to encourage continued involvement by the political branches.

Judges frequently work for the Ministry of Justice while adjudicating cases – despite bans on their employment outside the judiciary – in a manner which inevitably compromises their independence. Current draft legislation will actually exacerbate this problem. Indeed, judges seem to focus on threats to their independence stemming from the powers of the Ministry over judicial administration, but fail to recognize the dangers of excessive entanglement of their careers with the executive away from the bench.

## 2. Budget

The judiciary's lack of input into the budgeting process remains a problem. The budget is relatively low, resulting in insufficient investment. Compensation, while reasonably adequate, is lower than that for the political branches, which is perceived by many judges and observers as incompatible with the separation and equality of the branches. These problems are in part a function of the executive's continued control of the budget process and of the allocation of funding within the court system.

The political branches appear responsive to the problem. Two draft laws are now before Parliament: one concerns the ordinary courts and the other concerns the National Council of the Judiciary. Both drafts propose budgetary autonomy but they vary in the scope of autonomy proposed. In April 2001 Parliament sent the Draft Act on Ordinary Courts back to the Committee of the Judiciary for further discussions.

## B. Intra-Judicial and Public Attitudinal Problems

### 1. Uncertainty among Judges about Their Role

Some of the most serious problems affecting the independence of individual judges are intra-judicial and attitudinal; judges are not in agreement about their proper role and relationship to each other, the political branches, and society. Many judges, trained in a passive professional culture, have an excessively deferential approach towards higher judges. At the same time, influenced by the development of principles of judicial independence, some judges appear to believe that asking questions is also a form of curtailing judicial independence.[1]

Contemporary Polish law, having been developed in a short period of time, naturally raises numerous issues, which requires judges to be active. Yet many judges have concerns about posing questions to higher courts or the Constitutional Tribunal, either because of their passivity and deference or because of their unrealistic insistence on an all-encompassing independence. The result, in either case, is a corps of judges deciding cases, not independently, but in isolation, and unable collectively to defend its interests.

---

[1] See Section IV.C.1., discussing a regional court's ruling in defiance of a Constitutional Tribunal decision on the logic that making Constitutional Tribunal decisions binding would violate the court's independence.

A debate was conducted in the press in 1998 and 1999 on whether court judgements may properly be criticised. The judicial community, especially the National Council of the Judiciary, argued that court judgements should not be criticised. This stance was not, however, shared by the public, and judges' arguments have been more muted of late. Adopting the principle of separation of powers also assumes the allocation of accountability among all the state authorities. The judiciary, under these conditions, is subject to evaluation, just as other authorities are.

### 2. Uneven Public and Political Support for the Judiciary

Public and political support for the institutions of judicial independence has been uneven. In recent years, judges and courts have come under fire from the media and politicians. The criticism mainly involves the extended delays in legal proceedings, the growing backlog of cases, and corruption. There has also been criticism of excessively lenient verdicts. Critics, especially in the media, accuse the courts of being out of step with public sentiment, especially in regard to criminal sentences. Allegations of corruption have been raised against judges.

Such criticism and investigations of corruption have led to a drop in the public approval ratings enjoyed by judges. In 1994, 51 percent of respondents in a survey expressed confidence in the courts and 33 percent lacked confidence; in 2000, only 40 percent expressed confidence, and 44 percent lacked confidence.[2]

## C. The Judiciary and the EU Accession Process

In 1999 the European Commission commented that although judicial independence was respected, there had been only limited improvements in judicial capacity. The Regular Report noted the length of civil, penal and economic cases, and the lack of improvement with regard to the enforcement of judicial judgements and access to justice.[3]

In its 2000 report, the Commission noted some progress toward curtailing the length of court proceedings and reducing the case backlog. However, the Report also expressed concern that continued delays – especially in Warsaw – coupled with reports of corruption,

---

[2] OBOP (Centre for Public Opinion Research) report, "Do We Feel Safe?" April 2000.

[3] Commission's 1999 Report on Poland's Progress on the Way to Membership, European Integration Committee Office, Warsaw, p. 12.

discourages many citizens from turning to the courts, and contributes to the "generally negative perception of justice in Poland by the average citizen."[4]

Social expectations and the requirements promulgated by the EU demand changes in the performance of the judiciary. However, judges are not directly involved in the accession process. Thus far one meeting was held between EU representatives and representatives of the Iustitia Judges Association.

## D. Outline of the Court System

### 1. The Communist Legacy

Polish tradition long appreciated and supported the requirements of judicial independence; various parts of the future Poland employed the civil law system, as did independent inter-war Poland. The communist system introduced after the Second World War hampered the full realisation of this principle, however. Prior to 1989, the organisation of the judiciary was subject to the basic principle prevalent in all socialist states at the time, the unity of power.

In practice, this principle required the subordination of courts to the Communist Party, and dramatically altered the manner in which officials thought about the role of the courts. It was understood that courts must be involved in the execution of the state's political plan. Although the 1952 Constitution formally declared the independence of the judiciary, the law provided for a number of institutions that restricted this principle and in certain situations actually nullified it. Furthermore, the decisive role of the Minister of Justice concerning all personnel decisions involving judges and the absence of a self-regulatory body for judges also moulded judges' social awareness of their role as a body integrally connected to the executive[5] authority. The independence of any institution whatsoever, including the judicial authority, was treated as a threat to "socialist democracy".

The pledge principle was particularly harmful to judges' independence. The Council of State, acting upon a motion submitted by the Minister of Justice, could recall a

---

[4] European Commission's 2000 Report on Poland's Progress on the Way to EU Membership, European Integration Committee Office, Warsaw.

[5] The executive is generally referred to as the State Administration in Poland.

judge who did not exercise his judicial duties in accordance with the pledge.[6] The political authorities were not constrained by any defined criteria in availing themselves of such power; recall was possible even without granting a hearing for a judge in question. In combination with the explicit priority given to protection of the socio-political system, and the unwritten requirement that the local Communist Party committee had to approve any candidate for judicial office, the pledge principle significantly restricted the principle of independence or actually made it illusory. In effect, it deprived judges of their irremovability and their insulation from political influence, thus eliminating the basic guarantees of their independence.

When martial law was introduced in 1981, the principle of judicial independence came under serious threat, stemming both from binding laws as well as political practice; the Minister of Justice used his powers under martial law to remove from office those judges who refused to co-operate.[7]

## 2. The Transitional Period

As a result of the Roundtable Agreements in 1989, the Constitution was amended, leading to basic changes in the Act on Ordinary Courts[8] as well as the Law on the Supreme Court.[9] The changes effected in 1989 addressed all the key problems relating to judicial independence, in particular: (1) restriction of the role of the executive in the appointment and promotion of judges; (2) abolition of the pledge principle; (3) adoption of the principle of irremovability; (4) abolition of the Supreme Court's right to establish decisional guidelines for the lower courts;[10] and (5) withdrawal of the Supreme Court First President's power to review court adjudication outside of ordinary court proceedings.

---

[6] Act of 20 June 1985 on the Ordinary Courts, Art. 61, para. 1 (subsequently amended).

[7] A. Rzeplinski, *The Judicial System in People's Poland*, Warsaw, 1989.

[8] Law of 20 June 1985 on Ordinary Courts (amendments).

[9] Act of 20 September 1984 on the Supreme Court.

[10] An extensive discussion was conducted in the legal literature about the effects on independence of the courts' statutory duty to apply the "guideline for administration of justice and the practice of law" of the Supreme Court to their adjudication on an equal footing with laws. Some authors argued that the guidelines curtailed the courts' freedom to interpret provisions of law, and others argued that they facilitated the correct application of the law by judges. However, because in practice the Court's guidelines had been seen as safeguarding a specific political line of thought, it was deemed expedient to abolish the practice, and their removal was seen as an important constituent element of the guarantee of judicial independence.

The status of the judicial branch and guarantees of judicial independence were regarded as a key element of Poland's political transformation. Basic legal changes, creating a National Council of the Judiciary and introducing collective bodies – court colleges – for the appellate and regional courts were carried out during the initial months of the transformation process.

After 1989, the courts' competence was expanded quite abruptly, and has since been expanded further, with the transfer of numerous matters from the executive, including all registration activity, the right to order pre-trial arrest, jurisdiction over treasury crimes and misdemeanours (since October 1998), and lien-registration matters. Legislative changes in accordance with constitutional provisions designed to bring law into compliance with European standards have also endowed courts of law with new tasks. These tendencies, which in part arose from the public's initial confidence in courts as independent authorities, have contributed to their overburdening in recent years. This overburdening and the inefficiency it engenders are now the primary reasons behind negative evaluations of Poland's judicial system.

Still, on balance, the evolution of Polish legislation over the last decade clearly shows that the political authorities appreciate the significance of an independent judiciary. The extent to which judicial powers have been expanded is one of the outstanding proofs of this trend, along with the transfer of a host of competencies from the Ministry of Justice to the National Council of the Judiciary, which has curtailed the administrative authority of the executive.

## 3. *The Contemporary System*

The Supreme Court, the Supreme Administrative Court, the ordinary courts, and the military courts carry out the administration of justice. The Supreme Court and the Supreme Administrative Court are detached from the Ministry of Justice. The ordinary courts are structured in three levels: district courts, regional courts and appellate courts. At present, there are 294 district courts, 43 regional courts and 10 appellate courts. There is a single Supreme Administrative Court, although its members sit in offices throughout the country.

Since 1989 the number of judges in Poland has grown considerably. At the end of 2000 there were 8,343 judges and assessors in Poland, compared with 5,165 in 1989. (There are 4,875 judges and 956 assessors in district courts, 2,167 in regional courts and 345 in appellate courts).[11] But this increase has been far outstripped by the growth in

---

[11] Information from the Ministry of Justice, Autumn 2000.

the caseload, especially in public law registration matters; in 1989 there were roughly 70,000 registration cases before the courts while in 2000 there were more than 2,600,000 such cases. Judicial qualifications are not required to handle all of them, and for this reason a new position of court clerk was established in 1998 to handle registration matters; there were 403 court clerks by the end of 2000.

However, further expansions of jurisdiction are expected. Poland's 1997 Constitution requires the abolition of all quasi-judicial institutions. For this reason, as of 17 October 2001, all misdemeanour boards will be abolished, and their jurisdiction assumed by the courts. Tentative estimates suggest that the courts will take on another 800,000 petty offence cases. Another 400 full-time positions are envisaged in 2001.

*Military Courts*: Military courts handle the administration of criminal justice in the armed forces, but they are partly integrated into the bodies administering the regular courts. In 1997 military courts were brought substantially closer to ordinary courts from the point of view of administrative oversight – a step clearing the way for disbanding military courts in the future.

The Military Court Department is now one of the departments in the Ministry of Justice. Military court judges are independent in their adjudication and are subject only to statutes. The Supreme Court oversees the adjudicative activity of military courts; the Minister of Justice oversees military courts' organisational and administrative activity. The Minister of National Defence, in turn, oversees soldiers serving in military courts with respect to active military duty.[12]

*Constitutional Tribunal*: The Constitutional Tribunal is a part of the judicial system in the broad sense, as suggested by its inclusion in the same Chapter of the Constitution as that concerning Courts and Tribunals. It makes decisions that are binding upon other courts – although there have been assertions by some ordinary courts that they ought not to be bound by the Tribunal's rulings.[13] At the same time, it exhibits a series of characteristics that are less conducive to its inclusion as part of the judicial system in a strict sense. For instance, in contrast to the First President of the Supreme Court and the President of the Supreme Administrative Courts, the President of the Constitutional Tribunal is not a member of the National Council of the Judiciary. The Council in turn does not have any powers with respect to Constitutional Tribunal justices, who are elected by the parliament for nine years, and do not go through the same procedure as other judges.

---

[12] Act of 21 August 1997 on the Military Courts.

[13] See Section IV.C.1.

## II. Constitutional and Legal Foundations of Judicial Independence

### A. Guarantees of the Separation of Powers or Independence

The formal guarantees of judicial independence are generally satisfactory. The 1997 Constitution defines the position of the courts in general terms by establishing a division of powers: "(1) The system of government of the Republic of Poland shall be based on the separation of, and balance between, the legislative, executive and judicial powers. (2) ...[T]he judicial power shall be vested in courts and tribunals."[14] The Constitution further states that "the courts and tribunals shall constitute a separate power and shall be independent of other branches of power."[15]

The Constitutional Tribunal has repeatedly ruled in support of judicial independence.[16] The Tribunal's ruling of November 9, 1993 was significant; it clearly stated that "one of the elements of the principle of the separation of powers and of the foundations of the democratic construction of a law-abiding state is the principle of judicial independence."[17]

The Constitution also confers normative status on the principle of the independence of individual judges by stating that "judges, within the exercise of their office, shall be independent and subject only to the Constitution and statutes."[18] Commentators have emphasised that the Constitution thus defines, in a new and important way, the position of judges as subordinate not only to any particular regulation, but rather to the legal system, crowned by the Constitution,[19] thus further ensuring its independence from the other branches.

---

[14] CONST. REP. POLAND, Art. 10. See also E. Letowska, "Courts and Tribunals under the Constitution of Poland", in *Constitutional Essays*, M. Wyrzykowski, ed., Warsaw 1999. pp. 191–220.

[15] CONST. REP. POLAND, Art. 173.

[16] Compare ruling of the Constitutional Tribunal of 9 November 1993 (OTK 1993/2/37); ruling of the Constitutional Tribunal of 8 November 1994 (suspension of the valorisation of judges' salaries); ruling of the Constitutional Tribunal of 11 September 1995 (reply to a query by the Supreme Court regarding the principles governing judges' salaries); verdict of 24 June 1998; and ruling of the Constitutional Tribunal of 22 March 2000 (determination of the amount of judges' salaries within the context of the Constitution, 2 April 1997, *Journal of Laws*, No. 78, 1997, Art. 178).

[17] Ruling of the Constitutional Tribunal, 1993/2/106; compare K. Buchala, approving commentary to that ruling, *State and Law*, 1995, notebook 5.

[18] CONST. REP. POLAND, Art. 178(1).

[19] Compare E. Letowska, "Courts and Tribunals under the Constitution of Poland", in *Constitutional Essays*, M. Wyrzykowski, ed., Warsaw 1999. p. 392.

An extensive discussion was held during the constitutional debates from 1993 to 1997 on the scope of guarantees for judicial independence. The judicial community and political authorities generally see the current catalogue of guarantees as sufficient. However, while certain important guarantees are located in the Constitution, others are contained in statutes, such as the Law on the Ordinary Courts. As all statutes have the same legal rank – the institution of organic statutes is unknown in the Polish system – statutes concerning the status of the judiciary are subject to revision by the same rules as any other statute. It is therefore particularly important that the basic guarantees of judicial independence be set out in the Constitution, amendment of which requires a qualified majority.[20]

## B.  Representation of the Judiciary

From a legal standpoint, judicial authority is acknowledged as an equal partner with the legislative and executive branches; in practice, however, it has been difficult to precisely define the nature of this relationship. Further clarification of the National Council of the Judiciary's role and powers as a representative of the whole judiciary would be welcome.

### 1.  The National Council of the Judiciary

Under current law it would be difficult to regard any organ as the supreme representative of the judicial branch. In a certain sense, the National Council of the Judiciary provides such representation. The Council is defined in the Constitution as an organ guarding the independence of judges and courts,[21] though not necessarily the judiciary as such. In addition, the Council has standing to petition the Constitutional Tribunal to rule on the constitutionality of normative acts dealing with the independence of judges and courts[22] – a right the Council has actually invoked.[23] Still, the Council's powers concentrate in particular on the personal affairs of judges, rather than on the role and

---

[20]  CONST. REP. POLAND, Art. 235.

[21]  CONST. REP. POLAND, Art. 186(1). In reply to a legal question from the Supreme Administrative Court, the Constitutional Tribunal stated that in accordance with the Constitution the Council guards the independence of courts and judges.

[22]  CONST. REP. POLAND, Art. 186(2).

[23]  Compare the National Council of the Judiciary's resolution of 15 January 1998, and the verdict of the Constitutional Tribunal, 27 January 1999, OTK 1999/1/3 (upholding a complaint by the Council against a ban on judges' relatives being employed as lawyers or legal advisers).

status of the judiciary as a whole, and judges generally do not consider the Council to be the representative of the judicial branch as such.[24]

In 1989, when the Council was created,[25] there was discussion in Parliament about whether or not it constituted a representative body of judges. The prevailing view held that the Council had a special character, but that it was not strictly speaking an organ of judicial authority and that it did not seem to qualify as an organ of judicial self-government.[26] With the Council's *sui generis* status, representatives of the Council are invited to take part in discussions at meetings of parliamentary committees, although such an invitation is the prerogative of the parliamentary committee chairman rather than an obligation imposed upon him. Parliament is obliged to request the Council's present opinions on all bills concerning the judiciary; however, the Council's opinion is not binding upon Parliament.[27]

The membership of the Council is determined in the Constitution, and includes a majority of judges.[28] Council members are appointed for four years and may be re-appointed. It has become the practice for the State President to select a judge, although this is not directly prescribed by law.

---

[24] The Council is empowered to: (1) review the nominations of judges and petition the State President to appoint them; (2) review and decide on motions to transfer judges to other posts taking into account the high standing of the judge's office, with binding effect; (3) consent to a judge remaining in office upon reaching 65 years of age; (4) make pronouncements on issues involving the professional ethics of judges; (5) express its opinion on proposals to change the organisational structure of courts as well as other matters pertaining to the way courts function; (6) acquaint itself with draft normative acts pertaining to the judiciary; (7) express its opinion on training programs for legal apprentices and the manner in which examinations for prospective judges are conducted; and (8) express its opinion on matters relating to judges and courts submitted for the Council's deliberation by the State President and other state organs, as well as by general assemblies of judges. Law on the National Council of the Judiciary, Art. 2.

[25] The Council only acquired constitutional status in 1997.

[26] T. Erecinski, "The Role of the Judicial Council in a Democratic State", *Przeglad Sadowy (Judicial Review)* 1994/5/3; P. Przybysz, Commentary on the verdict of the Supreme Administrative Court of 5 November 1992, IISA 207/92, in *State and Law*, 1994/6/113.

[27] The notion has appeared in press commentaries that the NJC is a kind of trade union for judges.

[28] The membership includes the First President of the Supreme Court; the Minister of Justice; the President of the Supreme Administrative Court; one person appointed by the State President; fifteen members elected from among the judges of the Supreme Court and ordinary, administrative and military courts by the general assemblies of these courts, four members elected by Parliament from its members, and two members elected by the Senate from its members. CONST. REP. POLAND, Art. 187.

The role of the Minister of Justice in the National Council of the Judiciary does not differ from the role played by its other members; the Minister does not enjoy any additional powers, or a special position.

## C. Rules on Incompatibility

Judges are restricted from most potentially compromising work outside the judiciary. However, practices allowing judges to work within the Ministry of Justice – which the Draft Act on Ordinary Courts will further encourage – seriously entangles judges with the executive and endangers their independence.

Judges may not engage in public activities incompatible with the principles of judicial independence. The Constitution adopts a broad formulation limiting judges' public involvement: "A judge shall not belong to a political party, a trade union or perform public activities incompatible with the principles of independence of the courts and judges."[29] The Constitutional Tribunal noted in a 1993 case that

> [t]he concept of judicial independence has an unambiguous and well-founded substance providing a basic guarantee of impartial decision-making. Independence must therefore mean a judge's independence both from the parties to a dispute as well as from state organs. The corollary of the principle of independence on the part of the judge is the duty of impartiality[.][30]

The Constitution contains clear provisions restricting judges from holding other public offices, including a ban on judges' holding parliamentary mandates.[31] The constitutional ban is the logical consequence of the division of power and the guarantees for judicial independence; holding the offices of judge and parliamentarian simultaneously cannot easily be reconciled with the principle of judicial independence, given the explicitly partisan nature of parliamentary service.[32]

Judges may perform other extra-judicial public roles that are clearly allowed by law. Judges of the appellate, regional and district courts may be nominated by the Minister

---

[29]  CONST. REP. POLAND, Art. 178(3).

[30]  Ruling of the Constitutional Tribunal, 1993/2/106.

[31]  CONST. REP. POLAND, Art. 103(2). An earlier law had allowed a judge to take a leave of absence without pay for the duration of his parliamentary mandate. Act on Ordinary Courts, Art. 64, para. 4.

[32]  The two judges who took part in the 1997 election campaign and were elected to Parliament resigned from their judicial functions; the Parliament has elected both former judges as its representatives to the National Council of the Judiciary.

of Justice to serve on election commissions. In addition, the Board of the Institute of National Remembrance includes members – usually judges[33] – elected by the National Council of the Judiciary.[34]

Judges do not generally perform administrative functions outside the judiciary; they are not employed in the executive with the exception of the Ministry of Justice. A judge appointed or elected to duties in a state organ, provincial government, diplomatic or consular service, or with an international organisation is obliged to resign from his post.[35]

By tradition, judges may be employed at the Ministry of Justice in a variety of functions – some even as department directors. They do not become civil servants by the mere fact of their employment there, but rather retain the status of judge and may even adjudicate in court at the same time. No statute regulates this practice. Obviously, allowing judges to serve as both judicial and executive officials at the same time seriously undermines the effective separation of powers; because judges working at the Ministry are employed by the executive, they are susceptible to the sorts of pressures any employee might feel from an employer, which in this case threatens their decisional independence on the bench. Certainly, this practice damages the public's perception of judges' independence.

An unfortunate trend may be observed of late: judges focus mainly on limiting the direct powers of the Ministry of Justice over them and on securing financial guarantees for the judiciary; the performance by judges of functions in other bodies besides courts is not recognised as a threat to judicial independence. The new draft legislation for the Act on Ordinary Courts even envisages, for example, that a judge may be the deputy Minister of Justice. This development is potentially dangerous to judicial independence as it revisits institutions of the kind dismantled in 1989.

Judges may not participate in political activities,[36] and may not belong to political parties or trade unions.[37] It is interesting to note the way thinking on judicial independence and political involvement has evolved over the past decade. In 1989, during a debate

---

[33] The issue of electing judges to the Council of the Institute of National Remembrance prompted discussion at a National Council of the Judiciary meeting, with a small minority asserting that this trespassed upon the boundary between legislative and judicial authority. The majority nonetheless decided to propose judges for this position and Parliament accepted the choice.

[34] Law on the Institute of National Remembrance.

[35] Act on Ordinary Courts, Art. 79.

[36] Act on Ordinary Courts, Art. 64(3).

[37] CONST. REP. POLAND, Art. 178 (3). Trade unions play an important political role in Poland, and participate in electoral politics, so in context the ban on trade union membership can be seen as integral to an effective ban on political party membership.

on a draft law to amend the Act on Ordinary Courts, the problem of judges' membership in political parties was raised. At that time, however, attention focused mainly on a ban's potential to violate the constitutional rights of citizens to affiliate.[38] In 1997, no doubts were raised over the constitutionality of a ban on public involvement; rather, it was generally supposed that such involvement is irreconcilable with the principle of judicial independence – in contrast to the continued tolerance of sitting judges working in ministerial posts.

The Act on Ordinary Courts contains other restrictions on the outside activities of judges. Judges may not accept outside employment that impedes the exercise of his judicial duties, undermines judicial prestige, or weakens confidence in their impartiality.[39] Moreover, a judge may not accept additional employment without the consent of the president of the regional court; a regional court president may not accept additional employment without the consent of the Minister of Justice.[40] Exceptions are made for employment in academic teaching or research positions, again provided such employment does not impede the exercise of judicial duties.

Current law does not prohibit commercial activities. However, under the Draft Law on the Ordinary Courts, a broad range of prohibitions is contemplated. Under the draft law, a judge could not: be a member of a management and supervisory board or audit committee in a commercial law company or in a co-operative other than a housing co-operative; be a management board member in a foundation that conducts economic activity; hold more than a ten percent stake in commercial law companies or in the founding capital of any such companies; or conduct economic activity for his own account or jointly with other persons, nor manage such activity or be an agent or power-of-attorney in conducting such activity (except for running a family farm).

*Disclosure*: The Act on Ordinary Courts contains a special anti-corruption provision, according to which all judges must make an annual written disclosure of all the real property, stocks, and other financial assets they own.[41]

---

[38] Stenographic minutes of the 11th session of the Parliament of the Polish People's Republic, 30 October 1989.

[39] Act on Ordinary Courts, Art. 68, paras. 1 and 2.

[40] Additional employment in such a case might include, for example, employment in a foundation or in the editor's office of a trade journal. This kind of employment, however, is very rare in practice.

[41] Act on Ordinary Courts, Art. 68.

## D. Judges' Associations

Judges, as any citizens, have a right to freedom of association. There is a nation-wide association of judges, Iustitia, which also has regional branches; there are no other associations of judges. The association organises training programs for judges throughout the country that are partly financed with funds provided by the Ministry of Justice and foreign institutions. However, Iustitia does not have any formal standing before Parliament, the Government, or any other State body; its representative function is informal.

## III. Administration of the Court System and Judicial Independence

The Ministry of Justice continues to exercise considerable administrative control over judges, either directly or through the court presidents. Although administrative powers must vest in some body, the Ministry's supervisory powers and ability to initiate investigations or overturn administrative decisions of courts unnecessarily affords the executive opportunities indirectly to influence judges.

There is no independent judicial administration at the national level. The responsibilities of the National Council of the Judiciary are confined to safeguarding the independence of individual judges; it does not exercise administrative supervision. Under the Act on Ordinary Courts,[42] supervision of the administrative activities of ordinary courts is entrusted to the Ministry of Justice. The Minister has defined the scope of that authority to include ensuring efficient case handling and proper enforcement of court rulings.[43] The Ministry of Justice supervises administrative activities of courts directly as well as through designated individuals[44] – meaning, in practice, court presidents. Supervision is exercised through inspection visits, statistical analysis of courts' performance, examination of case backlogs, and review of complaints about judges' behaviour or rulings.[45]

The Ministry of Justice is authorised to create a supervisory department but it has not done so. Judges employed in the Ministry's Department for Courts and Notary Offices[46] or working in different courts may be assigned to perform supervisory tasks; in either case the choice is made by the Ministry, with the approval of the Minister, the judge himself, and his court president being necessary. The reports of supervising judges are sent to the Ministry, to the president of the affected court, and to the National Council of the Judiciary. A negative report can lead to the recall of the court president or disciplinary proceedings against anyone deemed responsible for infractions.

---

[42] Act on Ordinary Courts, Art. 10.

[43] Regulation of the Minister of Justice of 18 September 1995, *Journal of Laws* of 28 September 1995, 1995.111.538.

[44] Act on Ordinary Courts, Art. 29.

[45] Regulation of the Minister of Justice of 18 September 1995. The Ministry includes a special bureau that handles complaints.

[46] In the Ministry of Justice there are seven departments, including Legislative, Organisational, Courts and Notary Offices, Personnel, and Budgetary departments. Judges may be employed in these departments.

Court presidents manage the day-to-day activities of their courts. Organisational matters pertaining to archives and court records are in the purview of court presidents; at the central level these matters are handled by the Ministry of Justice's Organisational Department.

Court presidents supervise the administrative activities of courts in the judicial districts under their jurisdiction; thus regional court presidents supervise district courts beneath them, and appellate court presidents oversee the regional courts beneath them. These supervisory powers include: monitoring those courts' adjudication; updating the service records of judges; conducting periodic evaluations of the qualifications of other judicial employees on the basis of separate regulations; reviewing complaints pertaining to the performance of courts; issuing the proper directives and taking necessary measures in the event that flaws or infringements are detected in the activities of judges and other court employees.

Appellate and regional court presidents have oversight powers and may appoint visiting judges to conduct supervisory inspections, or may, by agreement with a court's college, designate a judge to conduct an informal, *ad hoc* inspection. During such inspections judges may sit in on proceedings, examine complaints, and may recommend that disciplinary proceedings be initiated.

Court presidents report up the chain of district, regional and appellate court presidents to the Minister of Justice on matters of administration. The Minister and the presidents of higher courts may draw lower courts' attention to infractions affecting the efficiency and organisation of judicial proceedings, and may demand that steps be taken to remedy the effects of the infraction. The Minister and presidents of higher courts may overturn administrative ordinances issued by lower court presidents.

The Act on Ordinary Courts also requires the Ministry of Justice to present a court activity report to the State President and the National Council of the Judiciary. The Minister determines the contents of this report and usually uses data collected by the Ministry's own departments, but also data forwarded by individual regional and appellate court presidents. The report includes information on the most significant issues for evaluating the operation of the judiciary: growth in caseload, case management and the average duration of proceedings, personnel in the administration of justice, computerisation of the courts, and court budget and investments, as well as issues relating to reform.[47]

---

[47] Information from the Ministry of Justice about the activity of ordinary courts, Warsaw, 2000.

*Judges' Administrative Bodies*: Judges participate in the administration of courts through collective court bodies. These are the general assemblies of regional and appellate judges and the court colleges.[48]

The general assembly of a regional court consists of all regional judges and an equal number of delegates elected by the district judges within the regional court's area of jurisdiction.[49] The Minister of Justice establishes bylaws for electing delegates. If a general assembly consists of more than one hundred members, it may elect a meeting of representatives; the general assembly determines the bylaws for the election and determines the delegated competence of the meeting of representatives.[50]

The general assembly discharges various advisory tasks prescribed by law, such as hearing information presented by regional court presidents on the operation of courts, and reviewing the activity reports filed by regional court colleges. In addition, they have a more substantive involvement in the selection and removal of judges and court presidents (discussed below).[51] The composition of general assemblies and their competencies suggest that they fulfil, in a very limited capacity, the role of a judicial self-governing body, although the statute does not use such a term expressly, and they seem more properly to be advisory bodies.

Besides the assemblies there are also colleges in the appellate and regional courts. A regional court college discharges those tasks prescribed by statute which are not reserved to the sole jurisdiction of the general assembly. In particular, it determines the division of activities in the courts, prescribes the rules for substituting judges and court clerks, as well as for allocating cases, and reviews motions which court presidents (who are heads of the colleges) raise based on the scrutiny of courts by visiting judges.[52]

The draft amendment to the Act on Ordinary Courts, currently before the Parliament, expressly states that judges form a court self-governing body, composed by the general assembly of the regional judges and the general assembly of appellate judges. The implications for the future form of court administration or the involvement of the Ministry of Justice are not clear.

---

[48] Law of 20 June 1985 on Ordinary Courts, Art. 12.

[49] Judges of each district court elect a number of delegates in proportion to the size of the court.

[50] Act on Ordinary Courts, Art. 38.

[51] Act on Ordinary Courts, Art. 39.

[52] Act on Ordinary Courts, Art. 41.

## IV. Financial Autonomy and Level of Funding

The judiciary has little control over or involvement with its own funding. Many judges see increased budgetary autonomy as an important factor in guaranteeing equality among the branches, while the executive feels that the judiciary must not participate in the budgetary process, at least during certain phases (such as discussions in the government) which are inherently political.

### A. Budgeting Process

There is no separate budget chapter for the regular judiciary within the overall State budget. Appropriations for the judiciary are part of the Justice Ministry's budget, which includes sub-lines for various functions within the framework of the Ministry, such as the judiciary, the prosecution, and the prison service. The Supreme Court, Supreme Administrative Court and Constitutional Tribunal have autonomous budgets.

The annual budget is drafted on the basis of budgetary parameters written by the Ministry of Finance. At the Ministry of Justice the annual budget is prepared on the basis of the evaluation of the previous year's performance, while giving consideration to the estimated growth in caseload in courts connected to increasing the number of full-time judge positions and the requirements for new investments. The regional and appellate court presidents prepare data for courts in a given area, which are then analysed by the Budget Department at the Ministry of Justice in consultation with the court presidents. The Minister of Justice's budget proposal is presented to the Ministry of Finance for consultation, and then to the Government.[53]

Neither judges nor court presidents participate in the official negotiations concerning the budget. The Ministry of Justice does discuss the budget with the National Council of the Judiciary, however. Council members can also meet with the Minister of Finance and members of Parliament to present the judiciary's needs against the backdrop of the State budget. They are also invited to parliamentary committee meetings on the budget. They do not, however, participate in the budget sessions of the Council of Ministers, nor are they involved in the detailed negotiations. While this prevents judges becoming entangled in disputes of a political nature, and so might accord with the principle of separation of powers, many judges are dissatisfied with their subordinate position in the budget process, believing that it places them at a disadvantage, to the detriment of their independence.

---

[53] The Supreme Court, Supreme Administrative Court, and Constitutional Tribunal prepare their budgets in co-operation with the Ministry of Finance, just as any ministry would.

In the course of the budget debate in the Government and Parliament, there were no instances in which approval of the judiciary's appropriation was made conditional upon enhancing certain "productivity" standards.[54] There is, however, a definite dearth of legal mechanisms to safeguard against such political interference.

The Draft Act on Ordinary Courts envisages that the income and expenditures of ordinary courts will constitute a separate part in the state budget. The Minister of Justice would, however, still be in charge of the portion of the budget allocated to the ordinary courts.

Since the Minister of Justice exercises administrative supervision and is responsible for preparing the budget, it is also the Minister who makes decisions on allocating budgetary resources. Court presidents submit applications to the Ministry outlining their financial needs. However, because the Minister operates within the general parameters of the budget approved by Parliament, he/she has limited discretion, and cannot, for instance, increase the number of full-time positions. On the basis of the adopted budget, the Ministry's Personnel Department allocates job appointments both for judicial and administrative posts for individual regional courts. Regional court presidents fill vacancies within their districts and allocate duties to new employees. The National Council of the Judiciary expresses its opinion on the job distribution proposals drawn up by the Ministry of Justice.

The actual allocation of funds for investments in court infrastructure and current court operations are handled by the Budget Department, which also evaluates how those resources are spent. During the year, it is not possible to transfer from one part of the budget to another, unless Parliament amends the budget law; to date, the judiciary's appropriation has not been subject to intra-budget cuts. The possibility does exist to transfer one court's budget to another court when resources allocated to a given court are not utilised at the end of a budgetary year and when concern arises that they will not be used.[55]

The regular courts' sub-line with the Ministry of Justice's budget has been increasing; in 1989 the judiciary's budget accounted for 34.3 percent of the Ministry's entire budget and in 1999 it accounted for 48.5 percent. In 2000, expenditures for the ordinary

---

[54] The chairman of Parliament's Budget Committee raised a solitary voice in the course of work on the budget, calling for budget cuts with respect to the judiciary owing to the ineffectiveness of the courts. The committee did not back the chairman's position. Compare the report on the Budget Committee's activities of 1999.

[55] This situation occurred at the end of 1998 when the resources awarded to the Warsaw District Court were not utilised and were transferred to another district court. The funds had not been used due to poor management by the court president, who later tendered his resignation.

courts account for 1.37 percent of the State's overall spending;[56] according to the 2001 budget, the judiciary received 1.29 percent.[57]

## B. Work Conditions

Work conditions for judges remain sufficiently poor that in some instances they may indirectly threaten judges' independence by increasing their reliance on the branches that control funding decisions or on outside parties.

The Constitution provides that judges shall be provided with appropriate conditions for work.[58] Recent appropriations have not provided adequately for the indispensable resources that courts require – in part, a result of more than four decades of under-investment. New court buildings were not constructed in the post-WWII period; old buildings were renovated or other buildings were adapted to meet the needs of courts. In connection with the expansion of judicial competencies and the concomitant increase in workload during the 1990s, this produced a constant deterioration in working conditions. In smaller courts, every judge has his own office, but conditions are considerably worse in courts in larger cities; the situation is most critical in Warsaw, where some judges' chambers have had to be converted into courtrooms.

It is obvious that decades of neglect cannot be remedied in a short period of time. Certain improvements have occurred, however. Between 1997 to 1999 investment expenditures for the judiciary jumped by roughly 40 percent, resulting in a significant increase in the construction of new office space and an improvement in the previously serious situation.

The level of computerisation is still insufficient, and is considerably less advanced in comparison with the offices of the executive. In 1999 the Ministry of Justice accepted a plan whereby resources for technology procurement and development were to be allocated to regional and appellate courts rather than centrally, which has resulted in some incompatible systems being adopted in certain localities. All newly commissioned court buildings as well as the modernised court buildings are computerised, as are departments dealing with registration issues. Current legislation is available on CD-ROM, updated every month and listing the more important literature in the field.

---

[56] By comparison, percentages of the State's overall spending in other areas were as follows: culture and art, 0.3 percent; higher education, 2.9 percent; education and training, 0.2 percent; and science, 1.95 percent.

[57] Information from the Ministry of Justice, Autumn 2000.

[58] CONST. REP. POLAND, Art. 178.

Every court has been equipped with such a program (but not every judge). Each court is supplied with current issues of the Journal of Laws.

Each court's staff size is determined by its share of the appropriation, which stipulates the amount available for officials' salaries. According to criteria developed by the Ministry of Justice, there should be three administrative employees for every judge. However, the budget over the past decade has not been sufficient to cover all of these posts, although the situation has improved considerably since 1997, with a roughly ten percent increase in administrative staff positions in 1998 and 1999.[59] At the beginning of 2000 there were 19,335 court employees in ordinary courts. In 2001, the number of court officials should grow to 20,235.

In 1997 the institution of court clerk was introduced. Clerks are to replace judges in the performance of various court duties that do not require high judicial qualifications, such as registration activities and keeping property records. There were 403 clerks at the end of 2000.

## C. Compensation

An essential change in the way judges' salaries are determined was introduced after 1989. Adequate remuneration for judges was intended to become one of the guarantees of their independence,[60] and was elevated to a constitutional principle.[61] However, this has generated controversy concerning the proper level of compensation for judges.

The profession of judge is an attractive one from an economic standpoint when compared with other professionals whose remuneration is set within the state budget, such as teachers. Moreover, judges are entitled to privileges that other professionals, including legal advisers and lawyers, do not enjoy, including job security and retirement benefits. The salaries of judges are fully comparable to those of prosecutors.

In comparing the social and material advantages granted to the three branches it should be noted that judges' salaries vary most widely due to the different levels of judgeships. In addition, judges enjoy rights to which the representatives of other branches of power are not entitled, including irremovability from office, longer recreational leave after

---

[59] Information from the Ministry of Justice, Autumn 2000.

[60] It should be remembered that we are dealing with Poland's relatively modest budget.

[61] CONST. REP. POLAND, Art. 178(2).

ten years of service, and better retirement conditions than representatives of the other two branches do.

The State President issues a directive pertaining to the salaries of regular court judges, in accordance with general rules established in law.[62] In practice, the State President relies on a directive prepared by the Minister of Justice with the opinion of the National Council of the Judiciary.[63] The basic pay of judges of equivalent courts is equal. The actual base salary is calculated according to principles set out in the Budget Law; for 2001 the base amount has been set at 1,303 zloty.[64] The multiple is determined by presidential directive; in accordance with the previous presidential directive, the base amount is multiplied by 4.4 for appellate court judges, by 3.6 for regional court judges and by 3.1 for district court judges. This means that the basic monthly salary of an appellate court judge was about € 1,860.[65] The latest presidential directive of 16 April 2001 raised the multiplication factor for judges at all levels by 0.3.

Because the total sum provided by the presidential directive must fit within the overall budgetary limits, there is always concern that increasing the compensation indicators, which satisfies judges, reduces funds available for other constituent elements, such as the courts' day-to-day activity, modernisation and new investments.

In addition to remuneration of judges, the presidential directive sets the amount of functional allowances, which are awarded to court presidents and vice-presidents, visiting judges, judicial training managers, and various other officials. Pursuant to the presidential directive of 2001 the functional allowance cap has been elevated from 1.1 to 2.0.[66] Compensation is also supplemented with the seniority bonus (one percent for every year of work up to 20 years). The highest allowances are awarded to court presidents, who receive discretionary allowance multiples ranging from 0.8 to 2.0 – which increases the executive's ability to reward or punish court presidents.

A judge's salary may not be decreased, except through disciplinary proceedings, when a disciplinary court may suspend a judge from his professional duties as the result of penal, disciplinary, or incapacity proceedings against him. The court then has the

---

[62] Act on Ordinary Courts, Art. 71 (1).

[63] The draft version of the presidential directive is written by the Minister of Justice. The presidential directive must be countersigned by the President of the Council of Ministers. CONST. REP. POLAND, Art. 144(2–3).

[64] 1,211 zloty was worth approximately € 350 at the time this Report was prepared.

[65] A member of Parliament's monthly salary is about € 1,740, comparable to that of an appeals court judge.

[66] *Journal of Laws* 2001/ 37/ 425.

option of decreasing the judge's salary by 50 percent for the duration of his suspension. That does not apply to individuals against whom incapacity proceedings have been instituted. If disciplinary proceedings have been dismissed or have ended in an acquittal, the withheld salary must be reimbursed.[67]

Judges are entitled to preferentially taxed loans for housing. The interest rate on such a loan is flexible and corresponds to the rate of inflation established in the budget law.[68] A directive of the Ministry of Justice issued in consultation with the Ministry of Finance determines the principles regulating the planning and deployment of funds for housing as well as terms of assistance.[69]

Detailed principles and procedures for determining and paying remuneration and family remuneration to retired judges and prosecutors and members of their families were laid down in a 16 October 1997 directive of the Minister of Justice.[70] It sets the remuneration of a judge *emeritus* at 75 percent of the base pay received at his last post, plus a seniority bonus. The entitlement provisions also apply to the family members of a deceased judge who had been receiving a family social security pension.

## 1. Constitutional and Court Challenges

The constitutional principle concerning judges' remuneration is very general, and in practice, the concept of "remuneration consistent with the dignity of judicial office" is controversial. Because provisions of the Constitution are applied directly unless otherwise provided,[71] many judges have lodged individual claims concerning their compensation. Judges, mainly those from district courts, are demanding salaries equivalent to those earned by members of Parliament; in 1999 and 2000, more than 500 such claims were lodged. On account of the complicated problems concerning direct application of the Constitution, the Regional Court in Cracow and the Regional Court in Czestochowa forwarded legal questions to the Constitutional Tribunal.

The questions concerned whether provisions of the Act on Ordinary Courts and the complementary provisions of the presidential directive of 23 December 1996 regulating

---

[67] Act on Ordinary Courts, Art. 103.

[68] The interest rate is adjusted according to the annual inflation index – in 2000, about seven percent. The interest on housing loans for other professional groups is between 21 and 23 percent.

[69] Directive of the Minister of Justice, September 1995, *Journal of Laws* 1995/114.

[70] *Journal of Laws*, 24 October 1997.

[71] CONST. REP. POLAND, Art. 8(2).

compensation complied with the Constitution. In October 2000, the Tribunal ruled that the Act and presidential directive violated the Constitution on other grounds;[72] however, the Tribunal noted *inter alia* that

[the Constitution] does not establish... the amount of compensation for persons holding judicial office in an unequivocal manner and... cannot form self-evident grounds for judges' claims against the state... The general and simply unspecified nature of the criteria contained in the constitutional provision under analysis unambiguously points to the necessity of stating them with greater precision; they must, therefore, be stated more specifically in ordinary legislation.

Despite the judgement handed down by the Constitutional Tribunal, the Regional Court in Czestochowa issued a judgement on 11 October 2000 finding a claim, arguing that the ordinary courts are not bound by the Constitutional Tribunal's decision, as this would violate the principle of judicial independence.[73] This issue has generated considerable repercussions; indeed, it is through such jurisprudence that the scope of Article 8(2) provisions on direct application of the Constitution is being defined.

## 2. Other Court Employees

In 1999 a very important statute for the administrative employees of courts came into force,[74] which established that a court official's basic compensation is linked to a judge's compensation, and shall be one-half that of a district court judge. For the first time in ten years, this statute created conditions to improve the basic financial terms for administrative employees and to stabilise the staffing situation in courts. Efficient and experienced administrative staff is of material assistance in a judge's work.

---

[72] The Tribunal found a violation of CONST. REP. POLAND, Art. 10(1) concerning the separation and balance of powers. See Section II.A. The Tribunal did not find a violation of Art. 178(2), the provision relating to judge's compensation in relation to judicial independence.

[73] For more information, see "W Czestochowie inaczej niz w Trybunale" ("Czestochowa Does It Differently from the Tribunal") in *Gazeta Sadowa 2001*, Nos. 2 and 3.

[74] Act of 18 December 1998 on Court and Prosecution Employees, *Journal of Laws*.

## V. Judicial Office

### A. Selection

In general, authority for appointments to the bench is divided between executive and judicial bodies in a way that does not harm judicial independence. However, the institution of court assessor – effectively a probationary judge – allows these bodies to grant or withhold a permanent post from a judge based on his rulings.

Individuals may be appointed to the position of a judge if, in addition to various general requirements, they have participated in a court or prosecution apprenticeship, passed a judicial or prosecution examination, and worked as a judicial or prosecution assessor for at least two years.[75]

In order to become a judge one must be nominated to a two-and-a-half year judicial apprenticeship[76] – a kind of internship. A judicial apprentice must fulfil the same general requirements as a judge.[77] Judicial apprentices are nominated and dismissed by appellate court presidents. Nominees must have successfully completed a competition organised by the of the appellate court presidents, under rules determined by the Minister of Justice.[78]

*Court Assessor*: After completing the apprenticeship and passing a competitive examination – whose scope is also determined by the Minister of Justice – an individual may be appointed by the Minister to be a court assessor. The Minister may assign a court assessor to judge's duties in district court for a specified term not to exceed two years, with the consent of the college of the appropriate regional court; it is possible to extend the assessor's term to three years.[79]

---

[75] In addition, a professor or a person holding a doctorate (*doctor habilitowany*) in legal sciences from a Polish university, the Polish Academy of Science, or some other scientific institution may be appointed as a judge. Act on Ordinary Courts, Art. 51.

[76] A part-time court apprenticeship is also possible. Under that arrangement, the apprentice serves in some other institution and works in court only twice a week, but must fulfil all the other conditions required of full-time court apprentices. Act on Ordinary Courts, Art. 117. The draft amendment to the Act on Ordinary Courts would increase the apprenticeship to three years.

[77] Act on Ordinary Courts, Art. 112.

[78] Act on Ordinary Courts, Art. 113.

[79] Act on Ordinary Courts, Art. 115.

The court assessorship has a lengthy history in Poland. It has never been challenged, even during the transition in 1989 and 1990 when institutions that violated the principle of judicial independence were dismantled in a systemic manner. Although the Polish system does not formally nominate judges for a probationary period, the assessorship – during which an individual may have the same duties as a judge – serves the same function. Thus, in practice, the assessorship allows the Ministry of Justice or court superiors to exercise undue influence on new or potential judges whose future employment is insecure.

*Appointment as a Judge*: Assessors are either nominated to a judgeship or have their employment terminated after their initial term has elapsed. If successful, an application for judgeship must pass through numerous phases involving both judicial and executive bodies. A court college nominates candidates for consideration by the general assembly of regional court judges.[80] The general assembly then forwards its candidates to the Minister of Justice, who forwards the names, together with his non-binding opinion, to the National Council of the Judiciary.[81] The Council then votes to recommend candidates to the State President, who may make the final appointment.

The Minister of Justice may also propose judicial candidates to the National Council of the Judiciary on his own initiative after consulting with the college of the relevant court. The Minister's proposal is reviewed by the Council and is otherwise subject to the same rules as other nominations.[82]

## 1. Court Presidents

The Minister of Justice appoints and recalls presidents of all district, regional and appellate courts after receiving an opinion from the general assembly of judges of the relevant regional or appellate court; the Minister, however, is not allowed to appoint or recall the president if the general assembly opposes such an action by a majority of votes. Court presidents are appointed for four-year terms, and may be re-elected for a second four-year term of office.[83] There are no additional legal requirements to be elected to be a court president. Local political authorities have no influence on the nomination or recall of presidents of the courts. These decisions are thus jointly influenced by the judicial body and the Ministry of Justice – although the Ministry's influence over whether

---

[80] Act on Ordinary Courts, Arts. 38–41.

[81] Law on the National Council of the Judiciary, Art. 3.

[82] Act on Ordinary Courts, Art. 41.

[83] Act on Ordinary Courts, Arts. 29(1), 30, and 30(1).

to initiate an appointment to a second term might afford it undue influence over a court president wishing to continue in his position.

## 2. *Military Judges*

Only a professional officer may serve as a military court judge, and must also fulfil all the conditions required of regular judges. The initial selection of candidates is made by the Department for Military Justice at the Ministry of Justice, which presents them to the General Assembly of Military Judges.[84] The General Assembly then selects candidates, from which the Minister of Justice in agreement with the Minister of Defence presents a candidate to the National Council of the Judiciary. However, the Minister of Justice may on his own initiative propose judicial candidates to the National Council of the Judiciary in agreement with the Minister of Defence.[85] The executive therefore has somewhat more influence over the process of appointing military judges, although the Council's influence is still decisive.

## B. Tenure, Retirement, Transfer and Removal

### 1. *Tenure*

The Constitution provides that judges are appointed for an indefinite term;[86] in conjunction with the provisions enshrining the irremovability of judges from office,[87] this amounts to an appointment until retirement.

### 2. *Retirement*

A judge must retire upon turning 65 unless the National Council of the Judiciary, acting upon a motion by the judge in question and in consultation with the college of the relevant court, consents to his continued service.[88] The length of an extension may

---

[84] Act of 21 August 1997 on Military Courts, Arts. 23 and 5(4).
[85] Act of 20 December 1989 on the National Council of the Judiciary, Art. 3(4).
[86] CONST. REP. POLAND, Art. 179.
[87] CONST. REP. POLAND, Art. 180(1) declares "Judges shall not be removable."
[88] Act on Ordinary Courts, Art. 59(3); Law on the National Council of the Judiciary, Art. 2.

vary, but in any case cannot be beyond the age of seventy.[89] There are no clear criteria for approving or refusing an extension, and it is therefore possible that judges will receive extensions based on their political acceptability to the Council. A Council decision not to consent to extend employment may be challenged with the Supreme Administrative Court – although, again, without clear criteria, it is not clear on what basis the Court would review the decision.[90]

The constitutionality of giving the Council discretion in deciding on retirement was questioned by the State President in a petition to the Constitutional Tribunal in 1998. The Constitutional Tribunal did not uphold that view and expressed the opinion that

> the basic question in this case is whether the introduction of that measure of flexibility is compatible with the principle of a judge's irremovability. That would be impermissible if, as during the period of the Polish People's Republic, consent to further judicial service were to be given by a political organ (Minister of Justice), situated outside the organisational system of judicial authority. The current provision, however, accords that prerogative to the Council, whose constitutional task is to protect the independence of judges and whose composition guarantees that a judge's fate is to be decided mainly by other judges. There exist no grounds to allege that the composition, manner of operation or tasks of the Council constitute a threat of using that forum to engage in activities violating the principle of judicial independence. The Council has enjoyed an analogous prerogative for many years, but no instances of abusing or deforming it have been noted.[91]

## 3. Transfer

In general, a judge may not be permanently transferred to another post without his consent. A judge's consent is not required in cases strictly specified by the law, under the following circumstances: elimination of a post or an entire court as a result of a

---

[89] Act on Ordinary Courts, Art. 59(3).

[90] The Supreme Administrative Court took a stand on the issue in its ruling of 22 April 1993, when it stated that a Council resolution denying consent to the continued service of a judge who has turned 65 is an administrative decision and may be appealed to the Supreme Administrative Court. ONSA, 1 January 1995. An identical position in the matter was expressed by the Supreme Court in a resolution taken by a panel of seven judges on 20 December 1993, OSNC 1884/6/119. Compare the approving commentary on the case by E. Smoktunowicz, *State and Law*, 1995, No. 6.

[91] Compare the ruling of the Constitutional Tribunal of 24 June 1998, K. 3/98, *Polish Monitor*, No. 22, 1998, item 331.

reorganisation; conclusion of a marriage contract between judges of the same court which is not divided into departments, or in the event that one of the spouses becomes the direct superior of the other; on the basis of a Council resolution, adopted on the recommendation of the college of the relevant court, when required to preserve the dignity of the judicial office; or disciplinary transfer.[92]

The Minister of Justice may assign a judge, with his consent, to duties in another court, the Justice Ministry or other organisational units reporting to, or supervised by, the Minister of Justice. The Minister of Justice may assign a judge without his consent for up to three months;[93] there are no regulations specifying how often this may occur. In addition, upon a motion by the First President of the Supreme Court, the Minister of Justice may assign a judge to duties in the Supreme Court. Since this secondment is made with the judge's consent, it may be for a specified or unspecified term.[94]

## 4. Removal

Recall or suspension requires a court judgement in circumstances prescribed by law.[95] A judgeship may be terminated if a judge resigns or retires,[96] or for disciplinary reasons or if the judge no longer fulfils the underlying criteria for serving on the bench, such as maintaining a clean criminal record.[97]

There is only one procedure for dismissing a court president, apart from disciplinary proceedings. The Minister of Justice may dismiss a court president only after receiving an opinion from the general assembly of judges of his court, and only if the general assembly does not vote to oppose the action. Dismissals of court presidents have not occurred frequently in previous years. In 2000 there were three such dismissals: two regional court presidents and one district court president were dismissed.

*a.* *Lustration*: Two separate acts limit the right of judges to serve based on their actions under the regime prior to 1989; neither appears to violate norms on judicial independence, although they have generated controversy within Poland.

---

[92] Act on Ordinary Courts, Art. 61. A judge has the right to file a complaint with an administrative court for transfer based on marriage or a Council resolution.

[93] Act on Ordinary Courts, Art. 63(2).

[94] Act on Ordinary Courts, Art. 63.

[95] CONST. REP. POLAND, Art. 180(2).

[96] Act on Ordinary Courts, Art. 59.

[97] Act on Ordinary Courts, Art. 60.

*Judges Active under Communism*: An effort in 1993 to mandate verification of judges was declared unconstitutional, but subsequently, the Act on the Disciplinary Accountability of Judges Who Violated the Principle of Judicial Independence from 1944 to 1989 was adopted in 1998.

Under the Act's provisions, judges are disciplinarily accountable for judicial service infractions, including infractions against the dignity of their office. The Act vacates the normal three-year statute of limitations for disciplinary offences for adjudicative acts undertaken between 1944 and 1989 in reprisal against individuals for involvement in political or independence movements, human rights activities, or for exercising basic human rights. The Act also lifts the statute of limitations for actions of judges which otherwise violated the oath of judicial independence as it was conceived at the time.[98] These provisions also apply to judges who, while exercising positions of leadership in the judicial administration or political organisations, violated the principle of judicial independence by attempting to influence the rulings of judges presiding over the types of cases mentioned above.

The Act envisages a special verification procedure for judges,[99] applied within the framework of disciplinary proceedings, and thus carried out by judges themselves under the course of disciplinary proceedings. For offences under the Act the disciplinary court may penalise the offender by expelling him from judicial service. Since the law went into effect, no such case has been brought to a legally binding conclusion.

*Co-operation with State Security*: Judges are also subject to investigation procedures pursuant to the Law on the Disclosure of Work or Service in State Security Bodies or on Co-operation with Them between 1944 and 1990 by Persons Holding Public Office[100] –referred to as the lustration procedure. All persons holding public office – including judges – are required to submit a declaration concerning their work or service in state security bodies or in co-operation with them in the period between 22 July 1944 and 10 May 1990.

A judge's declaration on having co-operated with the security service does not result in his removal. However, to assess the authenticity of the representations tendered, an ombudsman for public affairs and a court of lustration have been established.[101] If the

---

[98] Act on the Disciplinary Responsibility of Judges Who Violated Judicial Independence in 1944-1989, 3 December 1998, *Journal of Laws*, 99/1.

[99] Verification in this case implies the removal of judges who have violated the principle of independence.

[100] Act of 11 April 1997, *Journal of Laws*, 1999/42.

[101] One of the departments of the Warsaw Appellate Court fills the functions of the court of lustration. A separate court of lustration was not established. This court has jurisdiction over all persons (and not just judges) subjected to the scrutiny procedure throughout the nation.

court finds that the individual submitted an untrue declaration, this in effect means that the judge does not have the requisite moral qualifications to discharge a public function.

The Court's legally binding ruling that an individual subject to investigative proceedings has made an untrue declaration means the individual effectively forfeits the office or function for which the declaration was made. Following the court's ruling disciplinary proceedings must be held to decide on the forfeiture of the position. Thus far, no such incident has occurred. Ten years from the moment the decision becomes legally binding, the court's ruling is considered null and void; this means that after ten years a person can seek judicial office again.

## C. Evaluation and Promotion

The National Council of the Judiciary decides on appointment of judges to higher instance courts. Candidacies for the appellate and regional courts are submitted to the Council through the Minister of Justice by the various appellate and regional courts' general assemblies of judges, with two candidates proposed for each available vacancy. A visiting judge designated by the court president evaluates each candidate on the basis of performance. Efficient performance and the number of rulings overturned by a higher court as well as experience are considered in assessing a judge's performance.

There is no special promotion procedure, but only appointment to a higher court or appointment as a court president; the same process described above for the nomination of assessors as judges applies to the appointment of judges to higher courts.

## D. Discipline

### 1. Liability

A judge may not be tried by a penal or administrative court without the consent of the relevant disciplinary court. Media assertions of corruption are generally analysed by the Minister of Justice and by court presidents; in justified instances applications are submitted to commence disciplinary and criminal proceedings.

## 2. Discipline

There is no written code of ethics for judges. When appointed, a judge takes an oath to uphold basic standards of ethical behaviour, swearing to uphold the law, conscientiously fulfil his/her duties, impartially mete out justice in accordance with his/her conscience and legal regulations, keep state secrets and be guided by the principles of dignity and honesty.[102] A judge is required, first and foremost, to perform the judicial duties in accordance with the oath. A judge is also obligated, both on and off duty, to uphold the prestige of the judicial office and avoid anything that could undermine the dignity of the office or confidence in judges' impartiality.[103]

The provisions of the Law on the Ordinary Courts regulate disciplinary procedures.[104] A judge may face a disciplinary court for professional offences, flagrant contempt of legal regulations, or undermining the dignity of the office. All decisions to deprive a judge of immunity rest with a disciplinary court composed of judges.

Disciplinary proceedings are instituted by the disciplinary spokesman, a judge elected by the college of an appellate court from among the judges of the same college. The disciplinary spokesman is bound by instructions given by the official requesting proceedings, and therefore cannot expand the proceedings to other charges or other judges without additional authorisation. The Minister of Justice, the president of an appellate court or regional court, or the college of an appellate court or regional court may submit such a request. The disciplinary court reviews each motion by the disciplinary spokesman. If the disciplinary court accepts a motion, it adopts a resolution to institute disciplinary proceedings. After the elapse of three years from the commission of a deed, it is not possible to launch disciplinary proceedings.

Disciplinary courts of first and second instance have been established. The disciplinary courts are composed of judges elected in numbers determined by the National Council of the Judiciary by general assemblies of the Supreme Court, the Supreme Administrative Court, appellate courts, regional courts and military courts.[105]

Disciplinary proceedings take place behind closed doors. Only judges and assessors performing judicial functions may be present. The defendant may designate only another judge as defence counsel. Both the defendant and the disciplinary spokesman have

---

[102] Act on Ordinary Courts, Art. 56.
[103] Act on Ordinary Courts, Art. 64.
[104] Act on Ordinary Courts, Chapter 5.
[105] Act on Ordinary Courts, Art. 83.

the right to appeal to the Higher Disciplinary Court against the verdict of the disciplinary court of first instance. The disciplinary court may adopt a resolution to make its ruling public after it becomes legally binding. The institution of closed-door hearings – formally justified as necessary to protect the court's dignity – contributes to public mistrust of the process and encourages a corporatist and protective attitude among judges inclined to protect their own.

Disciplinary sanctions include admonition, reprimand, removal from a post (such as president of the court), transfer to another place, and expulsion from judicial service. An extraordinary review may be instituted with regards to every legally binding ruling resulting from disciplinary proceedings. The organs entitled to request such a review are the Council, the First President of the Supreme Court, and the Minister of Justice; the higher instance disciplinary court decides whether to grant a rehearing.

# VI. Intra-Judicial Relations

## A. Relations with Superior Courts

Some of the most serious problems of intra-judicial relations are attitudinal; many judges have an excessively deferential and passive approach towards higher judges that in effect limits their individual decisional independence.

The Constitution provides that the Supreme Court exercises supervision over the judgements of ordinary and military courts.[106] A court of higher instance may overturn the ruling of a lower court in its entirety. The higher court also provides direction as to which changes should be made upon retrial; a court that retries a case is bound by the guidelines given by the court of higher instance (both in penal and civil cases). In practice the scope of overturned rulings is growing increasingly narrow, and this includes the guidelines given by the higher courts to lower courts.

There is no system of formal consultation between higher and lower court judges. Regional courts organise training programs and hold conferences for judges from the entire judicial region, including judges of lower rank.

Some obstacles to the judiciary's being an effective and independent third branch of authority are actually internal to the judiciary itself. Judges have been trained in a professional culture given to a certain degree of passivity. Contemporary Polish law, having been developed in a short period of time, naturally raises numerous issues, yet many judges have concerns about posing questions to the Constitutional Tribunal. The Constitution, which provides for its direct application, requires judges to be active. Judges' passivity may form a material impediment to the correct application of European law. Yet judges frequently appear to believe that asking questions is also a form of curtailing judicial independence, which is, of course, an erroneous stance.[107]

---

[106] CONST. REP. POLAND, Art. 183.

[107] Statement of participant, OSI meeting, Warsaw, 9 April 2001. *Explanatory Note: OSI held a roundtable meeting in Warsaw on 9 April 2001 to invite critique of the present report in draft form. Experts present included representatives of the government, the judiciary, the media and civil society organisations. References to this meeting should not be understood as an endorsement of any particular point of view by any one participant.*

## B. Case Management and Relations with Court Presidents

The current rules do not provide sufficiently transparent and neutral criteria for allocating cases. Although court presidents are fairly powerful and have broad supervisory responsibility over administrative matters, there is no evidence of their attempting to influence or supervise judges' adjudication directly.

The court college specifies the general rules for allocating cases to judges, but cases are assigned by the chairmen of individual court departments. The chairman is supposed ensure a certain degree of fairness in the internal allocation of cases on account of case differentiation; the chairman's decisions are not, however, always transparent. Poland does not yet have a computerised system for allocating cases.

Courts are burdened with a huge backlog of cases. Both court presidents and department chairmen are responsible for the speed with which cases are handled.[108] In light of the bylaws, the chairmen set the timetable for court proceedings and indicate the days on which presiding judges may schedule new court sessions. In practice, however, judges set their own specific session schedules. The department chairmen assess the expediency and justification of postponing or adjourning court sessions, monitor cases that are particularly protracted, and attempt to prevent case backlogs. If backlogs materialise the department chairman must devise a plan to eliminate it, supervise the plan's execution and periodically inform the court president of progress.[109] There are no formal rules concerning revocation or redistribution of cases; in practice, this is up to the court president and division chairmen.

The court president has a dual role, as *primus inter pares* and chair of the assembly of judges. The court system is quite hierarchical and court presidents have considerable means to supervise or influence other judges in his/her court or in lower courts. The president may press judges for expediency, but there are no reports that presidents do so, just as there is no information that they remove cases from one judge to give them to another judge. The prerogatives of the presidents of higher courts in relation to lower courts are extensive and clearly defined.

---

[108] There has been considerable public criticism of a case that had to be dropped because ten years had elapsed since it was brought. In that case, the disciplinary spokesman was petitioned to launch proceedings against the court president who had failed to ensure timely review.

[109] Rules and Regulations on the Internal Procedures of Ordinary Courts of the Minister of Justice, 19 November 1987, with Subsequent Modifications, *Journal of Laws*, 87/38/218.

## VII. Enforcement

The separation of the judicial authority and the importance of court decisions are respected. The decisions of courts in penal cases are fully respected and executed. There have been no reports of attempts to press for a court decision to be altered after it has been given.

Problems do exist, however, in connection with the enforcement of court decisions in civil cases. A change in the Law on Court Bailiffs[110] is being prepared, because court bailiffs' ineffectiveness is seen as the reason for the unsatisfactory level of execution of court rulings.

---

[110] Act of 29 August 1997 on Court Bailiffs.

OPEN SOCIETY INSTITUTE 2001

# Judicial Independence in Romania

MONITORING THE EU ACCESSION PROCESS: JUDICIAL INDEPENDENCE

# Table of Contents

Executive Summary .................................................. 352

I. Introduction .................................................. 354

    A. Weak Commitment to Political Culture
       Based on Rule of Law ................................. 354

    B. Other Issues Affecting the Independence
       of the Judiciary ............................................ 357
       1. Ill-Defined Separation of Powers
          and Equality of the Judiciary .............. 357
       2. Insufficient Financial Autonomy ........ 357
       3. Executive Involvement
          in the Appointment and Promotion
          of Judges ............................................... 358
       4. Problems with Enforcement ............... 358

    C. Organisation of the Judicial System ......... 359

II. Constitutional and Legal Foundations
    of Judicial Independence ............................... 361

    A. Guarantees of the Separation of Powers
       and Judicial Independence ....................... 361
       1. Tripartite Division of Judicial Power ... 361
       2. Superior Council of Magistracy .......... 362
       3. Constitutional Court ......................... 363

    B. Representation of the Judiciary ................ 364

    C. Independent and Uniform
       Administration of Justice .......................... 365

    D. Military Courts and Executive Control .... 367

    E. Rules on Incompatibility .......................... 368

    F. Judges' Associations .................................. 370

III. Administration of The Court System
    and Judicial Independence ............................. 371

| IV. | Financial Autonomy and Level of Funding .... 374 |
|---|---|
| | A. Budgeting Process ....................................... 374 |
| | B. Work Conditions ........................................ 375 |
| | C. Compensation ............................................ 377 |
| V. | Judicial Office .................................................... 381 |
| | A. Selection ...................................................... 381 |
| |     1. Selection of Constitutional Court Members .................................... 383 |
| | B. Tenure, Retirement, Transfer and Removal ............................................... 383 |
| | C. Evaluation and Promotion ........................ 385 |
| | D. Discipline .................................................... 386 |
| VI. | Intra-Judicial Relations .................................... 389 |
| | A. Relations with Superior Courts ................. 389 |
| | B. Case Management and Relations with Court Presidents ................................ 389 |
| VII. | Enforcement and Corruption ........................... 392 |
| | A. Enforcement of Judgements ...................... 392 |
| | B. Corruption .................................................. 393 |

# Judicial Independence in Romania

## Executive Summary

Romania has taken some important steps towards consolidating democracy and embracing the rule of law. The 1991 Constitution and new legislation have settled the main features of judicial authority and proclaimed the independence of judges.

However, significant obstacles to the realisation of a fully independent judiciary remain, including insufficient separation of powers, intrusive involvement of the executive in judicial affairs, inadequate funding and control of the funding process, endemic corruption, and a persistent lack of respect for the principles of a legal culture supportive of the rule of law.

*Weak Commitment to the Rule of Law*

The decisions taken by many of Romania's judges, legislators and members of the executive do not evince a consistent commitment to the principles of judicial independence. Despite formal safeguards, judges are not effectively protected from political manipulation. During the first months of 2001, leading officials in the Government have repeatedly attempted to influence judges' decisions in particular cases. For many, including judges, these efforts raise very serious concerns about the Government's intentions in the area of judicial independence.

*Excessive Involvement of the Executive*

Most of the problems affecting the judiciary share a common feature: the excessive involvement of the executive in the affairs of the judiciary. Much of this involvement is entrenched in law, and is the single most significant structural problem facing the judiciary. Some of the most significant issues are briefly noted below:

*Separation of Powers*

The judiciary's separate role is proclaimed in law, but is ill-defined in practice, where its functions often overlap with those of the prosecutorial office – which is controlled by the executive. The judiciary has no independent legal representative in its relations with the other organs of the State; it has to rely on bodies such as the Ministry of Justice.

*Military Courts*

In addition, large areas of jurisdiction fall not under the regular courts, but under the separate system of military courts, which also tries cases involving the police and which responds to the imperatives of the military hierarchy. As a consequence, the ability of the judiciary to play a role in curbing excesses in the executive is severely hampered.

*Budget Authority*

The judiciary in Romania has almost no independent authority over its own budget process, which is in the hands of the Ministry of Justice. Although there is no evidence that this budgetary control has been used to exact political compliance, the very possibility may act as a limit on the judiciary's willingness to assert its independence.

*Compensation and Work Conditions*

Historically low compensation has improved considerably in recent years, although significant discretion in determining overall compensation threatens judges' independence. Moreover, working conditions remain at a very low standard, hampering the effective administration of justice and encouraging corruption.

*Appointments and Promotions*

The executive's involvement in the appointment, evaluation, and promotion of judges may impair their independence. In particular, justices of the Supreme Court and judges of the Constitutional Court seem vulnerable to political influence.

*Enforcement of Decisions*

Enforcement often takes a very long time. There is a poorly developed procedural framework, and some officials in charge are reportedly corrupt; reforms privatising enforcement are too recent to be fully assessed.

*Corruption*

There is a widespread public perception that the judiciary is corrupt. The procedures employed in Romanian courts themselves – such as the very limited recording of proceedings – often do little to protect against corrupt practices or to allow for their subsequent discovery.

## I. Introduction

Romania has taken some important steps towards consolidating democracy and embracing the rule of law. The 1991 Constitution settled the main features of judicial authority in Romania and proclaimed the independence of judges. New legislation has been established in various fields, including the organisation of the judiciary by a 1992 law[1] (amended through 1999[2]) and through the amendments to the Civil and Criminal Procedure Codes.[3] Many of the more egregious practices that limited the judiciary's independence during the Communist period have been rejected.

However, significant obstacles to the realisation of a fully independent judiciary remain, including: insufficient separation of powers, intrusive involvement of the executive in judicial affairs, inadequate funding and involvement in the budget process, and endemic corruption. Above all, politicians, the populace, and judges alike evince a persistent lack of respect for the principles of a political culture based on the rule of law. This last issue underlies and informs many of the other structural and political problems, and will therefore be considered first here.

### A. Weak Commitment to Political Culture Based on Rule of Law

In Romania, the development of an independent judiciary has strong support among intellectuals and professionals. However, the majority of the population and a significant number of judicial, legislative, and executive officials are not concerned with – let alone committed to – judicial independence. The decisions taken by many of Romania's judges reflect the fact that many continue to operate as they did under the communist regime, particularly in their unwavering defence of State interests and dutiful submission to the bureaucratic chain of command. For example, in cases in which State civil liability or claims to State property are at issue, most judges provide little redress. Many of the judges who served the previous political regime remain on the bench (particularly in the higher courts), which has done little to improve public opinion about the judiciary. Moreover, judges often consult their respective court president prior to taking decisions.

---

[1] Law on the Judiciary (92/1992).

[2] Laws 89/1996 and 142/1997; Emergency Ordinance 179/1999.

[3] Laws 45/1993 and 141/1996 amending the Code of Criminal Procedure; Laws 59/1993 and 17/1997 amending the Code of Civil Procedure.

Although the law prohibits the political branches from obstructing the judicial process, judges are not entirely safeguarded from political manipulation, in part because the political culture assumes that such behaviour is normal. There appear to be informal mechanisms, outside legal boundaries, by which judges can be put under pressure and coerced to act in accordance with certain political interests.

Attempts by high political officials to influence judges are not uncommon. A notorious incident of executive interference with judicial independence occurred in 1995, when the General Prosecutor filed a number of extraordinary appeals against final judgements restoring nationalised property to its original owners following a 1994 speech in which the State President publicly criticised the judgements and instructed the executive not to enforce them. Proving its lack of independence, the Supreme Court reversed a large number of these judgements.[4] (In 1998 – after a cycle of elections – the Court reversed itself, again providing the possibility of restitution.[5])

Two recent examples show how politicians do not show sufficient regard for the principle of judicial independence, interfering freely both with the decision-making process and with appointments. In March 2001, the prefect of the Caras-Severin County sent a letter to the Minister of Justice recommending a particular candidate for district court president in his County.[6] In another case,[7] the State President publicly attacked the judges of the Supreme Court who, by a final judgement, had convicted two army generals for ordering killings during the December 1989 events in Timisoara. The State President characterised the convictions as "a big political mistake and a judicial inequity";[8] the Prime Minister has also declared the trial "political",[9] and the General Prosecutor has suspended the enforcement of the judgement, apparently without legal basis.

Reform of the judicial system has not been well received by prosecutors or by military court officials, who oppose changes that would reduce their power and influence. Many judges are themselves unenthusiastic about reform.

---

[4] Supreme Court, Judgement No. 1/1995 followed by other similar judgements.

[5] Supreme Court, Judgement No. 1/1998.

[6] Letter published by *Evenimentul Zilei*, 4 April 2001. The letter was given to the human resources department within the Ministry of Justice.

[7] See also Sections II.C. and VII.A.

[8] *Evenimentul Zilei*, 2 March 2001.

[9] *Evenimentul Zilei*, 27 February 2001.

Public trust in courts is low, and there is a widespread public perception that corruption is in fact endemic in the judiciary.[10] Journalists frequently report on the judiciary in a very critical manner; on an April 2001 national television programme, a well-known journalist referred to judges as "people who do not obey anyone, not even God" and reproached the State President, also present on the programme, for having "made them irremovable".[11] In response, many judges claim that such critical media reporting contributes to low public trust.[12]

International organisations do not perceive the Romanian judiciary as fully independent or effective. The European Commission's "2000 Regular Report from the Commission on Romania's Progress towards Accession"[13] declares that the judiciary still has insufficient administrative capacity.[14] On 24 April 2001 EU Commissioner for Enlargement Gunter Verheugen told journalists in Brussels that the EU is worried by possible infringements on the independence of the judiciary; two days later, in Bucharest, he reiterated the EU's concerns and promised to continue monitoring the matter.[15] A World Bank survey finds a significant lack of public trust in the judiciary and a general perception of corruption within the judicial system.[16] In addition, the United States' State Department's 2000 Report on Romania notes that the judiciary remained subject to executive branch influence – a finding which had not changed since the 1999 Report.[17]

Despite these difficult conditions, many individual judges do indeed understand and defend their independence; the creation of judges' associations is a positive step in that direction.

---

[10] World Bank, Diagnostic Surveys of Corruption in Romania, RomRep80FINALA4.doc, 3/09/01, p. vii. The procedures employed in Romanian courts – such as the limited recording of proceedings – often do little to protect against corrupt practice or encourage their subsequent discovery.

[11] TVR, *Scurt pe doi*, 9 April 2001.

[12] Information from 40 judges in Cluj, March 2001 and five judges in Bucharest, April 2001.

[13] Eureopan Commission, *2000 Regular Report from the Commission on Romania's Progress Towards Accession*, November 2000 (hereafter *2000 Regular Report*).

[14] *2000 Regular Report*, Chapter on Political Criteria and Rule of Law.

[15] *Adevarul*, 27 April 2001; *Romania Libera*, 28 April 2001.

[16] World Bank, Diagnostic Surveys of Corruption in Romania, RomRep80FINALA4.doc, 3/09/01, p. vii.

[17] US Department of State, Country Reports on Human Rights Practices-2000, Romania, February 2001.

## B. Other Issues Affecting the Independence of the Judiciary

In addition to the general problem of weak legal culture, several other issues are discussed in the body of this report. Most share a common feature: excessive involvement of the executive in the affairs of the judiciary. Much of this involvement is entrenched in law, and is the most significant structural problem facing the judiciary. Some of the most significant issues are briefly noted here.

### 1. Ill-Defined Separation of Powers and Equality of the Judiciary

Although it does not explicitly proclaim a principle of separation of powers, the Constitution nevertheless provides distinct tasks and competencies for each branch. However, the division is blurred by the classification of judges and prosecutors jointly as magistrates with overlapping authorities. Although a 1997 amendment to the Law on the Judiciary clarifies the distinction between judge and prosecutor, nothing has been done to revise prosecutors' powers; in addition, because of the confusion at the constitutional level, an analogous constitutional amendment would seem advisable.

In part because of its ill-defined position, the judiciary has no independent legal representative in its relations with the other organs of the State; it has to rely on the Ministry of Justice, a part of the executive. The only other organ is the Superior Council of Magistracy, but it is itself dependent on the executive. The Council meets once a month; its budget is determined by the Ministry and it has no administration, but only a small secretariat. Moreover, the agenda of the Supreme Council seems to be driven by the Ministry; for example, the Ministry retains reponsibility for the court administration, and no question related to the career and disciplining of judges can be decided by the Council except on a motion (recommendation, proposal or request) of the Minister.

In addition, large areas of jurisdiction fall under a separate system of military courts, which also tries cases involving the police. The military courts are hierarchically dependent on the will of the executive; as a consequence, the ability of the judiciary to play a role in curbing police excesses is severely hampered. There have been some improvements in this area, as the Supreme Court is now the court of last resort for military court cases, but otherwise the entire military court system has been preserved.

### 2. Insufficient Financial Autonomy

The judiciary in Romania has almost no authority over its own budget process, which is in the hands of the executive. Although there is no evidence that this budgetary control has been used to exact political compliance, the possibility alone may set an implicit limit on the judiciary's ability to assert its independence.

Partly as a result, working conditions – including buildings, offices, access to adequate infrastructure and modern technologies – are poor, hampering effective adjudication and encouraging a culture of bribery to ensure expeditious services.

The role of drafting the budget of the judiciary should be located within the judicial branch. For instance, courts could send their budget requests to the Supreme Court, which would then submit the budget for all courts directly to Parliament.

## 3. Executive Involvement in the Appointment and Promotion of Judges

The executive's involvement in the appointment, evaluation, and promotion of judges unduly intrudes upon their independence. In particular, in the context of the weak political commitment to the rule of law, judges of the Constitutional Court and justices of the Supreme Court are particularly vulnerable to political influence, as they are appointed to limited terms by political actors: the State President appoints Supreme Court justices to renewable six-year terms on the recommendation of the Minister of Justice, and the State President, Senate and Chamber of Deputies each appoint three judges of the Constitutional Court to nine-year terms.[18]

The system for disciplining judges – which is both non-transparent and little used – mainly falls under the authority of the Minister of Justice, who has discretion to bring indictments, and the Superior Council of Magistracy, which is responsible for taking decisions on disciplinary matters.

## 4. Problems with Enforcement

The lack of a developed legal culture has had negative consequences for enforcement, as enforcement of judicial decisions is given a low priority within the executive and judiciary. Enforcement often takes a very long time and court personnel in charge are notoriously corrupt.

---

[18] The judges of the Constitutional Court are openly political appointees – although this openness does not mitigate the harm done to their ability to interpret the Constitution free of undue political influence.

## C. Organisation of the Judicial System

Prior to the Second World War, Romania had a continental-style civil law system. The communist judicial system introduced after the war essentially continued in the civil law tradition, although strongly amplifying its deference to the executive. The principle of unity of power precluded a separate and independent judiciary; law and its institutions were instruments of unitary state-party control, but lacked democratic legitimacy. Moreover, the prosecutors' body (*prokuratura*) was developed as the main legal arm of the communist state; prosecutors had broad powers to control the legality of activity outside the judicial system and to apply sanctions, leaving a limited sphere of activity to judges. Interference with judicial decision-making was common, and so-called "telephone justice" was widespread. Military courts formed a parallel system of justice that enjoyed a higher status in society. The legacies of communist rule continue to have a profound impact on the Romanian judiciary today.

The current court system in Romania follows a four-tiered pyramid structure. The lowest level consists of district courts, the next level is comprised of regional courts and the courts of appeal occupy the third level. The Supreme Court of Justice is at the top of the system, but is regulated by a separate law.[19] Constitutional matters are reviewed by the Constitutional Court,[20] although laws promulgated before 1991 may be reviewed for constitutionality by the regular courts.[21] In addition to the civilian courts, Romania also has a military court system;[22] military courts hear certain cases involving civilians, including all allegations of police abuses.

According to unofficial data from the Ministry of Justice, there are 3,434 sitting judges in ordinary courts,[23] as well as 86 in the Supreme Court of Justice and nine on the Constitutional Court. The support staff includes 2,337 clerks who take part in hearings and several thousand other clerical and archival workers. There are 351 judgement enforcement officers within the district and regional courts, who from 1 May 2001 were re-organised on a private basis.[24]

---

[19] Law 56/1993 on the Supreme Court of Justice.

[20] Law 47/1992 on the Constitutional Court.

[21] This power was identified in the regular courts in a number of Constitutional Court cases (2/1993, 4/1993, 5/1993, 28/1993, 11/1994). Courts seldom avail themselves of it, however.

[22] Law 54/1993, Art. 2.

[23] 1,989 in the district courts; 971 in the regional courts; 474 in the courts of appeal.

[24] Law 188/2000 on the judicial enforcement agents.

Prosecutors and judges alike belong to the professional category of "magistrates", both treated under the title "Judicial Authority" in the Constitution.[25] Prosecutors still perform certain judicial-like functions, such as issuing arrest warrants and authorising searches in addition to gathering evidence and developing cases. Prosecutors have the authority to verify compliance with the law at pre-trial detention and prison facilities, and to "uphold educational and safety standards."[26]

In keeping with the mixed judicial-prosecutorial model, prosecutors have considerable additional powers. The General Prosecutor has exclusive authority to file extraordinary appeals against final judgements, at his own initiative or if required by the Minister of Justice. Furthermore, a large part of a prosecutor's activity, such as searches and wiretapping, may not be appealed or challenged before the courts.

The powerful role enjoyed by prosecutors has been jealously guarded. During the last ten years there has been no effective reduction in the judicial functions of the prosecutorial service. The current Government appears unwilling to contemplate such a change, having withdrawn a draft amendment to the Criminal Procedure Code prepared by the previous Government that would have shifted most judicial functions from prosecutors to investigative judges. Indeed, the Government's "Governing Programme" provides, *inter alia*, that the "role of the Prosecutor's Office and of prosecutors shall be reconsidered and strengthened."[27]

The Ministry of Justice plays an important (though sometimes indirect) role in the administration of the court system, including budgetary matters, the selection and promotion of judges, and even decisions about substantive cases. As the majority of criticisms that have been raised about the independence of the Romanian judiciary concern the role of the Ministry, its various forms of influence over judicial functions will be considered in detail in the following sections.

---

[25] CONST. REP. ROMANIA, Chapter VI, which contains separate sections entitled "Courts", "Public Ministry", and Superior Council of Magistracy" (discussed separately below).

[26] Law on the Judiciary, Art. 27(h).

[27] Government Programme, Chapter 7.3, < http://www.kappa.ro/> (accessed 20 August 2001).

## II. Constitutional and Legal Foundations of Judicial Independence

### A. Guarantees of the Separation of Powers and Judicial Independence

The 1991 Constitution does not explicitly proclaim a principle of separation of powers. Nevertheless, the constitutional framework provides distinct tasks and competencies for each institution, in an effort to balance powers. According to the Constitution, "[j]ustice shall be rendered in the name of the law. Judges shall be independent and subject only to the law."[28] Moreover, constitutional provisions regarding the independence of the judiciary may not be amended.[29]

#### 1. Tripartite Division of Judicial Power

However, in its description of judicial power, the Constitution treats the "Courts of Law" and the "Public Ministry" (which supervises prosecutors) equally, under the heading "Judicial Authorities".[30] Similarly, the 1992 Law on the Judiciary classifies prosecutors and judges alike as members of the magistracy; the effect is to blur the functional distinction between the judiciary and the executive in ways that can limit judicial independence.

In defining the nature and scope of the prosecutorial power, the Constitution provides that prosecutors carry out their activities under the hierarchical control of the Minister of Justice.[31] By including prosecutors under the umbrella of "judicial authority", the constitutional provisions endanger the very core of the judiciary's independence.

In 1997, an amendment to the Law on the Judiciary introduced a welcome correction. While the definition of "judicial authority" remains unchanged,[32] a new paragraph stipulates that "Judicial Power" shall only be exercised by courts of law,[33] while another amendment

---

[28] CONST. REP. ROMANIA, Art. 123.

[29] CONST. REP. ROMANIA, Art. 148, para. 1.

[30] CONST. REP. ROMANIA, Chapter VI.

[31] CONST. REP. ROMANIA, Art. 131.

[32] Law on the Judiciary, Art. 1, para. 1 ("The Judicial Authority consists of courts of law, the Public Ministry and the Superior Council of Magistracy...").

[33] Law on the Judiciary, Art. 1, para. 2.

empowered the Minister of Justice to give instructions to prosecutors to enforce the law or to initiate investigations.[34] In addition, the Minister of Justice was given the power to control prosecutors' activity through general inspectors, councillors or other prosecutors.[35] The 1997 amendments place the prosecutors squarely in the executive branch; in addition, the Constitutional Court has affirmed that prosecutors are agents of the executive who do not belong to the judiciary and have no judicial powers.[36]

However, although the 1997 amendment and ruling clarify the distinction between judge and prosecutor, little has been done to delimit prosecutors' powers. In addition, because the co-identification of prosecutors and judges as "judicial authority" remains in the Constitution, a constitutional amendment would seem advisable.

Two other bodies should be briefly noted here in the context of separation of powers and independence of the judiciary.

## 2. Superior Council of Magistracy

The third component of the "Judicial Authority" – along with the Public Ministry (prosecutorial office subordinated to the Ministry of Justice) and the judiciary – is the Superior Council of Magistracy.[37] The Council consists of 15 members – ten judges and five prosecutors – nominated by various judicial and prosecutorial bodies and elected by Parliament to four year terms.[38]

---

[34] Law on the Judiciary, Arts. 33–34.

[35] Law on the Judiciary, Arts. 33–34.

[36] Constitutional Court, Judgements Nos. 339/1997; 73/1996; 96/1996;

[37] CONST. REP. ROMANIA, Chapter VI, Arts. 132–133.

[38] The Council consists of fifteen members elected by majority vote in a secret ballot in Parliament according to the following formula:
- four judges from 12 candidates nominated by the Supreme Court of Justice;
- three prosecutors from nine candidates nominated by the Prosecutor's Office established by the Supreme Court;
- six judges from 15 candidates nominated by the courts of appeal;
- two prosecutors from six candidates nominated by the Prosecutor's Office established under the Bucharest Court of Appeal.

The composition of the Superior Council of Magistracy is striking for two facts: one, only the judges of the higher courts are represented, leaving the more than 3,000 judges of the first and second instance courts entirely unrepresented in the Council; and two, prosecutorial bodies determine one-third of the membership of a body which has important powers of judges' career paths.

The Superior Council of Magistracy is an institution conjoining the powers of the judiciary and the executive. Although the Council is seen by public opinion and public authorities as the representative of the judiciary, one third of its members are prosecutors under the authority of the executive

The Council has broad-ranging powers, which it generally exercises in conjunction with the Minister of Justice or other bodies. Together with the Minister, the Council recommends nominees for judgeships to the State President; decides on the promotion, transfer, disciplining, and removal of judges; and has a general obligation to "safeguard the independence of justice."[39]

The Minister of Justice chairs the Council but does not have the right to vote. Nevertheless, the risk that the Minister's political position could influence Council decisions, in particular the votes cast by members who, as prosecutors, are his subordinates, is real – an important consideration, in light of its involvement in judicial appointments.[40]

The Government declared its intention to enlarge the composition of the Council by including respected scholars,[41] but has not expressed any intention to modify the role of prosecutors on the Council or its powers over judges' careers.

## 3. Constitutional Court

Although not part of the "Judicial Authority", the constitutional court exercises binding judicial power to decide on the constitutionality of laws adopted after the 1991 Constitution came into force, while ordinary courts may adjudicate the constitutionality of laws adopted prior to 1991. The Constitutional Court cannot be considered fully independent or as constituting a separate power, given the terms of its judges' election by the political branches, their limited tenure, and the political and legal culture in which it operates.[42]

The degree to which the Court is independent is of the greatest importance to the question of the regular judiciary's independence, as there is a continuing controversy over whether or not the regular courts are subject to the Constitutional Court. In a number

---

[39] Law on the Judiciary, Art. 18, para. 1.

[40] Moreover, the four members who are Supreme Court justices are appointed to the Court upon the recommendation of the Minister of Justice, who is Chair of the Council.

[41] Government Programme, Chapter 7.3.

[42] See Section V.A.

of cases between 1994 and 2000, the Constitutional Court held that courts must review pre-trial detention ordered by prosecutors every 30 days.[43] Although the judgements of the Constitutional Court are binding for all courts,[44] the Supreme Court has issued judgements contradicting the Constitutional Court rulings.[45] Moreover, the Supreme Court independently decided that Constitutional Court judgements require endorsement by the Parliament in order to have an *erga omnes* binding effect.[46] In response, the Constitutional Court ruled that courts failing to observe Constitutional Court judgements could be held liable.[47]

Certainly, this situation has led to confusion among the ordinary judiciary, which has been left to choose between ignoring the Supreme Court or the Constitutional Court. Following a period of contradictory solutions, judges appeared to apply the Constitutional Court's ruling and review pre-trial detention every 30 days. However, the beginning of 2001 brought a reversal, and some courts, with the support of the trial prosecutors, have again refused periodically to review pre-trial detention. The newly appointed Deputy General Prosecutor has publicly argued against periodical court review of pre-trial detention.[48]

## B. Representation of the Judiciary

A subsidiary problem related to the judiciary's imperfect position in the constitutional order is that the judiciary does not have an independent representative. In practice, the Ministry of Justice intercedes in matters related to the judiciary through its administration of the judiciary.[49] However, ministerial representation of the judiciary jeopardises judicial independence. The Minister of Justice should properly only represent the prosecutors under his direct authority.

The only other authority representing judges is the Superior Council of Magistracy. As noted above, the Superior Council of Magistracy is a hybrid institution that conflates

---

[43] Judgements No. 60/1994, final by judgement 20/1995; No. 1/1996; No. 546/1997; No. 10/2000.

[44] CONST. REP. ROMANIA, Art. 145.

[45] Supreme Court, Criminal Section, Judgement No. 1613 of 7 May 1999.

[46] Supreme Court, Criminal Section, Judgement No. 3277 of 28 September 1999.

[47] Constitutional Court, Judgement No. 186 of 18 November 1999; published in the Official Gazette 213/2000. It is not clear from the judgement how courts are to be held liable, or for what.

[48] A. Tuculeanu, *Pro Jure* 1/2001, pp. 53–58.

[49] See sections III and IV.

the powers of the judiciary and the executive, and where, as noted earlier, the Minister of Justice enjoys significant authority.

Due to the absence of a clear authority representing the judiciary, informal contacts between members of the judiciary and the executive or legislative branches may take place. This does not contribute to a measure of accountability consistent with judges' independence because such contacts lack transparency.

## C. Independent and Uniform Administration of Justice

Although formally proclaimed by law, judges' decisional independence is not effectively safeguarded against interference from the executive.

The Constitution provides that "[j]ustice shall be administered by the Supreme Court of Justice and other courts established by law[,]"[50] and further that the "[j]urisdiction and procedure of courts shall be regulated by law, mainly by the Civil and Criminal Procedure Codes."[51] Formally, the Supreme Court "oversees the correct and uniform enforcement of laws by all courts."[52] In practice the Supreme Court's supervision of lower courts' decisions is limited to the regular process of appeal or hearing extraordinary appeals filed by the General Prosecutor.

Instead, two other institutions have considerably more responsibility for supervising the actual decision-making of judges. The Law on the Judiciary provides that "the Superior Council of Magistracy and the Minister of Justice safeguard the independence of justice."[53] The Law further provides that "under no circumstances may such control lead to interference with pending cases or reopening decided matters."[54] However, the recent practice of the Minister of Justice in particular raises very serious concerns; powers granted to inspectors with the courts of appeal and the Ministry of Justice to verify courts' application of law in particular cases, and to the executive to intervene in cases through extraordinary appeals, provide avenues for influencing judicial decision-making.

In a letter dated 7 March 2001 and addressed to the presidents of all courts of appeal, the Minister of Justice required that judicial decisions aimed at enforcing judgements

---

[50] CONST. REP. ROMANIA, Art. 125, para. 1.

[51] CONST. REP. ROMANIA, Art. 125, para. 3.

[52] Law 56/1993 on the Supreme Court of Justice, Art. 1, para. 2.

[53] Law on the Judiciary, Art. 18, para. 1.

[54] Law on the Judiciary, Art. 18.

returning nationalised property should take into account the housing problems of the current tenants. In addition, the letter placed judges under implicit threat of being inspected by judicial inspectors and officials in the Ministry of Justice for their compliance with its terms.[55] In a letter of April 2001, addressed to all courts of appeal, the Minister of Justice recommended that proceedings relating to liquidation of bankrupt banks be suspended.[56]

The Law on the Judiciary further provides that "[t]he exercise of the right to appeal granted by law to the Minister of Justice shall not be considered an interference."[57] This refers to the power of the Minister of Justice to file two forms of extraordinary appeal with the Supreme Court, both of which can threaten judicial independence.

The first form of extraordinary appeal seeks uniform guidance from the Supreme Court on legal questions that have produced significantly different rulings in the lower courts,[58] aiming at guaranteeing the uniform interpretation and enforcement of laws throughout the country.

The second, and more problematic form, is extraordinary appeal (appeal for cancellation) to the Supreme Court – at the General Prosecutor's own initiative or at the request of the Minister of Justice – against final judgements, including in civil cases, after the normal time for appeal has expired. Especially when combined with other means that afford the executive undue influence, this power may be used to interfere with judicial independence, such as when the extraordinary appeal process was used to void final judgements restoring nationalised property to its former owners.[59]

Extraordinary appeals against final judgement, or the threat of their use, undermine the finality of court decisions in criminal cases as well. In the case of the two generals convicted by the Supreme Court for their involvement in the events in Timisoara in 1989,[60] the General Prosecutor suspended enforcement of the judgement pending an extraordinary appeal. In March 2001, a senator demanded that final judgement against M. Cosma, leader of the miners' union on trial for events in the early 1990s, be subjected to an extraordinary appeal, arguing that the conviction was political.[61] While extraordinary

---

[55] *Evenimentul Zilei*, 4 April 2001. See also Section I.
[56] *Evenimentul Zilei*, 19 April 2001. See also Section I.
[57] Law on the Judiciary, Art. 18.
[58] Code of Civil Procedure, Art. 329; Code of Criminal Procedure, Art. 414.
[59] See Section I.A.
[60] See Sections I.A and VII.A.
[61] A. Paunescu, *Evenimentul Zilei*, 14 March 2001.

appeals are not technically refusals to enforce judgements or an intrusion on court power, their exercise under the current system – especially when accompanied by open political denunciations of the prior final judgement by senior figures in the executive – inevitably places undue pressure on the Supreme Court.

By allowing the executive branch to decide which cases should be sent to the Supreme Court, the independence of judges' decisions may be put in jeopardy, having in mind the courts' tradition of extreme deference to the Ministry of Justice, judges' continuing indirect reliance on the Ministry for appointment or reappointment, and the potential for politically motivated executive intervention through extraordinary appeal. The need for the Supreme Court to resolve a contradictory legal matter could be assessed by the Court itself or by a designated group of judges, in order to minimise the potential for interference by the executive.

However, instead of limiting extraordinary appeal, the Government recently enlarged the grounds on which the General Prosecutor can file extraordinary appeals against final judgements in civil cases related to the interpretation of law and facts, and doubled the length of time in which an extraordinary appeal can be filed.[62]

## D. Military Courts and Executive Control

Another judicial function controlled by the executive is the parallel system of military courts, which constitutes an institutional obstacle to the independence of the judiciary. Military courts hear, *inter alia*, certain cases involving civilians and all allegations of police abuses. In Romania, police officers, prison staff, members of the secret services and Ministry of Defence personnel have military status and therefore are investigated and tried by military prosecutors and military judges, even if their crimes are unrelated to their official capacity and duties. All members of the military courts are military personnel subject to military discipline, and ultimately to the executive; consequently, their independence is severely hampered.

Only active military officers may be appointed to serve as military judges.[63] They enjoy all rights of military status including promotion in accordance with the military grading rules. Military court judges are paid by the Ministry of Defence, and their salaries are higher than those of their civilian counterparts. The selection and training of military court judges are conducted by both the Ministry of Justice and the Ministry of Defence.

---

[62]  Emergency Ordinance 59/2001.

[63]  Law 54/1993 on the Military Courts and Military Prosecutors' Offices.

Thus, military judges have a dual status as members of the judiciary and the military. As military officers, they belong to the executive branch and are essentially organised on a hierarchical principle of subordination to higher command. This dual status clearly hampers the independence and impartiality of the military judges. The low number of indictments and convictions in police abuse cases (in comparison with the number of allegations)[64] suggests the negative impact that granting the military jurisdiction over police abuse has had on the protection of individual rights.

A welcome improvement was the abolition of the Military Section within the Supreme Court in 1999.[65] Now the Criminal Section of the Supreme Court hears cases falling under the jurisdiction of the military courts. Nevertheless, all other military courts were preserved and are regulated by a special law on the military courts and the military prosecutors' offices.[66]

The Council of Europe noted some years ago that "[a]lthough many assurances were given that the police were under civilian control, the problem remains that complaints against police officers can be brought only before military prosecutors who alone can decide to bring charges. Given the apparent reluctance to bring charges in a number of cases... this situation, too, gives rise to legitimate concern."[67] Despite eight years of international criticism, the situation remains unchanged.

## E. Rules on Incompatibility

Various constitutional and legal provisions regulate the extra-judicial activity of judges in order to maintain their impartiality and independence. The office of judge is incompatible with any other public or private office, except for academic activities.[68] Magistrates are barred from membership in political parties and from public political activities;[69] consequently, judges may not attend political meetings and they are not allowed to write political articles or be involved in any political debates. Judges are allowed to write

---

[64] See 1993-2000 APADOR-CH (Romanian Helsinki Committee) reports; <http://www.apador.org> (accessed 20 August 2001).

[65] Law 43/1999.

[66] Law 54/1993.

[67] F. Konig, rapporteur for the Committee of the Political Affairs of the Council of Europe, "Preliminary Draft Report on the Application by the Republic of Romania for membership of the Council of Europe", Doc.AS/pol(44)62, Strasbourg, 7 May 1993, p. 9. The same issue was raised in the 1995 Report on Romania, adopted in May 1995 by the Committee on Legal Affairs and Human Rights of the Council of Europe.

[68] CONST. REP. ROMANIA, Art. 124, para. 2.

[69] Law on the Judiciary, Art. 110.

articles in legal, literary, academic, or social journals and to take part in "broadcasting programs".[70] The political ban is not seen as extending to issues relating to the courts and the administration of justice.

The Law on the Judiciary also regulates the involvement of judges in non-political governmental activities. Both judges and prosecutors can be appointed to various commissions or committees provided by law,[71] such as the elections commission, although they may not serve in administrative bodies of the executive. Magistrates may take part in legal drafting committees only if the Minister of Justice so decides.[72] Here again, the Minister of Justice is granted the right to make decisions regarding the judiciary, and judges and prosecutors are treated as having equal status

Judges are required to refrain from conduct compromising the dignity of the court.[73] Judges are not allowed to conduct commercial activities, by themselves or through agents, or to be active in the leadership and management of trading companies, civil partnerships or autonomous economic administrations.[74]

The Civil and Criminal Procedure Codes further regulate judges' conduct in the event of potential conflicts of interest in the court.[75] Judges must either disclose the conflict and recuse themselves or risk having the parties disclose the matter to the court president who can then remove him from the case.[76] In addition, judges are not allowed to give legal advice, orally or in writing, even in cases pending before other courts. They must also refrain from publicly expressing their views on lawsuits that are pending.[77] However, judges may plead in cases where their interests or the interests of their parents, spouses or children are involved.[78]

*Disclosure*: Judges must submit statements on their assets at the beginning and the end of their terms.[79] In practice, however, their statements are kept confidential and are never

---

[70] Law on the Judiciary, Art. 113.

[71] Law on the Judiciary, Art. 116.

[72] Law on the Judiciary, Art. 114.

[73] Law on the Judiciary, Art. 118.

[74] Law on the Judiciary, Art. 112.

[75] Code of Criminal Procedure, Arts. 46-48; Code of Civil Procedure, Arts. 24–27.

[76] There is no clear disciplinary provision governing a failure to recuse oneself, although it might be brought on the grounds of an "unjustified denial to fulfil a duty provided by law." Law on the Judiciary, Art. 122(h). There have been no disciplinary proceedings against judges on these grounds, however.

[77] Law on the Judiciary, Art. 115.

[78] Law on the Judiciary, Art. 115.

[79] Law 115/1996, Art. 1.

verified.[80] Some observers believe that judges' ownership statements should be public information[81] because otherwise the practice does little to achieve its ostensible purpose of discouraging corruption.

## F. Judges' Associations

Judges are free to set up professional associations or other organisations for the purpose of representing their interests, improving professional training and protecting their own status;[82] they may also join international professional organisations.[83]

At present, there are two associations, neither strong enough efficiently to represent judges' interests before the other branches. The Association of Romanian Magistrates includes judges, prosecutors and civil servants of the Ministry of Justice. Established in 1993, the association made certain attempts – if not successful – to defend the interests of magistrates. In May 2000, the Association proposed to make the Chief Justice of the Supreme Court head of the judiciary, and to shift some powers from the Ministry of Justice to the Superior Council of Magistracy, in order to foster judicial independence;[84] thus far, these requests have not been considered by Parliament. At present, half of its members are no longer within the judicial system, and the association is in the process of re-organisation.[85] A separate Union of Judges' Associations, with a membership formed exclusively of judges, claims half of the judiciary as members. However, the Union mainly focuses on professional training, and has not been active in defending judges' rights and independence.

Apparently, the two associations compete between themselves and the political branches do not see either as a serious interlocutor.[86] Neither has reacted publicly against recent political interference with the judiciary's independence.

---

[80] The same is true for all officials bound by law to make ownership statements.

[81] Statement of participant, OSI Roundtable, Bucharest, 26 March 2001. *Explanatory note: OSI held a roundtable meeting in Bucharest in March 2001 to invite critique of the present report in draft form. Experts present included representatives of the Government, the judiciary, academia, and civil society organisations. No statements are attributable to any particular participant.*

[82] Law on the Judiciary, Art. 120.

[83] Law on the Judiciary, Art. 120.

[84] *Ziua*, 16 May 2000.

[85] Statements of participants at OSI Roundtable, Bucharest, 26 March 2001.

[86] Statements of participants at OSI Roundtable, Bucharest, 26 March 2001.

## III. Administration of The Court System and Judicial Independence

For the most part, day-to-day administration of individual courts is conducted independently by judges. All court administration matters fall under the jurisdiction of court presidents,[87] although the Minister of Justice also exercises some administrative control functions. Court presidents administer procurement issues, control court space, distribute necessary materials to judges and other court staff, manage the caseload,[88] appoint administrative staff, and organise court records, archives and statistics. They also assess the number of judges needed in the court, although the Ministry of Justice takes the final decision.

The Ministry of Justice must provide assistance to the court president in court administration, and the Superior Council of Magistracy may advise on the management of the courts when requested by the Minister of Justice.[89]

However, the overall administration of the judiciary is entrusted to the Minister of Justice, who is responsible for ensuring that the justice system is well organised and functions properly. The Ministry maintains a team of inspectors, who together with supervising judges from the courts of appeal, brief the Minister of Justice about the activity of courts and any misconduct which could have a deleterious effect on the application of law.

A 1999 amendment to the Law on the Judiciary set up administrative offices within the regional courts, whose directors are appointed by the Minister of Justice. Presidents of regional courts may delegate their administrative tasks to the administrative offices' directors.[90] Reportedly, offices have not been set up within all regional courts and the efficiency of those that have been established is low;[91] no such offices have been created in the district courts. In practice, when they need more personnel or equipment, court presidents address matters to higher courts or to the human resources or administrative departments in the Ministry of Justice.[92]

---

[87] Law on the Judiciary, Art. 12.

[88] Caseload management is discussed separately in section VI.B.

[89] Law on the Judiciary, Art. 88, para.1(g).

[90] Law on the Judiciary as amended by Ordinance 179 of November 1999, Art. 133, para. 2.

[91] Information from 40 judges in Cluj Napoca, March 2001.

[92] Information from 40 judges in Cluj Napoca, March 2001, and five judges, April 2001, Bucharest.

The Ministry of Justice also exercises some administrative control functions. However, some judges from the lower courts, in particular those from the district courts, report that such control intimidates them and interferes with their decisional independence, as the inspectors from both the Ministry of Justice and courts of appeal look into the case files to verify the correct application of the law.[93]

In order to avoid the risk posed by the Minister of Justice's power to control how judges apply the law under the general rubric of administration of justice, a clear firewall should be maintained between decisional and administrative supervision, and to this end an institutional change would be welcome: the authority charged with administering the courts should be the Supreme Court or a sufficiently independent Superior Council of Magistracy, while the Minister of Justice should only supervise the prosecutorial sector.

*Executive Involvement in Judicial Training*: Judicial training is also, to a certain extent, in the hands of the court presidents, but the indirect influence of the executive is considerable. New judges and prosecutors are trained either in the courts according to rules decided by the court president or within the framework of the National Institute for Magistrates, which trains both judges and prosecutors.[94] The Institute is directly subordinated to the Ministry of Justice[95] and is led by a council of 11 members (judges, prosecutors, and civil servants of the Ministry of Justice) appointed by the Superior Council of Magistracy.[96] The Minister of Justice appoints the director of the Institute and his deputies.[97] The decisions of the Institute's council (including budget approval and staffing[98]) must be vetted by the Minister of Justice.[99] Obviously, to the degree judicial training is conducted through the Institute, the Minister of Justice is the effective decision maker, rather than the judiciary.

---

[93] Information from five district court judges, April 2001, Bucharest; statements of participants at OSI Roundtable, 26 March 2001.

[94] Law on the Judiciary, Art. 52.

[95] Law on the Judiciary, Art. 70.

[96] Law on the Judiciary, Art. 71.

[97] Law on the Judiciary, Art. 71.

[98] Law on the Judiciary, Art. 74, para. 4. At present, 90 percent of the training judges are presidents of courts or of sections within the higher courts. Some prosecutors also teach at the Institute. Information from the director of NIM, September 2000. Although the law allows for magistrates to be transferred to the Institute, most continue in practice while teaching.

[99] Law on the Judiciary, Art. 72.

The Institute is also responsible for the professional training of sitting judges,[100] which is an ongoing obligation throughout their careers.[101] In addition, the Institute has established a training centre for clerks.[102] Although the Institute is currently the only high professional body for training judges,[103] the Ministry of Justice does not offer strong support for its development. An order issued by the Minister of Justice on 9 April 2001[104] reversed a 2000 order by the former Minister granting the Institute access to certain premises,[105] despite the financial contribution of the EU to equip and furnish the premises.[106] As of June 2001, the Ministry had not responded to the concerns expressed by the EC Delegation in Romania about to the Minister's order.[107] The Minister, who recently declared that the present teaching staff would fail the second year exams at the law school,[108] has replaced the director of the Institute.

---

[100] Law on the Judiciary, Art. 70.

[101] Law on the Judiciary, Art. 119.

[102] The 1999 Phare Programme for Romania.

[103] The Institute teaching staff have been intensively trained in international law, supported by international funds and assistance.

[104] Order 716/C/2001 issued by the Minister of Justice.

[105] Order 2876/C/2000 issued by the Minister of Justice.

[106] European Union, 1997 National Phare Programme for Romania, Assistance for the Development of the National Institute of the Magistracy and its 1999 continuation.

[107] Letter of 29 March 2001 from the Head of the European Commission Delegation in Romania.

[108] *Adevarul*, 7 March 2001; *Romania Libera*, 7 March 2001. One teacher resigned following the Minister's statement.

# IV. Financial Autonomy and Level of Funding

## A. Budgeting Process

The judiciary has almost no authority over its own budget process, which is in the hands of the Ministry of Justice. Although there is no evidence that this budgetary control has been used to exact political compliance, the possibility alone may act as an implicit limit on the judiciary's willingness to assert its independence. In addition, as the Ministry of Justice must prioritise the budget requests of several different institutions, it is generally less able to ensure maximum or even sufficient funding for the judiciary than would the judiciary itself if it developed its own budget.

As the primary financial administrator of the judicial authority, the Ministry of Justice drafts the overall budget for the court system,[109] which must then be adopted by Parliament. The judiciary has little direct influence on the process of drafting and adopting the budget; courts are not formally consulted when the budget is drafted.[110] Regional courts, which are the secondary financial administrators, gather budget estimates from the courts under their jurisdiction, and submit these figures to the Ministry of Justice. The Ministry prepares its budget, which includes expenditures for the judiciary; in each of the last two years, the Ministry has simply incorporated the regional courts' budget requests without changes. After consultations with the Ministry of Finance, the Ministry of Justice submits it to the Government for inclusion in the national budget.[111] During the parliamentary debates, each minister defends the budget of his ministry. Usually, Parliament adopts the national budget without significant changes. Through this process, the initial figures provided by courts are substantially altered by the executive and the Parliament.

The distribution of the budget to the courts is also in the hands of the Ministry of Justice and there are no legal guidelines for distribution. Following parliamentary approval, the Ministry of Justice divides the budget among the 41 regional courts, which administer the budgets of the district courts and the courts of appeal within their territorial jurisdiction. Every month, the regional courts submit to the Financial Department of the Ministry of Justice their financial requests for the coming month. The funds' distribution is subject

---

[109] Law 72/1996 on Public Finance.

[110] Information from the President of the National Association of Magistrates, July 2000.

[111] Information from the Financial Department in the Ministry of Justice, and from the president of a regional court, April 2001.

to the Audit Court's control. The Ministry also determines the spending of judicial fees and taxes used for investments in the courts' infrastructure, such as renovation of buildings. This situation creates conditions in which the judiciary may be easily manipulated by the executive, although there is no evidence to date that the Ministry has used its power in this fashion.

In 2001, the Ministry of Justice received 2.26 percent of the national budget to cover its own needs and those of the courts, penitentiaries, the National Institute of Magistrates and the Superior Council of Magistracy.[112] The ordinary courts' budget is not distinctively indicated within this budget. By way of comparison, the Public Ministry (prosecutors) received 0.49 percent of the national budget; the Supreme Court, 0.06 percent; the Constitutional Court, 0.02 percent.[113]

Because budgeting decisions are largely left up to the executive and legislative branches, the judiciary has had no financial support in developing into a strong authority capable of providing a check on the other branches of power. To remedy this problem, the courts' budgeting system should be changed in order to avoid the executive's interference, and the courts should be allowed to determine their budgetary needs. For instance, the Supreme Court could collect the budgetary requirements of all courts, draft the total budget and submit it directly to the Parliament. Government should be allowed to make changes to the judiciary's budget only in exceptional circumstances and within very narrow limits. In addition, the budget for the courts should be fully separated from those of the Ministry, penitentiaries, the National Institute for Magistrates and the Superior Council of Magistracy.

## B. Work Conditions

Romanian judges endure difficult working conditions. Courts suffer profoundly from under-investment, due to the limits of state budget resources in general, and to the courts' small budget share in particular. Many court buildings are inappropriate, the equipment is old, and the archives and hearing rooms are small and overcrowded; these problems are particularly acute in Bucharest, where in many of the district courts four to six judges

---

[112] The shares are higher than the last two years when, for example, the Ministry of Justice had received 0.96 percent (1999) and 1.73 percent (2000).

[113] Law on the 2001 National Budget. The 2001 budget, as well as the former budgets, is defined as an "austerity" budget. The Ministry of Justice's budget covers the needs of all courts except the Supreme Court, which drafts its own budget. Similarly, the Constitutional Court and the Public Ministry (prosecutors) draft separate budgets.

share an office;[114] In Craiova district court, 15 judges share an office.[115] There are no legal requirements on office space or standard technology.

There is an acute shortage of court staff given the existing caseload. The small number of staff, the lack of electronic registration of the archives and court hearings, and the poor conditions for studying case files all contribute to the low quality of services. Average caseloads have remained at a high, though steady, level over the past five years,[116] which has contributed to the low efficiency of the courts. The district courts in particular, which hear the large majority of cases, face permanent resource shortages.[117]

In light of these conditions, it is not surprising that the administration of justice is far from adequate. Court presidents are left to deal with these problems, although many of the tools needed to resolve them are out of their hands. For instance, decisions regarding additional staff are taken by the Ministry of Justice (which determines the number of judges) and the court of appeal (which determines the size of the administrative staff).[118] And, as mentioned above, court presidents have no influence on drafting budgets, or even spending allocated funds.

Information technology has not yet reached an acceptable level in courts, and the Ministry of Justice lacks a coherent strategy for improvement in this area.[119] The first beneficiaries of technological upgrades have been the higher courts and court presidents; judges and archives are still waiting. There is no uniform system of registering hearings electronically, and clerks' reports are either hand-written or produced on old typewriters. However, the Ministry of Justice has claimed[120] that a judicial IT network has been designed, including

---

[114] Information from district courts judges in Bucharest, April 2001. With the exception of the Supreme Court based in Bucharest and some higher courts in cities other than Bucharest, where courts function in newly renovated buildings.

[115] Information from four district courts judges in Craiova, May 2001.

[116] The 1996–1999 White Book, published by the Ministry of Justice (updated in 2000) shows the changes in the case loads:

- 1995    –    1,679,118;
- 1996    –    1,746,266;
- 1997    –    1.802,142;
- 1998    –    1,740,088;
- 2000    –    1,775,282.

[117] Information from 40 judges in Cluj Napoca, March 2001 and five district courts judges in Bucharest, April 2001.

[118] Subject, of course, to Ministerial approval of the budgetary costs.

[119] Statement of participant, 26 March 2001, OSI meeting.

[120] *The White Book. December 1996–December 1999*, p. 20.

a complex data base (law and case law), Internet access, e-mail accounts and security mechanisms. In practice, access to the system is limited to the higher courts and the Ministry. Courts do receive legal journals and the Official Gazette, together with printed collections of laws. However, these materials do not always come regularly, and are not freely available to all judges – in practice, extra copies are often kept in the office of the court president.[121] Under these circumstances, many judges have to pay for copying or buying legal materials.[122]

Due to the insufficiency of state budget resources, the funds allocated for judicial training are far from adequate. Most judicial training has been funded by foreign donors.[123] The Ministry of Justice has sought international financial assistance to address some of these problems.

## C. Compensation

Compensation has improved considerably, reducing the economic pressures for corruption. However, significant portions of the overall compensation are subject to discretionary determinations by the executive or court presidents, placing the individual judge's decisional independence at risk.

In recent years there has been considerable progress towards removing possible economic restraints on judicial independence. In 1996, following organised protests, judges' salaries were significantly increased to a level commensurate with that of other high public officials. Such measures were seen as necessary in order to deter corruption and to halt the exodus of magistrates into the higher-paying private sector.

Nevertheless, noting that some private lawyers have significantly higher incomes, the Romanian Magistrates Association continues to claim that judges' income is disproportionately low.[124] This comparison seems dubious, since the competition among judges is not nearly as high as it is among private lawyers and many lawyers value job stability more than a high salary. These sentiments can be witnessed in practice through the current wave of young lawyers now abandoning private practice and migrating to the

---

[121] Information from four district court judges in Craiova, May 2001. The court president receives the Official Gazette well after the issue date.

[122] Information from 40 judges in Cluj Napoca, March 2001 and five district court judges in Bucharest, April 2001.

[123] *The White Book. December 1996–December 1999*, pp. 21–26.

[124] Information from the president of the RMA; September 2000.

bench.[125] (The salaries of military judges and military prosecutors are higher than those of their civilian counterparts, and are paid by the Ministry of Defence. Due to their military status, military judges enjoy a large number of additional financial and social security benefits.[126])

A 1996 law established the legal basis for judges' and other magistrates' compensation;[127] the law was modified and supplemented by a 2000 Ordinance adopted by the Government,[128] which eliminated some additional benefits in exchange for a higher monthly salary. At the same time, the 2000 Ordinance increased some supplementary payments, such as compensation for overtime hours, and provided for a supplementary one-month salary prior to the annual paid holiday.[129] However, the new Government, which took office in December 2000, issued an Emergency Ordinance[130] suspending supplementary payments until 1 January 2002.[131] (A separate law governs the compensation of Supreme Court justices.[132]) The use of ordinances to alter judges' salaries on an emergency basis circumvents statutory guarantees which should protect judges' economic independence.

As of March 2001, the average monthly salary in Romania was approximately € 115. At present, the average monthly salary of a district court judge is c. € 325, roughly three times the average salary. Judges in regional courts receive an average salary of approximately € 370, while judges in the courts of appeal receive approximately € 405.[133] Judges with the Supreme Court receive c. € 580 per month.[134] In addition, judges serving as court presidents receive higher salaries. For instance, a district court president receives a net salary of approximately € 405, a regional court president receives approximately € 440 and an appellate court president € 485.[135]

---

[125] Information from the dean and the teachers of the National Institute of Magistrates, September 2000.

[126] Law 50/1996, Art. 55.

[127] Law 50/1996.

[128] Ordinance 83/2000 issued in accordance with Art. 107 para. 3 of the Constitution and Art. 1.Q of Law 125/2000 by which the Government was granted the power to adopt ordinances in certain areas.

[129] Ordinance 83/2000, Arts. 38 and 40.

[130] Emergency Ordinance 33/2001.

[131] Emergency Ordinance 33/2001, Art. III.

[132] Law 56/1996.

[133] Ordinance 83/2000, Annex 1. The figures indicate the net and not the gross income.

[134] In accordance with Law 56/1993, Art. 64, justices with the Supreme Court receive salaries equal to those paid in the highest public authorities.

[135] Ordinance 83/2000, Annex 1.

Depending on the discretion of the Government, a judge's base salary may be increased through a wide variety of benefits, premiums and indemnities. These forms of contingent judicial compensation could potentially be manipulated by the executive or other officials, placing judicial independence at risk. Judges receive regular increases to their base salary based on length of service, generally five percent after every five additional years on the bench.[136] Judges serving in rural areas receive additional payments up to ten percent; the Minister of Justice determines the exact percentage depending on the degree of isolation and the living conditions.[137] In addition, judges may receive a "medal" awarded after five, ten, 15, 20 or 25 years of service on the bench with good qualification assessments, which entitles the recipient to tax reductions of 20 to 50 percent;[138] the medals are awarded by the State President on the proposal of the Superior Council of Magistracy. Because of the service requirements, the service and medals systems currently favour judges who also served the communist regime, a group representing the most vocal opponents to judicial reform.

In addition to base salary and service adjustments, judges may receive various other benefits. Many of these are awarded on a contingent or selective basis, and increase the opportunities for the awarding body – the Ministry of Justice and court presidents – to exert economic pressure on judges. Judges may receive bonuses equal to a month's salary;[139] however, those whose "professional activities" have been "unsatisfactory" (according to the court president's assessment) or who have been subject to disciplinary sanctions during the previous year are not granted such bonuses or receive a reduced amount.[140] Other financial bonuses may be granted to judges, in the course of the year, if the Ministry of Justice has extra money out of the salary fund due to unfilled positions.[141] Moreover, the Ministry of Justice is allowed to set up a monthly fund for bonuses given to personnel whose activity was considered "valuable".[142] Although the law does not provide for a body or person to decide on who receives these bonuses, in practice the court presidents exercise this power.

Local councils may provide housing to judges at their request. There are no special quotas for judges, and such requests are in principle fulfilled when there are free apartments available; because there are no criteria for allocation, this is seen as a method by which

---

[136] Ordinance 83/2000, Art. 8, modifying Art. 5 of Law 50/1996.

[137] Ordinance 83/2000, Art. 10. modifying Art. 11 of Law 50/1996.

[138] Law on the Judiciary, Arts. 107–109.

[139] Law 50/1996, Art. 34.

[140] Law 50/1996, Art. 37.

[141] Law 50/1996, Art. 35.

[142] Law 50/1996, Art. 36.

local governments may influence courts. Judges and their families have the right to free medical treatment and insurance.[143] Judges may also use holiday, health and sport establishments owned or administered by the Ministry of Justice. The particular benefits are bestowed upon judges by order of the Minister of Justice.[144] Additional benefits include: 50 percent reduction for 12 annual roundtrip inland journeys by air, ship and train; one free roundtrip journey within Romania for vacation; and low interest housing loans to judges under 45 years of age.[145] However, it has been reported that none of these benefits are regularly awarded.[146]

Upon retirement judges receive pensions equal to 80 percent of their last salary, and up to 100 percent for those who have served more than 25 years[147] or have been awarded medals.[148]

The 2000 Regular Report from the European Commission on Romania's progress towards accession commends the fact that judges' salaries have been increased in Romania, claiming that the move "has both strengthened their financial independence and increased the attractiveness of the profession."[149] The corruption of Romanian courts[150] is in part a function of traditionally low judicial incomes, and it is an open question whether or not the recently increased salaries will serve to insulate the judiciary sufficiently from economic pressures. However, even if incentives towards external corruption are reduced, because many of the additional benefits depend on the Government's or court presidents' will, judges' independence from the political branches or within the judicial hierarchy will still be at risk. More regularised payments, without recourse to contingent or merit-based payments, could reduce this risk.

---

[143] Law 50/1996, Art. 36.

[144] Ordinance 83/2000, Art. 37, modifying Art. 41 of Law 50/1996.

[145] Law on the Judiciary, Art. 105.

[146] Reported by the president of the Association of Romanian Magistrates, July 2000.

[147] Law on the Judiciary, Art. 103.

[148] Law on the Judiciary, Art. 109.

[149] *2000 Regular Report*, p. 18.

[150] See Section VII.B.

## V. Judicial Office

Although various other bodies are also involved, the Superior Council of Magistracy and the Ministry of Justice generally share significant responsibility for decisions regarding the promotion, transfer, disciplinary action and removal from office of judges; as a consequence, there is reasonable concern that individual judges' career paths are unduly subject to influence by the executive.

### A. Selection

The Commission's 2000 Regular Report states: "Concerning the independence of the judiciary, the Ministry of Justice continues to have a significant influence over judicial appointments and this is an issue that remains to be addressed."[151]

The State President appoints judges and Supreme Court justices upon the proposal of the Superior Council of Magistracy, following the recommendation of the Minister of Justice.[152] However, some judges must complete a probationary period prior to receiving a full appointment as a senior judge, which may limit their independence during the interim period.

Beginning in 2000, all law graduates applying for a judicial position must complete a course of training with the National Institute of Magistrates,[153] choosing between two courses of study. The Institute's students are appointed as junior judges by the Minister of Justice – that is, they are technically judges, but without full tenure. Candidates who study two years at the Institute may take an examination to be eligible for appointment as senior judges with full tenure. The examination is conducted by a commission composed of two Supreme Court justices, two law professors, and one representative of the Ministry of Justice. The Minister of Justice then recommends candidates to the Superior Council of Magistracy, which in turn proposes candidates to the State President for appointment as senior judges.[154]

---

[151] *2000 Regular Report*, p. 18.

[152] Law on the Judiciary, Arts. 47 and 88, para.1 (a-c).

[153] Statement of participant, OSI meeting, 26 March 2001. Previously, new candidates could apply to the bench without studying at the Institute, but would then serve a two-year probationary period. The competition to enter the Institute has become quite intense; in 2000, 4000 law graduates competed for 120 offices. Lawyers with five years' experience in practice can also apply for judicial appointments without attending the Institute; with eight years' experience, they are eligible for appointment to the regional courts and courts of appeal. Law on the Judiciary, Art. 67, para.2.

[154] Law on the Judiciary, Art. 47 (role of president); Art. 88, para. 1(c) (role of the Minister and the Council).

However, candidates who study only one year at the Institute then serve a six-month probation as a junior judge, during which they may adjudicate only a limited number of cases,[155] and at the end of which they may take the examination to be eligible for appointment as senior judges with full tenure. Only at this point is their tenure secure, meaning that both the Minister and the State President have the opportunity to consider the candidate's performance on the bench – including his rulings – prior to appointing him.

A candidate for a full judgeship may appeal to the Supreme Court a refusal by the Council to submit his name to the State President;[156] in such cases, the Minister of Justice represents the Superior Council of Magistracy before the Supreme Court.[157] There is no such appeal from the Minister's refusal to recommend him to the Council, or from the State President's refusal to appoint him.

Practising lawyers may be appointed as senior judges as well. Such candidates must have at least five years' experience[158] in one of a number of specified legal positions, such as lawyer, prosecutor, law professor, staff member in various executive or legislative organs.[159]

Court presidents are appointed by the Superior Council of Magistracy, upon the recommendation of the Minister of Justice.[160] The court presidents are appointed to four-year terms, with the possibility of renewal.[161] The process of appointing court presidents involves analysing the credentials of judges, their professional and social conduct, and their management skills. Furthermore, the law requires that presidents of a court of first instance have a minimum of four years' experience as judges, while presidents of a court of appeal must have at least eight years' experience. The Minister of Justice can request the Superior Council of Magistracy to recall a court president, before the end of the service, for "unsatisfactory fulfillment of the leading tasks or following a disciplinary sanction."[162]

---

[155] Law on the Judiciary, Art. 56. Those who complete the longer two-year course at the Institute may take the examination to become a judge without the intervening probation period. Law on the judiciary, Art. 84.

[156] Law on the Judiciary, Art. 64, para. 1.

[157] Law on the Judiciary, Art. 64, para.2.

[158] Eight years for the regional courts and courts of appeal. Law on the Judiciary, Art. 67 para. 2.

[159] Law on the Judiciary, Art. 65.

[160] Law on the Judiciary, Art. 69. In accordance with Art. 88 para. 4, the Council proposes three candidates to the State President for the position of President of the Supreme Court.

[161] Law on the Judiciary, Art. 66, para. 5.

[162] Law on Judiciary, Art. 66 para. 7.

The problems related to judicial appointments stem in part from the fact that many newly-appointed junior judges lack legal knowledge and experience. The failure to verify the capability, morality and integrity of candidates contributes to their lack of independence, impartiality and professionalism. A legislative change would be desirable, raising the minimum age for judicial candidacy, or setting higher standards for legal experience and requiring strong evidence of professional capability and integrity. The introduction of more extensive testing requirements through the Institute would be a welcome development.

### 1. Selection of Constitutional Court Members

Constitutional Court judges are appointed to non-renewable nine-year terms. The State President, the Senate, and the Chamber of Deputies appoint the judges to the Constitutional Court (three judges each). While this method of appointment in itself does not depart from European standards, it does unnecessarily politicise the selection process, and in practice appears to have had a negative impact on the independence of Constitutional Court judges. For example, in a 1996 judgement[163] the Constitutional Court ruled that the presidential candidate Ion Iliescu could run in 1996 for his second term despite a 1992 Court judgement stating that the 1992–1996 presidency was his second term in office.[164] The composition of the 1996 Court had been determined by Iliescu and his party's majority in Parliament. The same matter was brought before the Constitutional Court during the 2000 presidential elections, and the Court's ruling was identical to its 1996 ruling,[165] except for two dissenting opinions by judges appointed by then State President Constantinescu, who served between 1996 and 2000 while the party of current State President Iliescu was in opposition.

## B. Tenure, Retirement, Transfer and Removal

*Tenure*: The Constitution provides that judges appointed by the State President are appointed for life. An exception is made with respect to the justices of the Supreme Court, who are appointed to six-year terms with the possibility of renewal.[166] The combination of a relatively short term in office, term renewal contingent on decisions of the Superior Council of Magistracy and the State President on the recommendation

---

[163] Constitutional Court, Judgement No. 1/1996.
[164] Constitutional Court, Judgement No. 18/1992.
[165] Constitutional Court, Judgement No. 3/2000.
[166] CONST. REP. ROMANIA, Art. 124, para.1.

of the Minister of Justice, and the continuous involvement of the General Prosecutor in the Supreme Court's activity raises concerns over the independence and impartiality of the Supreme Court.

Some recent statements of high officials serving in the Government have provided further concern with regard to judges' irremovability. In April 2001, both the Minister of Justice and the State President expressed critical opinions about the irremovability of judges.[167]

*Retirement*: The law provides maximum age limits for serving on the bench: 65 years for judges in the district and regional courts, 68 years for judges in the courts of appeal[168] and 70 years for justices of the Supreme Court.[169] There is no possibility for a judge to continue in his position after the mandatory retirement age. However, because the general retirement ages in Romania are lower – 60 for women and 65 for men – judges may retire at those ages. Service up to the maximum retirement age is subject to the approval of a judge's court president (with the exception of Supreme Court justices).[170] This creates undue incentives for a judge wishing to stay on the bench to avoid offending his court president over a period as long as eight years.

*Transfer*: Judges may be transferred to other courts by order of the Superior Council of Magistracy following the proposal of the Minister of Justice.[171] Judges' consent is required prior to the transfer (as well as to promotion).[172] However, where a court cannot function properly due to temporary vacancies, the Minister of Justice, following the proposal of the court president, can temporarily re-assign a judge. The judge's consent is not required for assignments up to two months within any given year.[173] Longer temporary assignments of six months to three years require the judge's consent. Some observers have criticised this provision, since the judge does not have tenure in his temporary assignment, which may nonetheless be quite long, and may be subject to political influence following the termination of an assignment.

---

[167] TVR, *Scurt pe doi,* 9 April 2001.

[168] Law on the Judiciary, Art. 68.

[169] Art. 14 of the Law 56/1993 on the Supreme Court of Justice. However, at their own request, justices may retire at 62 (men) or 57 (women).

[170] Law on the Judiciary, Art. 68.

[171] Law on the Judiciary, Arts. 69 and 88 para.1/d.

[172] Law on the Judiciary, Art. 94.

[173] Law on the Judiciary, Art. 95.

*Removal*: The Superior Council of Magistracy decides judges' removal from office upon the proposal of the Minister of Justice. Removal can be decided in the following cases: resignation; retirement; transfer to another office; obvious professional incompetence or mental illness; criminal conviction; failure to fulfil any of the requirements for joining the profession; violation of the prohibitions against joining political parties, or undertaking political activities or commercial activities;[174] as well as for violations of the Code of Ethics or disciplinary provisions enumerated in the Law on the Judiciary.[175] The inclusion of prosecutors among the membership of the Superior Council raises concerns about undue executive interference with judicial independence flowing from removal decisions.

## C. Evaluation and Promotion

The current method for evaluating judges' performance raises serious concerns. First, judges may be influenced by those responsible for promotions and annual qualification assessments. Second, the Minister of Justice's duty to submit proposals to the Superior Council of Magistracy regarding which judges to promote and his influence over the Council unduly involve the executive in the promotion process.

The Superior Council of Magistracy plays a major role in the career advancement of judges, as it decides on promotions – but only following a proposal by the Ministry of Justice. In practice, therefore, the executive is in a position to act as gatekeeper for any judge's promotion prospects.

There are minimum criteria for promotion. Judges must have served a minimum number of years, ranging from four years for the regional courts to 12 years for the Supreme Court,[176] and four to 15 years for court presidents,[177] to be eligible. In addition, judges' promotion to higher courts requires "meritorious activity proved by the grades issued by the hierarchical chiefs."[178] These graded evaluations are produced annually by each judge's superior. The annual reports must reflect professional results, conduct inside and outside the court, skills, and prospects for professional progress.[179] The law does not provide any quantitative measures for evaluating a judge's activity; however, the Ministry of

---

[174] Law on the Judiciary, Art. 92 para.1.

[175] Discussed in section V.C.

[176] Law on the Judiciary, Art. 66, para. 4(a) and (c); Law 56/1993 on the Supreme Court, Art. 13.

[177] Law on the Judiciary , Art. 66, para. 4(a), (b), (d); Law 56/1993 on the Supreme Court, Art. 13.

[178] Law on the Judiciary, Art. 66, para. 1.

[179] Law on the Judiciary, Art. 66, para. 1, 2.

Justice has drafted an evaluation form which considers the number of cases assigned, number of cases decided, number of reversals, application of law, and conduct.[180] In practice, it has been observed that a high rate of reversals can lead to a low qualification assessment. For appointment as court presidents, managerial skills are also considered.[181]

The Superior Council of Magistracy has the right to ask the Ministry of Justice and the courts information about judges' professional performance and their personal conduct;[182] the Council therefore has considerable authority to evaluate the performance and efficiency of judges. However, it is clear that the Ministry is expected to keep records of judges' performance, and once the Council becomes interested in a judge's professional performance, the Minister of Justice becomes directly involved in the evaluation. In addition, keeping in mind that one-third of the Superior Council of Magistracy are prosecutors under the authority of the Minister of Justice, the active participation of the executive in the evaluation of the judiciary is undeniable.

## D. Discipline

In general, provisions relating to the liability or disciplining of judges comport with the requirements of judicial independence and accountability; however, the role of the Ministry of Justice is unnecessarily intrusive, especially if the Ministry's overall responsibility for administration and oversight were to be reduced to proper levels.

*Liability*: The law generally does not allow for civil liability arising from judges' decisions. The only such provision is for cases in which a judge's ruling leads to an incorrect conviction which is subsequently enforced, in which case the Ministry of Finance pays damages, and may then sue the judge to recover the amount paid if it proves that the judge had acted in bad faith or with extreme negligence.[183] However, no such suit against a judge has been brought for the last 50 years. A 1999 Ordinance adopted by the Government provides for the civil liability of State officials who had intentionally contributed to a violation resulting in the payment of damages. However, with respect to judges, the ordinance provides that their civil liability shall be regulated by future amendments to the law on the judiciary.[184]

---

[180] OSI meeting, Bucharest, 26 March 2001.

[181] Law on the Judiciary, Art. 66, para. 3.

[182] Law on the Judiciary, Art. 88.

[183] Code of Criminal Procedure, Art. 507.

[184] Ordinance 94/1999, Art. 12 para. 3.

Judges may not be prosecuted, detained, arrested, searched or indicted without the approval of the Minister of Justice.[185] The Regular Report of the European Commission stated that during 1999 four judges were indicted; their trials are still pending.[186] In practice, where there is strong evidence of criminal misconduct, the judge is asked confidentially to resign.[187] At the beginning of 2001, three judges and one prosecutor were arrested on bribery charges; proceedings are ongoing.

*Disciplinary Procedures*: The Law on the Judiciary enumerates activities considered to be judicial misconduct, including: frequent delay in completing paperwork, unjustified absence from work, interference with the activity of another judge, offensive attitude in the office, breach of secrecy in judicial decision-making, public political activities, activities affecting the judicial profession's integrity and honour, unjustified refusal to carry out duties, frequent negligence, breaking the Code of Ethics,[188] or tax evasion.[189] In addition, judges must refrain from conduct "compromising their dignity in the court and in society."[190]

Oversight of judges' conduct and initiation of disciplinary proceedings mainly falls under the authority of the Minister of Justice and the Superior Council of Magistracy. The Minister acts as the disciplinary prosecutor (except in cases concerning justices of the Supreme Court, in which case this is the Deputy Chief Justice).[191] Disciplinary proceedings may be initiated only after the Minister has ordered an inquiry by judges or general inspectors from the Ministry.[192] (A commission of five justices performs the inquiry into another Supreme Court justice's misconduct.) During the inquiry, the accused judge has the right to view the investigative case file and to ask for evidence in his defence.[193] When the investigation is complete, the Minister of Justice may decide to indict the judge, in which event the Superior Council of Magistracy initiates hearings.

---

[185] Law on the Judiciary, Art. 91, para. 2.

[186] *Regular Report 1999*.

[187] This information relies on informal contacts with judicial actors who were unanimous in their opinion.

[188] No Code of Ethics has yet been adopted. A 1999 Ordinance requested the Superior Council of Magistracy to draft and adopt a Code of Ethics for both judges and prosecutors. Emergency Ordinance 179/1999, Art. II. Although the deadline provided by the Ordinance was 17 February 2000, the Code has not been drafted yet.

[189] Law on the Judiciary, Art. 122.

[190] Law on the Judiciary, Art. 118.

[191] Law on the Judiciary, Art. 124.

[192] Law on the Judiciary, Art. 125, paras. 1 and 2.

[193] Law on the Judiciary, Art. 125, para. 4.

During the hearings before the Superior Council of Magistracy, the judge may be assisted only by another judge or prosecutor,[194] whose ability to provide an effective defence may be compromised by his own dependence on the Council for career advancement.[195] The Council's proceedings are not public, and the decision is communicated only to the parties. In some cases, a judge sanctioned by the Council may appeal to the Supreme Court. However, judges are not granted the right to appeal removal on grounds of inadequate professional experience, physical incapacity, or insufficient knowledge of the Romanian language.

If a judge is found guilty, the Council can apply various sanctions: warning, admonition, reduction of salary by up to 15 percent for one to three months, transfer to another court for one to three months, suspension without pay for up to six months, or expulsion from the magistracy. The Minister of Justice can request that the Council remove a court president, before the end of his term, for "unsatisfactory fulfilment of the principal duties or following a disciplinary sanction."[196]

Through the powers granted to the Minister of Justice and to the prosecutors in the Superior Council of Magistracy, the executive is unduly involved in determining the judges' disciplinary responsibility. By contrast, prosecutors do not fall under the Council's disciplinary jurisdiction but have their own disciplinary commission formed exclusively of prosecutors; there is no countervailing influence of the judiciary on disciplinary proceedings against prosecutors.

---

[194] Law on the Judiciary, Art. 128.

[195] Statement of participants, OSI Meeting, 26 March 2001.

[196] Law on the Judiciary, Art. 66, para. 7

# VI. Intra-Judicial Relations

## A. Relations with Superior Courts

Individual judges' decisions are often influenced by higher-level judges through informal and often non-public consultations, which reduce the transparency of the adjudicative process and may limit those judges' decisional independence.

In the appeals system, higher courts enjoy full control over the merits of the case. Lower courts are bound to implement the instructions issued by higher courts deciding on appeal. However, in practice, inferior courts do not always follow these instructions, which increases the probability that another appeal will be sought. Courts of appeal may also decide to completely change a decision based on the facts or law. The Supreme Court, following extraordinary appeals filed by the General Prosecutor, may issue binding judgements clarifying legal issues that have been given different interpretations by the courts.[197]

Higher courts are not allowed to give lower court judges instruction regarding a case other than through the processes of judicial appeal. Nevertheless, in practice, some judges seek informal advice from judges in the higher courts. In many cases, such advice is given by senior judges who were trained under the communist system and are therefore highly deferential to the executive. In addition, such a system reduces the level of transparency – and thus the accountability – in the system of adjudication.

Judges from the courts of appeal conduct inspections of lower courts, and the Ministry of Justice is briefed on the findings. The inspecting judges have a very broad mandate to inspect the activities of the lower courts, the application of laws, and judicial conduct.[198] The extremely intrusive nature of the inspections and the channeling of information to the Ministry can have a chilling effect on judges' decisional independence.

## B. Case Management and Relations with Court Presidents

Non-transparent and corrupt practices in assigning cases increase the opportunities for corruption, which is harmful to judges' impartiality and public standing, ultimately threatening their institutional independence. Court presidents exercise considerable

---

[197] Code of Civil Procedure, Art. 329; Code of Criminal Procedure, Art. 414.
[198] See Section II.C.

authority over judges in their courts, which, given their reliance on the Ministry of Justice, creates an opportunity for the executive indirectly to influence individual judges.

Cases are assigned to judges by court presidents at their discretion; there is no transparency in the process. Statutory or regulatory limits on the caseload of individual judges do not exist. Judges may be pressed to expedite cases, and frequent non-observance of such requests can lead to disciplinary sanctions.[199]

The assignment of a case to a particular judge may be a deciding factor in the outcome of a trial. For example, restitution of nationalised property has become a divisive issue in Romanian politics and most judges have strong personal opinions on this matter; as there are no objective criteria determining the assignment of cases, there is ample space for court presidents to manipulate the system to direct cases towards sympathetic or compliant judges.

Corruption has also been connected with the assignment process. A World Bank survey found that one of the most commonly cited reasons for bribery was "to assure that a certain person would be assigned to the case."[200] The survey also noted that requests to expedite a case were also frequent grounds for bribes.[201]

Nevertheless, it seems that in practice, court presidents take the overall caseload into account in keeping a balance among judges. Reportedly, the presidents in the district courts exercise this discretion fairly, by assigning cases to judges in the order in which cases are registered with the court.[202]

Case registration rules allow only a limited identification of the individual judge, clerk or other administrative staff working on a particular case file. Members of the registry or other administrative staff have largely uncontrolled access to the case files. In general, the registry does not record requests for the case files made by court officials or parties. While some courts practice the signature system for handling case files, their content is not verified when they change hands, leaving open the possibility of documents' disappearance without any chance of identifying the moment or the responsible person.[203]

---

[199] Law on the Judiciary, Art. 122. See section V.E.

[200] World Bank, Diagnostic Survey of Corruption in Romania, RomRep80FinalA4.doc, 3 March 2001, p. 15.

[201] World Bank, Diagnostic Survey of Corruption in Romania, RomRep80FinalA4.doc, 3 March 2001, p. 15.

[202] Information from five district court judges, April 2001, Bucharest; OSI Meeting, Bucharest, 26 March 2001.

[203] Statement of participant, OSI Meeting, Bucharest, 26 March 2000; interview with five judges, April 2001, Bucharest.

Although there is a judge in charge of supervising the registry in each court, his other duties generally prevent him from spending sufficient time in the registry, and his authority with the registry staff is low.[204]

It is widely believed that many court clerks are involved in petty corruption on a daily basis. When asking for information or case files, many parties or their lawyers bribe the staff. This is already such a notorious practice that the staff no longer need to ask for the bribe, which is offered automatically. The absence of an adequate case tracking system exacerbates this problem by making effective monitoring or *post hoc* auditing practically impossible, reducing the transparency of the whole system, and thus its accountability. Here public perception is also important; if court officials with whom they have contact are corrupt, the public will reasonably suppose that the courts as a whole are corrupt, reducing judges' reputation for impartiality which is a crucial justification for their grant of independence.

Following a verification of the registry and notification offices of some of the lower courts, the Ministry of Justice issued a press release in June 2000, noting the large number of errors in tracking case files. Some staff members were dismissed while others received disciplinary sanctions. The registration system should be substantially changed and computerisation of the data would be welcome.

Court presidents have significant powers over judges, which include evaluation of judges performance and playing an important role in awarding benefits, premiums, and indemnities. Court presidents have some say in judges obtaining housing as well. This contributes to creation of the bureaucratic chain of command and may lead to judges' excessive loyalty to court presidents, who are, in turn, quite dependent in their position on the Minister of Justice.

---

[204] Statement of participant, OSI Meeting, Bucharest, 26 March 2001; information from five judges, Bucharest, April 2001.

# VII. Enforcement and Corruption

## A. Enforcement of Judgements

Enforcement of judicial decisions, in particular those issued in civil, commercial and administrative matters, poses a significant problem for judicial independence.[205] Enforcement often takes a long time and bribery is common.[206] In addition, there are many possibilities for contesting the enforcement procedures, which further delays execution of judgements. There are no deadlines for enforcement, and in practice the responsible staff is not held accountable for failure to execute judgements.

Beyond questions of inefficiency or petty corruption, there are reasons for concern about the low level of political commitment to enforcement of court decisions. Government officials often openly express their refusal to consider routine enforcement of judges' decisions, especially in controversial cases; indeed, such attempts seem to be on the increase and to be more openly conducted. Recently, the Government expressed reluctance to enforce judgements returning nationalised property to pre-1945 owners. On 7 March 2001 the Minister of Justice sent a letter to all presidents of courts of appeal, stating that enforcement of such judgements raises "social problems" with regards to the tenants. The Minister asked the appellate court presidents to monitor such trials, and noted that "responsibility for the concrete measures to be taken by each court shall be verified by the General Inspection Corps, judicial inspectors, officials in ruling positions with the Ministry of Justice and the co-ordinator state-secretary."[207] In effect, judges were told to avoid ruling on the enforcement of decisions requiring the nationalised property to be returned, under threat of being inspected or sanctioned by the executive officials.

The General Prosecutor's decision in 2001 to suspend enforcement of final judgement against the two generals convicted for the events in Timisoara in 1989,[208] pending an extraordinary appeal, is apparently illegal, as the Constitutional Court has held that only courts have the power to suspend enforcement.[209]

---

[205] For instance, in *Ignaccolo-Zenide v. Romania*, (ECHR judgement 31679/96, 25 January 2000), the court found that a court's judgement had not been enforced for four years.

[206] Information provided during informal contacts with lawyers and parties involved in the enforcement process.

[207] *Evenimentul Zilei*, 4 April 2001.

[208] See sections 1.A. and 2.C.

[209] Judgement No. 73/1996. The Court's reasoning – that prosecutors belong to the executive branch and therefore should not enjoy the power to suspend final judgements, which properly belongs to the courts alone – applies equally to criminal and civil cases.

There are some efforts underway aimed at reforming the enforcement regime. Until recently, enforcement fell under the court presidents' jurisdiction. However, under a law passed in 2000,[210] the judicial enforcement corps became an autonomously organised profession under the authority of the Ministry of Justice. A re-organisation process is currently taking place. It is too early for an assessment of the practical effectiveness of the new law. Also, in late 2000, the Ministry of Justice expressed its intention to amend the enforcement rules of the Civil Procedure Code.[211] Improvements in enforcement will raise public respect for court rulings.

However, the courts themselves also need to improve their attitude towards enforcement and respect of court decisions. The dispute between the Constitutional Court and the Supreme Court[212] has had negative consequences for the development of a culture of respect for enforcement of judicial decisions, since the spectacle of courts' denying each other's authority can hardly encourage other parties to consider themselves bound by court rulings.

## B. Corruption

Corruption is a major obstacle to judicial independence and continues to be a widespread and systemic problem in Romania.[213] According to a recent survey performed by the non-governmental organisation "Pro Democratia", the public believes that courts, prosecutors' offices and the police are the most corrupt institutions in the country.[214] The 2001 World Bank survey also found that the courts are widely perceived to be corrupt, and that bribery is common.[215] The survey concludes that this practice illustrates that "corruption should be treated in a systemic way, including the legal profession, and legal education, in addition to the courts system *per se*."[216]

---

[210] Law 188/2000 on the judicial enforcing agents.

[211] *The White Book. December 1996 – December 1999*, pp. 57–58.

[212] See Section 2.A.3.

[213] *2000 Regular Report*, p. 18.

[214] *Cronica Romana*, 5 October 2000.

[215] World Bank, Diagnostic Survey of Corruption in Romania, RomRep80FinalA4.doc, 3 March 2001. The report also noted that most bribes are given to attorneys acting as intermediaries, and may not necessarily ever get into the hands of judges or court officials. However, the mere fact that clients hand money to attorneys believing it will be used for bribes demonstrates the low level of faith in an impartial and independent judiciary.

[216] World Bank, Diagnostic Survey of Corruption in Romania, RomRep80FinalA4.doc, 3 March 2001, p. 15.

Corruption in the judiciary goes largely uninvestigated and unpunished. However, there have been some cases where corruption was identified and sanctioned. As noted by the 2000 Regular Report, "concerning corruption in the judiciary, in 1999 the Superior Council of Magistracy handled 14 disciplinary actions against judges. Of the eight actions accepted, six judges received disciplinary sanctions and two were removed from office."[217]

This somewhat optimistic report on the fight against judicial corruption in Romania must be supplemented by certain considerations. First, any form of corruption is a crime requiring a court trial, not simply a (non-public) hearing in a disciplinary body. By applying disciplinary sanctions, the Superior Council of Magistracy avoided the courts' jurisdiction and public debate on such cases.

Moreover, the data provided by the June 2000 press release of the Ministry of Justice shows that during the first six months of 2000, although the prosecution requested approval to investigate six judges the Ministry gave its approval to investigate only three.[218] Recently, disciplinary and criminal proceedings have been initiated against three judges. However, the process is not transparent, and some fear that officials are more concerned with protecting the public image of the judiciary than with bringing the allegedly corrupt judges before the courts.

Although the sources of judicial corruption are principally economic and political, a series of procedural shortcomings in the judicial system encourage corruption and prevent judges from being punished. For instance, court proceedings are not recorded verbatim. In practice, judges use their own words to summarise the parties' and witnesses' statements, and dictate these summaries to the clerk. Oral debates between the parties, as well as the questions asked during interviews, are never recorded. In addition, there is no record of the questions rejected by the court. The lack of recording applies to all cases at every level of jurisdiction. Under these circumstances, a judge may easily distort what the parties and witnesses have stated in court. Moreover, the appeal hearings lack the means by which to identify possible mistakes in previous proceedings since there is no record of what was said. Finally, procedural rules allowing very long proceedings at the discretion of the courts may constitute another vehicle for corruption.

---

[217] *2000 Regular Report*, pp. 18–19.

[218] By law, the minister must only "advise" on the indictment, but it seems in practice his approval is required. The lack of "approval" raises a question about the objectivity of the Minister of Justice and of the prosecution process.

# Judicial Independence
# in Slovakia

# Table of Contents

Executive Summary .................................................... 398

I. Introduction .................................................. 401
    A. Incomplete Legal Transformation ............ 401
    B. Excessive Executive Involvement .............. 402
    C. Weak Commitment to a Culture Supporting the Rule of Law ..................... 402
    D. Organisation of the Judicial System ......... 404

II. Constitutional and Legal Foundations of Judicial Independence ................................ 407
    A. Guarantees of the Separation of Powers and Judicial Independence ....................... 407
    B. Representation of the Judiciary ................ 407
        1. The Planned National Judicial Council .................................. 408
    C. Rules on Incompatibility .......................... 409
    D. Judges' Associations .................................. 411

III. Administration of the Court System and Judicial Independence ............................ 412

IV. Financial Autonomy and Level of Funding .... 414
    A. Budgeting Process ..................................... 414
    B. Work Conditions ....................................... 416
    C. Compensation .......................................... 417

| | | |
|---|---|---|
| V. | Judicial Office | 419 |
| | A. Selection | 419 |
| | B. Tenure, Transfer, Retirement and Removal | 421 |
| |    1. Tenure | 421 |
| |    2. Transfer | 421 |
| |    3. Retirement | 422 |
| |    4. Removal | 422 |
| | C. Evaluation and Promotion | 423 |
| | D. Discipline | 424 |
| |    1. Liability | 424 |
| |    2. Disciplinary Procedures | 425 |
| VI. | Intra-Judicial Relations | 427 |
| | A. Relations with Higher Courts | 427 |
| | B. Case Management and Relations with Court Presidents | 427 |
| VII. | Enforcement and Corruption | 429 |
| | A. Enforcement | 429 |
| | B. Persistent Corruption | 429 |

# Judicial Independence in Slovakia

## Executive Summary

The Slovak Republic, or Slovakia, is in the middle of a process of reform in which it has made many important social, political and legal changes, and has definitively broken with the communist legacy. Many basic constitutional and legal guarantees of judicial independence are in place.

A number of necessary changes still need to be addressed, however, including the incomplete transformation of the legal and constitutional structures guaranteeing judicial independence, and continued excessive executive involvement. Underlying these is a continuing weak commitment to a legal culture, even among judges.

*Incomplete Transformation*
Slovakia is still in a transitional phase. Only in the past year have important legal and constitutional reforms been completed, and these still do not adequately address the institutional or corporate elements of the judiciary's independence, a fact the Commission itself has noted.

*Excessive Executive Involvement*
The judiciary remains unduly reliant on the executive in several important areas, such as court management, budgeting, and appointment of court presidents. The existing judicial councils are merely advisory in character. The level of routine supervision by the executive is far greater than is desirable for maintenance of an independent judiciary. The recent constitutional and legislative changes represent partial improvements – but even the new National Judicial Council may not go far enough in removing executive involvement.

*Weak Commitment to a Culture Supporting the Rule of Law*
The incomplete transformation of the judiciary, and its subordination to the executive are themselves functions of the weak commitment to a legal culture which continues to mark Slovak social and political life. While some officials have embraced the rule of law and support an independent judiciary, others continue to expect that judges will

act as loyal servants of the executive's political will – a view shared by many citizens. Quite simply, many politicians do not consider judicial independence a priority; very few acknowledge that strengthening judicial independence complements the system of checks and balances.

Judges' attitudes themselves present obstacles to the judiciary's transformation into an independent, responsible and equal branch. Many judges maintain a subservient attitude towards the political branches. Signs of apathy, timidity and dependence can be found even among judges who are relatively new to the profession. At the same time, ironically, some judges have embraced a rather immature conception of judicial independence, equating it with the right to be free from any public control or criticism, and resisting efforts to investigate judges' breaches of ethics, including widespread corruption.

Several other issues relating to these themes are discussed in the body of this Report. Some of the most significant are the following:

*Separation of Powers*

The corporate independence of the whole judiciary is insufficiently protected, as most legal guarantees only contemplate the individual judge. Plans for a new National Judicial Council with expanded powers, while unquestionably an improvement, may not go far enough in reducing executive involvement in the judiciary.

*Representation*

There is no legal norm in Slovakia that provides for equal status of the legislative, executive, and judicial branches, and in reality the position of the judiciary is weaker than that of the other two branches. The planned National Judicial Council is a constitutional body with some representative authority, but implementing legislation has not yet been enacted, and it is clear that the version introduced under the amendment does not meet the requirements proposed by the judiciary.

*Administration*

Even with the planned creation of the new Judicial Council, the Minister of Justice still retains significant policy-making and administrative authority. Through officials within the Ministry, the Minister can influence any decision of district or regional court presidents relating to court administration.

*Budget Authority*

Judges have almost no involvement in the process of developing or defending the judiciary's financial allocation. There is no evidence that the Ministry of Justice has attempted to condition funding for the judiciary on its performance, but the level of reliance on the executive in financial matters necessarily raises concerns about the judiciary's corporate independence.

*Work Conditions*

Work conditions are generally inadequate, and in some cases are poor enough effectively to interfere with judges' core decision-making functions.

*Appointment and Promotion*

Recent alterations to the rules on selection and career path of judges appear likely to reduce the undue influence discretionary career decisions can place on a judge's core decision-making, but there are still problems with the selection process and tenure in particular. Selection of judges is insufficiently grounded in transparent and neutral procedures. Court presidents serve at the executive's discretion, and judges serve beyond the retirement age at the discretion of the State President and the National Judicial Council.

*Liability*

Judges can be indemnified for damages paid by the State for miscarriages of justice. Because the decision to pursue repayment is discretionary, the executive effectively determines the insurance risk judges face in making decisions.

*Corruption*

Corruption is generally reported to be endemic among judges and court officials. Corruption is encouraged by the existing case management system, which is insufficiently systematic and transparent.

## I. Introduction

The Slovak Republic, or Slovakia, is in the middle of a process of reform, in which many social, political and legal changes have been made to definitively break with the communist legacy and move towards European integration. Almost eleven years after the change of regime in November 1989, after three free elections and with the tenth Minister of Justice in office, basic constitutional and legal guarantees of judicial in-dependence are mostly in place.

A number of changes still need to be addressed, however, including incomplete transformation of the legal and constitutional structures guaranteeing the independence of judges and the judiciary; continued excessive executive involvement in the organisation and administration of the judiciary, and, underlying these, a continuing weak commitment to a legal culture.

### A. Incomplete Legal Transformation

Slovakia is still in a transitional phase, in which basic structural changes still must be carried through. Although it has definitively rejected the communist legacy and divested itself of communist political structures, it has not fully replaced all the formal elements of that system with positive alternatives, but has rather abided with partial reforms only now being completed. Only in this past year have important legal and constitutional reforms been completed, and these still do not adequately address the institutional or corporate elements of the judiciary's independence; for example, the judiciary will still not have a satisfactory constitutional representative when the recent reforms take full effect.

Apart from having declared its orientation towards European structures, Slovakia has not yet adopted a comprehensive reform strategy to guide its fundamental direction, including the organisation of the judiciary. Efforts to develop comprehensive reform have been hampered by the political branches' insufficient appreciation of the importance of the judiciary to political and economic reform, by the polarisation of society and groups within the judiciary, and by institutional traditions favouring strong executive involvement in managing the courts.

Such a strategy, preferably adopted by all the leading political forces, should specify the full range of courts' activities and lead to the reform of criminal, civil, and commercial courts; it should also expand the competency of administrative courts. The documents "The Judiciary – Current Situation and Prospects" (adopted by the Ministry of Justice in 2000) and "The Conception of Stabilisation of Judiciary" (approved by parliamentary committee in 2001[1]) only partly meet the requirements for such a strategy.

The European Commission itself has noted this continuing failure to implement comprehensive reform:

Certain legal steps were taken to strengthen the independence of the judiciary. However, key parts of the reform, in particular the constitutional amendment with regard to the nomination and probationary system, which were set as a short-term priority, have not yet been adopted. Therefore, continued efforts are needed to ensure the independence of the judiciary.[2]

## B. Excessive Executive Involvement

In large part because the legal and regulatory framework has not been comprehensively reformed, the judiciary remains, both in structural terms and in daily practice, unduly reliant on the executive in several important areas, such as court management, budgeting, and appointment of court presidents. The existing judicial councils are merely advisory in character. Owing to this dependence, the level of routine involvement with and supervision by the executive (and legislature, to a lesser degree) is far greater than is desirable for maintenance of an independent judiciary. The recent constitutional and legislative changes represent partial improvements in this regard – but even the planned new National Judicial Council with expanded powers, while unquestionably an improvement, may not go far enough in removing executive involvement in the organisation and administration of the judiciary.

## C. Weak Commitment to a Culture Supporting the Rule of Law

The failure to complete the transformation of the judiciary, and the concomitant persistence of executive involvement in the judiciary's affairs, are themselves functions of the weak commitment to a genuine legal culture which continues to mark Slovak social

---

[1] Approved by the Constitutional Committee of the Parliament on 14 March 2001. Some experts have expressed the viewpoint that a doctrine is not needed; rather, they contend that improving the constitutional and legal environment should take precedence over formulating any kind of doctrine.

[2] European Commission, *2000 Regular Report on Slovakia's Progress towards Accession*, (hereafter *2000 Regular Report*), November 2000, General Evaluation section. The amendment was adopted in February 2001, and is discussed throughout this report.

and political life. To be sure, some public officials, including judges, have embraced a vision of political life consistent with the requirements of European democracy; others, however, fall along a spectrum of views, from a judiciary almost identical to the communist model, to an overreaching notion of independence as immunity from any criticism.

*Public and Political Attitudes*: Politicians at all levels declare their willingness to strengthen the independence of the judiciary; however, contrary opinions are sometimes voiced, particularly in unofficial settings. Some argue that a lack of independence is not the most crucial problem for the judicial branch, but rather that some judges assert an overreaching independence, refusing any kind of control and rejecting the system of checks and balances. While there is some basis for this opinion, it may also suggest an insufficient degree of support for the principle of judicial independence. Quite simply, politicians do not consider judicial independence a priority; very few acknowledge that strengthening judicial independence complements the system of checks and balances. Politicians have justified their reluctance to introduce systemic changes by arguing that judges are insufficiently mature to conduct their own affairs. This attitude has translated into extremely strained relations, especially between the Ministry of Justice and the judges' organisations.

Public opinion of judges is fairly negative, and there is a high level of criticism toward all judges and courts except the Constitutional Court. Moreover, there has been a marked decrease in public confidence in the judiciary,[3] which is seen as unable to deliver services efficiently, and most people still perceive the judiciary to be no more than an extension of the State administration, as it was before November 1989.

The media reports on court decisions in a comprehensive manner. There is no shortage of criticism, which cannot be considered undue influence. At the same time, some journalists write articles of substandard quality which do not reflect a balanced consideration of the reasons for specific, sometimes publicly controversial, judicial decisions.

*Attitudes among Judges*: Some judges' attitudes themselves present obstacles to the judiciary's transformation into an independent, responsible and equal branch.

In spite of the democratic changes in society, there have been few incentives for judges to change their attitudes, and some judges continue to behave as if they were no more than civil servants whose obligation is to fulfil the will of the political branch and to

---

[3] Information from spokesperson of the Ministry of Justice, June 2001, referring to a series of surveys by the Slovak Bureau of Statistics conducted between December 1998 and April 2001 which showed a consistent decline in public confidence in the judiciary.

accept, without reservation, the decisions of State officials. Although they formally express their support for democratic reforms, in specific situations they are reluctant to embrace the consequences of these changes. Signs of apathy, timidity and dependence can be found even among judges who are relatively new to the profession.

At the same time, ironically, some judges have embraced an overly broad conception of judicial independence, equating it with the right to be free of any public control or criticism, and failing to recognise the utility of criticism in supporting an independent and accountable judiciary.

Many judges have difficulty accepting the fact that media legitimately take a critical interest in their work. Until 1989, there was no real need to communicate with the media; judges were not prepared or trained to communicate with the media, and courts did not have the necessary media facilities. They expect that the media will present only objective and truthful opinions, although it is not clear who, other than a censor, would enforce a regime of neutral reporting.

Critical opinions expressed within the community of judges about specific breaches of judicial ethics are not always positively received. Some judges consider such criticism harmful to the judiciary, arguing that it unnecessarily attracts negative attention from citizens and the political branches which they feel reflects badly on the whole judiciary. The effect of this is to shield corrupt and incompetent judges from scrutiny, which over time in fact weakens public and political support for the institution's independent operation.

## D. Organisation of the Judicial System

Prior to the Second World War, Czechoslovakia had a continental-style civil law system. The communist system introduced after the war continued in the civil law tradition, although strongly amplifying its deference to the executive and introducing a number of totalitarian features. The principle of unity of power precluded a separate and independent judiciary; law and its institutions were merely extensions of unitary state-party control, but lacked democratic legitimacy. The courts in the Czechoslovak Socialist Republic did not have any impact on executive decision-making since appeals to the courts on administrative acts were not allowed. A Constitutional Court was never created despite being mentioned in the 1948 Constitution. Thus, the courts were just another state organ performing routine decision-making, not an equal participant in a system of checks and balances. The legacies of communist rule continue to have a profound impact on the Slovak judiciary today.

Following the collapse of the communist regime in 1989, reform of the judiciary and other State institutions was initiated, and some of the important legal documents date from that period. The process continued after the separation of the Czech Republic and Slovakia in 1993.

The current system governing the status of the judiciary and judges is outlined in a number of basic legal provisions, including the Constitution (Articles 141–148), Act No. 335/1991 on Courts and Judges, Act No. 80/1992 on the Administration of Courts, Act No. 420/1990 on Salaries of Judges and Act No. 385/2000 on Judges and Lay Judges. The Constitution's provisions related to the judiciary were amended on 23 February 2001, and Act No. 385/2000 is of relatively recent provenance; thus some of the provisions discussed in this Report have not yet been fully tested in practice.

The judicial system consists of the Constitutional Court and the courts of general jurisdiction. There are three instances of courts of general jurisdiction in Slovakia. The district courts handle the vast majority of cases, although the regional courts handle some cases of first instance as well. In general, however, regional courts serve as appellate courts; three also serve as bankruptcy courts. The Supreme Court in Bratislava acts as the appellate court in those cases that are heard and determined by a regional court acting as a first-instance court. In addition, it decides on extraordinary legal remedies (such as re-trial and complaints on points of law), and passes uniformity decisions to harmonise the decision-making of lower courts.[4] It is also the court of first instance for certain administrative cases. Its management and budget are quite separate from those of the other courts.

There is also a Constitutional Court, which exercises a parallel jurisdiction; the Constitutional Court does not have a superior position vis-à-vis the general courts and does not serve as appellate body for them. The main mission of the Constitutional Court is to check constitutionality at different levels of the decision-making process.[5] However, a recent constitutional amendment[6] has strengthened the decision-making

---

[4] Altogether, there are eight regional courts and 55 district courts. The Supreme Court has 81 judges, regional courts 391, and district courts 786. "2001 report on Slovakia's Progress in its Integration into the EU, September 2000–June 2001", <http://www.europa.sk/english/index.htm> (accessed 10 August 2001).

[5] CONST. SLOVAK REP, Arts. 124–140.

[6] The amendment was adopted by the Parliament by qualified majority on 23 February 2001, signed by the State President, Prime Minister and Chairman of the National Council on 5 March 2001, and published in the Collection of Laws on 19 March as Act No. 90/2001, and except for some provisions which enter into force at the beginning of 2002 it entered into force on 1 July 2001.

competence of this court, so that, as far as basic rights are concerned, it will be possible to challenge the decisions of general courts as well.

There is a system of military courts as well with jurisdiction over soldiers and police. There are three district military courts and one regional military court, and the Supreme Court is the last instance for cases heard by these courts. In comparison with other courts, military courts have significantly lower workloads and their necessity could be questioned. However, there have not been any reports of violations of the principle of judicial independence. Military courts are part of the general court system with all the attributes of the judiciary; though judges are military officers, the rules of their appointment, promotion, discipline are the same as for civilian judges. They are paid from the budget of the Ministry of Justice, although the Ministry of Defence makes additional payments for military ranks.

There is a system of local judicial councils at the regional level and at the Supreme Court, as well as a Council of Judges of the Slovak Republic.[7] The councils have only non-binding, advisory powers. A new National Judicial Council as a constitutional representative of judiciary and with broader powers is to be created by legislation required under the February 2001 constitutional amendment.

In general, the judiciary is not involved in the EU accession process, and there is no public or professional debate on the status and problems of the judiciary in the context of accession.

---

[7] Act No. 335/1991 on Courts and Judges, 1991, as amended under Act No. 307/1995, Secs. 58, 58a, and 58b. Judicial councils are headed by presidents of individual courts who have the right to appoint one-third of each council's members, with the remaining two-thirds elected by judges of the relevant courts at plenary meetings. Judges of the Supreme Court elect members of their council, and judges of regional courts and associated district courts elect members of the regional councils. The Council of Judges consists of presidents and vice-presidents of the various judicial councils, headed by the President of the Supreme Court; the Vice-President is elected by the other members of the Council of Judges.

## II. Constitutional and Legal Foundations of Judicial Independence

Slovakia is in transition as far as arrangements for the institutional independence of the judiciary are concerned. Recent constitutional amendments and legal reforms have partly clarified the individual and institutional independence of judges, although it is too early to confirm their effects in practice. In particular, plans for a new National Judicial Council with expanded powers, while unquestionably an improvement, may not go far enough in removing executive involvement in the organisation and administration of the judiciary. In addition, the corporate independence of the whole judiciary is insufficiently protected, as most legal guarantees contemplate the individual judge.

### A. Guarantees of the Separation of Powers and Judicial Independence

Although the Constitution does not identify an explicit principle of separation of powers, it unambiguously recognises the independence of the courts and individual judges: "(1) Justice in the Slovak Republic is administered by independent and impartial courts. (2) Justice at all levels is administered independently of other state bodies[,]"[8] and that "[j]udges are independent in making decisions and bound solely by the constitution, constitutional law, international treaty and law."[9] Changes to the constitutional provisions ensuring judicial independence require a two-thirds majority in Parliament. Courts and judges are clearly separated from other law enforcement agencies, such as police investigators and prosecutors, which form part of the executive.

### B. Representation of the Judiciary

There is no constitutional or legal norm in Slovakia providing for equal status of the legislative, executive, and judicial branches, and in reality the position of the judiciary is weaker than that of the other two branches. In part this has been due to a lack of clarity about which institution represents the judiciary in relations with other state branches, a matter only partly addressed by the February 2001 constitutional amendment.

---

[8] CONST. SLOVAK REP., Art. 141.

[9] CONST. SLOVAK REP., Art. 144(1).

Until that amendment, the judiciary did not have a constitutional representative of its own; instead, the Minister of Justice and the President of the Supreme Court acted as its spokesmen. This arrangement created several problems for representing the interests of an independent judiciary. The Minister is a member of the executive and therefore has primary loyalty to a different branch; the President of the Supreme Court is a member of the judiciary, but is principally concerned with the Supreme Court, and has no constituent or institutional link to other general courts. Thus, neither of these two officials' opinions and positions necessarily reflected those of the judicial community as a whole. In addition, the mere fact that representational responsibility was divided tended to weaken its effectiveness and bred uncertainty and competition.

## 1. *The Planned National Judicial Council*

The 23 February 2001 amendment mandates the establishment of a National Judicial Council as the constitutional representative of judicial power. The Council will be competent in a range of areas, including proposing candidates for judicial office, deciding on assignment of judges, presenting opinions on the budget.[10] However, important matters such as budgeting and negotiations with other Government institutions and Parliament on behalf of the judiciary will continue to be conducted by the Ministry.

The National Judicial Council will have a balance of judges and appointees from other branches, and will take decisions by simple majority. Nine out of eighteen members of the Council are to be judges of various courts (eight of them elected by the judges themselves) and nine members are to be nominated by other branches of government (three by the president, three by the Parliament and three by the Government). The head of the Council is to be the President of the Supreme Court. All members must have degrees in law.[11]

The Judicial Council has not been created yet, as implementing legislation has not yet been enacted; the process of drafting such legislation is underway. However, it is clear that the version planned under the amendment does not meet the requirements proposed by the judiciary. Before the adoption of the amendment, the Association of Slovak Judges[12] put forward what its own proposal for the composition of the Judicial Council.[13] Among other things, the Association requested that judges form a majority on the Council, and the judiciary should draft, submit and defend its own budget. In addition, the

---

[10] CONST. SLOVAK REP., Art. 141a. The various powers of the Council will be addressed in detail in the appropriate sections.

[11] CONST. SLOVAK REP., Art. 141a.

[12] See section II.F.

[13] Analysis of the Judiciary and the Concept of Judicial Reform, Association of Slovak Judges, 1999.

Association proposed that the Council should have a far broader range of powers, in keeping with the constitutional principles of the courts' independence.

## C. Rules on Incompatibility

Rules on incompatibility generally limit judges' outside activities in a reasonable fashion that contributes to judges' real and perceived impartiality. However, limits on work within the executive are insufficiently robust, and in practice the Ministry of Justice is engaged in an ongoing employer relationship with many judges, in a manner which creates unnecessary opportunities for influence.

Judges are considered to be public servants and judicial office is a public function; only the President and Vice-Presidents of the Supreme Court and judges of the Constitutional Court are considered constitutional representatives and higher State officials.[14] Certain constitutional restrictions apply only to these judges, such as bans on any entrepreneurial activity that could cause a conflict of interest and limitations on supplementary benefits. In addition, these officials are obliged to disclose their property holdings to the chairman of the Parliament and to report any public activity connected with the state or municipal self-governance.

However, the law lays down many restrictions for other judges as well. The office of a judge is incompatible with membership in Parliament, municipal self-governing authority or any office in public administration. In practice, however, the restriction on work in public administration is commonly bypassed, as judges are routinely seconded to the Ministry of Justice to work as directors of departments.[15] While working at the Ministry, judges keep their status as judges, although since 2000 they have not been allowed to adjudicate cases during their secondment. The routine connection with the Ministry defeats the purpose of having restrictions on judges' outside activity, reinforces the Ministry's improper dominance of administrative and managerial functions,[16] and unnecessarily affords the Ministry leverage over the careers of judges, as secondment cannot occur without the discretionary approval of the Ministry.

---

[14] Along with the State President, members of Parliament, Government ministers, state secretaries, heads of the highest State agencies, the Prosecutor General and the Deputy Prosecutor General, Constitutional Statute No. 119, 1995, Art. 2(a).

[15] See Section V.B.

[16] See Section III.

With the adoption and entry into force of Act No. 385/2000 on Judges and Lay Judges, judges are expressly prohibited from becoming members or activists of any political party or movement.[17] However, judges may still stand for election as a candidate for State President, member of the Parliament or a municipal council, in which case the performance of their judicial function is suspended upon registration of candidacy. The suspension lasts three months beyond the announcement of the election results if the judge is not elected, or three months past the term of office to which the judge has been elected – thus, the judicial office does not expire, but is only suspended, which may create conflicts of interest and blurs the distinction between service in the legislative and judicial branches.

Judges are not allowed to conduct any entrepreneurial activity, except administration of their own property, or scientific, pedagogical, literary, publishing and artistic activities. Even these activities are allowed only provided they "do not disrupt or otherwise impair the proper conduct of judicial function, lessen the dignity of the judge or undermine the trust of the public in the independence and impartiality of the judiciary."[18] In addition, all judges are obliged to submit a written statement affirming their compliance with the rules on incompatibility.

A judge may be disqualified from hearing specific cases due to bias for reasons specified in law. A judge is obliged to "refrain from anything that could disrupt the seriousness and dignity of the judicial function or undermine the trust in independent, impartial and equitable decision-making of courts."[19] In addition, judges are obliged to cultivate their professional knowledge, refute any pressure on the performance of their function, act without bias, ensure that their impartiality is not called into doubt, adhere to the (admittedly vague[20]) rules of judicial ethics and stay clear of any influences by interests of political parties.[21]

---

[17] In addition, the recent constitutional amendment provides that "where an appointed judge is a member of a political party or a political movement, he shall terminate his membership prior taking the oath of judicial office." CONST. SLOVAK REP., Art. 145a(1). There has been one case in Slovakia in which a judge manifestly expressed his support for a particular political party. In 1994 a Supreme Court judge ran on a party slate as a candidate for Parliament and issued several statements for the media on politically sensitive cases. Although arguably a violation of the disciplinary rules in force at that time governing judges' impartiality (under Act No. 412/1991 on the Disciplinary Responsibility of Judges, superseded 1 January 2001), no judge or other authority protested, and no competent authority petitioned the relevant disciplinary court. The judge's action would clearly violate the new rules.

[18] Act No. 385/2000 on Judges and Lay Judges, Section 23, paragraphs 1 and 2. Also Art. 145, paragraph 2, for a similar provision on incompatibility of functions.

[19] Act No. 385/2000 on Judges and Lay Judges, Action 30.

[20] See section V.D.

[21] Act No. 385/2000 on Judges and Lay Judges, Action 30; a similar (but less comprehensive) provision can be found in the previous Act on Courts and Judges (Act No. 335/1991, Section 54).

*Disclosure*: All judges are obliged to submit a property statement to the relevant Judicial Council and the Minister of Justice;[22] one former district court president involved in a bribery case refused to submit his property statement, arguing that it was not required by law.

## D. Judges' Associations

Freedom of association for judges is guaranteed in the same way as to any person. There are now three professional associations of judges, the largest being the Association of Slovak Judges, followed by the Union of Slovak Judges and the Association of Women Judges. All three address issues of judicial independence and corruption. However, many judges are not members of any organised association.

The Association of Slovak Judges, the first professional association representing judges, was founded in early 1990, almost immediately after the revolution of 1989. The newer Union of Slovak Judges was created by judges from the Zilina region as a response to the removal of the presidents of regional and district courts in that city by the Minister of Justice, in spite of a vote of confidence in them by a majority of their colleagues in 1999.[23] Thus, the creation of the Union of Slovak Judges in this sense is commonly perceived as a political step aimed against the personal policy of the Ministry of Justice; it is also evidence of the polarised state of the judiciary, which limits the associations' effectiveness in representing judges and protecting judicial independence.

Judges are allowed to join trade unions as well, and some of them are members of a trade union for public servants. There are no reports suggesting that membership endangers judicial independence; nevertheless, the majority of judges prefer membership in their own professional organisations. The main thing they expect their organisations to do is to come to their defence – especially against politicians and the media.

---

[22] Act No. 385/2000 on Judges and Lay Judges, Sections 31 and 32.

[23] The judges were defending a colleague implicated with another judge in a bribery scandal. See section V.D.

## III. Administration of the Court System and Judicial Independence

Even with the planned creation of the National Judicial Council, the Minister of Justice still retains significant policy-making and administrative authority, while the authority of court presidents is limited to specific administrative matters for which they are ultimately answerable to the Ministry. Through the officials within the Ministry, the Minister can influence any decision or policy of court presidents relating to court administration.

Management of the judiciary on a national level rests with the Ministry of Justice. The Ministry administers regional and district courts directly or through the court presidents. Only the Supreme Court is administered directly by its President without the involvement of the Ministry.

The Ministry of Justice is directly responsible for determining the rules on caseload,[24] the number of judges in individual courts, and allocation of the judiciary's budget to individual courts as well as supervision of expenditures.[25] In addition, on the basis of requests for court presidents, the Ministry also is responsible for assessing personnel needs and the creation of new positions within courts.

To date, no independent body for the administration of courts has been created, and it is not clear if the National Judicial Council will have any authority to manage the court system, as the constitutional amendment does not grant the Council any administrative powers, but does allow it to have other competencies stipulated by law. It is also unclear whether the National Judicial Council will have its own institutional structures or will rely on administrative support from the Ministry.

The day-to-day operation of the courts is supervised and managed by court presidents, who therefore act both as judges and as state administration officials with responsibilities and obligations towards the Ministry of Justice – a position that potentially compromises their independence. Court presidents are directly responsible for recruitment of court personnel and supervision of court premises and facilities. Regional court presidents distribute the funds allocated to them among the lower district courts; the Ministry of Justice and regional court presidents also jointly supervise the utilisation of allocated funds by the district courts. Court presidents are responsible for organisation of the system of court records, archives, and statistics in accordance with regulations issued by the Ministry

---

[24] See section VI.B.

[25] See section IV.A.

of Justice. In collaboration with the Minister of Justice and the judges' associations, court presidents also are responsible for determining how the benefits for judges and other court employees are to be distributed.

Responsibility for judicial training rests with the Ministry's Education Department and the presidents of regional courts; the Association of Slovak Judges is informally involved in the training of candidates for judicial office. No independent educational agency of training for sitting judges or systematic training system of training by the state exists. Such training is carried out sporadically on an *ad hoc* basis or, at most, within the framework of a six-month education plan by the Ministry of Justice.

Another problem is that the court leaders are responsible for the efficiency of any economic activity of their court, without special training in the field of economical or personal management. Instituting a system of independent professional court administrators might remove a potential source of pressure on court presidents and improve court management.

# IV. Financial Autonomy and Level of Funding

## A. Budgeting Process

Judges have almost no involvement in the process of developing or defending the judiciary's financial allocation, and are almost entirely reliant on the executive in financial matters, both for budgeting and for supervision of spending, to a level which necessarily raises concerns about the judiciary's corporate independence.

Approval of the budget of the judiciary involves annual intra-governmental negotiations, in which the Minister of Justice negotiates on behalf of the judiciary.[26] There is no separate budget for the regional and district courts in the state budget law, and regional and district courts are financed from the chapter of the Ministry of Justice; the Constitutional Court and Supreme Court (beginning in 2001) are the only courts with a separate chapter in the budget. Thus regional and district courts are fully dependent on the Ministry of Justice for their financing and, indirectly, on the Ministry of Finance, which sets restrictions on the amount of money spent by individual budget chapters' administrators.

Initial figures for the draft budget – including district courts under their purview – are collected by the regional court presidents and presented to the Ministry of Justice. There is no clear methodology for initial calculations either at the courts level or at the Ministry of Justice; the previous year's figures usually serve as a basis for a new draft, and the Ministry of Justice is also guided by the budgetary framework developed by the Ministry of Finance. The rest of the preparation process, including the budget's adoption by the Government and Parliament, takes place without judges' participation.

The Minister of Justice is the administrator and distributor of funds for general courts. Ministry officials may receive various requests from court presidents, but the decision as to the amounts allocated to individual regional courts is up to the Minister. Funds are allocated to the regional courts at the beginning of the year. The presidents of regional courts distribute the funds allocated to them among individual district courts.[27] This system of distribution is not sufficiently objective or transparent, and creates conditions for dependencies, both in the first phase (distribution from the Ministry to the regional

---

[26] The basic law regulating the budgeting process, in addition to annual budget laws, is Act No. 305/1995 on Budgetary Rules.

[27] Information from spokesperson of the Ministry of Justice, June 2001.

courts) and in the second phase (distribution from the regional courts to the district courts).[28]

As far as budgetary supervision is concerned, the principle that "everyone controls his own budget" is applied, meaning that court presidents, with the help of their financial managers, are responsible for fund utilisation, with certain supervisory competencies existing between regional and district courts. The Ministry of Justice exercises overall control over the budgetary discipline.

No transfers are permitted among individual chapters of the State budget, although there is no prohibition against a transfer between two courts by mutual agreement of the respective presidents and with the approval of the Ministry of Justice. During the fiscal year, state budget corrections are possible and have in fact been made, affecting the amount of funding available to the courts.

There is no evidence of any attempts to "blackmail" the judiciary in the budgeting process by making funding directly conditional on its performance. Nonetheless, the current system of budgeting can have indirect adverse effects on the independence of the judiciary. The introduction of a special budget chapter for the whole judiciary, within which every regional court would have its separate chapter, could improve matters, especially if objective guarantees, such as funding minimums or block grants, were employed. Such a "regional model" of fund distribution could limit subjective manipulation of the judiciary through the budget. However, the recent constitutional amendments have left the current court budgeting system intact.

The budget law for the year 2001 allocates 4.15 billion SKK (€ 95,555,780), to the Ministry of Justice, and 77.5 million SKK (€ 1,781,529) to the Supreme Court – in all, 1.95 percent of state budget expenditures.[29] From the Ministry of Justice's budget, 1.6 billion SKK are allocated for the judiciary – 0.72 percent of the state budget for 2001, or roughly one-third of the Ministry's total budget.[30]

---

[28] OSI roundtable, March 2001. *Explanatory Note: OSI held a roundtable meeting in Bratislava in March 2001 to invite critique of the present report in draft form. Experts present included representatives of the Government, the Parliament, the judiciary, the media and civil organisations. No statements are attributable to any particular participant.*

[29] Act No. 472/2000 on State Budget, Annex 3.

[30] Information from spokesperson of the Ministry of Justice, June 2001.

## B. Work Conditions

Work conditions vary dramatically between courts, but in general are inadequate. Often they are not of a sufficient standard to ensure that judges will be free to focus on their core decision-making function; in some cases, conditions are poor enough to effectively interfere with that function.

There are no objective norms developed for standard space, equipment, and technology. It appears, however, that judges' work conditions are better than those of police, at about the same level as those of prosecutors, and worse than in the state administration.

Judges often work in inadequately equipped and dilapidated offices, which they sometimes have to share. Judges receive printed collections of legislation only, and in some courts just one copy is provided per judicial panel. Availability of other necessary professional literature (such as annotated codes) is so limited so that even regional courts often assign certain publications to panels of judges rather to individual judges.[31]

Substantial differences in the working conditions of individual courts were created by the administrative-territorial reform instituted in 1996. In some regions new court facilities have been built or old ones renovated, but in others there has been little improvement.

Caseload has been increasingly heavy since 1992, and as a consequence the number of unsettled cases continues to grow.[32] The average number of cases assigned annually to one judge in 1990 was 217.5, and a judge settled an average of 162.9 cases per year. In 1992, these numbers rose to 368.4 assigned cases and 258 settled cases, and by 1999 they climbed to 531.8 assigned cases and 387.4 settled cases.[33]

Certain courts are almost unable to function because of a shortage of other professional and clerical support staff. There are no clear norms developed for determination of a necessary court staff, but even existing quotas concerning support staff traditionally go unfulfilled. Being employed as a member of court support staff is not considered

---

[31] Act No. 385/2000 on Judges and Lay Judges, Section 35, para. 1 provides, *inter alia*, that a judge is entitled to receive all the legal regulations, professional literature and other information indispensable to the performance of the judicial function.

[32] See "The Judiciary – Current Situation and Prospects, Ministry of Justice, April 2000", Annex 1. This is a conceptual document of the Justice Ministry that summarises the current status of the judiciary with suggestions for improving the situation.

[33] Figures for 2000 are not available.

to be a lucrative position, and the quality of the staff is therefore fairly low. By the end of 2000 there were 3,473 court employees, including the Supreme Court but not including military courts – a fairly low ratio of court staff to judges of 2.75:1.[34] Under these circumstances, judges waste much of their time on technical, preparatory tasks.

The state of computerisation of the courts is quite poor. There is no e-mail communication among judges and a vast majority of judges are not familiar with the use of the Internet. The efficient functioning of the judiciary cannot be improved without widespread introduction of information technology in courts and connection to information databases, in order to improve the quality of court documents, to speed up clerical work, and especially to ensure swift communication within the court system and with outside entities.

There are great differences between courts as far as computerisation is concerned. The judiciary, including the Supreme Court, as a whole utilises about 1400 computers, used mostly by court staff for typing and printing. Some 220 judges at higher of court levels have their own computers.[35] Some courts have a computer available to judges in the library, while other courts have no computer reserved exclusively for use by the judges.

There is an obsolete system of court reporting; no stenography is allowed and thus clerks must use typing machines during court hearings, although some courts have started to use computers for this purpose. The judges in criminal cases must dictate records to typists; in civil cases they are allowed to dictate into tape-recorders and the text is subsequently transcribed by typists. This means that there is no direct record of proceedings at courts. Judges are obliged to dictate every statement in direct speech. However, in spite of the opportunity for correction, this system is not only slow but also prone to misuse, abuse by a partial judge, or corruption.

## C. Compensation

Compensation is generally adequate to ensure that judges are not unduly exposed to economic pressures that might encourage corruption.

Salaries of regular judges are comparable with those public prosecutors or members of Parliament, to which they are scaled. Supreme Court judges receive salaries comparable to those of Government ministers. The current average salary of judges is about triple

---

[34] Information from spokesperson of the Ministry of Justice, June 2001.

[35] Information from spokesperson of the Ministry of Justice, June 2001.

the average salary in the Republic. Nevertheless, a judge's salary is not particularly attractive, given the more lucrative opportunities in the private sector.

Salaries of judges are fixed by law, and are calculated at the beginning of each year according the Government decree fixing the amount of average salary in the country. Moreover, it is possible to reflect also the rate of inflation every half a year, provided it is higher than ten percent.

There is no possibility to reduce salaries, although occasionally the Government has chosen not to make the recalculation to reflect the rate of inflation, which, in practical terms is the equivalent of a reduction. Also, the State budget law may provide that salaries for certain professions (such as State officials and members of Parliament) will remain at the level of the previous year; this has occurred several times during the last decade and has affected the representatives of all three branches of government. Judges' salaries can also be reduced for a limited period for disciplinary reasons.

Currently, the salary of a judge ranges from 70 to 130 percent of the salary payable to a Member of Parliament, which is around € 760 per month. The new salary scale introduced by Act No. 385/2000 – introducing ranges from 90 to 125 percent – will not enter into force until 2003. In accordance with this law, salaries of regular court judges will range from 90 to 125 percent of the salary of a Member of Parliament. Salary differentials depend on the instance of the court and experience as a judge. Experience in other legal professions may also be taken into account but the decision lies with the Minister of Justice. The salary of a judge of the Supreme Court is fixed at 130 percent of the salary of a Member of Parliament.[36]

In addition to their base salary, judges are entitled to a range of additional benefits, such as payments of ten to 20 percent of their base salaries for court presidents and vice-presidents, overtime, anniversary bonuses.[37]

Upon retirement judges do not enjoy any special treatment. Since the pension of a retired judge is considerably lower than the judicial salary, older judges have rarely been eager to retire. The new Act on Judges and Lay Judges introduces a change in this area; from 2003, retiring judges will be entitled to a supplement to their old-age pension commensurate to their length of service, which may amount to as much as 150 percent of the basic pension (3.75 percent of the basic salary for each year with a maximum of 40 years of performance).[38] Upon retirement, a judge is also entitled to a severance payment equal to ten months' salary.

---

[36] Act of 5 October 2000 on Judges and Lay Judges, Arts. 66–67.

[37] Act of 5 October 2000 on Judges and Lay Judges, Art. 65–80.

[38] Act of 5 October 2000 on judges and Lay Judges, Art. 95.

## V. Judicial Office

The rules addressing the selection and career path of judges have been significantly altered by the February 2001 constitutional amendment and Act No. 385/2000 on Judges and Lay Judges. While the full effects of those changes will not be clear for some time, they generally appear set to reduce the level of undue influence which discretionary career decisions can place on a judge's core decision-making. There are still problems connected with the selection process and tenure in particular.

### A. Selection

Even with the recent changes, the process of selecting judges is insufficiently grounded in transparent and neutral procedures that would limit the opportunities for undue executive or intra-judicial interference.

The Constitution does not stipulate in detail the procedures by which one may become a judge, saying only that judges are to be appointed by the State President on proposal of the new National Judicial Council.[39] The procedures have been relatively recently modified by Act No. 385/2000 on Judges and Lay Judges.

A judicial examination constitutes the basic precondition for appointment to judicial office.[40] Thereafter, candidates must complete a process of selection for the individual courts to which they ultimately hope to be assigned.[41] For each vacancy, the regional court president establishes an *ad hoc* selection commission, and appoints five members on the proposal of the judicial council of the relevant regional court; members of the commission elect their chair from among themselves.[42] The Commission will then forward recommendations to the new National Judicial Council, which will make proposals to the State President for appointment. There is no system of appeal against any decisions in the process.

---

[39] CONST. SLOVAK REP., Art. 145, paras. 1 and 2, providing that a prospective judge must be a citizen of Slovakia, at least 30 years old, have a university degree in law, and meet the conditions of eligibility to be elected to Parliament. Act. No. 385/2000 on Judges and Lay Judges further stipulates a clean criminal record and moral integrity as criteria for the appointment of judges and lay judges.

[40] The Minister of Justice may also recognise other examinations – such as that given to prosecutors – in lieu of the regular judicial examination or, under certain conditions, may waive this requirement altogether.

[41] Act No. 385/2000 on Judges and Lay Judges. Section 5.

[42] Act No. 385/2000 on Judges and Lay Judges, Sections 28 and 29. Under these provisions, the selection procedure is designed to verify the skills and capabilities, professional knowledge, health condition and mental composure of candidates.

Any judicial apprentices working at the court in question, may, at the discretion of the court president, be given priority for selection. There is no pre-established system for accepting candidates for apprenticeship. The Minister of Justice determines the number of judicial apprentices, while presidents of regional courts organise their selection and admission to various courts using a variety of methods, such as exams, interviews, and psychological tests. The selection of apprentices is therefore quite discretionary, and tends to encourage the apprentices to unnecessary deference towards the court president. The "Concept for Stabilisation of the Judiciary"[43] proposes the introduction of obligatory and transparent selection procedures for judicial apprentices, including examination by a board including representatives of the courts, the Ministry, and the Association of Slovak Judges.

*Court Presidents*: The selection and appointment of regional and district court presidents remains in the hands of the Minister of Justice. No objective standards have been adopted for their appointment. The Minister is obliged to ask the relevant judicial council for its opinion, but is not bound by what the council says.[44] After the 1998 elections, the Minister of Justice initiated informal co-operation with judges in the appointment of court presidents and vice-presidents. Judges, the Association of Judges and the local judicial councils were given an opportunity to freely express their opinions and nominate candidates for the above offices. Although under no legal obligation to do so, the Minister generally respects their opinion in making appointments.

Under the February 2001 constitutional amendment, the President and Vice-President of the Supreme Court are appointed by the State President from among Supreme Court judges, on the non-binding advice of its Judicial Council.[45]

There are no criteria for an appointment of the presidents of judicial panels who, prior to the adoption of Act No. 358/2000, were appointed by the president of the relevant regional court or of the Supreme Court. The new law introduces an obligatory appointment procedure for presidents of judicial panels; the president of the court still formally appoints the president of the judicial panel, but is bound by the order of

---

[43] See "The Conception of Stabilisation of Judiciary".

[44] Act No. 335/91 on Courts and Judges, Art. 58, para. 8(g), provides that the judicial council "gives opinions" on the nominations of court officials. During 1996 and 1997, however, there were two cases when the then Minister of Justice sought no opinion from the judicial council on the appointment of court officials.

[45] Under the previous rules, the Government proposed a candidate to the Parliament for a vote; both the Council of Judges and the Judicial Council of the Supreme Court opposed the nomination in 1996 of the current President of the Supreme Court.

candidates established by a selection commission.[46] In addition, the relevant judicial council issues opinions on individual candidates.

*Constitutional Court*: The Constitutional Court has ten members appointed by the State President from a list proposed by Parliament;[47] the recent constitutional amendment raises the number of members to 13. The process is openly political, even though the Constitutional Court exercises judicial functions.

## B. Tenure, Transfer, Retirement, and Removal

The rules addressing the career of a sitting judge have been significantly altered by the recent changes in the Constitution and law, and their full effects are not yet clear; however, the formal changes appear to increase judicial independence. Remaining problems include the susceptibility of court presidents to re-appointment pressures and discretionary termination of judges serving beyond the retirement age.

### 1. Tenure

The probationary period for judges has been recently abolished, and regional and district judges are now appointed to life terms. There is no term of office for regional and district court presidents or vice-presidents; the Minister of Justice can appoint and recall them at any time. The usual practice is that an incoming Minister replaces a number of court presidents and vice-presidents without explanation. In this context court presidents are undoubtedly susceptible to political pressures. The President and Vice-President of the Supreme Court and chamber presidents are appointed to five-year terms by the State President, and thus may be susceptible to pressure if they seek a second term.

### 2. Transfer

Judges may be assigned to a particular court or relocated from one court to another only with their consent, except on the basis of a final decision by a disciplinary court. With their consent, judges may be temporarily assigned to another court or to work as advisors at various other bodies, such as training institutes, the Constitutional Court,

---

[46] The selection commission is composed in the same fashion as the one described for judicial appointments.

[47] Act No. 38/1993 on the Organisation of the Constitutional Court and its Procedural Rules, Art. 2.

the Office of the State President, or the Office of Parliament; in practice, most judges are appointed to the Ministry of Justice. Temporary assignment may not exceed one year in a period of three years, with the exception of assignment to a "central body of the state administration of judges and to an institution undertaking judges' education."[48] In practice, these exceptions mean that a judge can be assigned to the Ministry of Justice indefinitely. Decisions on temporary assignment are generally made by the Minister. However, when a temporary assignment concerns transfer to or from the Supreme Court the decision is made by the President of the Supreme Court in agreement with the Minister; when a temporary assignment takes place within the circuit of a regional court the decision is made by the president of that regional court.[49]

The February 2001 constitutional amendment will necessitate modification of current law, as it vests the authority to decide on the assignment and transfer of judges in the new National Judicial Council.[50] The rules on temporary appointment are not affected.

## 3. Retirement

Judges may resign at their own will. There is no mandatory retirement age for judges; however, the State President may, on the advice of the new Judicial Council, recall a judge at any time after the judge has reached 65 years of age. Thus older judges who wish to continue in office effectively serve at the pleasure of the State President and the Council.

## 4. Removal

Under the February 2001 constitutional amendment, the State President, on the advice of the new National Judicial Council, may recall judges who have been convicted of an intentional crime;[51] have been sentenced to imprisonment or probation for any other crime; have committed a disciplinary offence incompatible with the judicial function; no longer meet basic eligibility requirements; or are prevented for reasons of health from performing judicial duties for more than one year.[52]

---

[48] Act No. 385/2000 on Judges and Lay Judges, Section 12(5).

[49] Act No. 385/2000 on Judges and Lay Judges, Section 13.

[50] CONST. SLOVAK REP., Art. 141a, para. 3b.

[51] Such a situation has occurred only once when, in September 2000, the Parliament removed a judge who had been sentenced by a Czech court for committing a criminal offence connected with corruption. See sections V.D. and II.F (referring to a colleague implicated in the same incident).

[52] CONST. SLOVAK REP., Art. 147 (amended).

In Summer 2000, the Government asked Parliament to remove the President of the Supreme Court before the expiry of his five-year term, on the grounds that he had not fulfilled his professional duties in accordance with the ethical principles governing the judiciary;[53] there was considerable debate concerning the constitutionality of such a move. Ultimately the President of the Supreme Court was not recalled, partly as a result of a report delivered by the independent UN Rapporteur on judicial independence, Mr Dato Param Cummaraswammy. The UN report argued that judges and officials for state administration of the judiciary have a right to fair procedures in the event of their removal, regardless of how they were nominated to their posts, as long as their nomination was *lege artis*.

*a. Lustration*: Two years after the change of regime in 1989, each judge was subjected to a "lustration" (screening) according to the Lustration Law.[54] Judges who co-operated with the former communist secret service were barred from continuing in office; members of the Communist Party were allowed to stay with the exception of those who held the highest positions at the level of the Republic, regions or districts. This means that, for instance, judges who chaired party organisations at courts were allowed to stay.

## C. Evaluation and Promotion

Prior to the adoption of Act 385/2000 on Judges and Lay Judges, evaluation of judges was the responsibility of court presidents; there were no criteria other than quantity of work measured against caseload standards set by the Ministry of Justice. The former law did not prescribe any obligatory system for the appraisal of judges and only provided that the regional judicial councils should "co-operate in the appraisal of judges[;]"[55] ethical considerations or assessments of the quality of court decisions played no part in the evaluation process, resulting in unsystematic, unbalanced, and subjective appraisals. The new Act improves matters.

The new law prescribes mandatory appraisal of judges once every five years, as well as during every selection procedure and whenever a judge so requests. Judges are appraised by their court presidents based on a review of their decisions prepared by a commission appointed by the relevant judicial council, opinions of appellate courts, and the president's own knowledge of the judge's work. The judge may express an opinion on the appraisal and request further specification or elaboration. In addition, at the end of 2000, the

---

[53] *Regular Report 2000*, section 2.
[54] Act No.451/1991 on Lustration, 1991.
[55] Act No. 335/1991, Section 58.

Ministry of Justice introduced a new system of evaluation that ranks cases in terms of difficulty, thus reducing the incentive for judges to avoid taking complicated or time-consuming cases. At this point, there is no data available to estimate the effectiveness of this new system.

These changes bring more transparency and more consistent standards into the evaluation process. On the other hand, the appraisal still remains largely in the hands of presidents who are appointed by the Minister of Justice. The Ministry of Justice retains the right to prescribe the number of cases, and the ratio of reversals remains a criterion for assessment. Furthermore, it is not yet clear what consequences a negative appraisal has for a judge. There is a proposal to empower the State President to remove a judge on the proposal of the National Judicial Council in the event a judge receives multiple negative appraisals.

The February 2001 constitutional amendment and Act No. 385/2000 on Judges and Lay Judges have introduced a new system of career advancement for judges moving to courts of higher instance. The new law establishes an obligation to publicise every vacancy and carry out a competitive selection process, while the constitutional amendment shifts the power to decide on advancement to the National Judicial Council.

## D. Discipline

### 1. Liability

The current system of liability for miscarriages of justice creates a serious risk of economic interference by the executive with judicial decision-making. The liability for damages sustained in connection with judges' wrongful conduct in the course of their duties lies with the State; however, the State has a right of recourse against the judge or another court official who took the decision which caused damage. In order to address the issue of potential personal liability, judges contract for personal insurance coverage. This arrangement seems quite extraordinary: Because the decision to recover damages would be at the discretion of the executive, judges may be reluctant to rule according their conscience in cases involving large sums or about which there is political controversy, especially if the executive signals its intention about pursuing any eventual repayment. In effect, the executive is in the position of increasing or decreasing the effective insurance risk the judge faces for decisions. To date, no cases testing how the system would work in practice have been reported.

A judge may not be sanctioned by an authority that is otherwise competent to penalise minor offences (such as the police issuing a fine for speeding). Rather, the competent authority must forward the case to the president of the court, who has discretion to decide how to proceed concerning minor offences, including possible prosecution. As regards serious criminal liability, as of 1 July 2001 the power to consent to criminal prosecution or detention of a judge was transferred from the Parliament to the Constitutional Court.[56]

## 2. Disciplinary Procedures

Ethical standards for the judicial profession are not defined in the law. However, Act No. 385/2000 on Judges and Lay Judges contains an indirect reference to ethical standards by, among other things, stipulating a clean criminal record and moral integrity as criteria for the appointment of judges and lay judges.

In addition, the provisions for holding judges liable for disciplinary proceedings suggest general ethical standards. A disciplinary offence is defined as the deliberate non-fulfilment or infringement of a judge's duties which creates justified doubts about that judge's independence, conscientiousness and objectivity in giving judgement, impartiality in regard to participants in proceedings, or efforts to end court proceedings fairly and without undue delays.[57] This is an exhaustive, though quite abstract, list of grounds for disciplinary responsibility.

The Minister of Justice and court presidents settle complaints against judges. There is no formal procedure of how to handle complaints; in practice, the court president investigates the complaint and answers the complainant, and in cases of serious or substantiated allegations, the case may go to disciplinary proceedings.

The number of disciplinary proceedings in the last ten years has fluctuated between seven to 14 cases per year. In 2000 there were 13 disciplinary cases.[58] The most common punishments are reprimands and salary reductions.[59] It seems that the members of disciplinary courts are reluctant to use more serious punishments, even in more serious cases such as altering case assignments in order to be assigned a particular case in which the judge is biased in favour of one of the parties.

---

[56] CONST. SLOVAK REP., Art. 136.

[57] Act No. 385/2000 on Judges and Lay Judges, Section 116.

[58] Information from spokesperson of the Ministry of Justice, June 2001.

[59] An elaborate system of disciplinary measures, which include reduction in salary, suspension, transfer to another court and removal, is envisioned in Act on Judges and Lay Judges, Art. 117.

Prior to the entry into force of Act No. 385/2000 on Judges and Lay Judges, individual judges faced serious constraints on their independence through the disciplinary process, which was controlled by the Ministry of Justice and the court presidents that appointed the disciplinary court members.[60] Act No. 385/2000 on Judges and Lay Judges now provides that the disciplinary court will be elected and dismissed by the new National Judicial Council from among candidates nominated by the relevant judicial councils, in a manner that ensures adequate representation of judges from all types and levels of general courts. Thus the disciplinary court of first instance will now consist of five members – two district court judges, two regional court judges and one Supreme Court judge. Only Supreme Court judges may sit as members of the seven-person appellate disciplinary court.[61] Under the new Constitutional amendment, the Constitutional Court is the responsible disciplinary authority for the President and Vice-President of the Supreme Court.[62]

Disciplinary proceedings are public, and the accused judge has the right to be heard and to retain counsel; indeed, the procedure is similar to the criminal procedure, with every right of the accused guaranteed, including a right of appeal.

*Code of Ethics*: Last year the Association of Slovak Judges adopted a "Code of Ethics", which, however, is only an internal document informally binding on members of the Association. At its 1999 annual meeting, the Association agreed to submit this document to the judicial councils for approval, though none have yet adopted it for use. Judges themselves are divided as to the appropriate approach to ethical rules, with some arguing for development of systematic and comprehensive ethical rules, others arguing that general principles or even no elaborated rules are preferable. Whatever the merits of these highly divergent opinions, the current lack of clear regulations for enforcement of ethical standards produces uncertainty among judges, and hardly encourages the general public to see the judiciary as a model of ethical behaviour, rather than as a corrupt group not subject to any rules.

---

[60] And, in the case of military judges, by the Minister of Defence.
[61] Act 385/2000 on Judges and Lay Judges, Section 119.
[62] CONST. SLOVAK REP., Art. 136.

# VI. Intra-Judicial Relations

## A. Relations with Higher Courts

There are generally no problems of decisional interference in the relationship between the higher and lower courts.

According to the law, judges are independent in the exercise of judicial functions, and interpret laws and other generally binding legal regulations according to the best of their knowledge and belief; they make decisions equitably, fairly, and without undue delay.[63] Appeal courts can uphold, change or reverse decisions of lower courts and, if they change the decisions, they can issue binding instructions for lower courts.[64]

Lower judges are not officially subordinated to higher judges, and there are no systems of supervision or mentoring. Such a system exists only for judicial apprentices, who during their entire training period are supervised by judges of the district court to which they are assigned. However, judges attend various training events and other educational activities, where more or less formal consultations with higher judges take place.

The jurisprudence of higher courts, including the Supreme Court, is not officially binding on lower courts. However, in practice, higher courts request that similar cases be decided similarly in order to ensure legal certainty and consistent interpretation and application of law. For this purpose, the Chambers of the Supreme Court select cases of general importance to publicise; courts are expected to conform to those rulings.

## B. Case Management and Relations with Court Presidents

The existing case management system is insufficiently systematic and transparent, and unnecessarily encourages corrupt practices harmful to the decisional independence and impartiality of judges.

As noted above, regional and district court administration is the responsibility of court presidents and vice-presidents, under the supervision of the Ministry of Justice. While court presidents are not allowed to influence the content of particular decisions,

---

[63] Act No. 385/2000 on Judges and Lay Judges, Art. 2, para 2. See also CONST. SLOVAK REP., Art. 144.

[64] For example, the Criminal Procedure Code and Civil Procedure Code provide that opinion of higher courts are binding on lower courts.

they can control the smooth functioning of the judicial system, including taking judges' level of activity in resolving cases into account when evaluating their performance.

Each court president formulates a system for assigning cases, with the non-binding advice of the relevant judicial council. Some presidents try to avoid subjectivism by assigning cases on the basis of a rotation formula; others do not make such an effort. Several district court presidents assign all defamation-related cases to the same pre-determined judge; as defamation complaints are most often filed by senior political figures, this practice has made it possible to exert political pressure on the judges assigned.

"Judge-shopping" is thus widely believed to be a common phenomenon, as is corruption of court presidents or court clerks responsible for the actual assignment of cases (or for picking the moment at which a case is introduced into the recording system, which in a rotation assignment model can determine which judge receives the case). Introduction of a truly randomised case allocation, perhaps employing special software, would minimise this danger; so far, only in Banska Bistrica district court has such a system been introduced.

Otherwise, case flow management of any particular case is in the hands of the judge assigned. The law prescribes no rules apart from certain time limits on issuing decisions. The system of recording is obsolete.

Under Ministry of Justice Regulation No. 66 of 1992, revocation of assigned cases is possible only when there is a significant imbalance between the workloads of different judges, or in the event of a prolonged illness or similar incapacity. However, court presidents retain a significant degree of discretion in determining when these conditions obtain.

To some degree, judges are dependent on court presidents in obtaining additional payments, such as substitution bonuses and anniversary bonuses.

# VII. Enforcement and Corruption

## A. Enforcement

The Government, prosecution, police, and other State authorities generally respect court decisions. Acting against a court decision would also invite strong criticism from the media. Enforcement problems have been encountered in the private rather than in the public sphere. A system of private executors has been in operation for four years. Using this system, the executors take about 20 percent of the value of executed property. Private execution of court decisions seems to have alleviated the problems of enforcement to some degree; however, there is also widespread suspicion of corruption in private enforcement.[65]

## B. Persistent Corruption

While difficult to prove definitively, corruption is generally reported to be widespread and endemic among judges and court officials. According to several opinion polls, judges are considered among the most corrupt groups in society, and from 15 to 25 percent of businessmen reported paying bribes to judges or staff. The Commission itself has noted a study in which one-fifth of parties to court proceedings reported having "experienced corrupt behaviour from judges. Bribes were given either to influence the outcome of the cases or to accelerate their proceedings."[66]

There is a general public perception that "corruption is widespread in the...justice system[.]"[67] Plaintiffs and defendants reportedly often seek to influence the result of a trial by using various illegal methods, and the situation has reportedly got worse over the past three years.[68] Even honest judges can be affected by this environment, and can be concerned their decisions will lead to suspicion that they have taken bribes.

---

[65] Information from spokesperson of the Ministry of Justice, June 2001.

[66] *Regular Report 2000*, Section 2.

[67] J. Anderson, "Corruption in Slovakia: Results of Diagnostic Surveys, Prepared at the Request of the Government of the Slovak Republic by the World Bank and the United States Agency for International Development", World Bank (Slovak version 18 September 2000), <http://www.worldbank.sk/data/anticorruption.pdf> (English version, accessed 22 August 2001) (hereafter World Bank Corruption Report), p. vii (noting also that half of enterprise managers surveyed by the World Bank reported that corruption is "very widespread in the justice system[.]").

[68] World Bank Corruption Report, pp. 34–35 (noting that one-quarter of all households involved in proceedings "gave something 'special' to a court employee, judge, or attorney.").

The most necessary reforms would strengthen not only the rights of judges but also systems of supervision, because as long as corruption is prevalent in society, judges' independence alone is no guarantee of impartiality, as even an independent judge may readily accept bribes – perhaps with even greater impunity. The effect, over time, will be to weaken public trust in and support of the judiciary – which will be seen as mere license or impunity – with consequent further weakening of societal support for fending off encroachment by the political branches. Therefore, transparency of court procedures and effective control by the media and watchdog groups are crucial elements in the endeavour to strengthen the judiciary.

# Judicial Independence
# in Slovenia

# Table of Contents

Executive Summary ........................................ 434

I. Introduction .................................................. 437

   A. Residual Areas of Undue Executive
      or Legislative Involvement ........................ 437
      1. Selection ............................................ 437
      2. Monitoring Structures and
         Ministry of Justice Involvement ......... 438
      3. Involvement in the Budget and
         Salary Determination ......................... 438
      4. Compensation .................................... 438

   B. Lack of Public Trust and Commitment
      to a Fully Independent Judiciary ............. 438

   C. Judicial Accountability ............................ 440
      1. Weak Efforts at Self-Policing
         of the Judiciary ................................... 440
      2. Disclosure .......................................... 440

   D. The Judiciary and the
      EU Accession Process .............................. 441

   E. Organisation of the Court System ............ 441

II. Constitutional and Legal Foundations
    of Judicial Independence ............................. 444

    A. Guarantees of the Separation of Powers
       and Judicial Independence ...................... 444

    B. Representation of the Judiciary ................ 445

    C. Rules on Incompatibility ......................... 447
       1. Disclosure .......................................... 448

    D. Judges' Associations ................................ 449

| III. | Administration of the Court System and Judicial Independence .......................... 450 |
|---|---|
| | A. The Judicial Council ............................... 451 |
| | B. Ministry of Justice .................................. 451 |
| | C. Court Presidents and Personnel Councils .......................... 453 |
| IV. | Financial Autonomy and Level of Funding .... 454 |
| | A. Budgeting Process .................................. 454 |
| | B. Work Conditions ................................... 456 |
| |     1. Training ........................................... 457 |
| | C. Compensation ....................................... 457 |
| V. | Judicial Office ............................................... 460 |
| | A. Selection Process .................................... 460 |
| |     1. Appointment of Court Presidents ...... 461 |
| |     2. Appointment of Supreme Court President ............... 461 |
| | B. Tenure, Retirement, Transfer and Removal ........................................... 462 |
| |     1. Tenure and Retirement ..................... 462 |
| |     2. Transfer ............................................ 463 |
| |     3. Removal ........................................... 664 |
| | C. Evaluation and Promotion ...................... 465 |
| | D. Discipline .............................................. 466 |
| |     1. Liability ............................................ 466 |
| |     2. Disciplinary Proceedings ................... 466 |
| VI. | Intra-Judicial Relations .................................. 469 |
| | A. Relations with Superior Courts ................ 469 |
| | B. Case Management and Relations with Court Presidents ............................. 470 |
| VII. | Enforcement ................................................. 472 |

# Judicial Independence in Slovenia

## Executive Summary

Slovenia has made very significant progress towards the establishment of a truly independent judiciary. The 1991 Constitution and accompanying legislation create a framework incorporating all the elements necessary to ensure judges a high degree of independence. The political branches and the public generally respect the principle of judicial independence.

Despite Slovenia's acknowledged progress, however, there are certain limited areas of concern, including the residual undue involvement of the executive and the legislature in judicial administration, the lack of public trust in the judiciary, and continuing, if isolated, political resistance to the consolidation of judicial independence In addition, because of the relatively strong institutional position of the judiciary in Slovenia, further attention should be paid to ensuring the intra-judicial integrity of the system, and its accountability to society.

*Ministry of Justice Involvement in Administration*

The executive and the legislature are still involved in certain aspects of judicial administration that might more properly be assigned to independent bodies with greater judicial representation. The Ministry of Justice is generally limited to a supporting role. However, the Ministry has on some occasions attempted to improperly extend its administrative power over the courts, and in general, its influence over the appointment of court presidents affords it an unnecessary level of influence over administrative matters.

*Executive Involvement in the Budget*

The political branches continue to control the budget process and remuneration of judges. The judiciary does not control or prepare its own budget – although it has some advisory authority – and the funds Parliament allocates for the judiciary are generally insufficient to cover the courts' legitimate costs.

*Compensation*

The compensation package of judges is generally competitive with that of other State employees. Nonetheless, many judges believe their compensation is not sufficient to ensure material security consistent with the requirements of a professional and independent judiciary. Reduction in judges' compensation is possible.

*Lack of Public Trust and Commitment to a Fully Independent Judiciary*

Despite the gains made in the past decade, public trust in the judiciary remains low, and the political branches have not demonstrated a thoroughgoing commitment to support the legitimate requirements of judicial independence beyond the existing institutional arrangements.

Some parliamentarians have called for abolition of judges' life tenure. Although their efforts have been firmly rejected, they do suggest that respect for the most basic principles of judicial independence are still not universally accepted.

In addition, lack of political commitment hampers the efficiency of the courts and undermines public support for the judiciary and arguments for its independence. Enforcement of judgements is inconsistent at best, suggesting that an automatic habit of compliance with court decisions is not ingrained in the political branches or the population as a whole.

*Judicial Accountability*

The judiciary as an institution is fairly strong in Slovenia; because of that institutional strength, areas of concern relate to intra-judicial independence and ensuring the accountability of judges to society.

Judges have not proven willing to discipline themselves; few judges have been convicted of any disciplinary transgressions. The procedures themselves overly favour confidentiality, which is damaging to public confidence in the accountability of the judiciary as a whole.

At present, preventing conflicts of interest is mostly left to the individual judge's discretion, which does not encourage public confidence in the judiciary. It would be prudent to further guarantee judicial neutrality through annual public statements listing judges' property, assets, holdings and income.

In addition to these general issues, the following matters of particular concern are discussed in the body of the Report:

*Constitutional Guarantees*

The Constitution does not guarantee the independence of the judiciary as an institution, but only of judges individually. There is no formal constitutional representative of the judiciary. In practice, the judicial branch is represented by the Supreme Court on financial issues and by the Judicial Council on personnel and status issues – a position that can somewhat undercut the formal guarantees of judicial independence.

*Working Conditions*

Working conditions of the judiciary are generally insufficient – particularly with regard to office and courtroom space – and may contribute to a weakening of judicial independence. Computerisation is adequate.

*Judicial Tenure*

Support for judicial tenure is particularly weak, and there have been a number of attacks on the principle that judges should be irremovable, including a current effort to introduce a five-year probationary period. Most other provisions for the conduct of judges in office do not pose significant problems for judicial independence.

*Enforcement*

In general, judicial decisions are respected but there have been several reported cases in which the Government or Parliament has failed to comply with court decisions. In effect, failing to comply with court decisions and maintaining a large number of pending cases are partly a matter of Government policy to avoid paying judicial settlements. Parliament has demonstrated a similarly ambivalent attitude towards implementation of Constitutional Court decisions.

## I. Introduction

Slovenia has made very significant progress towards the establishment of a truly independent judiciary integrated into a political system that respects the rule of law – a fact which various international observers, including the EU, have noted. The 1991 Constitution and the major legislation create a framework incorporating all the important elements necessary to ensure judges a high degree of individual and institutional independence.[1] The public and the political branches generally show respect for the principle of judicial independence.

Despite Slovenia's acknowledged progress, however, there are certain limited areas of concern, including the residual undue involvement of the executive and the legislature in judicial administration, and the lack of public trust in the judiciary. In addition, because of the relatively strong institutional position of the judiciary in Slovenia, further attention should be paid to ensuring the intra-judicial integrity of the system, and its accountability to society, which accepts, but is still not convinced of the need for judicial independence.

### A. Residual Areas of Undue Executive or Legislative Involvement

The executive and the legislature are still involved in certain aspects of judicial administration which might more properly be assigned to independent bodies with greater judicial representation.

#### 1. Selection

Although diminished with the newly amended Courts Act, the Minister of Justice's authority in the process of appointing court presidents remains a matter of concern. Members of the judiciary have sought to strengthen the role of the Judicial Council by empowering it to appoint court presidents; these efforts should be encouraged.

---

[1] The Commission has judged that "Slovenia is a democracy with stable institutions which guarantee the rule of law…" (See Commission Opinion on Slovenia's Application for Membership of the European Union, 15 July 1997, at <http://europa.eu.int/comm/enlargement/slovenia/op_07_97/b1.htm>, accessed 18 August 2001). Another Commission study notes that "further assistance in building up the institutional independence of the Slovenian judiciary is unnecessary." Woratsch, "Report on Expert Mission of the European Commission in Slovenia", 1998, p. 10.

## 2. Monitoring Structures and Ministry of Justice Involvement

The powers of the Ministry of Justice are generally limited. However, the Ministry does retain significant supervisory and reporting powers, which can be used to bring pressure on judges. Moreover, the Ministry has on some occasions attempted to improperly extend its administrative power over the courts. It would be advisable to strengthen the self-governing role of the judiciary, rather than contemplating new administrative functions for the Ministry of Justice.

## 3. Involvement in the Budget and Salary Determination

The political branches' continue to control the budget process and the remuneration of judges. The judiciary does not prepare its own budget – although it does have some advisory authority – and the funds Parliament allocates for the judiciary are generally insufficient to cover the legitimate costs of the courts. There is some concern that the judiciary's financial dependence on the executive and legislative branches may affect its corporate independence. Due to the increasing disparity between the caseload of courts and the static budget allotments, the judicial budget has the potential to become the most effective means to extend improper control over the judiciary.

## 4. Compensation

The compensation package of judges is generally competitive with that of other government employees, and is considerably higher than the national average. Nonetheless, many judges believe their compensation is not commensurate with the dignity of the office, nor sufficient to ensure their material security consistent with the requirements of a professional and independent judiciary. Under the current system, reduction of judges' compensation is possible. Amendments to the Judicial Service Act already have been drafted to prohibit reduction of judicial salaries except as a disciplinary sanction; these should be encouraged.

## B. Lack of Public Trust and Commitment to a Fully Independent Judiciary

Despite the gains made in the past decade, public trust in the judiciary remains low, and the political branches have not demonstrated a thoroughgoing commitment to support the legitimate requirements of judicial independence beyond the existing institutional arrangements.

In general, media treatment of the courts respects the requirements both of a free press and of an independent, accountable judiciary.[2] Several courts, especially regional courts and the Supreme Court, have recently begun taking a more active approach towards media and the general public using various methods such as press conferences, and the establishment of spokesmen or information offices. Further development of such activities is advisable.

Public criticism of judges occasionally occurs in the form of written articles or public statements mostly from parties dissatisfied with a particular judicial proceeding. On occasion, government officials have decried the inefficiency of the judiciary as a whole.[3] No evidence of political blackmail of or personal insults directed at individual judges has been reported.

Some parliamentarians have called for abolition of judges' life tenure, arguing that it discourages greater efficiency. Although their efforts have been firmly rejected, they do suggest that respect for the most basic principles of judicial independence are still not universally accepted.

In addition, lack of political commitment hampers the efficiency of the courts in ways that undermine public support for the judiciary. Enforcement of judgements[4] is inconsistent at best, suggesting that an automatic habit of compliance with court decisions is not ingrained in the political branches or in the population as a whole. The Slovenian Ombudsman has declared that the main problem facing the judiciary concerns long delays in court proceedings.[5] This assessment is shared by the European Commission, which has consistently expressed its concerns regarding judicial backlogs.[6] Lack of public trust in the judiciary certainly closely links with inefficient judiciary.

---

[2] The judiciary received strong support from the mass media in its successful effort to persuade Parliament to increase the 1999 budget for the courts. See Records of the Committee for Judiciary and Internal Affairs, from 19 November 1998, No. 411-01/98-53/4.

[3] See e.g. Radio Slovenija 1, 24 May 2001, "Dogodki in odmevi", 15:30; POP TV, 24 May 2001, "24 ur", 19:15; Radio Slovenija, 25 May 2001, 15:30; Slovenske novice, 26 May 2001, "Kdaj sojenje Loncaricu", 26 May 2001.

[4] See Section VII.

[5] *Delo*, 8 April 2001, p. 2.

[6] European Commission Regular Reports 1998, 1999 and 2000, <http://www.europa.eu.int/comm/enlargment/slovenia/index.htm.> (accessed 10 August 2001).

## C. Judicial Accountability

The judiciary as an institution is fairly strong; because of that institutional strength, the areas of greater concern relate to intra-judicial independence and ensuring the accountability of judges to society.

### 1. Weak Efforts at Self-Policing of the Judiciary

No case of judicial corruption has been uncovered to date. However, there is a public perception that corruption within the judiciary does occur, and that judges extend protection to their colleagues on the bench who violate rules and regulations. Media articles spotlighted a 2000 Council of Europe report,[7] which recommended the adoption of anti-corruption measures for the judiciary, such as regulations relating to financial disclosure.[8]

Indeed, judges have not proven particularly willing to discipline themselves. Although disciplinary proceedings have been initiated on a number of occasions, few judges have been convicted of any disciplinary transgressions. Instead, some judges have quietly resigned following investigation.

Existing disciplinary procedures strongly favour confidentiality, which is valuable for protecting public confidence in individual judges, but damaging with regard to public trust in the accountability of the judiciary as a whole. Moreover, an informal approach to the rules can encourage their selective application against lower judges in a way that may discourage their independence. Judges themselves have expressed the opinion that disciplinary bodies should be encouraged strictly to apply disciplinary rules, as a means of increasing public trust and confidence in the judiciary.

### 2. Disclosure

At present, the prevention of conflicts of interest is primarily left up to the individual judge's discretion, which does not encourage public confidence in the judiciary. It would be prudent to further guarantee judicial neutrality through annual public statements listing judges' property, assets, holdings and income.

---

[7] Council of Europe, Group of States Against Corruption (GRECO) Eval I Rep (2000) 3E final, 12–15. December 2000.

[8] "Financial disclosure in judiciary", *Vecer*, 25 March 2001, p. 4.

## D. The Judiciary and the EU Accession Process

The Commission's 2000 Regular Report focused on judicial efficiency and concluded that while progress has been made in judicial reform, it is still too early to assess the effectiveness of new measures aimed at reducing the backlog of pending court cases. Reinforcement of administrative and judicial capacity was designated a medium-term priority.[9] In 2000 Slovenian courts adjudicated 558,779 cases – a considerable increase over 1997, when 450,380 cases were decided.

Judges, members of political branches of government and the general public are aware of what the Commission states about the judiciary. Excerpts from regular reports are published and commented upon in the media.

The judiciary is marginally involved in the accession negotiations, in that the Ministry for European Affairs and the Ministry of Justice solicit the opinions of the Supreme Court on certain judicial issues. Additionally, in the "National Programme for the Adoption of the *Acquis* by the End of 2002" the President of the Supreme Court is named as the person responsible for the judiciary in the accession process. The Delegation of the European Commission in Slovenia and the Supreme Court have had several meetings in order to make a joint assessment of progress with regard to issues raised in the reports of the Commission.[10]

Through the end of 2000, no EU funding had been used for strengthening the judiciary and no Phare horizontal programme for the judiciary has been planned for the year 2001.[11] Judges and judicial administrators generally are not sufficiently familiar with the existing European Union support programmes and have not received sufficient information on how to apply for funds.

## E. Organisation of the Court System

Although judges first formed an association in 1971, and the civil legal system has been in use since the late Habsburg period, the principal outlines of judicial organisation were defined under the 1991 Constitution.

---

[9] 2000 Regular Report, <http://www.europa.eu.int/comm/enlargment/slovenia/index.htm>.

[10] The National Programme for the Adoption of the Acquis by the End of 2002, <http://www.gov.si/svez_ang.htm> (under documents) (accessed 10 August 2001).

[11] Judicial conference, 4 May 2001.

The judicial system is comprised of 44 district courts, 11 regional courts, four courts of appeal and the Supreme Court. Regional and district courts are courts of first instance.[12] There are also four specialised Labour Courts, a Social and Labour Court, and a Social and Labour Court of Appeal. In 1998, an Administrative Court was established as a specialised court with divisions in four cities.[13] Extraordinary courts may not be established, nor may military courts be established in peacetime.[14]

The Constitutional Court is the highest body of judicial authority for the protection of constitutionality, legality, human rights and basic freedoms.[15] The Constitution treats this court separately from other courts,[16] and law provides that in relation to other state bodies, the Constitutional Court is an autonomous and independent state body.[17] The Constitutional Court acts as a part of the judiciary only when it is deciding on constitutional complaints by individuals alleging violations of their constitutional rights by the decision of another court.[18]

Specialised courts have been established to deal with minor offences.[19] Minor offence court judges, who serve until the mandatory retirement age, are elected by Parliament on the proposal of the Judicial Council in the same manner as other judges,[20] although the requirements for office are slightly less stringent than for other judges. Minor offence court judges receive rights, benefits and education under the same provisions of the Law on Judicial Service as do other judges. Minor offence courts are listed as a single item in the State budget, separate from other courts.

---

[12] District courts are vested with jurisdiction over criminal cases under penalty of fine or prison sentence of up to three years, civil disputes concerning damages or property rights not exceeding two million SIT (c. € 9,200), enforcement cases and non-litigious matters. Regional courts are vested with jurisdiction over other cases. Courts Act, Arts. 99 and 101.

[13] Although the Administrative Court is a court of first instance, administrative judges have a position and salary equal to that of judges from the courts of appeal.

[14] CONST. REP. SLOVENIA, Art. 126, para. 2.

[15] The Constitutional Court Act., Art. 1 (1), Official Gazette, (hereafter "OG"), Nos. 33/91–1, 42/97 and 66/2000, <http://www.us-rs.com/en/basisfr.html.> (accessed 10 August 2001).

[16] See CONST. REP. SLOVENIA, Chapter VIII.

[17] The Constitutional Court Act., Art. 1(2). OG, 15/94.

[18] CONST. REP. SLOVENIA, Art. 160.

[19] Minor Offences Act, OG 25/83, with amendments.

[20] See Section V.A.

Slovenia has 786 judicial posts.[21] 505 judges serve in regional and district courts, 97 judges in courts of appeal, and 33 judges in the Supreme Court. Another 27 judges serve in specialised administrative courts and 56 judges sit in labour courts.[22]

---

[21] Except minor offence judges.

[22] Annual Statistical Report of Ministry of Justice for the year 2000, April 2001.

## II. Constitutional and Legal Foundations of Judicial Independence

### A. Guarantees of the Separation of Powers and Judicial Independence

The Constitution creates a system of separation of powers,[23] and the independence of judges is likewise guaranteed by the Constitution.[24] Important elements of judicial independence are also embedded in the Constitution, such as the separate role of the Judicial Council with a majority composed of judges elected by their peers,[25] the mode of elections of judges,[26] life tenure,[27] judicial immunity,[28] and the requirement that grounds for termination be provided by statute.[29] The Constitution does not, however, expressly guarantee the independence of the judiciary as an institution, but only of judges individually. Indeed, the constitutional jurisprudence does not appear to require fully separate branches, but rather mutually interdependent ones. In holding constitutional Parliament's power to appoint the President of the Supreme Court, for example, the Constitutional Court noted:

> The principle of the separation of powers does not mean the autonomy of individual branches of authority, but the establishing of mutual interdependence between them. The institution of checks and balances is an essential element of the principle of the separation of powers, from both a functional and organisational point of view. Since judges are bearers of responsibility for which no direct responsibility to electors is established, it is in compliance with the demand for

---

[23] CONST. REP. SLOVENIA, Art. 3(2).

[24] CONST. REP. SLOVENIA, Art. 125.

[25] CONST. REP. SLOVENIA, Art. 130.

[26] CONST. REP. SLOVENIA, Art. 130. The Government has formally initiated proceedings for a constitutional amendment addressing the manner in which individuals become judges. "Constitutional Changes before Summer in the Parliament", *Delo*, 11 April 2001, p. 2. Under the draft amendment, the State President would appoint and remove judges upon a decision by the Judicial Council. Only the President of the Supreme Court would still be appointed by Parliament upon the recommendation by the Judicial Council.

[27] CONST. REP. SLOVENIA, Art. 129.

[28] CONST. REP. SLOVENIA, Art. 134.

[29] CONST. REP. SLOVENIA, Art. 132(1); Judicial Service Act, Art. 74(1).

mutual interdependence of the holders of various functions of state power that the executive and legislative powers co-operate in the appointment of judges.[30]

Other elements are elaborated in statutory law, in particular the Courts Act and the Judicial Service Act: retirement rules,[31] protections against non-statutory transfers of judges against their consent,[32] personnel councils composed of judges elected by their peers which advise the Judicial Council selection and promotion of judges,[33] and, notably, a judge's right to appeal to the Judicial Council when he considers his independence has been infringed.[34]

Constitutional guarantees of judicial independence are further entrenched by the requirement of a two-thirds majority for their amendment. The statutory guarantees of judicial independence in the Courts Act and Judicial Service Act do not have a privileged status. Since important guarantees of judicial independence are provided only in statutory law, it might be desirable to require a supermajority or more complex procedures for their alteration.

The Constitution also establishes a parliamentary system, which to some degree subordinates the judiciary to the executive and legislature. This constitutional subordination causes some tension between the branches in practice, and the actual relations between the judiciary and other branches of government are less than balanced.[35] The main source of tension derives from the fact that the executive and the legislature determine the judiciary's budget allocation and the level of remuneration of judges.[36] There is some legitimate concern that the judiciary's financial dependence on the executive and legislative branches may limit the scope and effect of the constitutional and statutory guarantees of independence.

## B. Representation of the Judiciary

There is no formal constitutional representative of the judiciary. In practice, the judicial branch is represented by the Supreme Court on financial issues and by the Judicial

---

[30] Decision of the Constitutional Court U-I-224/96 from 22 May 1997, OG, No. 36/97.
[31] Judicial Service Act, Art. 74(1).
[32] Judicial Service Act, Art. 4(2).
[33] Courts Act, Art. 30(1); Judicial Service Act, Arts. 16 and 18(1).
[34] Courts Act, Art. 28(1). To date, no judge has filed such an appeal concerning a violation of his independence.
[35] Interviews with judges at various levels of the judiciary.
[36] See Section IV.A and C.

Council on personnel and status issues – a position that can somewhat undercut the formal guarantees of judicial independence.

The Supreme Court is commonly considered the representative of the judiciary although there is no constitutional or legal basis for this role. The president of the Supreme Court is regularly invited to the parliamentary sessions of the Committee for Judiciary and has annual meetings with the president of the Parliament and the Prime Minister.

The other constitutional institution which co-ordinates contact between the judiciary and the legislature is the Judicial Council.[37] The Judicial Council is an autonomous state body, composed of judges and other lawyers. According to a decision of the Constitutional Court, the Council is not the formal representative of the judiciary.[38] Nevertheless, it performs an important role, since it proposes judicial candidates to the National Assembly,[39] and is empowered to give an opinion on the Government's proposal for the judicial budget.[40]

The Council is composed of 11 members elected for non-renewable five-year terms. Five of the 11 are elected by the National Assembly upon the nomination of the State President; candidates must be lawyers or professors of law. The remaining six members are judges elected by their peers in a secret ballot. One member is elected by the Supreme Court, one by the courts of appeal, one by regional courts, one by district courts, and two by all judges jointly. After the Council is formed, its members elect their President from among themselves. The Council therefore represents a balance of judicial and non-judicial appointments.

A draft constitutional amendment would enlarge membership to 15; six members would be nominated and elected by Parliament (and thus the State President would no longer be involved), seven members by judges, while the Minister of Justice and the President of the Supreme Court would be members *ex officio*. Critics of this proposal maintain that the new make-up of the Council and the new system of appointment will to some extent politicise the Council.

---

[37] CONST. REP. SLOVENIA, Arts. 130–31.

[38] The Court reasoned that members of the Judicial Council do not exercise a judicial function within that institution. Judges exercise judicial power as members of a court established by law when they adjudicate cases; the Judicial Council, therefore, is not representative of the judicial branch before other branches of government. Decision of the Constitutional Court U-I-224/96 from 22 May 1997, OG, No. 36/97.

[39] CONST. REP. SLOVENIA, Art. 130.

[40] Courts Act, Art. 28(1).

*Parliamentary Investigations*: The establishment of parliamentary investigations poses a problem for judicial independence. Under a special parliamentary proceeding aimed at determining the political accountability of public office holders,[41] the Investigative Commission of the National Assembly has investigated the legal proceedings in particular cases. The Investigative Commission is empowered to adopt conclusions finding that a public office holder is politically accountable. Such investigations cannot lead to the dismissal of a judge, but their findings could erode public confidence in the judiciary or engender confusion about judges' political accountability. The Investigative Commission's mandate extends even to pending cases, as it could bring undue pressure on a judge to rule in accordance with an already established parliamentary preference for a particular outcome.

## C. Rules on Incompatibility

Judicial office is incompatible with office in any other State body, local government body or any organ of a political party.[42] If a judge is elected or appointed to a political office, or to the Constitutional Court, or as ombudsman, his office and all rights and obligations deriving from judicial service are suspended.[43] To avoid any public doubts regarding improper political influence on the exercise of the judicial function, it would be preferable for a judge to be obliged to resign his office prior to standing for election or taking office.[44] The draft Code of Judicial Ethics notes that the principle of incompatibility has to be understood and explained in relation with due political restraint of judges.[45]

Not all political activity by judges is prohibited. Judges are allowed to be members of political parties.[46] In general, judges seem politically restrained, and there have not been any serious allegations about improper influence on adjudication stemming from their political engagements.

A judge may not accept any other employment that would obstruct his performance as a judge, harm the reputation of the judicial service, or create the impression that he

---

[41] Parliamentary investigation is regulated by the Parliamentary Investigation Act, OG No. 63/93.

[42] CONST. REP. SLOVENIA, Art. 133.

[43] Judicial Service Act, Art. 40.

[44] The Slovenian Association of Judges considers the current provision of the Judicial Service Act to be inconsistent with the principle of the "appearance of independence".

[45] A draft code of judicial ethics was adopted at the general session of the Slovenian Association of Judges on 8 June 2001.

[46] CONST. REP. SLOVENIA, Art. 133.

is not impartial in administering justice. The Judicial Service Act further specifically prohibits judges from working as advocates, notaries public, or in any commercial or other profit-making activity,[47] including positions in management, administration or supervisory boards.

A judge may teach, publish, or conduct research or similar work within the legal profession, provided this activity does not interfere with his judicial performance.[48] Nonetheless, judges' complaints concerning insufficient salaries[49] have clear repercussions on issues of incompatibility. In an effort to raise their income, many judges give lectures at conferences and seminars organised by private or public enterprises and institutes; such practices sometimes give the impression that judges accept fees for lecturing to groups that have interests before the court. Comprehensive financial reform should therefore combine salary increases with additional limitations on extra-judicial activities, such as allowing lectures only at law schools or professional associations.

The civil and criminal procedural codes prohibit judges from hearing cases in which they or a relative have been a party or witness, if they have issued a decision in any earlier stages of the proceeding, or if other circumstances raise doubt about their impartiality.[50]

Court personnel, such as clerks and apprentices, are also subject to incompatibility rules; they may not engage in other activities unless they are "compatible with the independence and reputation of the court[,]" as decided by the president of the court.[51]

## 1. Disclosure

There are no public disclosure rules, and little consideration is given to the prevention of potential financial conflicts of interest. This renders judgements about levels of corruption highly uncertain. Moreover, prevention of conflicts of interest is largely left up to the individual judge's discretion, which does not encourage public confidence in the judiciary. It would be advisable to further guarantee judges' impartiality through a requirement that they release annual public statements of their assets, holdings and income.

---

[47] Judicial Service Act, Art. 41.
[48] Judicial Service Act, Art. 42.
[49] See Section IV.C.
[50] Criminal Procedure Code, Art. 39 (OG, Nos., 63/94, 72/98) and Civil Procedure Code, Art. 70 (OG, No. 26/99).
[51] Courts Act, Art. 57.

## D. Judges' Associations

Judges are free to form and join associations and other organisations to represent their interests, to promote their professional training and to protect their judicial independence. Judges are also allowed to form trade unions, although no judges' trade union currently exists. The Slovenian Association of Judges was established in 1971 and more than 90 percent of judges are members. To ensure its independence, the Association is funded solely through membership fees. The Association actively co-operates in all legislation projects concerning the judiciary and judges, and its expert observations and opinions have an important informal value during parliamentary procedures. There have been no reports of restrictions on the operation of the Association.

## III. Administration of the Court System and Judicial Independence

Administration of the judiciary is under the jurisdiction of the Ministry of Justice,[52] but the Judicial Council, the court presidents and personnel councils also have important roles, and in effect there is a mixed model of administration.

The management and supervision of courts' operations, as well as control over its performance and efficiency is divided between the Judicial Council, the Ministry of Justice, and presidents of courts; court presidents, assisted by the personnel councils, manage individual courts while the Judicial Council and Minister of Justice share management responsibilities on a national level. In addition, the Supreme Court is involved in the budgetary process.[53]

This mixed system of administrative control by judicial and non-judicial bodies distributes control and accountability across the various branches and institutions, and taken as a whole, could contribute to an effective and neutral system for administering the justice system. However, courts still rely on the executive branch for a variety of services, such as drafting laws and regulations on the organisation and operation of courts, providing personnel, material, and infrastructure support, as well as statistical research and enforcement of penal sanctions. Moreover, the Ministry of Justice retains a key role in appointing and removing court presidents,[54] and thus retains an indirect but decisive influence on the daily administration which those court presidents control.

In light of attempts by the Minister of Justice to assert greater authority over court presidents (discussed below), it would be advisable to strengthen the self-governing role of the judiciary rather than establish new monitoring structures within the Ministry.

---

[52] Courts Act, Art. 10.

[53] See IV.A.

[54] The Minister appoints court presidents from among three candidates proposed by the Judicial Council. Courts Act, Art. 62. The President of the Supreme Court is appointed by Parliament on the proposal of the Minister, who must solicit the opinions of the Council and the regular session of the Supreme Court. Courts Act, Art. 62. The Minister dismisses court presidents (except the President of the Supreme Court); he must solicit the opinion of the Judicial Council, but is not bound by it, although if the Council opposes a dismissal, the Disciplinary Court of second instance rules on the matter. Courts Act, Art. 64.

## A. The Judicial Council

The Judicial Council has explicit statutory authority to administer courts and judges at the national level.[55] It decides on matters relating to incompatibility with judicial service and is empowered, but not obliged, to adopt standard work norms. Upon the proposal of the Minister of Justice, the Council also decides on the number of judges in each court.[56] The Council gives opinions on the judicial budget proposal and on statutes regulating the status, rights and duties of judges and of court staff.

The Judicial Council has its own administration, which consists of a judge seconded to the Council for a term of six years, who is responsible for preparing all relevant materials for sessions, and a secretary.

Although formally the Judicial Council has an autonomous position in financial matters,[57] it does not have its own budget. Its funds are separately allocated to the Supreme Court, against the recommendation of the Parliamentary Committee for Internal Affairs,[58] giving rise to the impression that the Government is actively resisting the financial autonomy of the Council.

## B. Ministry of Justice

In addition to the Judicial Council, the Ministry of Justice continues to exert significant control over judicial administration, giving the executive unnecessary and improper influence over the judiciary. In particular, the Minister's involvement in the selection of court presidents, who have important administrative functions, is problematic.

The Ministry of Justice ensures the general conditions for the successful functioning of the judiciary by preparing draft laws and regulations on court organisation and operation; providing human, material, and technical support; co-ordinating international legal aid; and enforcing penal sanctions.[59] The Ministry also determines the need for new personnel and court facilities. The Ministry, together with the court presidents, is responsible for

---

[55] Courts Act, Art. 28.
[56] Courts Act, Art. 38.
[57] Courts Act, Art. 29(3).
[58] Proposal of the State Budget, Parliamentary Reporter No. 16/2001.
[59] Courts Act, Art. 74.

compliance with the Court Order regulating the organisation of court records, archives, and statistics.[60]

The Ministry of Justice also has authority, together with the presidents of superior courts, to supervise and monitor court presidents' administrative activities, except at the Supreme Court.[61] In practice, the Minister requires court presidents to submit reports on various issues or proposes to a given court's hierarchical superior that an inspection be conducted.[62] Such supervision is limited in scope: the Ministry generally requires court presidents to submit regular reports assessing the reasonableness of complaints filed by parties alleging unreasonable delay or other deficiencies in court operations. In any event, monitoring and supervision may not interfere with individual judges' independence in deciding particular cases.[63]

Every six months the Ministry of Justice publishes statistical data complied by the courts, including the number of cases received and their status, as well as comparative data across different courts of the same instance. The statistical report also includes figures regarding the number of judges, vacant posts and gender structure of the judiciary. The report, which is submitted to all courts and the Judicial Council, provides an objective basis for making an assessment of the burden on courts and judges. The report should properly be completed by the Council, but the Ministry still retains responsibility for this task.

Because the Ministry of Justice appoints court presidents,[64] it retains an undue level of influence over those presidents' administrative decisions, which can be a means of bringing indirect pressure on judges in their decision making. The Ministry of Justice's residual powers have been improperly asserted in the past. In the period between 1998 and 2000, the Minister of Justice tried on several occasions to remove the President of the District court of Nova Gorica, arguing that he had failed to administer the court in accordance with legal regulations; the Administrative Court vacated the dismissal. The Minister also demanded internal review of the operation of some courts of first instance, but the presidents of the court of appeal refused.

---

[60] Court Order, Art. 6(1), Official Gazette No. 17/95. The Court Order is the only regulation prescribed by the Constitution.

[61] Courts Act, Art. 67.

[62] Courts Act, Arts. 72, 73.

[63] Courts Act, Art. 60, para. 2.

[64] See Section V.A.1.

## C. Court Presidents and Personnel Councils

The day-to-day operations of a court are controlled and managed by the court president. The Presidents of the Supreme Court and the Courts of Appeal exercise some limited supervisory control over the operation of their own and lower court presidents' administrative activities.[65] However, the presidents' supervisory competence is limited to the right to demand written reports about lower court presidents' performance of their administrative activities, and the right to review petitions filed by parties complaining of unnecessary delay in a particular case.

The competencies of the personnel councils differ at each level. In general, however, personnel councils decide on the assignment of judges to different divisions, the system of case assignment, and determination of judges' specialisations, on the proposal of court presidents. In addition, the personnel council of a regional court gives an opinion on candidates for district or regional court judgeships, while the personnel councils of higher courts also assess judges' performance.[66]

Personnel councils are created for every regional court, court of appeals and the Supreme Court. The personnel councils are composed of seven judges elected by their peers, except for a regional court, which includes four regional and three district court judges.[67]

This system of decentralised self-regulation prevents the accumulation of power in one judge or in one central body. Nevertheless, the Government, on the initiative of the Ministry of Justice, recently proposed the abolition of eleven personnel councils of regional courts and the transference of their competence to the personnel councils of the courts of appeal. During parliamentary discussions this proposal failed, due to opposition from the judiciary.[68]

---

[65] Presidents of courts of appeal also supervise the administrative activity of district and regional court presidents.
[66] See Section V.C.
[67] Courts Act, Art. 30.
[68] "Jeopardising Judicial Independence?", *Delo*, 10 February 2000.

## IV. Financial Autonomy and Level of Funding

### A. Budgeting Process

The judiciary's extensive control of its own administration is significantly undercut by its reliance on the executive in budgetary matters and its lack of meaningful input into key budget discussions.

The judiciary does not control or prepare its own budget, although it does have some advisory authority. The judicial budget is a separate line within the State budget, prepared by the executive with some input from the courts. The presidents of each regional court (in consultation with the presidents of district courts), court of appeal and the Supreme Court prepare a financial plan for the next fiscal year. On the basis of these financial plans, the Supreme Court prepares a draft budget for all courts and submits it to the Government.[69]

In preparing its budget proposal for submission to Parliament, the Government is not bound by the proposal of the Supreme Court; in practice, the Ministry of Justice is supposed to represent the judiciary in the intra-governmental discussions. Parliament adopts the final version of the state budget, which includes the judicial budget.[70]

The only means at the judiciary's disposal to defend its budget requirements is the competence of the Judicial Council to give an advisory opinion to Parliament on the draft budget submitted by the government.[71] It has become standard practice that representatives from the Judicial Council, the Supreme Court and the Slovenian Association of Judges participate in the sessions of the Judiciary Committee in Parliament when it examines the draft budget. For example, representatives of the judiciary (with unanimous support from the mass media) successfully persuaded the Parliament to increase the 1999 budget for the judicial branch.[72]

Due to the increasing disparity between the rising caseload of courts and static budget allotments, the judicial budget has the potential to become the most effective means for controlling the judiciary. To date, neither the Government nor the legislature has

---

[69] Courts Act, Art. 75(2).

[70] Courts Act, Art. 4.

[71] Courts Act, Art. 28(1).

[72] See Records of the Committee for Judiciary and Internal Affairs, from 19 November 1998, No. 411-01/98-53/4.

made provision of sufficient funding contingent on the judiciary's performance. Some politicians have expressed their expectations for a better, faster and more effective judiciary.[73] However, such expectations have mainly been expressed by Members of Parliament on occasions which cannot be directly linked to the actual budget negotiation process.

Nonetheless, the main obstacle to sufficient and stable financing is the absence of judicial involvement or input into the most important stages of the budget process. The Ministry of Justice has no legal obligation to provide sufficient financial resources for the judiciary. Therefore, it is up to the Minister to decide whether or not he will take part in the negotiations over the judicial budget.

In 1998, the Minister of Justice chose not to participate in the negotiations, which partly contributed to the near financial collapse of the district and regional courts by the end of 1999. In 1999, the Minister of Justice did participate in these negotiations, which was positively reflected in the judicial budget allocation that year. In 2000 and 2001 the Minister again did not participate in negotiations over the judicial budget. A firm legal obligation on the Ministry to take part in the negotiations would therefore be desirable, or an open commitment by the Government and the Parliament to ensure a given level of funding from year to year.

The president of each court[74] is accountable to the Court of Auditors for expenditure of budgeted funds.[75] Court presidents are therefore not directly accountable to Parliament or to the Government for their spending.

The funds allocated are generally insufficient to cover the legitimate costs of the courts. In 2001, 1.6 percent of the State budget was allocated to the judiciary,[76] a decrease from previous years; the budget for the judiciary in 2000 represented 1.7 percent of the State budget. The budget for 2001 is sufficient to cover the material expenses of courts only for nine or ten months. During discussions of the parliamentary Committee for Internal Affairs in 2001, the President of the Supreme Court warned that most of the courts would be forced to "shut their doors" in September 2001 if the governmental proposal of judicial budget were adopted,[77] a concern which was echoed by the Judicial

---

[73] *Delo*, 7 January 2000.

[74] Except district courts, for which regional court presidents are responsible.

[75] The Court of Auditors is not a part of the judiciary. After making its review of public funds, the Court of Auditors reports to the Parliament; its recommendations are not binding.

[76] Budget of the Republic of Slovenia, OG, No. 32/2001.

[77] Committee for Internal Affairs, opinion on draft state budget for 2001, 19 March 2001, No. 411-1/00-65/01.

Council.[78] However, the Government did not respond by making significant changes to the budget proposal for 2001.

## B. Work Conditions

The working conditions of the judiciary are generally insufficient – in particular with regard to office and courtroom space – and may contribute to a weakening of judicial independence. Computerisation is adequate.

In general, court buildings, especially in Ljubljana, are in critical need of repair. Despite the general consensus about the need for construction and repairs, no funds have been allocated. In 1997, the new Government rejected a previously planned "facilities project", and as a result the demand for office space in the Supreme Court, the Court of Appeal, and Regional and District courts in Ljubljana has risen to a critical level. The main problem is a serious shortage of courtrooms, which limits judges to two hearings days a week. None of the 25 judges from the commercial division at Ljubljana Regional Court has had the opportunity to conduct hearings in a courtroom during the last decade; instead, all such hearings have been conducted in the judges' personal offices, which are not suitable for this purpose.[79]

The investment shortfall is not simply a function of a general lack of funds. Considerable construction and renovation has been undertaken in the capital for different ministries or other governmental agencies in the past several years, but none for the judiciary. The limited influence of the judiciary in budget negotiations seems to be the principal cause of this imbalance. The situation might be improved if the office space shortage were seen in terms of its impact on judges' capacity, efficiency and independence.

The Ministry of Justice determines the number of staff for courts on the basis of court presidents' proposals. However, court presidents do not have the right to employ new court staff – even if approved by the Ministry of Justice – if the annual court budget does not include finances for salaries for the court in question. The Government makes a proposal for additional staff positions on the basis of an informal proposal of the Supreme Court. This practice is widely criticised by judges as a means of exercising improper influence on the judiciary, as the Ministry and the Government can use the budget process as leverage to discourage overly independent courts, by favouring or discouraging requests for needed funding to hire necessary staff.

---

[78] "Always the same old story", *Vecer*, 6 April 2001, p. 4.
[79] Annual reports on Ljubljana District Court 1999–2000.

In general, courts have adequate equipment, such as computers, typewriters, and faxes; every judge has a computer, although not all have Internet connections. The Information Technology Centre of the Supreme Court has exclusive authority to select, buy and distribute personal computers. Case law, legal opinions of the Supreme Court, and Constitutional Court judgements are stored on computer; in addition, every judge receives an official legislative journal and printed collections of legislation.

## 1. Training

The Judicial Training Centre adopts the overall curriculum for training of judges and court staff.[80] The Centre is not financially autonomous, since its budget is included in that of the Ministry of Justice. In addition, the Centre does not have its own facilities or management board; instead, the Centre is managed by an employee of the Ministry of Justice. Until recently, the Centre had been provided with sufficient financial resources for planning and implementing its curriculum, although there has been a lack of funding for postgraduate grants for study in Slovenia and abroad in all fields related to judicial work.[81] In 2001, however, financial restrictions were placed on planning the annual curriculum of training for judges. The Centre received 53.5 million SIT (c. € 244,405) in 2000 and 43.7 SIT (c. € 199,636) in 2001.

## C. Compensation

The compensation package of judges is generally competitive with that of other State employees, and is considerably higher than the national average,[82] although significantly lower than incomes of advocates and notaries.

Nonetheless, many judges believe their compensation is not commensurate with the dignity of the office, nor sufficient to ensure their material security consistent with the requirements of a professional and independent judiciary.[83] Economic restraints have provoked a considerable "brain drain" from the judiciary since the organisational reform in 1995; as a consequence, judges of first instance courts in particular are relatively young and

---

[80] Courts Act, Art. 74a.

[81] See the record of the session of JTC, 19 March 2001.

[82] The annual average salary of a judge in 1999 was € 23,641.38 (€ 12,959.97 net). Annual salary of a Supreme Court judge was € 42,050.44 (€ 20,833.86). The average income in the country as a whole for 1999 was € 9,884 (gross).

[83] Comments made at annual meeting of the Slovenian Association of Judges, Portoroz 1999.

inexperienced. On the other hand, actual incidents of judicial corruption – which one might expect if judges were seriously underpaid – have not been reported or alleged.

The executive and the legislature determine the remuneration of judges, but their discretion is statutorily limited. By law, a judge is entitled to receive a salary corresponding to his judicial post.[84] Judges' economic equality with the other branches is also partly guaranteed by statutory provisions stipulating that the base for calculating a judge's salary shall be the same as for parliamentary deputies.[85] Supreme Court judges receive a lower salary than do Members of Parliament or governmental ministers and deputy ministers, while judges from regional courts receive higher salaries than most ministerial officials at the rank of under-secretary of state.[86]

However, a reduction of judicial compensation is possible under this formula, and judges' salaries – together with parliamentarians' salaries – have been reduced by 20 percent since the Judicial Service Act was enacted in 1994. However, such a reduction has a greater impact on judges, as Members of Parliament receive additional payments for participating in parliamentary Committees. Unlike other public officials, judges do not receive any additional salary on the basis of their efficiency.[87]

Draft amendments to the Judicial Service Act would prohibit the reduction of judicial salaries except as a disciplinary sanction.[88] The prohibition should serve to shield judges against financial threats to their independence. An individual judge's compensation can also be reduced as a disciplinary sanction.[89]

Judges are divided into three pay groups, within each of which three salary classes are defined. Therefore, judges move through a number of pay classes during their careers, a factor that can affect their independence when promotions and pay raises are not made subject to clear criteria. In practice, pay increases are generally automatic. Presidents of

---

[84] Judicial Service Act, Art. 44.

[85] Judicial Service Act, Art. 45.

[86] Press conference of the President of the Supreme Court, Radio Slovenia, press release 17 April 2001.

[87] Every state official is entitled to receive up to 20 percent of his salary as a performance bonus.

[88] The draft amendments to the Judicial Service Act are published in the Parliamentary Reporter No. 90/2000.

[89] Judicial Service Act, Art. 82(1), p. 3.

courts and heads of divisions of courts also receive a specific allowance depending on the level of the court over which they preside.[90]

Judges are legally entitled to receive health, disability and other social insurance, as well as various additional benefits, including: reimbursement of official travel expenses; meal allowances; annual holiday allowance; housing compensation; reimbursement of moving expenses; reimbursement of education expenses; a long service bonus; and solidarity assistance in the event of a death in the family, long illness, or natural disaster. Upon retirement, a judge receives a bonus and pension (equivalent to approximately 70 percent of his last salary). The pension system is the same for all state employees.

A small number of official apartments intended only for the judiciary and other legal officers are distributed according to criteria established by a housing commission at the Ministry of Justice. The commission is composed of judges and representatives of the Ministry. Judges, state prosecutors, state attorneys and minor offence judges have priority in requesting apartments.

---

[90] Judicial Service Act, Art. 47. The allowances range from five percent for heads of small divisions, to 16 percent for presidents of regional courts and courts of appeals, and 20 percent for the President of the Supreme Court. Maribor and Ljubljana district court presidents receive a slightly higher allowance than their colleagues elsewhere.

# V. Judicial Office

## A. Selection Process

The selection process for all levels involves numerous steps with judicial, executive and legislative input. One current proposal, which would provide for initial five-year appointments, poses a particular threat to judicial independence. The Ministry of Justice also retains unnecessary influence on the appointment of court presidents.

When there is a vacancy in a particular court, the Ministry of Justice determines which applicants meet the minimum criteria for candidacy, including through an assessment of their training during the two-year apprenticeship.[91] The Ministry then forwards a list of qualified candidates to the personnel council of the court with the vacancy. The personnel council chooses a shortlist and prepares a written justification for each choice. The shortlist, justification, and all relevant documents are returned to the Ministry of Justice, which formulates its own opinion on the candidates and submits both its opinion and that of the personnel council to the Judicial Council; when selecting candidates for appointment, the Judicial Council is not bound by either opinion.[92] The Judicial Council then nominates one candidate for each vacant judicial post to Parliament for a vote. The Judicial Council's nomination procedure is subject to review by the Administrative Court.[93]

On at least four occasions Parliament has rejected, without explanation, the candidate proposed by the Judicial Council, most recently a candidate for Supreme Court judge in July 1999. In practice, for Parliament to reject a candidates is relatively rare, and a certain balance between the Council and Parliament has been achieved by the Council's practice of resubmitting rejected candidates.[94] For example, the current President of the Supreme Court had to be resubmitted as a candidate after Parliament initially rejected him in 1997. To date, the Parliament has always accepted resubmitted candidates.[95]

---

[91] Apprenticeship is required for all lawyers who want to pass the state legal exam.

[92] Judicial Service Act, Art. 18(2)

[93] CONST. REP. SLOVENIA, Art. 157(2)

[94] See Judicial Service Act, Art. 19, para. III.

[95] The current draft Constitutional amendment provides that judges would be appointed by the State President rather than Parliament.

The draft constitutional amendment would introduce an initial five-year appointment, in effect a probationary period before judges would receive life tenure. This would dramatically reduce the decisional independence of judges for a significant portion of their career.

## 1. Appointment of Court Presidents

Court presidents are appointed by the Minister of Justice from among three candidates proposed by the Judicial Council for a term of six years with the possibility of re-appointment.[96] There are no set criteria for the post, which is left to the discretion of the Council and the Minister.[97] If the candidate proposed by the Council is rejected, the Minister must explain the decision and the rejected candidate may request the Administrative Court or the Constitutional Court to review the decision.[98]

Although diminished with the newly amended Courts Act,[99] the Minister's authority in the process of appointing court presidents still remains a matter of concern. Some judges have called for the role of the Judicial Council to be strengthened by empowering it to appoint court presidents.

## 2. Appointment of Supreme Court President

The President of the Supreme Court is appointed by Parliament upon the proposal of the Minister of Justice. The Minister of Justice consults the opinion of the Judicial Council and Plenary Meeting of the Supreme Court prior to making a proposal to Parliament.[100] This procedure, which affords the courts very little influence, has been ruled constitutional by the Constitutional Court.[101]

---

[96] Courts Act, Art. 62.

[97] Judicial Service Act, Art. 29(7) only stipulates that the candidates shall have the ability to perform a leading post.

[98] CONST. REP. SLOVENIA, Art. 157.

[99] Amendments to the Courts Act, OG, No. 28/2000 from 30 March 2000.

[100] Judicial Service Act, Art. 62(5).

[101] Decision of the Constitutional Court U-I-224/96 from 22 May 1997, OG, No. 36/97.

## B. Tenure, Retirement, Transfer, and Removal

Support for judicial tenure is particularly weak, and there have been a number of attacks on the principle that judges should be irremovable, including a current effort to introduce a five-year probationary period before tenure is granted. Most other provisions for the conduct of judges in office do not pose significant problems for judicial independence.

### 1. Tenure and Retirement

The Constitution stipulates that "[t]he office of a judge shall be permanent."[102] Nevertheless, the principle of secure tenure has been called into question. On 23 July 1999, several Members of Parliament initiated a debate on the propriety of life tenure,[103] and proposed amending the Constitution to abolish life tenure. Advocates of reform argued that the backlogs in the courts were a consequence of judges' irremovability, and proposed that judicial tenure should be based on performance. The Slovenian Association of Judges strongly opposed the proposal,[104] as did other legal experts and a former constitutional court judge.[105] As a result, Parliament never initiated constitutional amendment proceedings, and the proposal has been dropped.

The abolition efforts were a fairly isolated phenomenon, and probably did not reflect broad-based public or political sentiment. However, other attempts to curb tenure have received broader support. As noted above,[106] current draft amendments to the Constitution would provide for permanent appointment only after five years in office, meaning that judges would not have tenured irremovability until they had served five years. Judges themselves have criticised the current tenure system, concerned that new judges are granted irremovability despite insufficient training. However, introducing probationary periods would create unnecessary risks to judicial independence that could well outweigh the benefits of screening new judges.

---

[102] CONST. REP. SLOVENIA, Art. 129.

[103] See the records of the National Assembly, <http://www.sigov.si/dz/index_an.html> (accessed 10 August 2001).

[104] See "Permanent office, privilege for judges or citizen's right?", (article by the President of the Slovenian Association of Judges), *Delo*, 21 August 1999.

[105] Mladina, Krivic 1999, 30 August 1999.

[106] See Section V.A.

The Slovenian Association of Judges has suggested introducing a special judicial exam instead of relying on the general state legal exam, an idea supported in principle by the Minister of Justice and representatives of the Law Faculty of Ljubljana. This would be clearly superior to any system restricting judges' tenure. However, as yet no steps have been taken to develop and enforce this plan.

The Judicial Service Act prescribes mandatory retirement at 70, and extensions are not allowed.

## 2. Transfer

Generally, judges may be transferred to another court or to work in another state organ temporarily or for an extended period only with consent.[107] The transfer of a judge to work in another court can only take place upon a mutual proposal to the Judicial Council by the presidents of both courts concerned.

Transfer of a judge without his consent is possible only as a temporary disciplinary measure,[108] or in other enumerated instances such as the abolition of the court, a significant decrease in the volume of work, or a re-organisation of the courts, in which case his status and salary must be protected.[109] In such cases, the judge may appeal to the Judicial Council. Since the enactment of the Judicial Service Act in 1994 no Slovenian judge has been transferred without his consent, and exceptions appear to be founded on legitimate administrative concerns and contain sufficient safeguards against abuses.

In order to reduce backlogs, the Supreme Court has proposed the introduction of the Hercules programme, under which approximately 20 judges would be transferred, with their consent, to overburdened courts for no longer than one year. They would keep their position and salary and they would receive additional payments for resolving a greater number of cases than the standard norms.

The Slovenian Association of Judges has voiced its opposition to such a system, arguing that it would introduce performance-based remuneration, which in turn would jeopardise

---

[107] Judicial Service Act, Art. 4(2).

[108] Judicial Service Act, Art. 82(1), p. 1.

[109] Judicial Service Act, Art. 66 notes that "[in the event of a non-consensual transfer], the judge must be ensured an equal judicial post and the same salary class as he had prior to the transfer. If this is not possible, the judge shall be allocated to a different judicial post, but shall be entitled to retain his previous office of judge as his title, his previous salary class, if higher, and the same right to promotion as before the transfer."

the appearance of impartiality by placing the personal interests of judges over those of deliberative justice.[110] The Hercules programme would require statutory authorisation, and is being debated in the parliamentary Committee for Internal Affairs.[111]

## 3. Removal

Parliament may impeach and remove a judge from office upon a proposal of the Judicial Council.[112] The judge must have acted in violation of the Constitution or have committed a major breach of the law. When a judge is convicted of having abused his office to commit an intentional crime, Parliament must dismiss him.[113] To date, however, no judge has been impeached or convicted on any of these grounds.

If criminal proceedings are initiated against a judge for an offence involving abuse of his judicial office, the President of the Supreme Court must order the temporary removal of the judge from service.[114] The judge may appeal the decision of suspension to the Judicial Council.[115]

A court president may be dismissed from his function if he fails to administer his court in accordance with regulations or if he unreasonably delays proceedings, if he violates the principle of independence of judges in adjudication, or if he violates the rules concerning distribution of cases. The Minister of Justice dismisses judges with the concurrence of the Judicial Council; if the Judicial Council opposes the decision, then the Minister may request the disciplinary court of second instance to decide on dismissal.[116]

Slovenia has not adopted a lustration law; thus, there is no procedure for the removal of a judge based on his having worked under the previous regime. However, the Judicial Service Act makes it a general condition for election that "judges who have adjudicated or decided in investigative or court proceedings in which fundamental human rights and freedoms were violated by the judgement, shall no longer fulfil the conditions for

---

[110] Written proposal of the Slovenian Association of Judges to the Parliamentary Committee of internal affairs from 18 December 2000.

[111] Parliamentary Reporter No. 19/2001.

[112] CONST. REP. SLOVENIA, Art. 132(2).

[113] CONST. REP. SLOVENIA, Arts. 132(2) and (3).

[114] Judicial Service Act, Art. 95.

[115] Judicial Service Act, Art. 96.

[116] Courts Act, Art. 64.

election to the function of judge after the expiry of their mandate."[117] This provision was implemented only in one case and is no longer relevant since all judges remaining from the communist period have life tenure.

## C. Evaluation and Promotion

Judicial promotion is based both on seniority and evaluation of performance, for which there are established rules. Judicial service is assessed by the following criteria: professional knowledge; ability to deal correctly with legal questions; reputation for impartiality, conscientiousness, reliability, diligence; ability in written and oral communications; ability in communication and work with parties; relationship with colleagues; and behaviour outside work.[118] The measures of a judge's performance are principally qualitative. The rate of reversal is also used as an indicator for promotion although it can never be the sole reason for deciding on promotion.

Judges are promoted both through salary classes and in rank. Generally, a judge is given an automatic salary increase every three years unless he does not meet the criteria for promotion. A judge is eligible to be promoted to the next highest judicial post after every two salary class increases. The title of councillor is awarded to judges when they reach the age of 45 or after the third successful promotion in the same post.[119]

The Judicial Council decides on judges' promotions upon the proposal of the relevant personnel council. Personnel councils assess the performance of each judge[120] every six years to determine if the judge is not suited to judicial service, if he meets the conditions for promotion, or if he meets the conditions for accelerated promotion.[121] With the exception of the appointment of court presidents – itself a kind of promotion[122] – the system of promotion is therefore entirely in the hands of the judiciary itself.

---

[117] Judicial Service Act, Art. 8(3).

[118] Judicial Service Act, Art. 29.

[119] Judicial Service Act, Art. 27(3).

[120] The personnel council of the Court of Appeal assesses judges from district and regional courts, while the Personnel Council of the Supreme Court assesses judges of courts of appeal and the Supreme Court.

[121] Judicial Service Act, Art. 32.

[122] See Section V.A.

## D. Discipline

The disciplinary provisions for judges are insufficiently transparent and overly protective of judges' reputations at the expense of legitimate concerns about public accountability.

### 1. Liability

Sitting judges are not directly liable for harm arising from the exercise of judicial power. While the Constitution stipulates that every person has the right to compensation for any damage he suffers due to the malfeasance of any State actor,[123] and normally compensation may be demanded directly from the actor,[124] where judges have caused the harm the State undertakes to guarantee payment. The State may then indemnify the judge, although there are no reports that this has happened.

A judge suspected of criminal activity may not be detained, nor may any judicial proceeding be initiated against him, except with the permission of Parliament acting upon the demand of a court.[125] A draft constitutional amendment would give the Judicial Council, rather than Parliament, the power to lift a judge's immunity. Unless implemented with careful attention to the specific arrangements, such a provision could serve to weaken judges' individual and collective accountability.

### 2. Disciplinary Proceedings

Disciplinary sanctions for judicial misconduct are applied by the Disciplinary Courts,[126] composed of judges elected by their peers, three to a Disciplinary Court of first instance and five to a Disciplinary Court of second instance.

Disciplinary action may be taken against a judge for breaching his judicial obligations or for undefined irregularity in the performance his duties.[127] Therefore, to a certain extent, it is up to the disciplinary authorities to define what attitudes or behaviour demand

---

[123] CONST. REP. SLOVENIA, Art. 26.
[124] CONST. REP. SLOVENIA, Art. 26.
[125] CONST. REP. SLOVENIA, Art. 134.
[126] Judicial Service Act, Chapter VII.
[127] Judicial Service Act, Art. 81.

disciplinary consequences.[128] The extremely abstract formulation of disciplinary offence is one of the reasons why few disciplinary proceedings have been initiated to date.[129]

Ethical rules for the judiciary are included in the Judicial Service Act, but only in the form of principles, such as the obligation to behave impartially, to refrain from commenting on pending cases, or to refrain from accepting gifts.[130] Breach of these ethical rules can result in disciplinary proceedings. A draft Code of Ethics was adopted by the Slovenian Association of Judges on 8 June 2001.

Only the president of a judge's court can initiate disciplinary proceedings against that judge, although the Minister of Justice may propose disciplinary proceedings to the court president. Delay in procedural activities has been the most commonly cited grounds for initiating disciplinary proceedings.

Disciplinary sanctions include transfer to another court for between six months and three years, denial of promotion for three years, and a 20 percent salary reduction for up to one year.[131] A judge may appeal decisions of the Disciplinary Courts.[132]

The Disciplinary Courts sit under a fixed set of procedural rules. The right to be heard and the right to defence counsel are secured by law. There have been no reports of infringements of the procedural rules for disciplinary hearings. The problem instead has been the effectiveness of the disciplinary proceedings in policing the judiciary. Although disciplinary proceedings against judges have been initiated on a number of occasions, so far no judge has been convicted of a disciplinary transgression. There have been several examples of voluntary retirement or resignation following disciplinary procedures, but the actual number of such cases is not available because of their confidentiality.

Disciplinary proceedings are not made public until the legal decision becomes binding, unless an accused judge explicitly protests against the exclusion of the general public.[133] In addition, a judge subject to a pending disciplinary proceeding is not suspended from deciding cases. Both these provisions serve to protect public confidence in particular judges

---

[128] E. Markel, "Judicial Independence: Ethics and the problem of corruption", presentation at the Meeting of the presidents of the supreme jurisdiction, San Francisco 2000.

[129] Judicial Service Act, Art. 81 stipulates: "Disciplinary action shall be taken against a judge accused of breaching his judicial obligations or of irregularity in the performance of the judicial service."

[130] Judicial Service Act, Arts. 37–39.

[131] Judicial Service Act, Art. 82.

[132] Judicial Service Act, Art. 87(1).

[133] Judicial Service Act, Art. 91.

in the event they are not found in violation of the rules. Of course, at a broader institutional level, they may not encourage confidence in the judiciary as a whole.

The inevitable consequence of such informal and non-transparent resolution of disciplinary problems is that the public believes that judges protect each other when mistakes are made. Moreover, such an informal approach can encourage the selective application of rules against lower judges in a way that may discourage their decisional independence. Judges themselves have expressed the opinion that disciplinary bodies should be encouraged strictly to apply disciplinary rules, as a means of increasing public trust and confidence in the judiciary.[134] Judges must also show that disciplinary action against judges is taken seriously in order to avoid a situation in which other branches of government would intervene or attempt to gain control over the judicial disciplinary process.

---

[134] Annual meeting of the Slovenian Association of Judges, Portoroz, 13 June 1999, National Conference on independence and accountability of judges.

## VI. Intra-Judicial Relations

### A. Relations with Superior Courts

In general, judges in lower courts are free to decide cases without undue interference, outside the normal processes of appellate review. Some judges believe the procedures for ensuring uniform adjudication – such as binding uniformity decisions by the Supreme Court – unduly limit their decisional independence.

Upon review, the court of appeal may affirm, amend or cancel a decision of a lower court; it may give binding instructions, but only as to which procedural action to carry out and which legal questions to deal with upon retrial. Thus, a system of full appeal still exists, but the court of appeal cannot instruct a lower court regarding the outcome of a retrial.

No other channels through which lower courts could be induced to conform to the rulings of higher courts are evident. There is no system of appointed supervisors in higher instance courts acting as either formal or informal mentors to lower judges, nor are there any formal consultations with superior court judges in specific cases, although informal consultations among fellow judges on particular legal problems cannot be avoided. There is no administrative subordination between judges of different levels.

Within the corps of judges, there is some disagreement over the priority to be given to measures ensuring uniformity of decisions or to protections maximising individual judges' decisional independence. Currently, different panels of appellate courts adopt different decisions in similar cases, which has the effect of confusing case law and limiting its uniformity throughout the country.

Some judges believe their adjudicative independence should prevail over the principle of legal certainty that uniformity of case law promotes. However, so long as uniformity is obtained through regulated appeals procedures, and no firm link is made between individual decisions (or the number of reversals) and a judge's prospects for advancement, there is no reason to suppose this unduly restricts the independence of the judge in any individual case. Indeed, uniformity in case law may strengthen the public's confidence in the judiciary's fundamental competence and may discourage fears of corruption.

The proper role of the Supreme Court's binding uniformity decisions is more controversial. The general assembly of the Supreme Court issues binding opinions on the uniform application of laws, as well as opinions on matters relating to questions of judicial practice and methods for adopting judicial practices in courts. The binding nature of these rules makes them, in the eyes of some judges, operate like parliamentary laws – but as they are issued by judges, not lawmakers, they ought not bind other judges in their decision-making.

## B. Case Management and Relations with Court Presidents

*Caseload*: Cases are assigned to judges at random. They are distributed according to the daily order of entry of petitions for legal action and assigned to judges in alphabetical order. These procedures[135] do not seem to raise concerns for judicial independence.

Norms for caseloads are determined by the Judicial Council for judges of all levels of courts, including Supreme Court judges; these norms identify the number of cases a judge is annually expected to resolve. Caseloads are one measure which personnel councils rely on in assessing judges' performance; the great majority of judges exceed the norms, suggesting they do not impose unreasonable pressures on individual judges that might affect the independent exercise of their judgement.

A judge may only be removed from a case in the event of an extended absence that prohibits him from attending to the case; the court president makes this determination.[136]

*Court Presidents*: A court president is considered *primus inter pares*, and a judge is not dependent on the court president in obtaining due benefits and promotion. The president does not formally assess a judge's performance, although he does supervise the collection of statistical data, case flow, and the promptness of trials, which are linked to assessments of a judge's performance. The court president performs these monitoring or supervisory functions' powers in relation to individual judges in two contexts: in response to requests for assessment of the judicial service and in connection with disciplinary proceedings.

The president is entitled to request that the personnel council issue an assessment of a judge's service more often than the mandatory six years,[137] which may lead to accelerated promotion or salary rise. In addition, as noted above, only court presidents can initiate disciplinary proceedings against judges in their court.

---

[135] Caseload is regulated by the Court Order issued by the Minister of Justice, OG, No. 17/95.

[136] Court Order, Art. 162.

[137] Judicial Service Act, Art. 31(1) stipulates: "The personnel council shall issue an assessment of judges' service every six years. The personnel council shall issue an earlier assessment at the request of the Judicial Council, president of court or a judge himself but not earlier than two years after the previous assessment."

Obviously, these powers could provide opportunities for presidents to reward co-operative judges or punish overly independent ones; however, in both cases, the president only initiates the proceedings, while the personnel council of the court of higher instance or the disciplinary court makes the final decision.[138] This dispersion of power somewhat mitigates the risks that a court president could use supervisory harassment or the threat of disciplinary hearings to bring pressure to bear on a judge.

In exercising his administrative and supervisory capacity, a court president is not allowed to infringe the independent position of a judge making decisions on cases;[139] he may be dismissed if he infringes the principle of independence of judges by violating regulations in any other way.[140] Perhaps as a result of this clear normative distinction between the court administration and the adjudication process, no complaint relating to a court president's conduct has been reported.

---

[138] Courts Act, Art. 30.

[139] Courts Act, Art. 60(2).

[140] Courts Act, Art. 64 (1), p. 2.

## VII. Enforcement

In general, judicial decisions are respected but there have been several reported cases in which the Government or Parliament has failed to comply with court decisions.[141]

The lack of compliance with court decisions, even as increasing numbers and kinds of disputes are being referred to courts, is related to budget limitations; the State Attorney has to secure the consent of the Ministry of Finance before he signs any judicial or non-judicial settlement or admits a claim. In effect, non-compliance with court decisions, as well as the maintenance of a high number of pending cases, is partly a matter of governmental policy. Of course, such a policy also undermines the standing of the judiciary.

Parliament has demonstrated a similar attitude towards the decisions of the Constitutional Court. As of the end of 2000, thirteen rulings of the Constitutional Court were not being enforced because the term of the legislature had expired before it replaced or supplemented the unconstitutional provisions.[142] Parliament has a continuing obligation to enact legislation conforming with the Court's rulings, but an automatic habit of compliance with court decisions does not appear to be ingrained in the political branches.

---

[141] In several prominent cases, judgements affecting 5,237 State employees' salaries have been ignored. Monitoring judicial independence conference, Ljubljana, 5 March 2001.

[142] Legal Information Centre of the Constitutional Court, Report No. 143/00-1 from 27 March 2001,